# The
# DIRECT
# CONNECT

# *The* DIRECT CONNECT

Simple Measures Those in Grief
Can Call On to Bring About Healing

Reginald T. Stanton

Copyright © 2018 Reginald T. Stanton

Published by Hereford House

All rights reserved. No part of this book may be reproduced in any form or by any electronic or mechanical means including information storage and retrieval systems without permission in writing from the author. The only exception is by a reviewer, who may quote short excerpts in a review.

ISBN Paperback: 978-0-578-21280-7

Printed in the United States of America

Interior Design: Ghislain Viau

*Dedicated to my beloved wife Doris
and our daughter Beverley Joy.
Two special ladies who have consistently
enriched my life in countless wondrous ways and
who continue to be my principal source of joy,
inspiration and spiritual sustenance.*

# CONTENTS

Preface . . . . . . . . . . . . . . . . . . . . . . . . . . . . xiii
Introduction . . . . . . . . . . . . . . . . . . . . . . . . . . . 1
CHAPTER 1 | **GRIEF** . . . . . . . . . . . . . . . . . . . . 9
   Spousal Death . . . . . . . . . . . . . . . . . . . . . . .13
   Job Sharing—and Other Things We Miss. . . . . . . . . .17
   Invisibility . . . . . . . . . . . . . . . . . . . . . . . . .23
   Isolation . . . . . . . . . . . . . . . . . . . . . . . . . .25
   Expectations . . . . . . . . . . . . . . . . . . . . . . . .29
CHAPTER 2 | **MEDIUMSHIP—IT'S *ALL* ABOUT LOVE** . .37
   The Case For Mediumship . . . . . . . . . . . . . . . . .40
   Historic Precedents . . . . . . . . . . . . . . . . . . . .42
   We All Allude To It . . . . . . . . . . . . . . . . . . . .44
   The Mediums—a Hard Sell . . . . . . . . . . . . . . . .49
   The Religion of Spiritualism . . . . . . . . . . . . . . .53
   Endorsements . . . . . . . . . . . . . . . . . . . . . . .56
CHAPTER 3 | **THE SKEPTICS** . . . . . . . . . . . . . . .63
   Those Skeptical Scientists . . . . . . . . . . . . . . . . .68
   The Value of Readings—Priceless . . . . . . . . . . . . .76
   Why Such Fervent Meanness? . . . . . . . . . . . . . . .80
   A History of Skepticism—the Blooper Reel . . . . . . . .82
   Things That Science Can't Explain . . . . . . . . . . . .84

Our Brain. . . . . . . . . . . . . . . . . . . . . . . . . . . . 90
Replicability . . . . . . . . . . . . . . . . . . . . . . . . . .92
More Priceless Value . . . . . . . . . . . . . . . . . . . . 96

CHAPTER 4 | **IT'S MUCH MORE THAN JUST
"A READING"** . . . . . . . . . . . . . . . . . . . . . .99
Our Allusions to a Soul Plan . . . . . . . . . . . . . . 102
Our Soul Plan . . . . . . . . . . . . . . . . . . . . . . . 105
Duality . . . . . . . . . . . . . . . . . . . . . . . . . . . 108
Helping it to Sink In . . . . . . . . . . . . . . . . . . 112
Ways In Which Spirit Supports Us . . . . . . . . . 116
Reading Between the Lines . . . . . . . . . . . . . . 121
Another Myth Debunked. . . . . . . . . . . . . . . 122
Angels and Spirit Guides . . . . . . . . . . . . . . . 123
Invoking Spirit Collaboration. . . . . . . . . . . . 127

CHAPTER 5 | **THE JOY OF READINGS—
IT'S MUTUAL** . . . . . . . . . . . . . . . . . . . . 133
Preparing For Our Reading. . . . . . . . . . . . . . 136
The Reading . . . . . . . . . . . . . . . . . . . . . . . 139
Messaging—Spirit Style. . . . . . . . . . . . . . . . 142
Electricity—the 'Light' in Enlightenment. . . . . . . . 146
The Games Those Dead People Play . . . . . . . . 148
Separating the Wheat from the Chaff. . . . . . . . 154
Spirited Counteractivity . . . . . . . . . . . . . . . 157

CHAPTER 6 | **MY READINGS** . . . . . . . . . . . . 161
Thirty Years On. . . . . . . . . . . . . . . . . . . . . 164
The Clincher . . . . . . . . . . . . . . . . . . . . . . 165
More Readings—From the Highlights Reel. . . . . . . . 166

CHAPTER 7 | **FACILITATING CONNECTION** . . . . . . 175
   Meditation—It's as Old as the Ills. . . . . . . . . . . . . 176
   Meditation—Simple but not Necessarily Easy . . . . . . . 180
   Choices Aplenty . . . . . . . . . . . . . . . . . . . . . . 182
   Manner of Procedure—Taking Our Meds. . . . . . . . . 183
   Our Watchword is......Relax. . . . . . . . . . . . . . . . 186
   Meditation—The Guided Type. . . . . . . . . . . . . . 188
   The Silent Type . . . . . . . . . . . . . . . . . . . . . . 190
   Taking Out the Garbage . . . . . . . . . . . . . . . . . 192
   Whoa—Not so Fast. . . . . . . . . . . . . . . . . . . . 193
   Are We There Yet? . . . . . . . . . . . . . . . . . . . . 194

CHAPTER 8 | **SIGNS—LOVE MADE MANIFEST** . . . . 197
   Sign Types . . . . . . . . . . . . . . . . . . . . . . . . . 201
   Spirit Assistance. . . . . . . . . . . . . . . . . . . . . . 203
   Electric Signs . . . . . . . . . . . . . . . . . . . . . . . 204
   The Signs of Music . . . . . . . . . . . . . . . . . . . . 206
   Old Habits—They Really do Die Hard. . . . . . . . . . 208
   Signs of Synchronicity . . . . . . . . . . . . . . . . . . 209
   Attestations . . . . . . . . . . . . . . . . . . . . . . . . 213
   Oracle Cards . . . . . . . . . . . . . . . . . . . . . . . 214
   Animal Signs . . . . . . . . . . . . . . . . . . . . . . . 217

CHAPTER 9 | **THESE ARE A FEW OF MY
                FAVORITE SIGNS** . . . . . . . . . . . . . . . . . 225
   Our Friend Flicker . . . . . . . . . . . . . . . . . . . . 229
   My Musical Signs . . . . . . . . . . . . . . . . . . . . . 230
   Synchronistic Signs . . . . . . . . . . . . . . . . . . . . 234
   Synchronicity at Work . . . . . . . . . . . . . . . . . . 236
   Synchronistically Forward to the Past . . . . . . . . . . 244

Oracle Cards—Our Personal Medium-in-Residence . . . . 252
Animal Signs . . . . . . . . . . . . . . . . . . . . . . . . 260
My Golden Crown Affair . . . . . . . . . . . . . . . . . 267

CHAPTER 10 | **DIY RECUPERATIVE MEASURES** . . . . 271
Suggested Measures: Our Health Matters . . . . . . . . . 281
Our Soul Plan . . . . . . . . . . . . . . . . . . . . . . . 283
Hitting the Books. . . . . . . . . . . . . . . . . . . . . 286
Fear, Begone . . . . . . . . . . . . . . . . . . . . . . . 289
Television: Commercials . . . . . . . . . . . . . . . . . 292
Television: Newscasts . . . . . . . . . . . . . . . . . . 294
Other Media Fearmongerers . . . . . . . . . . . . . . . 297
Fear: It's Like WiFi . . . . . . . . . . . . . . . . . . . . 299
Other People (Don't Get Me Started) . . . . . . . . . . . 300
People: They Can Say the Darnedest Things . . . . . . . 304
People: They're Known to Use and Abuse. . . . . . . . . 308
People: Spread the Word By All Means—But Carry
   an Umbrella . . . . . . . . . . . . . . . . . . . . . . 313
Acts of Kindness—The Other Best Medicine . . . . . . . 316
Kind Acts: More of 'Less is More' . . . . . . . . . . . . . 321
Kind Acts: Instant Karma . . . . . . . . . . . . . . . . . 323
Acts of Self-Kindness: Credit Ourselves . . . . . . . . . . 326
Act of Self-Kindness: Supersized . . . . . . . . . . . . . 327
A Brief Pertinent Afterword. . . . . . . . . . . . . . . . 327
Affirmations: Emboldening Words to the Wise . . . . . . 328
Affirmations: The Nature of Them . . . . . . . . . . . . 331
Affirmations: The Mechanics of Them . . . . . . . . . . 334
Photographs: Utilizing Their Energy . . . . . . . . . . . 337
Photographs: My Own Validations by Mediums . . . . . 343

Loneliness and Aloneness: Not Necessarily the
    Demons We've Been Led to Believe . . . . . . . . . . . 345
Loneliness and Aloneness: Join the Club—It Has a
    Huge Membership . . . . . . . . . . . . . . . . . . . . . 348
Reverence for Life: It's a Two-Way Treat. . . . . . . . . . . 350
Reverence for Life: It's a Healing Golden White Light . . . 353
Walking: Literally Steps on Our Road Back to Wellness . . 355
Walking: A Reverent Stroll in the Park . . . . . . . . . . . 356
Walking: Nothing Like a Stroll Through the
    "Oxygen Factory" . . . . . . . . . . . . . . . . . . . . . 358
Walking: More Ions in the Fire—(not a typo) . . . . . . . 359
Walking: To the Beat of the Thymus Thump . . . . . . . . 360
Walking: To Nature's Musical Accompaniment . . . . . . . 361
Walking: Doing it Mindfully . . . . . . . . . . . . . . . . . 363
Music: Nutrition for the Soul. . . . . . . . . . . . . . . . . 364
Music: It's Magic Disseminated en Masse. . . . . . . . . . 366
Music: The Other Universal Health Care . . . . . . . . . . 368
Music: "Has Charms to Soothe a Savage Breast" . . . . . . 368
Music: Trailblazing its therapeutic benefits . . . . . . . . . 370
Singing: It's Not Just for the Birds . . . . . . . . . . . . . 372
Singing: Those Lighter-Than-Air Ditties Can Lift the
    Heaviest of Hearts . . . . . . . . . . . . . . . . . . . . 374
Laughter: It Truly is the Best Medicine . . . . . . . . . . . 376
Are We There Yet? . . . . . . . . . . . . . . . . . . . . . . 381
Are We There Yet?: Typical Touchstone Moments. . . . . 383

CHAPTER 11 | **THE CASE FOR MEDIUMSHIP—
    GOING FORWARD** . . . . . . . . . . . . . . . . . . 389
The Case For: A Magical Confluence of Energies? . . . . . 392

 The Case For: Spirit's Ability to Adapt . . . . . . . . . . . 395
 The Case For: Brand Recognition. . . . . . . . . . . . . . . 398
 The Case For: A Television Programming Genre Upgrade. . 402
 The Case For: Universal Acceptance By Default . . . . . . 407
 The Case For: "Keep Soldiering On" . . . . . . . . . . . . 409
 The Case For: Possible Prospects for Scientific Verification. . 411
 The Case For: Quantum Physics . . . . . . . . . . . . . . 412
 The Case For: My Rationale . . . . . . . . . . . . . . . . 415

CHAPTER 12 | **NO WONDER IT'S CALLED HEAVEN** . . 419
 Welcome to Paradise . . . . . . . . . . . . . . . . . . . . 421
 Rest In Peace—and Other Myths . . . . . . . . . . . . . . 423
 Small Wonder It's Also Known As Paradise . . . . . . . . 426
 In the Meantime . . . . . . . . . . . . . . . . . . . . . . 429

AFTERLIFE AFTERWORD . . . . . . . . . . . . . . . . . 431
 A Few Final Words . . . . . . . . . . . . . . . . . . . . . 435

ACKNOWLEDGMENTS . . . . . . . . . . . . . . . . . . 437

READING SUGGESTIONS. . . . . . . . . . . . . . . . . 445

# PREFACE

> If you have knowledge,
> let others light their candles at it.
> —*Margaret Fuller, 19<sup>th</sup> century American Journalist*

I think it's safe to say that most of us have been fortunate to have had someone in our lives, at one time or another, who have had a positive and lasting influence on us—a role model, a mentor. My mentor was a gentleman by the name of Mr. Bill Simmonds, he was Company Director of a printing company I worked for in my early twenties in Birmingham, England. I have remained forever grateful for his many kindnesses to my wife and I, but especially so for the nuggets of wisdom he gladly shared daily with this gauche novice.

One dictum in particular found a permanent home in my psyche: "Knowledge," he would often say, "is not the personal property of anyone—knowledge belongs to all of us and should be shared." It was his firm belief that any knowledge we come by is a gift, a blessing bestowed upon us by the Universe, and as beneficiaries it is incumbent on us to share it whenever an appropriate opportunity presents itself. (He would have fully approved of Margaret Fuller's observation)

This simple maxim went on to serve me well through my half a dozen careers which included a four year stint teaching at a printing school, then subsequently during the thirty five years I operated my own illustration and design firm. But there was never a time when it was more foremost in my mind than when I complied to a publishing company's request to write a "How-to" book on Architectural Illustration.

It turned out to be pretty successful, for a book in that category, and went to a second printing, with international distribution. My satisfaction with that though was nothing compared to the positive feedback I received, and still do, from readers. The most wonderfully heartwarming accounts from people the world over, crediting the book with having taught them skills that had opened up rewarding new careers And interestingly, for many of them, at an uncannily fortuitous time in their lives. Naturally I've found touching people's lives in such a positive way to be an enormously gratifying experience and I often say a "thank you Bill" because I know Mr. Simmonds is observing all this approvingly.

Needless to say, it was this same spirit of knowledge-sharing that was the principal progenitor of the book you're now holding.

At this point I'd like to share with you the role played by spirit of another kind in my decision to share my experiences with you through this book.

# Preface

I'll be telling you in the introduction that follows of how a synchronous chain of events led me to books about the wonderful world of mediumship. Of how it wasn't long before just reading about the magic of the mediums wasn't enough—my appetite had been whetted, I had a burning desire to experience the magic myself, up close and personal. And so it was, that over the ensuing four years I consulted with six highly rated world class mediums.

In four of the readings, after undeniable verification of who exactly was coming through, I received what was basically the same message, "This lady who's here is saying that you should write a book about your experiences because many people will be helped by it.

So, when four mediums of their stature relayed the same message to me, I could only conclude that I had, in no uncertain terms—been given my marching orders.

So that is how this book came about. You heard the lady—she says it will help!

That's the spirit.

# INTRODUCTION

I'd never been in the park this late in the day. I walked here most days but I was usually out of here by 8 a.m. at the latest, it was now pushing 11:30. I'd been delayed today by several changes to a project demanded by a client who had started to be annoyingly unreasonable. I was beginning to realize though what a beautiful day I'd have missed if he hadn't been so fastidious.

As I was nearing the end of my final lap around the lake, I became aware of the need to visit a restroom and as luck would have it, the city library complex was just up ahead. Again, a flash of gratitude for the earlier delay, if I'd been on my usual schedule the library wouldn't have been open.

Access to the facilities for which I now had an urgent need is off the entrance lobby, so there's no need to go into the library itself. But on my way out, despite having had no previous intentions whatsoever of doing so, I found myself being inexplicably drawn to turn right into the library gallery instead of exiting left to the park. The next thing I know, I'm sitting in front of a computer—not exactly my favorite place in the world to be, incidently (those things don't seem to like me very much, I think it must have been something I said). I remember thinking how unusual it was that there weren't the usual half dozen or so people waiting to use the computers.

Well there I was, wondering what I was doing sitting in front of a blank screen. I certainly hadn't had any intention of looking for a book when I came in here, but I thought I may as well, seeing as how the screen is asking me to type in a title or author. My mind though, like the screen, was blank. At such times as this I sometimes turn to a trick I picked up during a meditation course I took years ago, I call it a mini-meditation. I've found it very useful in my creative work when I want to focus on a specific subject or I have a need to remember something that doesn't automatically spring to mind. Depending on where you are of course, you simply close your eyes and for two minutes or so take slow deep breaths while focusing on the subject and maybe asking a question. In this case, I asked—"What subject do I have a need to read about right now?" My meditation mentor used to call this, "percolating prompts."

After no more than thirty seconds, I "heard" the words—"Healing grief." I remember thinking, as I clicked on the 'submit' button—"Wow, that couldn't be more appropriate—where on earth did that come from?"

The image that formed on the screen wasn't the usual list of book titles I'd been expecting. What came up was just one book title—*"Healing Grief,"*—the author—James Van Praagh.

Over the years, in my work as an illustrator and designer, I'd made many title and subject searches on these very same computers, but I can't remember a time when the book I'd wanted had actually been

*Introduction*

on the shelves at this library. This had never been a problem as it would be sent over the following day from one of the other branches in the county system.

Not this time. We have a 'theme' in progress here—this has been a 'coincidence day' from the get-go. So, true to form, the screen informed me that "This book is on the shelf at this library." That's very nice, I thought, but how do I go about finding it. In the past, between the Dewey System and this library's shelf layout, I'd usually end up walking about a mile—been there—done that this morning. I leaned back in my chair and swiveled around to get my bearings and my jaw must have dropped at what immediately met my eyes. On the nearest shelf—at eye-level and no more than two and a half feet away, were two volumes of—*"Healing Grief."*

It hadn't been lost on me that, as I alluded to before, a pattern of fortuitous coincidences had been playing out throughout the morning. Granted, nothing earth shattering, nothing that would register on the Richter Scale, but nonetheless, collectively—decidedly curious. I'd learned that such a string of events warrants our attention.

Like most of us, I'd experienced many such sequences of related events over the years and they'd turned out to be a portent to matters of special significance too many times for me to pass them off as mere coincidences. I've since learned that this phenomenon has a name, it's called 'synchronicity'. ( we'll be discussing it more later on). It used to be that whenever I'd become aware of such a clustering of events, I'd say to friends, "Someone's trying to tell me something." It would invariably transpire that indeed 'someone' had been, and a significant change in the status quo had been in the offing. A shift that had often turned out to be a veritable life-changer.

This was one of those times. It's also time for me to explain.

*The Direct Connect*

It had been nine months or so since I and my daughter Bev had lost my wonderful, beautiful wife and her mother Doris to breast cancer.

As hideously horrifying the three year ordeal had been for us, I was finding the ongoing grieving process to be also relentlessly excruciating. I'd recognized the advice of a friend to, "Try to stay busy" to be very sound counsel, so after spending five months doing what was practically the only thing I was seemingly fit for—namely crying, I'd started accepting assignments from clients again. Several of whom had kindly and flatteringly put projects on hold till I was, as one of them put it, "back in the saddle."

Grief is a notorious energy vampire, both mentally and physically. I'd worked hard to surmount it's debilitating effects, but I'd found that coping with just the day-to-day basic functioning plus the unpredictable and erratic waves of despair, were themselves enough to deal with. So when the current project had turned out to be stressful, and nowhere near the quality my clients had a right to expect, I reluctantly had to face the fact that I just wasn't ready. My clients were being short-changed and that's not the way we operate—it's also a sure fire way for any kind of business to self destruct. Work hadn't helped in the way I'd hoped it would, it would have to be put on hold, healing would have to be my project for a while—one thing at a time.

I desperately wanted to learn how to accept what had befallen me and adapt to whatever that new condition turned out to be—my new "normal." I was looking for any kind of path that I felt would possibly lead me back to some degree of wholeness.

*Introduction*

This wasn't the first time I'd embarked on this quest, I'd set about seeking help and guidance a few weeks after my wife's passing and had explored a whole range of the conventional sources available. I'd tried a grief support group—individual counseling—church counsel etc., plus a wide variety of recommended books and CD's by "grief experts." After seven months, as earnestly as I'd wanted to, I couldn't honestly say I felt any benefit to speak of, nothing had "spoken to me." It had all seemed to be hackneyed boiler plate stuff—dispensed sincerely by well intentioned people but consisting, in the main, of theories that lacked the authority of "down-in-the-trenches" personal experience. I'd explored every avenue I could think of and the disappointing unfulfillment had only served to deepen my despondency.

And so, it had been in this frame of mind this morning that I'd turned to an old trusted ally who had rarely let me down—a long walk. Over the years, whenever I'd found myself creatively blocked or facing a perplexing problem, I'd make the time, an hour or so, for a few laps around the park lake or on the beach and turn things over to my subconscious. This is a trick I'd picked up long ago from somewhere and it had rarely failed to result in an answer of some kind. It just seems the uncluttering of one's head make us more easily accessible.

This had been such a time. I'd taken my walk and had wound up holding a book that promised to "heal grief." I had an intense sense of having hit pay dirt.

I would soon come to realize that what had started out as a walk in the park had actually been the first steps of what would wind up being an extraordinary journey. Culminating not just in the healing to which I'd aspired but also to an undreamed of level of enlightenment.

## The Direct Connect

By the time I got home from the library it was lunchtime, so I fixed myself a quick sandwich and brewed a pot of tea (I'm English—it's the law). I really wanted to start reading my book but a librarian friend once told me that sometimes when people return a book, you can tell what they've been eating and drinking, so I decided to watch television instead. The TV was tuned to the channel you have to go through to use the VCR (remember those days?) and one that I hardly, if ever, watch. I couldn't help watching though because as the picture faded to a commercial break it struck me that the show's host looked familiar. Something made me turn to the library book I'd placed on the end table next to my chair and there was the author's photo, it was the guy on the screen—it was James Van Praagh. When the program came back from the commercial break I learned it was his show called *"Beyond."*—I'd never heard of it.

This had been a busy day at the Department of Synchronicity. They were clearly so determined to get my attention and confirm that there was indeed 'something of significance' going on here, that they'd followed me home. I'd better take notice—I was being stalked.

I watched the remainder of the program in absolute awe. I was transfixed, this guy was incredible. The rest of the day, late into the evening and the next two days, was spent out on the deck ( my exterior office), equally enthralled by the book's theme—mediumship—communicating with those in spirit (dead people). Finally, I'd found an approach that spoke to me, or more correctly, I would later come to realize—*it* had found *me*.

On that first afternoon, I hadn't got very far into the book before I went online and ordered my own copy. Up came that piece of marketing genius—'*Those who ordered this book also bought...*' and two books were displayed by "the internationally renowned medium George Anderson."—They too went into my cart. My magical journey was well and truly off and running, so too was what would become quite an extensive library of wondrous knowledge, generously shared by psychic mediums, about the role those in spirit play in our lives.

Please know that I don't want to give the impression that I regard the approach to healing to which I was led, to be the only way to go. And I certainly would not presume to try dissuading anyone from exploring any approaches that come into their purview that appear to have healing potential. I only know that the approach to which I was led has worked for me. I hope it will be self evident that if this approach hadn't been effective, I wouldn't have been sufficiently motivated or would I have been up to the rigors of researching and writing a book about it.

I acknowledge and respect the fact that there may be those who, for one reason or another, may not feel ready to be fully acceptive of a medium's ability to communicate with those who have passed on. It is my hope however, that they don't allow their reticence to embrace this aspect prevent them from availing themselves of the other measures we'll be discussing. I feel they'll be found to be wholly compatible and even augmentive to any other steps and I don't think any of us need think they're at all contingent on relinquishing our existing beliefs.

I have to say though, that for me, the key element of my healing has undoubtedly been this wonderful gift of knowledge about the continuance of life after what we call death. This revelation and the attendant realization that we can continue to enjoy an ongoing connectivity with our loved ones in spirit and that we are never, ever alone, can not only mollify our grief but can enrich our lives to a degree that we hadn't previously dared think possible. Exalted enlightenment such as this enables us to transcend a lifetime of societal conditioning to which most of us have been subjected. Inarguably, a wondrous gift.

George Anderson, considered by many to be the world's greatest living medium, refers to it in his book *Walking In the Garden of Souls* as, "perhaps the greatest gift we will ever receive while we remain on the earth."

The kind of gift that just has to be shared. Wouldn't you agree? So here is my attempt to spread the light. Offered along with my fervent hope that it helps each and every one of you in every way you desire it to.

CHAPTER 1

# GRIEF

A report by the American Mental Health Association declared that the loss of a loved one is life's most stressful event. Now for anyone who *has* lost a loved one, this may appear to be stating the obvious and is not telling us anything we don't already know. But the reality is that unless they've had personal experience, people generally haven't had a reason to give much thought to how devastatingly debilitating the death of a loved one can be. And why would they? It's not something we're taught in school after all, and it's hardly the kind of subject that lends itself to conversations around the dinner table.

As a consequence, even when it's a case of simply being in the presence of someone in bereavement, we're simply not equipped to handle the situation very well. So we end up either detaching ourselves from it poste-haste or making banal and usually inappropriate comments.

Any of which can easily give the impression (albeit unintentional) that the innocent offender is heartless and disdainfully aloof to the griever's pain. Under normal circumstances, not likely to be a big deal, but someone in the throes of mental anguish and emotionally fragile can find it to be pretty hurtful.

The majority of those in grief rarely expect, or even want, anyone to get down in the abysmal quagmire with them, for heaven's sake, they wouldn't wish what they're experiencing on their worst enemies. To the contrary, these courageous souls recognize this as *their* challenge to face up to and hopefully overcome, they don't understand it but they own it. Lengthy speeches are neither necessary or expected, just a few well chosen commiserative words expressed with an attitude of sincere compassion will do it both for them—and the bestower.

So, in the spirit of "spreading the light," I don't think it would be at all amiss for us to pay a brief visit to this vexatious world of grief—that place populated by our direfully distressed brothers and sisters that our societal conditioning has had us uncomfortably tiptoeing around.

It's not going to be pretty (there is no "scenic route"), but it is hoped that the uninitiated amongst us will find this information enlightening enough to provide them with a valuable point of reference for the future. For our purposes here then it will be best, I feel, to corral this unpleasantness in one place rather than have it scattered throughout the book—this will also serve to get it behind us where it belongs.

We need this book to be about going forward—we've had enough of that other ghastly stuff. Begone with it!

I've found one of the ways in which people deal with the discomfort that being in our company induces in them, is to diminish our condition to the level of something they *are* familiar with, something they can then equate it to. Problem solved—for them.

I've met people for instance, who consider a person's grief following the death of their loved one to be, as one acquaintance put it, "On a line with a mental imbalance of some kind. Y'know, like depression. They have a pill for that now." There are days when it seems like everyone we meet is a "grief expert."

As the observation Shakespeare had Benedick make in *Much Ado About Nothing* goes—"Everyone can master grief but he that has it."

As someone who has experience of both grief and depression I think a little clarification is in order here. Depression is a component of grieving certainly, and is in fact one of the immutable standards known as *"The Five Stages of Grief"* introduced by the preeminent Swiss-American psychiatrist Elisabeth Kubler-Ross in her 1969 book *On Death and Dying*. So I suppose there is some affiliation, and grief brought on by the death of a loved one could be construed as depression. Ernest Hemingway for instance, referring to his own depression in a letter to his writer friend John Dos Passos, described it as, "That gigantic bloody emptiness." A term could certainly be applied to grief, but the depression that we're dealing with is 'depression industrial strength'—'turbo-charged—'super sized.' Inexorably, inexpressible anguish that is so far off the charts it defies description.

Whether the deceased loved one was our spouse, child, parent, sibling or friend, for the one in grief, none of the words we have in our language come close to adequately conveying the searing rawness of our pain. Even the carefully chosen words on a condolence card, proffered as they undoubtedly are, with sincere love, aren't able to alleviate for very long the abject despair and desolation which encases us during every waking minute.

*The Direct Connect*

Author Madeleine L'Engle in her foreword to C. S. Lewis's book *A Grief Observed*, referring to her own feelings following the death of her husband wrote, "The death of a beloved is an amputation."

Singer/actress Queen Latifah still struggles with her grief over the death of her brother Lancelot in 1992. He was killed while riding the motorcycle she'd recently bought him (just imagine.) She too describes her loss as being, "Like suffering an amputation."

President Dwight D. Eisenhower's first born child, Doud, died at three years of age in January 1921, from scarlet fever. In 1977 the former president looked back on Doud's death as, "The greatest disappointment and disaster of my life, the one I have never been able to forget completely." He is also quoted as saying, "There is no tragedy in life like the death of a child. Things never get back to where they were."

Grief, as I said earlier, is a notorious 'energy vampire.' Every bereaved person with whom I've spoken have attested to this, and referred also to their constant state of mental exhaustion. Even the effort required to deal with just the basic chores that getting through a normal day entails, can leave us thoroughly depleted. Oh—and let's not forget those intermittent out-of-the-blue bouts of crying. There are times, in the earlier days, when the crying hobgoblin isn't satisfied with mere bouts but locks us in it's contemptible grip and we sob, and we sob, and then we sob some more—till we ache in every bone. The we cry that we're aching. (Honestly, there's no pleasing some people.)

We recall having read somewhere that it's not good to "hold it in,"—that it's better if we "let it all out," that the flow of tears actually has a beneficial cleansing effect by flushing away harmful toxins. We figure that sounds quite plausible and praying that it is, we let it all go. Later, when the aching abates somewhat, we grudgingly have to admit to feeling curiously better—a little less depressed, clearer headed and strangely lighter.

We find it disquieting that we seem to be in a constant state of bewilderment—out of sync with whatever is going on around us. We feel it isolating and unsettling to live with the ceaseless sense of being "off kilter"—out of step with the rest of the world.

The author and intellectual C. S. Lewis, in his eloquently written book, *A Grief Observed* written following the death from cancer of his wife Joy, described it this way, "It feels like being mildly drunk or concussed. There is a sort of invisible blanket between the world and me. I find it hard to take in what anyone says."

A lady I once met described her grief after her husband's passing as feeling like some noxious contaminant had permeated her brain and every nerve and cell. Another widow I met just the other day said, "It's been over ten years since I lost Ted and there's never been a day when I've felt like a whole person, I part of me died with him."

A widower I met in line at the Post Office (we had a very long chat) told me, "After twelve years I still feel there's a huge gaping hole where my heart used to be. It's like my senses have closed down, everything's colorless, the whole world seems drab somehow. My daughter tells me I hardly ever laugh much anymore."

Welcome to the lamentably woeful world of the bereaved.

## Spousal Death

More than 2,500 books have been published on the subject of grief, that is a prodigious body of data. Now we don't presume to be anywhere near qualified to add anything new to a subject that has obviously already been covered six ways to Sunday, but there are unassailable 'knowns' that I feel are pertinent to our discussion here so it behooves us recognize them.

No doubt we are all aware of the accounts of widows and widows who have died shortly after losing their spouse. "Died of a broken heart" has traditionally been the often heard lament in many cultures following such tragedies. Well it turns out that we really *can* die of a broken heart. It's known as the "broken heart syndrome," also as "the widowhood effect" and has been the subject of many studies worldwide. They've shown irrefutably that the grief brought on by the death of a loved one can itself be a killer.

We all have hormones such as cortisol, epinephrine and norepinephrine, known as the stress hormones. During the brief periods of stress that most of us experience from time to time, the level of these 'chemical messengers is automatically raised to deal with it. Commonly known as the "flight or fight syndrome," it is a harmless, normal defense mechanism.

The grieving process however, is anything but brief or normal, as anyone with experience of it knows, it is an intensely unrelenting bombardment on our bodily systems. The grieving process can be a diabolical demon that can hold us in its grip for many months—even years.

Many studies have demonstrated that when our stress hormones are raised to abnormally high levels for a prolonged length of time, our defense mechanism becomes severely compromised. As a consequence, our immune system also becomes seriously compromised, rendering us susceptible to all manner of health problems in addition to the possible worsening of any existing conditions we may have.

A cursory search came up with a veritable catalogue of disorders the griever can be smitten with. Not necessarily actually *caused* by grief mind you,—no definitive cause and effect here, but unequivocally linked nonetheless. Grief expert Dr. Elizabeth Harper Neeld, in an article on the subject for *connect.legacy.com* offers just a partial list of such diseases:

> cardiovascular disorders, cancer, pernicious anemia, ulcerative colitis, leukemia, lymphoma, lupus, pneumonia, diabetes, influenza, glaucoma.

I suppose it's inevitable that there will always be those who choose to discount someone's grief or trivialize it as being a 'state of mind' and therefore we can just 'snap out of it'. Perhaps from now on, whenever we find ourselves in the presence of such an uninformed individual, we can share this with them to show them that grief is far more consequential than the 'green apple bellyache' level of malady they seem to think it is.

Researchers at the University of St .Andrews in Scotland studied more than 58,000 married couples going back to 1981. The study indicated that surviving spouses were most likely to die within six months of their loved one. Forty people had become victims of the widowhood effect within just ten days after their loved one's passing and a staggering 40 percent of women and 26 percent of men died within three years of their spouse's deaths. These direful outcomes were not exclusive to just the elderly either,—couples in their thirties and forties also succumbed at the hands of "the effect."

Another study, this one in Jerusalem, found that the bereaved spouse's risk of death during the first six months rose by up to a whopping 50 percent.

A study by Dr. Abhishek Deshmukh, a cardiology fellow at the University of Arkansas found that women are likely to suffer 'broken heart syndrome' up to nine times more than men. In 2007 he found

6,229 cases from a federal data base of 1,000 hospitals, and only 671 were men.

The passing of a surviving spouse isn't always isn't always measured in terms of months—weeks or even days. Would you believe minutes? In March 2010 the British newspaper the *Daily Mail* carried a report of just such an incident. A 56 year old gentleman found his 61 years old wife on their kitchen floor in a comatose state following, it was later determined, a massive heart attack. He called the 999 emergency service but when the paramedics arrived at the home they didn't receive a response so they broke in the front door, only to find the bodies of both of them. The pathologist's post mortem examination determined that they had both died of heart attacks *within minutes* of each other.

Another British newspaper, the *Daily Express*, reported in September 2012 that an 84 year old lady had died while actually traveling in a funeral car. The car was following the hearse that was carrying the body of her husband who had died two weeks earlier. The funeral was cancelled so that they could have a joint funeral.

For those with a leaning towards the persuasiveness of 'celebrity endorsements' (they do seem to be effective in most everything else), there are plenty of those on record too.

Former President Nixon passed away on April 22nd 1994, just *ten months* after the death of his wife Pat.

Country singer icon Johnny Cash's death in September 2003 followed the death of his wife of 35 years, June Carter Cash by less than *four months*.

William F. Buckley Jr., esteemed author and political commentator lost his beloved wife of 57 years Patricia, in April 2007. Speaking at her memorial service, former Secretary of State Henry Kissinger said, "Theirs was one of the greatest love affairs of our time." Bill couldn't go on without her—he died *ten months* later.

The legendary Annie Oakley *(Annie Get Your Gun)* was the sharpshooting superstar of Buffalo Bill's Wild West Show in the early 20th century. On her passing in November 1926 at the age of 66, her husband of 50 years Frank Butler, became so grief stricken that he died just *eighteen days* later.

Such is the boundless, incalculable power of love. Amazing isn't it?

I once saw the love between two people defined as "the inextricable intertwining of two souls." These accounts would seem to bear that out.

The ancient Roman rhetorician Lucian de Croszonza enchantingly visualized it this way, "We are, each of us, angels with only one wing. And we can only fly while embracing each other." A particularly poignant and appropriate epilogue to the foregoing examples I think.

Let's take a look at some of the ways we're affected by this 'flying alone on one wing.'

## Job Sharing—and Other Things We Miss

The Pulitzer Prize winning poet Edna St. Vincent Millay wrote, "Where you used to be, there is a hole in the world which I find myself walking around in the daytime and falling into at night."

We've no doubt heard it said that, "Nothing in our life's experience prepares us for the death of a loved one." It's possible truer words may have been said by someone somewhere, but I doubt it. Any presumptions we may have had regarding how losing a loved one affects people probably came from a range of disparate sources over the years, many of them unreliable—some of them fallacious misconceptions, and many of them proverbial old wives' tales. Many of those preconceptions that may have stuck with us are now in the process of being dashed, as we attempt to grapple with the realities of the horrendous and perplexing situation in which we now find ourselves.

What articulated the situation for me, as much as anything, was a casual remark made by Suzie, one of my wife's friends who had dropped by one afternoon to see how I was doing, and had used a term that I don't remember ever having given much thought to. We were chatting over a good old pot of English tea when she asked me how I was coping with the household chores, (while at the same time glancing at the stacks of dishes, pots and pans cluttering the sinks and counter tops).

Busted! I sidled over and closed the door to the laundry room—( that wouldn't have qualified for the Good Housekeeping Seal of Approval either). I'd just been telling her about how exhausted I felt all the time when she said, "I imagine you really miss the job-sharing you had with Doris." Suzie had deftly put her finger on it,—it's the job-sharing stupid!

We've all heard those old sayings many times I expect, "Two heads are better than one," and, "A burden shared is a burden halved."

Those wise old-timers could have been referring to what we now call 'job sharing.' Or, in our case—*used* to call. For many of us bereaved it's just not part of our lives now, for us, it simply doesn't exist any more. Sure, all those ubiquitous chores and tasks are still there. (Boy, are they?), but the sharing?—Gone!

We were a team and, like most solid, loving and caring partnerships we had never really thought of them as tasks, we'd always implicitly regarded them as simply 'just doing things for each other.' You could say that's what we had both lived for. There is

*Grief*

no team now, no 'awesome twosome'—no 'dynamic duo', we're a solo act now.

There's been a general consensus among the many surviving spouses with whom I've discussed the subject. The most burdensome challenge we have to deal with and get accustomed to, after the absence of their partner of course, is undoubtedly that of coping with the overwhelming number of tasks and duties that we are now solely responsible for. The myriad decisions, from the piddling to the jumbo size, that are now ours alone to make, with all the attendant anxieties about the consequences of making wrong ones. Make no mistake, this is heavy stuff we've been saddled with, the term "multi-tasking" gets redefined.

met a very nice lady for instance, whose late husband had always taken care of every detail of their household finances. The poor dear was barely capable of writing a check let alone balancing her check-book. And how about us men whose wives had always been the full-time homemaker? How many of us can claim to be fully conversant with all those appliances? How about the laundry, have you been in there lately? It's like the bridge of the Starship Enterprise in there these days. My wife had been a cooking teacher/nutritionist. For forty years, the only time I'd been allowed near *her* kitchen was when she wanted my help with the dishes. There are days now when it seems like I'm hardly ever out of there.

The countless chores, tasks, and endless errands are, of course, integral to everyone's daily life and because they don't demand much from us in the way of mental effort, they're regarded as drudgery—'the daily grind'. They do however, collectively, require what adds up to a considerable amount of *physical* effort, and now that 'sharing' is no longer in our life and we're carrying the full load, it can often get to be more than a little wearying. This is especially true if we're also working a regular job, an aspect which can sometimes be lost on the unconversant among us.

Case in point: My friend Joani is a very talented interior designer who operates her own successful business. She had always remained mindful of the fact that she probably couldn't have done so if it hadn't been for the assistance and support of Roger, her husband of seven years, in the running of their home and the parenting of their daughter, now six four years old.

Several months after Roger's tragic death, she told me that although she fully recognized how being busy running her business was helping her handle her grief, she was finding it such a strain juggling so many things. She had one client who was being particularly demanding and giving her a hard time in general so, in an attempt to get him to understand her situation, she listed the many reasons why she couldn't put in the hours that she'd previously been able to, when she'd had Roger's help. His thoughtless response was, "Oh we all have that problem."

No we don't sir. Many people have partners—job sharers!

When we consider the fact that not only are our bodily systems already severely burdened and our resources depleted and stretched to the max by our grievous state, it becomes clear to us that we have a lot on our plate.

We've seen earlier what happens to us when our stress hormones are elevated for an extended period of time—how our immune systems become seriously compromised, leaving us vulnerable to all manner of diseases. Our lack of job-sharing is this type of stress manifested. We can't expect everyone to have a thorough understanding of it's implications, but we can at least try to spread the word among those around us. Those close to us know we're not given to whining.

## Grief

For us, it's by no means a trivial thing and I think those who really care would want to know this.

Job-sharing is not the only type of sharing we no longer have and miss terribly.

The old adage quoted earlier—"A burden shared, is a burden halved," is actually itself a half. The other half goes, "A happiness shared is a happiness doubled."

Isn't the sharing of pleasurable experiences what partnerships, and especially marriages, are all about? The sharing of our pleasures is one of those needs that are fundamental to the human condition. You might say, "It completes us."

One of the platitudes proffered by the well-meaning commiserators offers this piece of profundity, "Remember the happy times you had together." Are you kidding me? That's exactly what we *don't* want ro remember—yet. The operative word here is "had,' we *had* them, but now we *don't*. In the future—down the road somewhere, sure, that would be nice and we look forward to it, but not right now. Reminders of the happy times are everywhere but right now the realization that there will never be any more does not hold one iota of joy for us. C. S. Lewis, in *A Grief Observed* said, "Her absence is like the sky—spread over everything."

It's the flashes of these kinds of remembrances that elicit from us a wince as we brace ourselves in anticipation of the inevitable wave of torturous heartache that can swamp us at the slightest provocation. That, together with the cold hard fist of abject grief right in the gut—and off we go again. "Remember the happy times," is excellent advice, but it's much too soon. We have a lot of serious healing to go through before we feel comfortable about re-visiting happy places. It's just too soon.

We're going have to learn how to cope with a number of these "Spoiler alert—brace yourself—reminders of good times shared" occasions. Birthdays, anniversaries, thanksgiving etc., and that daddy of them all—Christmas. Then there's the one that comes around more regularly that we had eagerly anticipated as families—the weekend. With it's distinctive segments of time, each with its own blend of flavors, tastes, colors, tempos, adventure and laughter, each with its own unique appeal. Memories re-kindled and now missed—every long, long weekend.

Our weekends now are characterized by the "sameness" of everything, regardless of what we do, where we go and, unfortunately at times, whom we go with. Just a "thoroughly boring blanket of blandness"—is how my fellow widower friend Michel puts it, and the kind of time I imagine Shakespeare must have had in mind when, in *Richard II*, he had Bolingbroke say, "Grief makes one hour ten."

Yes, it's all about the sharing—it's what we live for. Our existence feels desolately devoid of meaning without it. The 19th century novelist Charlotte Bronte put it this way:

"Happiness quite unshared can scarcely be called happiness; it has no taste."

I don't think any discussion about the things we now miss would be complete without mentioning *the* one that most of us bereaved would definitely like to miss. I'm talking about that annual jolly frolic—Christmas. A fellow griever friend referred to it as, "the time of year when I envy bears their ability to hibernate."

Week and weeks of 'happy'—'merry'—'joy to the world,' in your face every way you turn, and with glitter. Then there are those merriest of missives—the Christmas letters. Each one giddily documenting in detail the glorious achievements of every family member, including the family pooch and little Timmy's gerbil. Four scant months after my wife had lost her valiant three year battle with the horror that is breast cancer, I received six such letters from friends(?). I have no way of knowing what thoughts and considerations, if any, went into the sending of them, but I certainly know what thoughts (tearful), the receiving of them engendered.

Ah, the joys of Christmas and goodwill to all men—the griever's version. Yikes! Move over Mommy Bear. Set the alarm for February.

In all this talk about *our* concerns, problems and pain, let's not lose sight of the fact that we are by no means the only ones who are deeply affected by all this. Our children (regardless of their ages), siblings and other relatives and friends have *also* lost someone they hold dear. We shouldn't allow ourselves to forget for a minute that they too have all been hit just as grievously hard. For a daughter for instance, the loss of her mother, the super-mom nurturer and general factotum, can be especially devastating. The impact of my wife's passing on our daughter Bev, (we had both held her hands as she died), had always been a source of great concern to me, as had hers for me. I felt that another type of sharing had been at play here, one that warrants the addition of another line to our proverb—"A pain shared, is a pain halved."

## Invisibility

Another bugaboo of bereavement is how we can easily feel isolated by the reticence of people to being in our company, in effect, rendering us invisible. I realize it's probably an innocent automatic reflex with no malevolence intended, and there are some who are very good at it and carry it of with a measure of grace that we find quite acceptable. But there are those who give themselves away by being

*The Direct Connect*

so flustered and blatant about it that their awkwardness gets to be comical, we might even find it amusing if it wasn't so hurtful. While they are obviously aware of their *own* discomfort they seem strangely unaware of ours. The renowned and highly talented medium Allison Dubois is aware of it. In her book, *Secrets of the Monarch*, she talks about the ways in which people who have been emotionally wounded become invisible to those who avoid getting pulled into another person's pain by going into a self-protection mode.

Invisibility isn't exclusive to those in grief, friends, even those of longstanding, can also mysteriously suddenly disappear. I remember how crushingly disquieting it had been when it first happened to me. Over my years in business, I'd been gifted with a number of great relationships with work associates around the country. We'd cooperated on many challenging and innovative high-profile projects—down in the trenches, as it were, and had stayed in touch via phone and e-mails between assignments. When I conveyed to them the news of my wife's cancer diagnosis however, several of them, inexplicably, went completely incommunicado. Not a word. Doris made the observation, "I think your so-called friends must think the cancer is contagious and you're a carrier."

A friend of mine, Gina, told me about her experience with neighbors and how they'd become invisible after her husband's passing. Then one day, while out shopping, she happened to come face-to-face with one of them and confronted her about this. The neighbor's lame response was, "Well we don't know what to say."

Now Gina, while not a great fan of organized religion, is one of the most spiritual souls I've ever met—not a bigoted cell in her system. "It's like every time you call one of them they're at the church. If it's not pizza night it's bingo, if it's not that it's choir—they practically live at the place. Don't know what to say? What the blazes are they sermonizing about over there?"

At a time in our lives that we don't need it, our self esteem takes a hit. We feel discounted and inadequate. We like to think that we possess *some* attributes, *some* recognizable qualities that make us worthy enough to warrant them making a benevolent effort to overcome their discomfort and not add to our pain.

Dr. Jackson Rainer is a nationally known grief expert and a professor of psychology at Georgia Southern University. Quoted by Harriet Brown in an essay in *The New York Times*, he refers to this distancing as "stiff-arming"—creating as much space as possible from the possibility of trauma. It's magical thinking in the service of denial: If bad things are happening to you and I stay away from you, then I'll be safe.

We will learn not to take this kind of thing too personally and we will eventually inure ourselves to it and be more resilient. In the meantime, it sometimes helps if we remember what the German philosopher Nietzsche said, "That which does not kill us makes us stronger." After all, being invisible must have a bright side—if we can only see it.

## Isolation

Grief experts, in their books and essays, invariably emphasize how important it is for those in grief to maintain their social ties. Excellent advice of course, but another instance of "easy said." I think we all have an intuitive awareness of the part that social contact plays in our lives, we are principally social animals after all, and our desire for fellowship and companionship is inherently basic to us. It's in our DNA, in computer-speak—we're hard-wired for it.

## The Direct Connect

The fact that since our loss, we're not exactly the gregarious extroverts everyone once knew and loved, shouldn't be taken as an indication that we're blind to its importance. Does anyone really think that we revel in this unnatural isolation? There may be some who actually do, out of choice, and for the time being. Who knows? That's their prerogative. In *A Grief Observed,* C. S. Lewis suggests that, "Perhaps the bereaved ought to be isolated in special settlements like lepers." Many of the grieving people I've met who've shared their disheartening socializing stories with me would doubtless agree with him.

Socializing, for those in grief, can often turn out to be a miserable experience. Is it any wonder we're reluctant to subject ourselves to more of the same? Wouldn't that align us with one of the definitions of insanity?

For those of us who've 'been there—done that' it's quite understandable why socializing doesn't remain as high on a griever's list of priorities. It's likely that our diffidence stems from the fact that we've been on the receiving end too many times, of those "stiff arms" Dr. Rainer speaks of, and have the emotional bruises to prove it.

It's no accident that women, in the main, fare better than men at the socializing aspect. We must admit social networking is one of those things (there are many), that women are better at than men, and why they're the "social secretary." We have a tacit understanding that it's they who take care of those elements necessary for of our social connectivity—the address books—Christmas card lists of all friends and relatives—those all-important "Thank You" notes they're required to answer. When we figure in things like all those phone chats and the girls doing lunch at "Chez Crepes" it adds up to a much broader base of social connectivity than men are usually used

# Grief

to, and is indicative, I feel, of why it is that women appear to deal with widowhood better than men.

There are any number of isolating ways our social ties can become unraveled. Our new single status for instance, can completely change the dynamic of friendships where we'd done things as "couples," and we get an interesting insight of how insecure some marriages can appear to be. We're now, for instance, perceived by a wife or husband to be a potential threat—you know—on the lookout.(an absurd notion of course, but quite flattering). We realize it's probably going to be uncomfortable being around someone who's adopted that mind set, so we elect to use the "prior commitment" excuse if we're invited to any of their future soirees. In modern day parlance—we unfriend them.

This kind of attitude isn't defined by age group the way one might expect—it's not necessarily a case of "the young divorcee" cliche anymore. A widow lady friend told me about an embarrassing confrontation she'd recently had when an old friend had accused her of "setting her cap" for her husband. "Is she serious?" my friend laughed, "I'm 73 for heaven's sake."

I've heard many other accounts of the perceived threat of a surviving spouse's singleness being the reason for friendships becoming no longer tenable. I met Martin for instance, a man with such movie star good looks, he makes George Clooney look almost homely. A friend who belongs to the same tennis club as Martin told me that when Martin started getting out and about after the death of his wife, he'd scared the other male club members out of their wits and they'd been avoiding him like the plague. He hasn't been seen around the club for months, preferring instead to stay home and tend his garden. He finds his azaleas far more accepting of him.

It goes without saying that maintaining social connections and mixing with people *is* an important factor in our attempt to "get on with our life," but unfortunately, when we make the effort to carry this into effect we often find that it's not quite as simple as we'd expected it to be. Our ventures into this realm can often be fraught with all manner of disheartening rebuffs. There are aspects to this that are naturally conditional to each individual's unique circumstances and whenever we're dealing with other people (a requirement), we are of course faced with a wide range of attitudes. We ourselves can be as comfortable with our intentions, motives and desires as it's possible to be, but that gets us nowhere if people are uneasy about being in the company of someone who's circumstances spook them out. The old saying about, "withholding judgement till you've walked a mile in their shoes," comes to mind here. Along, perhaps, with John Bradford's observation, "There but for the grace of God, go I."

Betrayal. It's an ugly word with odious connotations. A word synonymous with treachery, duplicity and stabbed-in-the-back. Psychologists, recognizing it's hurtful nature, gave it a name—"The Betrayal Trauma Theory." My Funk and Wagnalls defines "trauma" as, "A severe emotional shock having a deep, often lasting effect upon the personality."

In talking with people who have lost loved ones, I've noticed that they often, when relating their experiences involving other people's attitudes to their grief, the same word would come up time and again—betrayal. "I felt betrayed." they'd say. "For years we'd been like brothers, I can't believe he betrayed me like he did." "It will take me a long time to get over her betraying me like that. We'd always been so close."

Hurt heaped upon hurt—it's a jungle out there. Some days we're reminded of the wildlife documentary we once saw that showed a lion stalking a herd of gazelle and hoping to find one with a limp.

Those grief experts ( the qualified ones) are by no means steering us grievers wrong when they prescribe socializing—maintaining our social ties. Excellent advice—point well taken. But from what we've seen in our discussion so far regarding the ignorance of many people about grief, mixing with people just for its own sake is a medicine with possible negative side effects. As my introvert friend Waggish Wally says, "The trouble with these social affairs is they attract so many bloody people."

In discussing the miseries that those grieving the loss of a loved one must endure, we've been compelled to deal with the negative aspects of the roles people play in our dire drama. To have glossed over this unpleasantness would have served to sugar-coat the excruciating anguish of the bereaved, and would have been a disingenuous depiction at best. Such a less than an honest approach would have fallen way short of providing the enlightenment that I feel this situation sorely needs.

## Expectations

We'll stay on the subject of the role that other people play in our aggrieved situation for a little while longer, but with this aspect we can relax—with these folk there's no intent to be disdainful or haughtily indifferent, just a genuine concern for our well being together with a desire to proactively help us.

It's only natural for those around us to have expectations of how long our recovery should take. It's also quite understandable that they feel it's important that they share this with us—their prognosis so to speak. Bless their souls, but it's here that we should be wary of possible flaws in their methodology.

For instance, the times lines they put forward will more than likely be unrealistically optimistic, wishful thinking if you like, out of their desire to give us some much needed encouragement. This may indeed lift our spirits somewhat, but unfortunately can be problematic for us down the road, in the event it becomes clear that we're not going to come anywhere near to meeting that goal that's been planted in our psyche. As a consequence, in our fragile state, we can all too easily convince ourselves that this is a sure sign that we're not only failing miserably, but that we may never succeed at all.—Not good for our morale.

I remember how incredulous I'd found it to be that so many people I met would state, quite authoritatively, that I could expect to "get through this" in eighteen months to two years. Are you kidding me? Honestly, where do they get these numbers? Well the fact of the matter is of course, they're not, by any means, authentic experts, they're *pseudo experts*—they're not required to get their numbers from any officially ratified source. Neither is it axiomatic that they have any personal experience whatsoever, it's just simply a case of them wanting to do something nice for us—that's all. Let's just leave it at that and accept it for what it is—opinion misrepresented as fact. Just their own totally uninformed idea of what constitutes an acceptable recovery time.

"Pseudo experts"—we can find our world to be super-saturated with them. I was raised to believe that it's possible for *anyone* to learn something from literally *anyone*, a concept I've benefitted from many times over the years. So I feel it behooves us to humbly brace ourselves to the deluge of opinions and lend them an ear, we never know when we'll come across a gem.

I'd concluded early on that despite what the "experts" (pseudo or legitimate) would like to think, the estimated time of recovery from the death of a loved one defies the dictates of some sort of formulistic system. That would be like the 'tipping chart' a friend fishes out in restaurants. There is no set timetable for grief—period! For any "expert" to insist that there is, is thoughtless, insensitive and irresponsible.

As former U.S. Secretary of State General Colin Powell once said, "Don't be buffaloed by experts and elites."

Neither is it wise to compare our perceived rate of recovery with that of anyone else. We are all different, the rate of one person's progress (even if that were quantifiable) can be vastly dissimilar to that of another's.

There was a time, two years or so after my wife's passing, when the relentless disapproving views expressed by people around me regarding my progress (or rather the lack of it) really got to me and I found myself even deeper down in the dumps. Around this time though, as if on cue, I started to become aware of a series of synchronous happenings that were unmistakably germane to my concerns. From all manner of sources they came—newspapers and magazines—television interviews—news items—snatches of conversations overheard, they were everywhere. It was obvious to me that someone was trying to get my attention. It turned out that I was being gifted with precisely what I was in need of, and it served to put the whole situation into a coherent perspective. It was like this pattern of events was a slide show formed to demonstrate how long various other people had grappled with their heartfelt loss. Here's a sampling:

In a recent local newspaper interview, an ex-New Yorker admitted to have never really gotten over the Dodgers baseball club leaving Brooklyn—*in 1957!*

## The Direct Connect

During a chat with a client's receptionist, she told me that she reaches for a tissue when she recalls how much she misses her favorite television Soap Opera that was cancelled—*eleven years ago!*

In a television magazine segment, CBS correspondent Susan Spencer, interviewing Alex Trebek, host of the long running quiz show *Jeopardy*, divulged that she herself had once taken the show's candidate test and failed it. "That was *fifteen years ago,*" she said, "and I'm still devastated by it."

I came across an internet report on a Grey Cup luncheon held by the Canadian Football League Alumni Association in November 2011 in Vancouver. During the proceedings, two of the celebrity attendees, both ex-players, who'd had a history of animosity towards each other, became embroiled in a bout of fisticuffs. It was all over a controversial hit in the 1963 Grey Cup Final—just a mere *48 years* before!

While sketching on a local dock one afternoon recently, I couldn't help eavesdropping on a group of anglers sitting nearby. They'd been trotting out their cliche "one-that-got-away" tales, and one of them wound up his woeful saga about losing "the big one" with a plaintive, "I tell ya.—I was crushed. To this day I feel sick to the stomach whenever I think about it."

A recent event? Hardly, it had occurred *sixteen years ago!*

Well, as they say, "My mom didn't raise no fools," I'd recognized the synchronicity for what it was.—Message received.

It would, of course, be ludicrous to infer that a direct comparison exists between these instances and the abject agony of losing a loved one. But they had for me, at that time, served to put things into perspective. I resolved that never again would I allow any self-appointed arbiter to get to me in the way they had—in future I'd be ready for them with a few pertinent comparisons. The poor guy

*Grief*

who'd been given the slip by a flipping fish would be a good one to keep in mind.

Two or three years eh?—Good luck with that!

Having that special person who has been, virtually our very life, taken from us is an indescribably brutal experience—for spouses, children, parents, relatives and friends. It is simply preposterous for anyone to seriously consider themselves qualified to give a bereaved person who's gone through such a horrifically harrowing ordeal, an estimate of how long their recovery to anything resembling normalcy is going to take. Sorry—can't be done.

The nature of bereavement just does not lend itself to this kind of facile prognosis. Those in grief would be far better served if wannabee therapists would practice a little forbearance by reining in their egos. This would at least spare those in grief the unnecessary pressures that plucked-from-the-air time lines can easily engender. Besides, there are karmic benefits for such acts of benevolence.

There's been general consensus among the fellow grievers with whom I've discussed this that the low-ball estimate of two or three years serves very little useful purpose, and the little that there might be is cancelled out anyway when it becomes apparent that our expectations had been false all along. The act of casually dispensing phony expectations is really the stuff of "fantasyland."

Don't just take my word for it. Let's take a look at a few noteworthy real world examples that I've come across:

In an article published in the British *Daily Mail* in April 2013, the film actor Pierce Brosnin, famous for his James Bond role, talked about the death of his first wife Cassandra, *twenty two years ago.* Pierce explained, "To watch someone you love have their life eaten away—bit by bit—by this insidious and horrid disease—becomes an indelible part of your psyche.—Memories of Cassie are with me every day."

I saw a television interview with a Presidential candidate who had lost his young son in a tragic car accident *twelve years* before. When asked by the interviewer if he had thoughts about his son while he was campaigning so intensely, like every day for instance. The candidate responded, "Try every twenty minutes."

The legendary comedy duo Gracie Allen and her husband George Burns were together for over forty years. After Gracie's death in 1964, George regularly visited her grave at Forest Lawn Memorial Park every month for decades. He would tell reporters that he used to chat with her about what he'd been up to and what old friends he'd bumped into.

Anne Diamond was the popular host of the British television program *Good Morning Britain*. She had tragically lost her four month old son Sebastian to Sudden Infant Death Syndrome (SIDS). In an article published in the *Daily Mail* in 2011, she spoke poignantly about how the awfulness of that summer morning when she'd found her beloved baby dead, never wanes, and how those emotions still flood back and hit her like a hammer blow. She added, "The tears are surprisingly near the surface even after *twenty years*."

I hope these examples have served to evidence the fact that recovery from the trauma of losing a loved one is inevitably, going to take time. Regardless of how tirelessly and diligently we work at it, no matter how assiduously we apply ourselves to the measures we decide to adopt, our journey back to any kind of normalcy is probably not, going to be the short quick trip that we, and those around us, would like it to be. We *will* reach our destination though. *Know it!*

## Grief

The universe has chosen to hand us a challenging assignment at this time and we have no option but to accept it. But you know what? We are a surprisingly resilient, courageous group of troopers us grievers, and we *will* be triumphant, we *will* prevail, never, *ever* doubt that for one minute. We may have trouble believing that at this moment, but mark my words—we'll see.

I'm aware that in discussing the various ugly aspects of the grieving process, I probably haven't said one thing that those in grief aren't already all too familiar with. But there are times when it's necessary to "preach to the choir" in order to reach those for whom the message is intended.

This has been such a time. You see, in talking to grieving people over the past few years, I've been struck by how often they would say, plaintively, "People just do not know." Over and over I would hear this, together with crestfallen expressions like, "Nobody understands you see." and, "If they only knew." Usually coupled with accounts of how a dismissive encounter with someone had left them hurt and saddened, sometimes for days, even weeks.

I know from experience how easily those in grief can find their misery re-kindled by someone's careless and inconsiderate comments—casual remarks that, to them, seem to be of little significance. Those in grief though have suffered torturous agonies that will continue to hover around the edges for some time. They are after all, let's face it—"post traumatically stressed," so it's not surprising that they're vigilant and sensitive to anything that could potentially trigger a relapse back down into that hell-hole.

Obviously there's no malicious intent here whatsoever and I'm convinced that if it could be brought to their attention that their purely innocent lack of understanding could be the cause of such distress, they would genuinely welcome the opportunity to be better informed.

So, as I said at the beginning of this chapter, I felt it would be a good idea to cluster our discussion on grief and it's distressing aspects into a single opening chapter—rather than scattering references to them throughout the book. Hopefully, this will facilitate the dissemination of this information to those whom we consider might be open to receiving enlightenment on the subject.

Plus—an added bonus, it doesn't hurt that this will also serve to get this wretched dolorous stuff behind us. After all, we want the tenor and disposition of this book to be buoyant, optimistic and above all else—*recuperative*.

CHAPTER 2

# MEDIUMSHIP— IT'S *ALL* ABOUT LOVE

If the number of books by and about psychic mediums is any guide, interest and belief in mediumship is growing like a prairie fire. Yet while the mystery and timidness that has traditionally surrounded the subject are obviously dissipating, it seems that for the seller's of these books there remains one mystifying aspect—what category to list them under. I've seen them in bookstores and catalogues under "Parapsychology"—"Metaphysics"—"Self-Help" and "New Age." The latter one I find kind of curious considering the practice of mediumship goes back over 250 years.

After a dozen or so years of researching the subject plus many readings and getting to know a number of mediums, one can't help acquiring some sense of the *essence* of mediumship—what it's essentially all about. So, based on the conclusions I've come to, I think I

## The Direct Connect

can make it simple for them. I think the most appropriate place for books on mediumship would be the "Romance" section.

You see, the spirits have told us over and over again, through the mediums, that the principal reason they make the considerable effort required of them to come through in a reading and also the prime motivator for those of us on this side of the veil to seek a reading, are both borne of the same driving force—*love*. It is *all* about love! This is the love energy in its purest and most unconditional form—love of the highest order—and it survives after physical death.

Physics has long established the absolute that energy, in any of its many varied forms, cannot be destroyed, it can only be transformed.

The energy of love is one that has fascinated philosophers since time immemorial:

The French philosopher Pierre Teilhard de Chardin described love as, "The most powerful and still most unknown energy in the world."

The classicists, of course, also had their take on the subject, Aristotle for instance said that "Love is a single soul inhabiting two bodies."

"Love," declared the poet Robert Browning simply, "is the energy of life."

The old cliché, "You can't take it with you." may very well be one of the greatest truisms of all time—in matters materialistic anyway, but it certainly doesn't hold true in matters of the heart. The spirits, from their fully enlightened perspective on the other side of the veil, have confirmed that love does survive death, in other words—you *can* take it with you. This isn't just conjecture or assumption on the mediums' part, they receive this information via the unique direct line they have with the souls in spirit—"straight from the horse's mouth," if you will. The great medium James Van Praagh, in his seminal book *Reaching to Heaven* writes, "love is so far-reaching that it transcends death. Love is the strongest force in the universe.......... it is a concentrated energy that has no boundaries."

The renowned medium Patrick Mathews has also received this information. In his book *Never Say Goodbye,* he writes "The love bonds we share with others never die even with passing over." and then this wonderful affirmation, "By having love for someone on the other side and knowing they are still with you, you are making them happier than you could possibly ever realize." Isn't that a soul-nurturing thing to hear? The highly esteemed New Zealand medium Jenny Crawford tells us in her book *Through the Eyes of Spirit,* of how she's learned from the spirits that "the spiritual and emotional link leaves us with part of our heart leaving the earth plane with our loved one." It's no wonder that the bereaved are often heard to say something like "I feel like there's a huge hole inside me."

The mediums have relayed these kinds of messages to survivors from their loved ones in spirit hundreds of thousands of times, and they talk passionately of the gratification they experience as they bear witness to the miraculous consoling effects these tidings have on the bereaved sitters. Just think about it—the sitters have just been informed, after receiving irrefutable verification that it is indeed their loved one who is present, that not only is their loved one in spirit now enjoying perfect health but they are actually with them in every way but the physical, and furthermore, always will be—come what may.

Could there possibly be a more effective grief therapy? Such is the prodigious power of mediumship—potent stuff.

The foregoing parallels my own experience as I started to absorb the awesome knowledge that streamed from the pages of those books by James Van Praagh and George Anderson. The mediums' books afford us the opportunity to avail ourselves of this same magic vicariously through their transcripted readings. As I said earlier, I'd explored the other avenues available to me and none of them had shown any signs that they would lead me to the recovery I was seeking. These books, on the other hand, immediately began gifting me with a positive intuitive knowing that I was receiving my marching orders—it wasn't long before I became convinced, without a shadow of a doubt, that this was the road I was being guided to take.

## The Case For Mediumship

The decision to take this route does call for a measure of courage and resoluteness on our part, we are after all—"going against the herd," and that usually invites challenges, but what worthwhile venture doesn't? I tend to get nervous and suspicious if those gatecrashers *don't* put in an appearance. Like Robert Frost says in his poem *The Road Not Taken*, we've opted to take "the road less traveled" so not everyone in the herd is necessarily going to embrace the mediumship aspect of our approach. There are those who feel that to do so would be to abandon the safety of cherished long-held beliefs and replacing them with something of which they have no personal knowledge, (we hear terms like "that stuff's a bit woo-woo," and its equivalents). Our independent stance can make them feel uneasy, resentful, and even those close to us can "turn on a dime" and become quite confrontational. In our depleted condition we may not feel up to being combative, but if we can steel ourselves and rise above such onslaughts we can use the situation as a springboard to impel us up to a dogged determination to stay the course—it's our choice.

## Mediumship—It's All About Love

When we do stay on this road, at some point it will undoubtedly become clear to us that, again, like Robert Frost, we chose the road "that has made all the difference." The realization that we're at last on the right track to recovery may have us feeling so elated that we want to share it with everyone, but it might be prudent to keep it under wraps, at least for the time being. For our own protection, it will be safer not to expose ourselves to the opinions of others and allow them to define us right now—we don't want to provide them with the opportunity to "rain on our parade," which they're often apt to do because one of those cherished long-held beliefs is that such happiness is inevitably short-lived and temporary.

There's no rush—we have plenty of time. We just need to steadfastly stay with the courage of our convictions and relax in the peace and knowing that we are now safely and assuredly on the road to the recovery for which we yearn. By learning to open our hearts and minds to the unique enlightenment that those spirit impart to us through mediumship, we will establish our own direct line to them. We will be gifted with the absolute knowing that we are receiving their spirit guidance, assistance and protection, and will continue to from now on. Plus—we will experience the thrill of being aware of it's presence as it manifests regularly in our daily life.

Can any of us honestly claim to know many people to whom we can entrust this kind of information at this stage? Anyone who does is very fortunate but one has to admit that this is pretty heavy stuff for average persons to get their heads around, they're probably not ready for it just yet. In any event, it's probably not in our best interests to expose ourselves to the possibility of discord that might hinder our progress. Why risk it at this stage? Much better that we wait till our recovery is unmistakably apparent so that people can plainly see for themselves.

So, as much as we would like to share (being the benevolent and caring people we are), there's no pressing need for us to "go public," no matter how much we'd like to shout it from the rooftops—or Facebook it—or Tweet it. If my experience is anything to go by, full disclosure too early could result in two guys in white lab-coats showing up at our door carrying a large net.

Foremost among the sacrosanct beliefs that people are so protective of, is of course those that pertain to their religious persuasion, but there really shouldn't be any cause for concern whatsoever in this regard. There is simply no sectarian cant or anything of that nature involved here, and I see no reason for anyone to feel that the notion of the continuance of consciousness after the change we call death in anyway conflicts, or is incompatible, with anyone's religious convictions. Belief in an afterlife in one form or another has been at the core of the great majority of religions and cultures throughout the world for thousands of years. I have yet to hear of a medium who is anything other than devoutly committed to the Divine. As a medium friend of mine once told me,"Mediumship emanates *from* Divine Source and not at the *expense* of it."

## Historic Precedents

According to the *Christian Science Monitor*, the belief in life after death is both timeless and global, with almost every culture believing in an afterlife. In many cultures worldwide, death is not regarded as an *end* but rather as the *beginning* of a new and better life in the next world. Our belief in an afterlife is generally regarded as a way of a coming to terms with death. The Indian poet and recipient of the Nobel Prize in

Literature, Rabindranath Tagore said "Death is not extinguishing the light; it is putting out the lamp because dawn has come."

In a three-year 2.8 million dollar research project at Oxford University, 57 researchers conducted 40 separate studies in 20 countries. The studies concluded that humans are in fact actually *predisposed* to believe in gods and an afterlife.

We have evidence that indicates that even prehistoric man believed in an afterlife—that our personal identity survives the end of our physical lifetime and continues in a non-physical form. Archeologists have discovered prehistoric remains that indicate that their dead were buried along with personal possessions such as tools and weapons that they would presumably have a need for in their next life.

The Ancient Egyptians believed that following death they went to a place that duplicated life here on earth. So their dead were also buried along with their favorite possessions, together with *everything* they would need (that expression that refers to the kitchen sink comes to mind here).

We know for sure what these items were, thanks mainly to generations of grave-robbing westerners, our museums are full of them. The articles they packed for their journey included jewelry, furniture, clothing, knives, spoons, plates, cosmetics, ornaments, statues, tools, and interestingly—*a supply of food!*

They were also fond of decor that symbolized portals, such as large granite carvings of doors through which to pass on their way to the afterlife.

Later on, the ancient cultures of Greece and Rome showed a similar faith in an afterlife which was reflected in their elaborate burial rituals and ceremonies. The Greeks believed that all souls go to a place they called Hades—the land of the dead. To get there, they were required to cross the Acheron, one of five rivers. The dead were buried with a coin in their mouth because their spirits were transported to other side of the river by a ferryman named Charon. A bit of a capitalist was our Charon—apparently he demanded a gratuity for his services. I think I met one of his descendants a few years ago, driving a cab on the island of Crete.

In 850 B.C., the Greek author Homer wrote "'Tis true; 'tis certain; man though dead retains part of himself; the immortal mind remains"

Ancient Romans too were convinced that on dying they were transported to another land. They called theirs Paradise, a land of immortality, and their transport of choice was a four-horse fiery chariot—a stylish hot-rod.

Closer to home, our neighbors to the south of us in Mexico, like most other Latin American countries, celebrate All Souls Day on November 2nd known as the Day of the Dead. Many Mexican people living in American communities recognize the Day of the Dead every year with elaborate and colorful celebrations. It is believed that during the Days of the Dead the souls of the departed return to visit with and give counsel and advice to their surviving loved ones and family.

The famous 19th century historical novelist Sir Walter Scott said "Is death the last sleep? No– it is the last and final awakening."

## We All Allude To It

A 2009 CBS News poll found that as many as 78 percent of Americans across all age groups believe in an afterlife. In an article in *The American Sociological Review* in 2000 the Rev. Andrew Greeley, the well known Catholic priest and a University of Chicago sociologist, submitted compelling evidence that peoples' belief in life after death is increasing. Even among those with no particular religious affiliations, belief in a hereafter is growing—from 44 percent thirty years ago to 63 percent today. That is a trend of some considerable significance. In the jargon of Wall Street,—leading indicators like that are considered to be a presager of significant stock market gains.

When I came across these impressive statistics that reveal that a great majority of us believe that life survives death, I couldn't help wondering about what kinds of ways people's belief in the hereafter is reflected in their day to day lives—in our attitudes, approaches and responses to the many varied situations we encounter in a typical day. Does our belief manifest and impact on them in any discernible ways?

As if on cue, it seemed like the moment I started to ponder and reflect on possible ways this could occur, instances relevant to it began to serendipitously pop up. No *direct* references to there being an afterlife per se but comments and observations expressed idiomatically that tacitly acknowledged that there is by *alluding* to it. Examples were suddenly everywhere.

On a television sit-com, a mother berated her son with the kind of expression we hear often, "Your grandaddy must be turning in his grave at the way you speak to me." Surely a consciousness alluded to, right? And the variations of it that refer to spinning...rolling over etc. (Seems those dead folk stay pretty active. Are they into aerobics or something?).

Then there are all those acceptance speeches at the awards ceremonies, with their predictable "I just know my proud daddy is up there watching this tonight."

Mourners offering words of condolence at a funeral or memorial service often unthinkingly speak in banal clichés like, "He's gone to a better place" and, "She's reunited with her husband now." Undeniable inferences to there being 'something' after this—a place, a venue, but it stops right there. Nothing more—never any attempt to elaborate further, and none expected apparently. There's obviously a tacit understanding that such remarks are proffered only as conversation closers rather than openers anyway. But alludes to an afterlife nevertheless.

After I'd become aware of how frequently the many expressions like these are used, I couldn't help but wonder how those people would respond if they were asked whether it indicated they believed in an afterlife. I imagined them saying something to the effect, "Well, I can't say I've ever given it much thought, but when you put it that way—yes I suppose it does."

So for several months, whenever the opportunity presented itself in social situations, (and it did, more often than I'd anticipated) I would pose the question to people. Sure enough, that was invariably the answer I got. I was left with the feeling that if these kinds of responses were factored in to those polls, the numbers could conceivably be much closer to 100 percent.

Here are a few other examples that have recently come into my purview:

Sports and entertainment figures, in their celebrations of their achievements, are notorious for acknowledging the presence of spirit. The famous jockey Calvin Borel for instance, after winning the Kentucky Derby in 2010 for the second consecutive year, threw a red rose from the winner's wreath up towards the heavens. In a post race interview he explained, "That was for my deceased mom and dad watching."

New England Patriot's quarterback Tom Brady displayed his belief in similar fashion. In the game following the death in 2011 of

Patriot's owner Robert Kraft's wife Myra, after throwing a touchdown pass, he touched his team patch while pointing and looking up to the heavens as if to say "That one was for you Mrs. Kraft."

The English golfer Justin Rose won the U.S. Open Golf Championship on Father's Day 2013 (coincidentally, the official flower of Father's Day is the rose). On being presented with the winner's trophy he held it up to the heavens in honor of his beloved father Ken, who'd died of cancer in 2002. In an interview he said, "It wasn't lost on me that today is Father's Day. For it all to have worked out for me on such an emotional day, I just couldn't help but look up to the heavens and think that my old dad Ken had something to do with it."

Then there's that happily expectant expression "The best is yet to come,"—an allude to an afterlife possibly? "Old blue-eyes"—the great Frank Sinatra himself, appeared to think so—he had those words etched on his tombstone. It was also the title of the very last song he ever performed in public, on February 25th 1995.

In her speech at the Democratic Party Convention in 2008, soon-to-become First Lady Michelle Obama revealed her belief in an afterlife by acknowledging the presence at the proceedings of her deceased father, when she said "I can feel my dad looking down on us just as I've felt his presence in every Grace filled moment of my life."

In a CBS *60 Minutes* segment, correspondent Morley Safer spoke with the acclaimed historian David McCullough, two-time Pulitzer Prize winner and recipient of the Presidential Medal of Freedom. They sat together in front of Carpenters' Hall in Philadelphia, which hosted the First Continental Congress of the United Colonies in 1747.

Expounding on the emotional attachment he has for the location that's served as the backdrop in his works, Mr.McCullough said "Now you know I don't believe in ghosts. But at night, walking along

*The Direct Connect*

Market Street where they all lived and convened, it gets very quiet—I know that they're there. They really are—you feel it. You feel it!"

I think the great David McCulough just alluded to an afterlife. I'd love to see the look on his face when he discovers (which he surely will, one day) that those Founding Fathers have, all along, actually been assisting him in writing those wonderful books he's famous for.

For much of the almost 47 years that the late Senator Ted Kennedy spent in the United States Senate he passionately championed a universal health care system. He often referred to it as "The cause of my life."

*The Washington Post* reported in March 2010, that a few days after President Obama signed his historic health care bill into law, when the Senator's son Patrick J. Kennedy (D-R.I.) visited the grave in which his father had been laid to rest just seven months prior, he left behind a handwritten note that read simply "Dad, the unfinished business is done."

In anticipating his father would read those words the Honorable Congressman was clearly alluding to the survival of life after death, was he not?

Hearing declarations like these, expressed as they are so frequently and with such cogency and conviction would lead one to believe that a universal understanding and acceptance of life after death is just as firmly established and accepted as death itself, but that's hardly the case. If any conjectural thoughts *are* ever present they come to a stop right there and leave us hanging. "No admission past this point," seems to be the tacit injunction.

In an age where it seems every facet of our lives is becoming increasingly more scrutinized and every thought and feeling analyzed to a fare-the-well, there appears to be little discernible interest in examining the possible ramifications of what is inarguably such an extraordinary notion beyond these types of casual, almost offhand, alludes to it. An inquiring mind can't help but find this puzzling, it goes against our nature—people are more nosier than this as a rule.

As a consequence, like a promise unfulfilled, there exists an extensive knowledge gap between the two factions, an area where fallacies flourish.

## The Mediums—a Hard Sell

This is where the mediums come into the picture. Through the amazing abilities with which they have been gifted, connections are made—bridges are built that connect us to those on the other side of the veil. But despite the fact that the mediums have this ability to "flesh out" and substantiate a notion that everyone already habitually alludes to, people are fearful of crossing that bridge. There's a medical term for that, gephyrophobia—the fear of crossing bridges.

I'm reminded of a magazine item I came across some years ago. It told of how, back in the forties, a Madison Avenue advertising executive had long held the view that the main task of advertising copy was to overcome the public's inherent suspicious nature. His partner suggested that he put his theory to the test, so he set himself up with a vendors cart and signs that read. "FOR SALE – Genuine five dollar bills—Three dollars each." Then, early each morning, armed with his props, he took up a position on a busy block of Fifth Avenue. At the end of the week he'd had all of two takers. Man, we're a suspicious breed aren't we?

It seems to me that it's possibly the "supernormal" aspect of this ability the mediums possess that makes it so difficult to accept. "What makes these weirdos think they can talk to dead people?" they ask incredulously. They just don't buy it, and no amount of explaining can convince them. What they *do* see, they've often indicated to me, is that mediums, rather than conforming and marching in lockstep with some established high-minded doctrine, choose instead to dauntlessly follow some kind of discipline of which only *they* have any knowledge. This tends to make many people ill-at-ease, suspicious and even seems to scare some of them half to death, to the extent they flatly refuse to even discuss it. Not rationally anyway.And therein lies the rub—methinks. For this reason: Most every field of endeavor has its "stand-outs" or "phenoms," exponents who have been gifted with skills that surpass and go way beyond those of their contemporaries. No one seems to have difficulty accepting that there are people who are gifted with such extra-special abilities because the activities at which they excel, like baseball, football, chess, and tennis for instance are in our sphere of experience. But mention the special ability with which mediums are gifted and it's hard to find anyone who doesn't scoff at the notion—those expressions like "That's woo-woo stuff"are heard.

I feel that it must be the much greater degree of visibility and the higher profile of these other fields of endeavor that gives them the credence and the universal acceptance that's afforded them. In a word—they're cool. All things that mediumship has historically lacked. No globally lionized luminaries here—and I've yet to see a medium anywhere near a confetti cannon.

We refer to this ability with which the standout performers are gifted as "genius" they have "it," and "it" cannot be taught, (assisted to some degree by development and practice perhaps) but the essential "it" must be present in the first place—at birth.

I'm thinking of the Da Vinci's—the Beethoven's—the Einstein's—the Bjorn Borg's—the Charlie Chaplin's, all beneficiaries of huge helpings of God-given exalted talents.

# Mediumship—It's All About Love

I remember a wonderful filmed lecture by acclaimed composer/conductor Leonard Bernstein, in which he analyzed for us Beethoven's manner of creating his symphonies. At one point, in passionately reverential awe, he proclaimed that "The man clearly had a direct line to God!"

Then there was an interview I saw with the Romanian tennis star Ilie Nastase, in which he discussed his experience playing against the Swedish legend Bjorn Borg. Nastase, himself a singularly gifted player, said "The rest of us were out there playing tennis, God only knows what Bjorn was doing—the man's a robot."

Both instances were cited because they serve to reference the ways their special abilities are manifested, providing us with the means of evaluating their specialness. Coincidently, the skills of both these geniuses actualize in their respective scores—Beethoven's in his musical scores and Borg's on the scoreboard.

For me, this is entirely analogous to the mediums situation in that *they* also work with unique abilities about which no one can really claim to have a definitive understanding.

The mediums however, operate without the benefit of demonstrable notability, their special abilities are employed for the most part in personal one-on-one situations with a sitter. They too create unforgettably glorious moments, but without the fanfare. Even in message services or public demonstrations in front of audiences, the genuineness of messages relayed from spirit can really only be determined by the sitter for whom they're intended. Other people in the audience can only try to judge by the sitter's facial expressions and reactions whether or not the medium is getting "hits." But this can be misleading because the experience of receiving undeniably accurate evidence of a loved presence can be so powerfully stunning

## The Direct Connect

that the recipient often just freezes in absolute awe. The mediums though, recognize these kinds of reactions and for them they serve as their "rave reviews."

So the quality and accuracy of the medium's abilities really comes down to the personal judgement of those receiving the messages, with no such thing as audience feedback in the form of outbursts of applause or laughter etc., on which regular performers thrive—we're not exactly talking concerts at Carnegie Hall or the Gentlemen's Singles Final at Wimbledon. As long as mediumship is largely misunderstood and inexplicably unrevealed and unappreciated it will continue to be a hard sell. A friend of mine quips that, in an effort to level the playing field and bring some perspective to the proceedings, she's seriously considering attending a Medium's Message Service equipped with an illuminated scoreboard on which those receiving a reading can record their 'hits,' a confetti cannon and a tee-shirt stand.

It is a great, great pity that mediumship is not more widely understood and accepted. Not only because of its astonishing power to heal but also because it has the capacity, by extension, to provide us with the answers and solutions to many, if not all, of those vexatious and problematic challenges we're all called upon to face from time to time.

The mediums have been told, in millions and millions of readings with those on the other side of the veil, for more than two hundred years, that they maintain a constant loving presence in our lives. For those grieving over their loss of a loved one, hearing this "straight from the horse's mouth" can bring about tremendously healing levels of peace, comfort, solace, amelioration and hope, to a degree that up until now, they had not even dared dream of. What had been agonizingly unbearable becomes decidedly bearable. Such is the power of this wonderful ability with which our mediums have been gifted—and which they in turn gift us. There is simply nothing that warrants such fearfulness—there's just nothing at all mysterious about it.

Why anyone who's living the nightmare that is grief would be reluctant to avail themselves of a therapy about which millions of testimonials to it's efficacy have been made, over many generations, is the *real* mystery here.

So that is the role of the psychic medium. I've been privileged to know a number of them in the years since my wife made her transition. I know them to be just ordinary regular people who happen to have been Divinely gifted with wondrous abilities that they've worked diligently to develop and hone them even further. I know them to be acutely aware of the responsibility that their gift comes with, they reverentially accept this as their calling and they carry it with all due humility. They are dedicated to applying their abilities unerringly for the universal good and in service to those who have a need for them. They are above all, genuinely guileless simply splendid people. You can go near them—they won't hurt you, honest.

## The Religion of Spiritualism

My friend Tommy told me recently about a social gathering he'd attended the previous weekend where the host, when introducing him to a fellow guest, had mentioned that Tommy was a Spiritualist. The man said "That's interesting, I met a chap just the other day who said he's into Spiritualism. Tell me, what *is* Spiritualism exactly, it's not one of those fads like that macramé thing my wife was into once is it?"

A fit-to-burst indignant Tommy exclaimed "A fad? *A fad?* They're equating us with the macarena, hula-hoops and bloody beanie-babies now!" So, if only for the sake of Tommy's blood pressure, let's get a few things straight.

## The Direct Connect

First of all, the beginnings of this Spiritualism "fad" go back to around 1848. It is an officially sanctioned, fully accredited religion. It has its own churches and ministers who are granted the same rights and privileges as other religions.

The National Spiritualist Association of Churches define a Spiritualist as "one who believes, as the basis of his or her religion, in the communication between this and the Spirit World by means of mediumship and who endeavors to mold his or her character and conduct in accordance with the highest teachings derived from such communication."

We talked earlier about how mankind's belief in an afterlife has been traced all the way back to prehistoric times. The fact that the mystics, shamans and priests of ancient cultures were revered for their abilities to communicate with those in the spirit realm would indicate that they were actually the very roots of mediumship and subsequently Spiritualism—the Van Praagh's and John Edward's of their time.

Modern Spiritualism here in the west is generally acknowledged to have come about as a result of the controversial events involving the two young sisters, Margaret and Katie Fox at their family's small farmhouse home in Hydesville, New York in March 1848. The two sisters maintained that they had been communicating with a spirit entity using a coded word system of knocking and rapping sounds. After passing numerous rigorous tests by various experts they quickly became national celebrities. When their older sister, Leah organized the Society of Spiritualists it spun off into the formation of many Spiritualist societies throughout America

It was around this time that an English social reformer named David Richmond came to America to check out the Spiritualist phenomenon first hand. He was inspired by what he witnessed and on his return to England he founded the first Spiritualist Church in the United Kingdom in 1853 in the town of Keighley, Yorkshire. This church still exists but unfortunately not in its original building.

In 1885, back in America, Marcellus Seth Ayer, described as a progressive and free-thinking man, founded the First Spiritual Temple in Boston, the first temple in the world dedicated to religious Spiritualism. The temple remains active to this day.

By 1897, it was reported that there were eight million followers of spiritualism in the United States and Europe.

Among the many notables who supported Spiritualism in the U.S. was the eminent Dr. William James, known as the father of American psychology. He was a professor of psychology at Harvard University for thirty five years and became the first president of the American branch of the Society for Psychical Research founded in England in 1882. It was after being impressed by the quality of a personal reading he'd had with the well known medium Leonora Piper in 1885, that Dr. James made the much-quoted succinct statement he's become widely known for, "If you wish to upset the law that all crows are black, it is enough if you prove that *one* crow is white. My white crow is Mrs. Piper."

The practice of mediumship continued to flourish in both the United States and Europe despite being subjected to vigorous scrutiny and challenges to its legitimacy. Naturally some instances of fraudulence were exposed. But has there ever a field of activity where that *hasn't* been the case?

As the renowned English writer G. K. Chesterton, known as the "Prince of paradox" said, "A false ghost disproves the reality of ghosts exactly as much as a forged banknote disproves the existence of the Bank of England— if anything it *proves* its existence."

In any event, it turned out that any attempts to discredit the mediums' abilities were completely negated by the solid support for mediumship of many highly regarded scholars of the day together with numerous eminent men of science who, after their own investigations, had the courage and forthrightness to publicly endorse the mediumship phenomenon.

The movement continued to flourish into the twentieth century with a significant surge in interest taking place during and after World War One. This has been attributed to the tremendous carnage of the war but due also, in no small part, to support given by such prominent public figures as Sir Arthur Conan Doyle, creator of the hugely popular Sherlock Holmes, and his friend the celebrated scientist Sir David Lodge. Sir Arthur published his book on spiritualism *The New Revelation* in 1918, followed in 1926 by his two volume *History of Spiritualism*. He became a lifelong advocate and supporter of the movement. He was called the "St. Paul" of Spiritualism and traveled the world lecturing on the validity of the mediums' ability to communicate with the spirits of the dead.

By the late 1920's there were some two thousand Spiritualist Societies in the U.K. After more than two hundred years, Spiritualism continues to grow in stature and acceptance. It has been estimated that there are now over 15 million adherents world-wide.

Some fad.

## Endorsements

I read in an advertising trade magazine that fifteen billion dollars a year is spent on celebrity endorsements and corporate sponsorships.

The article went on to cite a Harvard Business School study that showed that ads featuring celebrities can increase sales by twenty percent. Those ubiquitous endorsements obviously work, they make believers out of us, or in modern day parlance—they improve "brand recognition."

Celebrity endorsements are by no means a modern phenomenon. Back in the 1800's, a sketch of Pope Leo XIII was featured on posters for Vin Mariani—a French red wine. In 1875, the renowned American author Mark Twain allowed his name to be used to endorse three brands of cigars, one of which survives to this day.

They certainly didn't hurt the Spiritualism brand during its establishment and growth during the late nineteenth and early twentieth centuries. In those days, the celebrities whose words carried the most weight regarding the validity of mediumship both in Europe and the U.S. came in the form of distinguished men of science, esteemed scholars of the day and officials of the church. Originally, there had been no shortage of these "experts" eager to weigh in with their repudiations of this preposterous phenomenon that had captured the imagination of the general public to such an extent. Many of them made no secret of the fact that it was their intention to "denounce these charlatans." There were also those who actually believed the mediums to be hallucinating.

However, after thoroughly investigating the mediums and subjecting them to the most intensive and stringent tests they could devise, many of them relented and associated themselves with those who had been the movement's loyal standard bearers. Some holdouts and fence-sitters of course but that's only to be expected with a subject of this nature. It's really impossible not to respect and admire the forthrightness of those who did choose to publicly acknowledge their findings and admit to their misjudgement.

Many of these men were the intellectual giants of their time after all, distinguished figures in their respective fields. People of prominence who, despite their professional and social status, courageously put it all on the line. Not in the interests of self-aggrandizement, not for monetary gain, but for no other reason than that it was for the greater good. We've gotta give it to 'em.

Here are a few of these celebrity endorsers. A comprehensive listing can be accessed on the website of the Academy for Spiritual and Consciousness Studies—www.aspi.org.

In the United Kingdom:

Sir Oliver Lodge (1851–1940)—World renowned physicist. As a pioneer in the development of radio he was actually the first to transmit a message by wireless signal in 1894—ahead of the better known Marconi. He didn't consider there to be any conflict between mainstream science and psychical research, he wrote "For myself, I do not believe that physics and psychics are entirely detached, neither is complete without the other." Like his friend Sir Arthur Conan Doyle, he also studied Leonora Piper closely, and the experience convinced him of the validity of survival after death and a medium's ability to communicate with spirit. Although a practicing Christian, he never wavered from what he believed to be the truth. He wrote "I am as convinced of continued existence on the other side of death as I am of existence here."

Sir William Crookes (1832–1919)—Described as one of England's most celebrated scientists. As a physicist and chemist, he was noted for his discovery of thallium and the high vacuum tubes that contributed to the discovery of the x-ray. Initially one of those "switchers" we mentioned, he'd originally set out in 1870, to "drive the worthless residuum of spiritualism into the unknown limbo of magic and necromancy" (charming). He studied several leading mediums of the day and obviously concluded that mediumship wasn't "just a trick", as he'd previously pronounced it to be, because he later became president of the Society for Psychical Research.

Rev. William Stainton Moses (1839–1892)—Ordained as a clergyman of the Church of England by Bishop Samuel Wilberforce in 1870, he was a psychical researcher and himself a gifted medium. He was appointed English Master at University College, London and in 1884 became a founding member of the London Spiritual Alliance. Prior to his own psychic abilities coming to light, he'd declared all mediumship to be "fraudulent and demonic."

Professor Augustus De Morgan (1806–1871)—Considered to be one of the most brilliant mathematicians of the 19th century. He was professor of mathematics at the University College of London and at the age of twenty one was appointed chairman of that department. He was one of the first English scientists to investigate Spiritualism and became convinced of its genuineness. We know this because in the Preface of a book, *From Matter to Spirit* written by his wife, De Morgan wrote "I am perfectly convinced that I have both seen and heard, in a manner that should make unbelief impossible, things called spiritual which cannot be taken by a rational being to be capable of explanation by imposture, coincidence or mistake"

Vice-Admiral W. Usborne Moore (1850–1918)—A mathematician and logician. On his retirement from the British Navy in 1904 he became a devoted psychical researcher. Sir Arthur Conan Doyle described him as "among the greatest." Besides studying dozens of mediums in Great Britain, his investigations also involved three extended visits to the United States where he sat with many mediums, notably with the gifted Etta Wriedt of Detroit, Michigan. He'd previously written two books on Spiritualism and his third book *The Voices* dealt solely with Etta's mediumship. In it he said about her, "For my part I can only say that, in her presence, I obtained evidence of the next state of consciousness so clear and so pronounced that the slightest doubt was no longer possible."

Notable endorsers in the United States:

Judge John W. Edmonds (1816–1918)—The judge enjoyed an extremely distinguished public career. Besides being a member of the New York State Legislature he also served as President of the Senate and subsequently became Chief Justice of the New York State Supreme Court.

In 1851, after his interest had been aroused by the controversy surrounding the Fox Sisters and the supposedly psychic events involving them, he embarked on an investigation of Spiritualism and the claims made by mediums, with the express intention of publicly exposing their fraudulence. His investigation was characterized as being logical, hard and indicative of a man of the law.

In August 1853 however, in an article in the *New York Courier* in which he related his experiences, he audaciously confessed to his complete conversion to Spiritualism. The resultant outcry and the attacks by the press, the church and politicians, forced him to resign his position on the Bench. The judge remained steadfast in his beliefs though and continued to unwaveringly champion the cause of Spiritualism, becoming perhaps the staunchest adherent of Spiritualism in America.

Governor Nathaniel P. Talmadge (1795–1864)—A lawyer by profession, he was a United States Senator from New York and the Governor of the Wisconsin Territory. Originally a firm non-believer in mediumship (he'd referred to it as a "delusion,") he was persuaded by Judge Edmonds to personally investigate the subject. This he proceeded to do—quite thoroughly apparently, with many personal readings and séances.

He became convinced of its veracity after a series of positive experiences that included communications with his old friend from the Senate the late John C. Calhoun, former Vice President of the United States.

Dr. Robert Hare (1781–1858)—A professor of chemistry at the University of Pennsylvania and a world renowned inventor. In July 1853 he wrote to the *Philadelphia Enquirer* denouncing the "popular madness" called Spiritualism. His letter elicited a response from a Amasa Holcombe who challenged Hare's views and suggested he make a scientific investigation and not just assume that it was all fraudulent. In a reading he had as a consequence he received accurate evidential messages from his deceased parents and sister that induced his conversion to Spiritualism.

Professor James J. Maples (1806–1866)—An analytical chemist and inventor. An attempt to save his friends from "running into imbecility," is the reason he originally gave for his investigation into Spiritualism. The way in which he framed that explanation must have incited the spirits to have a little fun with him, because a reading he had with the medium Cora Richmond produced evidence that defied explanation. And another successful conversion was chalked up. It turned out some time later that both his wife and daughter discovered their own previously latent mediumship abilities and went into practice.

So, that's a brief sampling of some of the pioneers of Spiritualism—the dew-beaters. Bold and intrepid stalwarts to whom the world owes a sizeable debt of gratitude.

CHAPTER 3
# THE SKEPTICS

As we've seen, psychic mediums have been effectively ministering to the needs of people in grief for over 160 years now. Yet despite this impressive record, there remain those who are skeptical of mediumship's genuineness, maintaining that it is just some kind of trickery designed to separate vulnerable people from their money in exchange for false hopes. Most skeptics are just regular well-meaning folk with our best interests at heart and may even include friends and family. But then there are the "professional skeptics," these are the ardently fervent ones with extremely strong feelings on the subject that they love to share with us at every opportunity. The passions of some of them run so high that they do actually make a career out of it, they operate websites and form clubs of like-minded zealots. They have also been known to insinuate themselves into the mediums' lectures and demonstrations where they behave obnoxiously and carry on in ways designed to be disruptive to the proceedings.

## The Direct Connect

Unfortunately their fervency is so intense there doesn't appear to be much chance of them opening their minds anytime soon, to the possibility they may be mistaken. Just recently, I was having a pleasant and quite rational discussion with a nice lady whom I knew to be a firm non-believer. Something I said though must have pushed the wrong button, because what had up until then, been a pleasurable chat with a reasonable and good-humored person turned suddenly into a "Beam me up Scotty" moment when she referred to mediums as "those agents of the anti-Christ," followed shortly afterwards by "they're the spawn of Satan." My waggish friend Alicia, who'd overheard this, commented later "I know about survival of intelligence *after* death, but there are times when these debunkers make me wonder if there's much of it around *before* death."

What *I* say about the debunkers is—"bless their little hearts!" I don't know whether it has ever occurred to any of them, but they could very well be performing the very kind of service that mediumship needs in order to stay healthy—they're the watchdogs needed to help make sure people stay honest and above board. All of society benefits when its various sectors have some form of checks and balances, our country's Founding Fathers recognized this when they built it into our Constitution after all.

That authentic skepticism is healthy, is a given. For skepticism to qualify as genuine however, it must be in compliance with the definition of the original Greek word *skeptikos*, from which the word 'skeptic' is derived. Various dictionaries define it as: thoughtful examination—consideration—one who thoughtfully reflects upon—a suspension of judgement. I don't think many of the skeptics I've come across could honestly claim to have spent much time on "thoughtful examination" or have "suspended their judgement."

## The Skeptics

I find it quite intriguing that in spite of the highly vocal adversarial posturing of the skeptics and debunkers, I have yet to meet a medium who responds to their churlish barbs with anything other than a reflexive genuinely amused smile and at times accompanied by a knowing wink. No harboring of enmity, like one might expect, at all. It's a response that seems to say "That's okay, we've heard it all before—the truth will out—bring 'em on."

What *does* concern the mediums, and all believers, is that the raucous ranting of the skeptics could dissuade someone who's valiantly battling the tyranny of grief, from seeking the relief that a medium's reading can bring about. The mediums know this to be true, this is their "wheelhouse" after all and they have been witness to a reading's recuperative powers time after time after time. This is what they live for and they give generously of themselves—knowing this to be their "calling." They know their unique abilities to be a contribution of a pure positive energy for the universal good. So it does vex them that those in dire need of their God-given abilities could be cowed by the skeptics' fear-mongering pronouncements that mediumship is quackery. Let's face it, there *are* fraudulent mediums out there. But isn't it true that, in these times, anyone would be hard-pressed to name a profession or area of activity where that's *not* the case?

The skeptics make their prejudgements however and, human nature being what it is, they have the tendency to stop looking any further the instant they come across any evidence that conveniently supports their presumptions, and for them—the die is cast.

The standard rationale that skeptics are fond of invoking, is that they're merely trying to protect the vulnerable from charlatans. That's a noble motive certainly, but there are many in the mediumship community who feel the public would be better served if they expressed their benevolence by suspending their judgement about mediumship while they give the subject some objective and thoughtful consideration. The truth is there—just waiting to be discovered.

The prevailing stance adopted by the skeptics, I feel, unjustifiably demeans and belittles the bereaved. We are quite capable of deciding for ourselves what is in our best interests but the skeptics appear to be of the opinion that our grief has caused us to somehow become too mentally enfeebled to do so. Unfortunately, as long as they choose to remain ignorant of the facts, these self-appointed vigilantes will continue to unfairly and undiscerningly cast a blanket indictment over the entire field of mediumship. In the process of which, the reputations of the many unquestionably genuine and ethical practitioners can become sullied and besmirched, resulting in many poor souls being deprived of their healing abilities.

There have been many mediums over the years whose exceptional abilities, combined with serendipitous events, have raised them to an elevated status of public fame and recognition. Of course this makes them the target of even more scorn from the skeptics. The criticism now directed at these "celebrity mediums" (as they disparagingly refer to them), is that they're "only in it for the money." One well known professional skeptic described one famous medium as "A ruthless money-making confidence trickster." Unfortunately for him, he'd chosen the wrong one on whom to vent his wrath.

The target at whom he'd aimed this diatribe was none other than the legendary and much beloved English medium Doris Stokes. Her life story, which she documented in several wonderful books, doesn't exactly fit the skeptic's profile of her. Doris, although she'd been aware of her special gift since early childhood, didn't achieve the international fame for which she was destined until her mid-fifties.

## The Skeptics

Prior to this, she and her war-wounded husband had lived in quite humble circumstances in England's industrial north. For years she worked as a hospital nurse and practiced her mediumship at weekends in the services of Spiritualist Churches around the country for just modest travel expenses. For any other readings she was asked to do, she would charge the princely sum of two or three dollars. Doris and John only ever lived in rented apartments till late in their lives and on her death in 1987 this "ruthless money-grabbing huckster" left all of 22,900 dollars.

There's a Chinese proverb that goes "Just as tall trees are known by their shadows, so are good men known by their enemies." This certainly applied to Doris because as her fame grew, so of course did the criticism leveled at her. She was not one for suffering fools gladly however, and reveled in meeting their unmerited diatribes head-on. There must have been something in the water in Grantham, the town of her upbringing, because she was born and raised just down the street from another girl who grew up to be quite well-known—a girl who went by the name of Margaret Thatcher. Yes *that* Margaret Thatcher—and like the "Iron Lady," Doris too was a master of acerbic banter and also refused to be bullied. Any critics foolhardy enough to lock horns with these ladies did so at their own peril. She discusses many of these amusing confrontations in her books.

Another fatuous gibe that the skeptics are fond of trotting out to mediums is the question "Why is it your dead friends only talk about trivial things? Why don't they address things of importance like world peace or world hunger?"

The spirits have thoroughly explained their reasons for this. They've told us over and over, through the mediums, that as part of their spiritual evolvement on the other side, they are given various assignments. One such task requires them to make contact with their surviving loved ones with the express purpose of providing them with conclusive evidence of their continued existence (albeit in non-physical form), that they are blissfully happy, entirely free from pain and in perfect health. Also, that the love bond between us is stronger than ever and they will always be with us, come what may.

Achieving all this, while at the same time offering irrefutable confirmation that this could not possibly be coming from anyone but them, requires references to specific details of our every-day lives. Events and aspects that, as mundane and inconsequential they may appear to be to others, are the stuff our average days are made up of. Something that's never merited any more attention than a fly-speck will, when referenced in a reading, assume a significance so colossal it can literally change one's life forever. Such is the awesome potential of every validating detail of a reading that unquestionably attests to the continued presence of our loved one.

Meis van der Rohe was a highly celebrated architect who is famous for a very succinct observation that is pertinent here, "God," he said "is in the details."

World peace, world hunger and the other hundred and one topics of concern? They too are assuredly being addressed by spirits on the other side of the veil—just not in this particular venue at this particular time. So, skeptics, debunkers and naysayers alike—please, just back off—shut up—go away and—do your homework. You're making fools of yourselves.

## Those Skeptical Scientists

"When I see a bird that walks like duck and swims like a duck and quacks like duck, I call that bird a duck."

## The Skeptics

I'm sure we're all familiar with this much quoted astute statement by the writer and poet James Whitcomb Riley. When he made it, he could have been of the mind that we don't always need the permission of the scientific establishment in order to know what we know—and that good old-fashioned common-sense often serves us very nicely thank you. And is, at times, all that we really need.

So one might expect that the overwhelming preponderance of evidence to mediumship's genuineness that has been piling up around the world over the years in millions of validated readings, would by now, like the duck—speak for itself and be proof enough. Not so, the skeptical scientists aren't buying. "It's not supported by science," is their mantra, along with "Where's the proof?" or "Where are the peer reviews?" And that's quite understandable when one thinks about it, after all that duck could very well be an obese crow with a good paint job and and a knack for bird impressions.

As Victor Hugo said "Common sense is in spite of, not the result of, education." And the German philosopher Johann Wolfgang von Goethe said that "Common sense is the genius of humanity."

The following is what three other eminently qualified scholars have to say on the subject of science and scientists in the books they've written for us:

In the introduction to his absorbing book *Reincarnation: The View From Eternity*, Dr. O. T. Bonnett maintains that "Scientists are wrong when they insist that, to be valid, the observations and experiences of men must be proven by established scientific methods." He later cites examples of things we all live by that are rarely provable by science and that no one demands proof of anyway. "For example, prove to someone that you like butterscotch ice-cream," he challenges, then "How can you prove they love their spouse, parent or children?" he asks, then later: "None of the things you do or say can validate your love in any scientific or provable fashion."

Dr. Gary E. Schwartz in his definitive work on mediumship *The Afterlife Experiments* makes the point, as a scientist himself, that "In science we hypothesize; we do not believe. And science ultimately does not establish "proof" as much as provide evidence for or against a hypothesis."

In his eloquently enlightening New York Times Bestseller *Healing Words*, Dr. Larry Dossey asserts "It is nowhere written down that science is the only or the best gateway to do what is real. We *invented* the scientific method; it did not descend from on high." ( Cartesians take note.)

I salute these men of science for their courage in standing steadfast to their convictions in publicly expressing their views. Because one can't help feeling at times that mainstream scientists must have allowed themselves to become too unhealthily steeped in self-glorification for them to find it so galling when it's suggested that they accept something that can't be actually seen, measured or MRI'd. But they've been conditioned into believing that anyone who has the temerity to expect their approval of something that can't be quantified by any conventional method is a knuckle-headed ninny—a looney-toon, stay away from him he's not to be trusted.

This, unfortunately, has been the prevalent position of the scientific establishment since the seventeenth century when they bought into the beliefs expounded by the French philosopher Rene Descartes. When his postulations became augmented later by the findings of the English physicist and mathematician Isaac Newton, a new world view emerged that became known as the Scientific Revolution.

## The Skeptics

Although historians still debate its validity to this day, it has continued to hold that *all* elements of scientific experimentation be rendered exclusively in terms of numerical values and statistical analysis of recorded data etc. etc. This is the "scientific method" that, as Dr. Larry Dossey reminds us—*we invented* and that "did not descend from on high."

In consequence, the Universe was effectively reduced, (at least in the minds of scientists) to little more than a piece of machinery. With everything required to be quantifiable with no allowance whatsoever for spiritual considerations of any kind. So it was, that down through the ages, science itself in effect became a god. Is it any wonder that scientists get a little haughty at the mere mention of something like mediumship? That must really spook them out.

Lynne McTaggart is an award-winning journalist and the author of several successful books. She travels the world holding seminars and master classes on the science of spirituality. In her brilliant, thoroughly researched and documented bestselling book *The Field*, she offers this intriguing insight regarding the predicament facing today's scientists, "the entire structure of science, with its highly competitive grant system, coupled with the publishing and peer review system, largely depends upon individuals conforming to the accepted world view."

To the participants involved in a reading, the spirits, the medium and the sitter, it matters not one jot or tittle that science hasn't deigned to confer their blessing on mediumship. The mediums and the sitters are not the imbeciles that skeptical scientists would have us believe them to be. As for the spirits, well, they're having a good old laugh at all this nonsensical stuff—I know this to be a fact because my wife-in-spirit told the legendary George Anderson to tell me so—just after she'd told him her first and middle names. As the celebrated drama critic and editor George Jean Nathan said, "The path of credence is through the thick forest of skepticism."

Marc Bekoff is one of the world's foremost experts on animal emotions and behavior, and the author of numerous wonderful books on the subject. In his highly absorbing book *The Emotional Lives of Animals* he discusses some of his own experiences with scientists in that field who reject anecdotal evidence on the grounds it doesn't meet their requirement of "hard data." (Sound familiar? Recognize the myopia?) But Bekoff likes to remind them that "the plural of anecdote *is* data," and "in the end, anecdotes are only data that are perhaps gathered more slowly, but that doesn't make them any less useful or reliable." And so, regardless of the scientists' disdainfully dismissive attitude, like the mediums, our animal friends too will just carry on happily doing what they do.

The evidence—an outrageously massive body of it by now—attesting to the mediums' ability to communicate with spirit is out there in plain sight for anyone to examine, they can see for themselves that it clearly goes way beyond the "beyond a reasonable doubt" that our legal system calls for. I fail to see how any thinking person who's prepared to invest a little time acquainting themselves with it, could ever again, in all good conscience, regard mediumship as anything other than "the real deal,"

There is one book in particular on the subject that is a "must read," because it is *the* seminal book on mediumship. We mentioned it earlier, it's the compelling *The Afterlife Experiments* by Dr. Gary E. Schwartz, A former Yale University professor, he's professor of psychology, medicine, neurology, psychiatry and surgery at the University of Arizona. (With many professors like him they wouldn't need many sofas in the Faculty Lounge.) His book definitively details, without hiding behind scientific jargon, the impressively successful series of *triple blind* tests conducted by the professor and his staff with many of our very top mediums.

In a summation, Schwartz writes "Statistical analysis of the experiments indicated that the results could have occurred by chance fewer than one in a trillion times."

That's—*one in a trillion!* But, amazingly, the scientific community still choose to doggedly stick to their perverse guns determined to appear to be unimpressed. For anyone to ignore studies with such solidly supported authentication, would call for them to be actually *working* at it. Does it ever occur to them, how patently silly and juvenile such a stance is? If this attitude was directed just towards lay people, one could put it down to some kind of snobbish elitism, but for them to be like this to each other is kind of quirky, like the following example.

Dr. David R. Hawkins was an internationally renowned psychiatrist and consciousness researcher, the author of an intriguing book on his years of research into the science of kinesiology titled *Power Vs. Force*, and translated into over twenty languages. He writes about how his "Kinesiology demonstrations often result in paradigm shock for people who have an investment in strict materialism." (Those Cartesians again.) He writes of how one observer of his demonstrations, a research psychiatrist himself, tried to prove they were fake. When he failed to do so. He walked away huffily saying "Even if it's true, I don't believe it."

Dr. Schwartz tells of a similar instance in *The Afterlife Experiments*. A visiting professor gave a colloquium at the University of Arizona on his analysis of studies on telepathy conducted by established researchers on the subject. The results had turned out to be extraordinarily significant, producing values in the billions compared with just the hundreds required for the publication of mainstream findings. When Schwartz asked a senior member of the University's Friendly Advocates committee for his views, he responded "We must remember, just because the probability values are less than one billion, they still could have occurred by chance." With that kind of thinking, is it any wonder they have a problem accepting mediumship?

When engaging these kinds of adversaries in debate, we have to anticipate them shifting the goalposts—that's a given. But sometimes that's not enough, it's so important to them to be right that these guys will try to move the entire stadium.

The skeptics, amateurs, professionals and science wonks alike, are known for expressing their rigidly held views with such radio-talk-show like vehemence, that one can't help but wonder sometimes where on earth they get this stuff. What's behind their fanatical fervency? Could it be the lack of substantive evidence that mediumship is anything other than legitimate that frustrates them so much?

We are all of course, to a large extent, products of the social conditioning that we begin to be subjected from the moment we come into the world. It's generally acknowledged that the quality of our basic nature that defines us throughout our lives can be determined during those early formative years. People are known to hold on unshakably to dogma that stemmed originally from a casual remark overheard—or *miss*-heard, that may have been a careless oddball comment made while in a crotchety mood by an authority figure—which, when we're toddlers, is literally everyone. I came across an item just recently about the many people who'd grown

## The Skeptics

up and gone around thinking that one of our country's Founding Fathers was someone by the name of Richard Stands. It turns out that when they'd started reciting the Pledge of Allegiance way back in first grade, they'd misheard the part that goes: "...and for the Republic for *which it stands.*"

During those impressionable formative years we can also be greatly influenced by all those well-meaning parental cautions, dispensed with such relentless regularity that they qualify as mantras. This would be all well and good but for the fact that many of these old saws come under the heading of "old wives' tales," a title that's used facetiously more than in deference to any wisdom they afford. The very day after I'd read an article that said a recent study had revealed that 69 percent of us believe in them, and 72 percent of them said they pass them on to their children, I came across another article that cited many old wives tales that are seriously flawed, accompanied by a lengthy list of examples of ridiculous "facts" many of us have been swallowing over the years. We can only speculate about what kind of irrational myths have been indelibly embedded in tender young minds where they sit unchallenged and fermenting for years, rendering them difficult, if not impossible, to expunge.

I don't feel it unreasonable to equate the foregoing with the skeptical scientists' hang-ups about a phenomenon like mediumship. Is it possible that their paranoia resulted from scary myths they were fed in their impressionable early years? It's as though they're fearful that the integrity of their cherished Cartesian and Newtonian scientific methods are under threat—man the ramparts, those mediums are at the gates with torches and pitchforks.

Enough with the "siege mentality," the devotees of mediumship are merely suggesting that it would be a good, healthy and progressive thing for everyone concerned if science's present rigid position on the subject was allowed to be a little more flexible. They might like to consider the fact that are many people of eminence who consider the term "scientific proof" to be a contradiction in terms anyway—that an assertion expressed in scientific jargon does not, by any means, establish it forever as an absolute. It is often more of a convenient serviceable description in the absence of something more apropos. It is a fact that over the years there have been many adamant scientific claims that have had to be revised to conform to new data.

One example of this would be the case of the coelacanth. This was a prehistoric fish that paleontology scientists *knew* had been around about 400 million years ago and they also *knew* that it had become extinct around 80 million years ago. That all changed however when a coelacanth was discovered alive and well off the coast of South Africa in 1938. Apparently, to paraphrase Mark Twain: "News of its demise had been greatly exaggerated." Since then, over 200 have been caught.

## The Value of Readings—Priceless

"She told me after our reading that she had been to see priests and psychiatrists in an effort to get over the depression caused by the loss of her children, but only now, after her sitting, did she feel any hope for the future."

In the above paragraph from her book *More Voices In My Ear*, the great medium Doris Stokes provides us with an example of a sitter's typical reaction to one of her readings. It also serves to explain the reason why I have a tendency to come down so hard on those who are skeptical of mediumship and would, for some inexplicable reason, discourage anyone availing themselves of its proven amazing benefits—you could say it's the "raison d'etre" for the book you're now holding.

This sitter Doris is writing about had tragically lost both an infant daughter *and* a son but had just received a string of amazingly detailed validations of their continued presence in her life. There is just no way we can even begin to imagine the priceless value of this reading to this young grief-stricken mother. And this is just one of thousands like it that have been taking place every single day for generations. (And there are actually people who begrudge them this?)

Doris was always able to empathize and relate with sitters like this young mother, she herself had tragically lost her only child John Michael, when he was just five months old. In her book *Innocent Voices In My Ear*, she recounts how she still can remember well the day when she herself had received undeniable proof, in a reading with a medium, that her beloved son still lived. She writes "There is not enough money in the world to pay for that wonderful joy and truth. It's given through God's love so it is beyond price." Later in the book, she gives us another example of how tremendously transforming the information received in a reading can be, when she speaks of the body-language of sitters, especially those who've lost children—they arrive "droopy and desolate," she says, but after the reading they walk out with "heads held high, the spring back in their step because suddenly they can face the future."

In another instance of a reading's effect, she tells of a letter she received from a recent sitter. She wrote about how she'd been so unable to get over her grief following the loss of her son that her friends had been afraid of what she might do. But since her reading with Doris she'd been on cloud nine and her friends and co-workers

## The Direct Connect

had all commented on how different she now looked with the strain of sadness gone from her eyes.

The books written by and about the mediums are replete with joyful accounts such as these from sitters whose lives had been magically transformed. The mediums bear witness to this delightfully exultant process over and over, and they've told me that the sense of gratification they derive from being a part of it never wanes. "It's what I get up in the morning for," one medium told me, "it's my calling, it's what I live for, you can't put a price on it."

The renowned medium James Van Praagh knows as much about this as anyone, in his *New York Times* number one best-selling book *Talking to Heaven*, he writes "The moment I relay a spirit message to a loved one, a person's life is changed forever." then later, "When a connection between two worlds—physical and spiritual—has been bridged, nothing short of a miraculous reunion occurs." I well remember a lady on Van Praagh's television show *Beyond* who summarized the experience of having her loved one coming through, with "You could spend thousands of dollars on therapy and it wouldn't do what this reading did."

I can't help but notice that the therapy comparison came up quite a lot. Is that therapy stuff "supported by science," and has its "replicability" been scientifically proven? Oh—and the fees that therapists charge, do they too bear any comparison to a medium's fees?—Just asking.

The New Zealand medium Jenny Crawford, in her eloquently written book *Through the Eyes of Spirit* writes "I say to those who question or mock this work that through readings, many people are given hope, strength, guidance and faith to trust in themselves in a positive and loving manner."

The sitters whose post-reading reviews we've been instancing had, previous to their readings, been living (sometimes for years,) in the grip of paralyzing grief that had been magically mitigated by a single reading by a medium. It takes longer than that for an aspirin to work on a headache, for goodness sake. The comments cited are typical of the hundreds of thousands of such testimonials to the effectiveness of mediums' readings. Mediums whose talents, if the skeptics had their way, would not be available because of their "deceptive practices" and lack of "scientific proof." The loss of such a unique resource, not to put too fine a point on it, would be a tragedy of global significance.

Those "questioners and mockers of this work" that Jenny Crawford refers to are those same skeptics we've been denouncing, the ones who habitually trot out their sanctimonious mantras like "We are just protecting the vulnerable from those quacks," and "They're selling false hopes." What patently disingenuous, histrionic clap-trap that stuff is. There is a plethora of Consumer Watchdog groups and Consumer Advocacy groups out there whose very existence attests to the fact that, as unfortunate as it may be, there are "quacks" and "purveyors of false hope" in most every sector of commerce—some of them on a gargantuan scale.

A CBS *Sixty Minutes* segment, aired in February 2012, reported on an investigation into the sales of anti-depressant prescription drugs. Apparently 17 million hopeful Americans are taking some form of them, making it an *11.3 billion dollar industry*.

Research carried out by a Harvard Scientist, and corroborated by a Clinical Professor of Psychiatry at Brown University's Medical School however, found that the drugs are no more effective than placebos. That is an FDA approved 11.3 billion dollars worth of "deceptive practices" and "false hopes." Now *that's* depressing.

We know how grievously debilitating grief can be, and we've seen how miraculously effective a reading can often be in releasing the bereaved from it's grip. We know there to be phonies out there, so certainly let's rid the scene of these shameless frauds—but in a manner that judiciously *weeds* them out. To needlessly endanger a resource of such immeasurable value by using indiscriminate scattershot tactics would be unforgivingly irresponsible, surely we are too heavily invested in this unique treasure for us to stand by and allow it to be squandered in that kind of way.

## Why Such Fervent Meanness?

We made mention earlier of how healthy genuine skepticism can be. But there are times when the outpourings of the more vocal skeptics of mediumship sink to a level of meanness that is anything *but* healthy, and we can't help feeling that there's something strange about the shrillness of their denunciations—that something else is going on here. For one thing, they obviously don't have any compassion for the bereaved, who are suffering such indescribable grief that they turn to a medium for some blessed relief.(or as a medium friend of mine puts it: "Desperately seeking the Balm Of Gilead."). And can they relate at all, on any level, to the *love* aspect of mediumship? Do they have even an inkling of what the love that the bereaved have for their lost loved one is all about? Then there's the concept of an inextricable intertwining of two souls—is that beyond their comprehension too? Just asking, but sadly, it appears that's the case. All in all, the picture that emerges is not very attractive.

Is it possible that these "don't-haves" are due to a lack of love in their own lives? The ever-rising divorce rates do attest to the sad fact that there's a lot of that going around. I also wonder too, if the positive outcomes of readings have a bearing on the skeptics' attitude. Could it be that it's the comfort, solace and contentment the bereaved derive from a reading that gets them so riled? It's and old saying, but there's usually a lot of truth in it: "Misery loves company."

I'm not convinced that those heartless skeptics who would delight in depriving grieving people access to mediums constitute a majority, it's just that they're more vociferous. I remain convinced that the less vocal and impassioned skeptics could easily render the more fractious element irrelevant if they would just allow themselves to be better informed on the subject.

I fail to see why the skeptics, assuming their professed desire to protect the vulnerable is genuine, couldn't direct their energies in more positive and productive ways than they currently are. For instance, seeing as how it's universally agreed that it's not possible to prove that life after death *doesn't* exist (a fact that seems to gall them no end), wouldn't the sensible solution be for them to join forces with us believers in a combined effort to prove it *does* exist. By agreeing to this it's possible we could finally put this contentious issue to rest once and for all—and maybe, just possibly, even to the satisfaction of those fastidious mainstream scientists.

Such a radical shift would call for a quantum leap in attitude of course, but it would surely be preferable to the non-constructive stand-off that's prevailed for so long. As long as the skeptics remain in their current unenlightened negative mode, they will continue to be perceived as not being very serious about their purported concern for the vulnerability of the bereaved. Standing on the sidelines taking cheap potshots and yelling a lot at those who are doing such good works, doesn't require much brain-power—literally anyone can do it.

## The Direct Connect

The phenomenon of mediumship is undeniably a potent and sacred force for the greater good, but its glorious potential has been fettered by the ignorant bellicosity of its skeptics. Although there are already millions of enlightened devotees, they still only account for a comparatively tiny fraction of the people whose lives could potentially be enormously enriched by science's "seal of approval."

The truth will, in any event, assuredly come about. The Nobel Prize winning German physicist Max Planck spoke to the inevitability of this when he told us: "A new scientific truth does not triumph by convincing its opponents and making them see the light, but rather because its opponents eventually die, and a new generation grows up that is familiar with it."

## A History of Skepticism—the Blooper Reel

There have been many occasions, over the years, when the mockers became the mocked, George and Ira Gershwin even wrote a romantic song around them titled *They All Laughed*:

"They all laughed at Christopher Columbus
When he said the world was round
They all laughed when Edison recorded sound"

The song listed in verse after verse, some of the many things people questioned and mocked over the years. Things that, as the song later tells us, resulted in *"now they're eating humble pie."*

So mediumship is by no means the first time that people have balked at accepting something on the grounds that it was different to other things in their life experience. It appears we've always been this way, almost to the extent that the skeptics' initial questioning and mocking is practically a requisite for the success of any proposition. If historic precedent is the guide that it usually is, we can rest assured

## The Skeptics

that the day will come when we'll need to come up with a word that rhymes with mediumship when we're adding a couple of lines to the Gershwins' song. And don't forget that order of humble pie.

Here are a few standouts I've come across:

It's reported that Colonel Harlan Sanders' secret recipe, for what would later become his legendary Kentucky Fried Chicken, was rejected by over *a thousand* restaurants before he made his first sale.

In the early 1800's the noted English chemist and inventor Sir Humphrey Davy scoffed at the suggestion that London could one day be lighted by gas-lamps.

That was around the same time that Thomas Gray was spending most of his adult life promoting the idea of a passenger railroad system—a notion that prompted *The Edinburgh Review* to call for him to be "put in a straight-jacket." Humble pie must have been a menu staple after these times because this was also the time when "experts" were testifying that Stephenson's locomotive would never be able to attain a speed of twelve miles an hour.

When Benjamin Franklin submitted the subject of lightning conductors before the Royal Society, he was laughed at as a dreamer and his paper wasn't admitted.

The great scientist and inventor Alexander Graham Bell approached the British Post Office with a little gadget he'd come up with, called a telephone, yes *the telephone*. Only to be turned away by the Chief Engineer (who should be eating his 6 billionth humble pie by now) by the name of Sir William Preece. His reason—because "England has plenty of small boys to run messages." ( I hope Mr. Bell hadn't had to stand in line very long at the Post Office).

In 1878, a British Parliamentary Committee referred to Thomas Edison's light bulb as "Good enough for our transatlantic friends...

but unworthy of the attention of practical or scientific men." Did I detect a hint of that "science is God" complex there? Uh-uh here comes another. In 1850, the President of the Stevens Institute of Technology said about Edison's invention: "Everyone acquainted with the subject will recognize it as a conspicuous failure."

I heard that he'd later been offered free passage out of the country, but had declined on the grounds that he was fearful of venturing too far in case he fell off the edge. Speaking of which—did you know that there *actually is* a *Flat Earth Society?* True. Apparently they're still enjoying a good laugh at Columbus's expense.

## Things That Science Can't Explain

In Shakespeare's *Hamlet*, after Hamlet and his friend had been spooked out by a visitation from the ghost of his deceased father, he made the famous observation: "There are more things in Heaven and Earth, Horatio, than are dreamt of in your philosophy." The Bard of Avon was making the point that there are things that even the best educated among us can't explain, or to put it another way, there is more to this world than meets the eye. A notion that seems to drive our mainstream scientist friends up the proverbial wall. If it doesn't meet the eye then it cannot be "supported by science." Ergo—there's no such thing—it doesn't exist, if it did—I'd know about it. Honestly, is it any wonder that this haughty air of infallibility, (the God factor we spoke of) comes across as arrogant, not to mention downright disingenuous? Such a dogmatic stance is simply not consistent with reality. The fact is, as Shakespeare implied, our world abounds with mysterious stuff that defies scientific explanation. An hour or two spent with our internet search engine of choice will reveal enough examples to fill a sizable book. Here are a couple that, if you're not

## The Skeptics

already familiar with, you may like to check out, look up Pumapunku and the Nazca Lines, I think you will be fascinated. Yet science doesn't appear to have much of a clue about either of them.

One of my favorite reading subjects is that of animal behavior, a topic that draws from a wide variety of species types and brimming with enthralling accounts of studies conducted by teams of ethologists throughout the world. The baffling mysteries surrounding migration for instance, like the annual excursions made by the Monarch butterfly. Up to 100 million of these delicate little marvels navigate up to 2000 miles, flying as fast as 30 mph, to the warmth of Southern California and Mexico, where they each hibernate in the *very same tree* every year. Incredibly, they are not the same butterflies—they are by now, four generations from those that left the year before. Can scientists explain this process? They haven't so far. They'll invariably *attempt* to give an explanation, but that's probably because they feel duty-bound never to utter the words "I don't know" about anything.

Our friends in the animal kingdom are a constant rich source of fascinating events that we can only marvel at and that elude the hidebound mainstream scientists' ability to explain.

Dr. Jonathan Balcombe is a world renowned animal behavior scientist—an ethologist, who has, on occasion, knocked heads with the pedantic dogma of mainstream science on various issues over the years. In his absorbing book *Second Nature* one of the things he discusses are the many ways in which various animal species have evolved perceptual abilities that far exceed our own. On the subject of their long distance homing instincts for example, we're all familiar with those stories of pet cats and dogs who've gone missing from their new home then turned up at their old home a hundred miles

## The Direct Connect

away. But crocodiles? Balcombe tells of an instance involving three dangerous estuarine crocodiles in Australia that had been caught near public bathing beaches. They were promptly relocated to remote areas, only to have one show up back home three weeks later, after being released—250 miles away. In one of his other books, *Pleasurable Kingdom*, Dr. Balcome cites many other examples that scientists have difficulty in explaining. Here are just two:

There is evidence that dolphins can amazingly detect that their human teachers are pregnant before the women themselves even know it.

Then this account of a study involving sheep, an animal that unfortunately is not traditionally regarded as being very smart. The study showed however that they have this extraordinary ability to recognize fifty or more members of their flock from photographs alone. Not only that, but they retain this memory—*for two years*. Any explanations? None forthcoming as yet. But we need to realize the next time we honk our horn at them for blocking a country lane, that that stare they give us isn't as vacant as we've been led to believe—they'll be keeping our mug-shot on file.

Another phenomenon that baffles the experts could be regarded as another kind of migration mystery, it takes place on a dry lake bed in Death Valley National Park, California. Known as Racetrack Playa, it owes its uniqueness to the fact that it has things that "migrate" across its surface. That may not seem at all unusual until we learn that these things are not birds or even creatures of any kind—they're *rocks*. Known as "Sailing Stones," they are rocks that can weigh up to 700 pounds and travel anywhere up to 800 feet, leaving long trails behind them in the sediment. The scientific explanation? There isn't one yet.

# The Skeptics

Back around 3000 B.C., the ancient Egyptians wrote about the use of willow leaves to reduce fevers and swelling. Later, in the 5$^{th}$ century B.C. in Greece, Hippocrates wrote about a powder made from the bark of willow trees that reduced fevers and eased headaches and other pains. The basis of this "wonder drug" apparently, was a chemical known as *salicin,* and it's a staple in most peoples' medicine cabinets to this day—we call it *aspirin.* There's another "wonder" aspect about it—apparently no one seems to know how it works.

Dr. Roy Herbst is Chief of Medical Oncology for the Yale Cancer Center. In an article for the *How Stuff Works* website, the good doctor says: "We don't understand how aspirin works..... after 200 hundred years of scientific work, how it works, we're not very clear, but it works." I've searched high and low but I haven't been able to find any reports of the Bayer Company being subjected to those ubiquitous stridently shrill protestations from skeptical scientists when something is "not supported by science." However, in the event they ever are— they'll just take a couple of aspirin. It works. Science can't explain *how* exactly—but like mediumship, it just does!

Homeopathy is a form of medicine that millions of people worldwide know and accept, without any doubt, to be an effective remedy for a vast array of ailments and conditions. But the mere mention of it can drive mainstream doctors crazy.

Homeopathy has enjoyed a following in Europe since its invention by the German physician Samuel Hahnemann in the late 18$^{th}$ century. Today it is the leading "alternative medicine" treatment used by doctors there, with around ten percent of German doctors specializing in it.

In India, for over 100 million people, it is the only form of medicine used. The British national newspaper *Daily Mirror,* reported in August 2012 that more than 10 million British people swear by homeopathy, and listed the laudatory comments of several of the many celebrities and top athletes, some of whom even have a homeopathic doctor on speed dial. Over 600 doctors in Britain prescribe homeopathic remedies and it has been widely known for years that the British Royal Family use homeopathics, the Royal Warrants of Appointment that's been officially conferred on the Ainsworths Homeopathic Pharmacy attests to this.

There's a reason for homeopathy being the modality of choice for so many people—it works. But unfortunately many mainstream doctors doggedly refuse to recognize this, and those that do find themselves at risk of being censured by their Medical Boards. Their medieval stance was exemplified by a doctor speaking at the 2010 British Medical Association conference when he dismissed homeopathy as "Nonsense on stilts." After having previously described homeopathy as "witchcraft" but now wished to "apologize to witches for making the link."

What was probably the most notable scientific explanation of how homeopathy works came out of the several years of research carried out by the French scientist Jacques Benveniste. His findings were published in 1988 in the prestigious magazine *Nature*.

In her brilliant book *The Field*, Lynne McTaggart gives us a detailed account of Benveniste's work and the subsequent systematic savaging of him by the professional establishment and professional skeptics. This, in spite of his years of impeccably conducted randomized double-blind and placebo-controlled studies, the results of which had been successfully replicated by five laboratories in four countries.

These establishment mainstreamers get to be so beset with paranoia and insecurity at times—I'm sure there's a homeopathic for that.

## The Skeptics

Meanwhile though, homeopathy continues on its inexorable path—selling itself by example and growing in stature every day—fueled by one simple, irrefutable truth—it works! My family and I have been using homeopathic remedies with great success for over forty years, and my wife used them on countless occasions to treat the many cats who owned us over the years. Our daughter Bev continues the tradition with her cats, and often uses the services of a veterinarian who uses homeopathic remedies.

These have been just a few of the many examples I've come across of things in our world for which, as of yet anyway, scientists cannot offer an explanation. There probably always will be things that we can't fully explain but accept nonetheless, I myself have yet to figure how a Pez dispenser works but, like so many other things—I don't have to concern myself with *how* it works—it just *does*. Not that anyone would ever need it,(except maybe a skeptical scientist) but the data regarding the technicalities involved in the dispensing of a piece of candy are there for anyone to avail themselves of, should they desire to. In much the same way that all the evidential data regarding the authenticity of mediumship is available to anyone. Going to the trouble of availing themselves of it objectively however, doesn't appear to be something the skeptics feel they *need* to do. It's as if they think the knowledge they have already is thorough enough for them to make their determination and that's the end of it. There's an arrogant implication here that anything not concordant with their life experience just simply cannot be—period. How old are these people—six? Psychiatrists have a term for this—arrested development.

There's another thing that scientists, do not have a thorough knowledge of. It's our brain.

## Our Brain

When skeptical scientists assert that mediums can't possibly communicate with spirit, or as they like to disdainfully put it—"talk to dead people," they're implying that they have a thorough knowledge of what the brain is, or is not, capable of. But I've been learning that there's a lot we don't know about this three pounds of grey stuff that sits between our ears. In regard to mediumship, obviously speaking, the brain of the medium is integrally involved in the processing of communications from spirit, so I feel it's quite reasonable to assume that a medium's ability to receive these transmissions from spirit is possibly due to the uniqueness of a part of the brain about which no one, as yet, has any knowledge whatsoever. The skeptical scientists though resolutely stick to their belief that anything outside of their knowledge cannot be worthy of their consideration, so I suppose we'll just have to wait until they catch up. This could take a while—their development is under house arrest.

This attitude reminds me of the story about a one time head of the U.S. Patent Office who, it's reported, in 1898 wrote to President McKinley urging him to permanently shut down the Patent Office since "Everything that can be invented has already been invented."

After what I've learned, I think that an observation once made by the illustrious inventor Thomas Edison still holds true, the great one said: "We don't know one millionth of one percent about anything." I think posting that on our bathroom mirror so that it's the first thing that we gift our brain with every morning, could help us stay humble—at least until around lunch-time.

Consider the following accounts of amazing brain power that recently caught my attention:

## The Skeptics

Magnus Carlsen is a young Norwegian man who possesses phenomenal mental abilities. Magnus is a brilliant Chess Grandmaster and prodigy who, at the age of nineteen became the youngest person to be ranked number one in the world.

In a CBS *60 Minutes* segment that aired in February 2012, he was shown playing against ten opponents *simultaneously*, and not just playing, but playing with his back to them and all boards out of sight. Achieving this required him to mentally keep track of 320 pieces.

Then there was the account of the incredible mental feats of a Japanese gentleman named Akira Haraguchi. Akira-san is a retired engineer who has always been fascinated by "pi"—the circumference of a circle divided by its diameter, and he can recite, entirely from memory, the first 100,000 decimal places of the equation.

Can science explain how the brains of these remarkable individuals can accomplish such impressive feats? Apparently not, scientists don't know how this works any more than Magnus and Akira-san themselves do. Just like the mediums, they too have no idea how *their* extraordinary ability works—they just know that it does.

Dr. Rafael Yuste is a professor of biological sciences at Columbia University, he's one of the experts involved in the Brain Activity Map Project announced by President Obama in April 2013. In talking about the brain—with a frankness and humility rare in his field, the Professor said: "I can guarantee you that we don't have a clue."

Jeffrey Hawkins is the inventor of the *Palm Pilot* and *Treo*. In his book *On Intelligence*, he writes: The U.S. has thousands of neuroscientists yet we have no productive theories about what intelligence is or how the brain works as a whole."

David Eagleman, an eminent neuroscientist at Baylor College of Medicine, is very familiar with things that we *do* know about the brain and he shares them with us in his best selling book *Incognito: The Secret Lives of the Brain*. For instance:

— Our brains consist of cells called neurons—a hundred billion of them, (give or take one or two) and they all carry messages and make connections to neighboring neurons.

— Each cell sends electrical impulses to other cells at a rate of hundreds per second.

— Each cubic millimeter of brain tissue has some one hundred synaptic connections between neurons.

One or two brain cells of Magnus Carlsen and Akira Haraguchi would appear to be "up to something" about which scientists have no knowledge. So, in regard to mediumship, as audacious a concept as this may be: Isn't it plausible that among all the nooks and crannies of the *mediums'* grey matter, there are also one or two of those hundred billion neurons that are also "up to something?" And I can't imagine scientists disdainfully ascribing momentous mental feats like those of Magnus and Akira-san to trickery. (Why is that? I wonder).

## Replicability

The ability to replicate any experiments and achieve precisely identical results each time is the "chiseled-in-granite" criterion that's fundamental to science's "seal-of-approval."

Faced with such dogmatic dictates, the chances of mediumship ever receiving a passing grade must be somewhere between slim to none. For the simple reason there is such a multiplicity of variables inherent in the nature of communication between medium and spirit. When we reflect on the numerous elements of the process that would hardly qualify as absolutes, it becomes wholly apparent why psychic readings are a phenomenon that just do not lend

## The Skeptics

themselves to any of the conventional methods of measuring and tabulating data.

The ultra-conservative formalized structure of Cartesian and Newtonian philosophies with their insistence on mathematical explanations for everything and upon which modern western science was founded, demands unreserved compliance. With no tolerance whatsoever for considerations like intuitive wisdom, unpredictability or, heaven forbid—any suggestion of humanness. Their inflexibility appears to be curiously disingenuous when one considers the fact that Newton himself warned us against using his "Laws of Motion" to view the universe as a mere machine, and is on record as proclaiming that "God governs all things and knows all that is or can be done." This isn't the only sign of a chink in their ostensible solid structure. Why, for instance isn't science the least bit amenable to be as yielding to mediumship in the way it is with other propositions—there's a disconnect here that puzzles. As an example, it's interesting to note that a hundred years after he began to revolutionize physics, Albert Einstein's theories are still being questioned by many scientists because they are, like most hypotheses, known to be based on assumptions, In the case of mediumship though, nothing less than unimpeachably pure scientific replicability is acceptable—no assumptions accepted here. They can't all be unaware of this inconsistency. So why the double-standard?

In the light of what has been known, testified to and thoroughly documented about mediumship over the past 160 years, such a rigidly hidebound stance is patently absurd. The world renowned expert on animal behavior, Marc Bekoff, knows something about this kind of arrogant elitism. In his absorbing book *Emotional Lives of Animals*, he tells of an incident at the 2005 convention of the Society of

## The Direct Connect

Neuroscience. No less a personage than His Holiness the Dalai Lama, a strong supporter of scientific inquiry and who himself had been a research subject, was slated to present a paper on Neurotheology. There was one particular group of scientists though who lobbied against His Holiness appearing, on the grounds that his claims regarding meditation are not substantiated and are not scientifically rigorous. (Assumptions in other words.) Even the word of His Holiness wasn't deemed to be good enough—that "God factor" again.

I'm reminded of what the author Edgar A. Shoaff said: "A skeptic is a person who would ask God for his ID card."

Another example of a double-standard that mediumship has to contend with is the difference between the expectations skeptics have of it compared to other things—and the leeway they habitually afford to them. I imagine, for instance that there are many skeptics, pros and amateurs alike, who attend or watch sporting events. If so, it must be an excruciatingly frustrating experience for them. Because, if their stance on mediumship is anything to go by, they do so with an expectation of the leading PGA golfer making a "birdie" at every hole, the basketball whooshing into the net every time a certain star performer throws it, their favorite batter hitting every pitch into the bleachers—you get the picture. Ridiculous of course, but that's the level of performance they appear to require from mediums in order for their abilities to be regarded as legitimate. All hits—no misses. That's the level of absurdity we're dealing with!

Communication between a medium and spirit is hardly comparable to that of a conversation via a single telephone line, they have a wide array of methods from which to choose and a single reading can often consist of a complex intermixture of several of them, all variable (We'll be discussing them in later chapters). The nature of

## The Skeptics

these methods are such, that there is no way they could possibly be compliant with the degree of replicability that science demands in order to merit its blessing. There are many factors at play, here are just a few:

Psychic messages, in common with the other methods of communication we're familiar with, radio, cell-phones television, semaphore, are all susceptible to the same vagaries of signal quality such as fading in and out, interference from various electrical sources, distortion and overlapping of outside frequencies. All due to causes over which we have no control (I'm told semaphore is practically useless on a foggy day).

It's my understanding that the transmission of messages by spirit calls for skills that have to be learned, so this factor alone, when combined with the difference in levels of proficiency between mediums, could account for a significant number of variables and misinterpretations.

Another consideration to bear in mind in our assessment of both a reading's accuracy and the medium's skill-level, is that mediums are only human, and like everyone else are prone to those days when, for any number of reasons, we just don't feel on top of our game. There are also times when messages are delivered with what the medium perceives as ambiguities that have to be interpreted before sharing them with the sitter.

I was recently fortunate to receive an excellent reading, that included several unquestionably genuine validations, from the medium Carole J. Obley—this lady is good. In her book *I'm Still With You*, she writes: "Every reading is a unique experiment because of the variables of the medium's abilities, the strength of the communicating spirit and receptivity of the sitter. Because of this, I (or any medium for that matter) cannot ever guarantee the outcome of a reading."

The millions of mediumship's adherents around the world are very comfortable with not feeling an overwhelming need for the sanction of either skeptics or science. But as impervious as they themselves are to anyones' denunciations, it does concern them that all the discordant negativity could dissuade other grieving souls, in their depleted and confused condition, from seeking a medium. Which would tragically deprive them of the miraculous alleviation from grief that knowing our loved ones are still a part of our lives can undoubtedly bring about.

## More Priceless Value

The renowned medium John Holland, in his excellent book *Born Knowing*, gives us a touching and poignant account of a reading he gave for a grieving mother. She'd been utterly devastated by the death twelve months before of her seventeen year old daughter, in a horrendous accident on an amusement park water-slide ride. John's remarkable reading was replete with one accurate evidential fact after another that included things like the special nickname she'd called her by, her fondness for pink frilly clothes and confirmation of the many signs she'd been leaving around the house since her passing. And all topped off with her assurance regarding that aspect of violent deaths that haunts the bereaved more than anything else—that she is well and not in any pain, and that the accident had all happened so quickly she hadn't felt a thing.

Through John's classically transformational reading, this formerly defeated and devastated mother received gifts more miraculously wondrous than she had dared hope for—not only had she been liberated from a year-long nightmare that she'd been convinced

## The Skeptics

would never end, but she'd also received confirmation from her dear daughter that she is still very much a part of her life, and furthermore—always will be. That's priceless.

Is there anyone who seriously thinks that this lady, and the countless millions like her, ever lose one minute's sleep because mediumship "isn't supported by science" or care one scintilla that "it's not replicable," or even give a damn what anyone thinks?

Mediumship is a sacred God-given resource that promises deliverance from the wretched pain and misery that grips the bereaved in such grotesquely cruel ways that their lives can be ruined forever. Yet there are those who, through ignorance, are skeptical of its genuineness and would, in their irrational arrogance, discourage anyone from recognizing it—based on nothing more than their stridently shrill say-so.

I find it interesting that, while it's their conviction that consciousness does not survive death, they don't seem inclined to present any kind of proof to support their claim. There will surely come a time though, when they will be in a position to put the matter to rest once and for all, and they'll find it to be surprisingly easy. All they have to do is wait until they themselves cross over and then simply send us a sign when they get there. Mystery solved—piece of cake.

CHAPTER 4

# IT'S MUCH MORE THAN JUST "A READING"

George Anderson, considered by many to be the world's greatest living medium, was not overstating the matter when he wrote in his book *Walking in the Garden of Souls* about knowledge of the afterlife being the greatest gift anyone could ever receive in an entire lifetime. Since those words first resonated with me about nine years ago, I've been the fortunate recipient of numerous excellent readings (including one from George himself)—studied many many books by and about the mediums and have come to know several mediums personally. But I've yet to come upon any evidence that in any way invalidates George's assessment.

The full value of this gift however, isn't limited to that aspect of mediumship that deals with providing us with proof of our loved one's continuance on the other side and their supportive presence in our lives. As awe-inspiring and comforting that unquestionably is, it pales in comparison to the knowledge it leads us to. It turns out that this level we've reached is actually a mere gateway to a path that takes us to a level of enlightenment that surpasses any expectations we may have had. This revelation is centered around what the spirits have told us, via the mediums, regarding our soul plan, a stratagem that was compiled before we incarnated here. In effect, a shopping-list of lessons we need to learn in order for us to advance to a higher level of spirituality—the reason for our incarnating here. We soon come to understand that acquiring knowledge of our soul plan is of enormous benefit in releasing us from our grief, but it also doesn't take long for us to realize that it's really much, much more than that.

Now I fully realize that a comprehensive detailed dissertation on *all* the many aspects of this soul plan is way beyond the intent and scope of this book (not to mention my ability to do so). The aim of this book—its "raison d'etre"—is to assist those in grief in their struggle to accept their loss and rebuild their life, so we'll try to limit our discussion here to just those aspects of our soul plan that are pertinent to that goal. There are several books that cover the topic much better than I possibly could, I'll be mentioning my personal favorite later, but I do urge you to familiarize yourself with this fascinating subject because it really is worthy of that overused expression—"mind-blowing." I think it's safe to say that one of the most prevalent and persistently agonizing features of our grief is our yearning for some kind of meaning—some kind of reason our loved one was taken from us and, by extension, the reasons behind our own sufferance. In that regard alone, learning about our soul plan holds the promise of being a unique recuperative step of inestimable value to us—even life transforming.

Dr. Viktor Frankl was an Austrian neurologist, psychiatrist and a Holocaust survivor. He wrote and lectured extensively on mankind's enduring search for meaning, drawing from his own harrowing experience during three years in Nazi concentration camps.

Dr. Frankl used to say that "If there is meaning in life at all, then there is meaning in suffering."

Our loved ones is spirit, as part of their own ongoing soul growth in their new existence, have acquired a knowing of this "meaning in life" of which Dr. Frankl speaks, and have lovingly shared the gift with us via the mediums. The acclaimed authority on all matters of mediumship, the illustrious James Van Praagh, confirms this in his wonderfully enlightening book *Unfinished Business*, when he tells us that "Thousands of spirits who have passed over have communicated to me that their departure was a gift to their loved ones left behind on earth." This is entirely consistent with the soul plan premise.

It would seem that the Irish author and scholar C. S. Lewis also had some knowledge of this principle. His dear friend, the author and poet Sheldon Vanauken, had tragically lost his beloved wife Jean at the early age of forty. In a letter of condolence to Vanauken, Lewis wrote "She was further along than you, and she can help you more where she now is than she could have done on earth. You must go on."

A clear reference to his wife's departure being a form of gift, wouldn't you say?

Many mediums attest to the spirits having told him this. When we consider the fact that thousands of mediums over the years have been receiving the same kind of messages, the spirits are clearly screaming for our attention on this matter.

## Our Allusions to a Soul Plan

People, going back to ancient times, have alluded to our life paths being governed by some kind of Divine plan—that our lives are scripted by a higher power. We seem to have an inherent need for the feelings of security that such a premise confers. Theologians like John Calvin in the 16th century, and Saint Augustine before him, espoused the doctrine of predestination.

Earlier in the book, in chapter two, we discussed how people, while stopping short of openly admitting to an actual belief in an afterlife, nevertheless often allude to one in the form of various habitual and clichéd expressions. Much the same situation exists regarding the concept of a soul plan. For instance, after someone has narrowly avoided a serious accident or someone who's been critically ill miraculously goes into remission and recovers, invariably we hear the situation summed up by someone saying "God spared him because He still has work for him to do." Surely an allusion to our lives operating in accordance with some unidentified plan. It would appear that William Shakespeare too had some knowledge of our lives being scripted when he wrote, in *As You Like It*, "All the world's a stage, and all the men and women merely players; They have their exits and their entrances....."

Here are a few other examples of ways we hear allusions to a life-plan typically expressed;

We frequently hear someone referring to an occurrence as being "Part of the great scheme of things."—part of some undefined grand plan apparently.

On those occasions when there's no discernible reason or cause for an incident, people will often assume there is one because they'll

## It's Much More Than Just "A Reading"

say "Ah well, there's a reason for everything." Implying that even though *we* may not be able to put our finger on it, we can rest assured that there's some higher power who can—that's all we need to know—puzzle solved—end of conversation.

A lady unexpectedly lost her job, a catastrophic blow akin, for her at the time, to the end of the world. Through a series of serendipitous events however, she soon secures a position that turns out to be infinitely better in every way to her previous job. Now, whenever she mentions being laid off, she says "It was a blessing in disguise." Implying that this had been part of some kind of plan all along, there was just no way she could have recognized it at the time.

Even the often heard mournful melancholic "Why me?" connotes a belief in there being a reason behind what has befallen the questioner.

On occasion we'll hear someone, in a well-intentioned attempt to mollify a widow's grief, say "It was his time," or "It was just meant to be." My sister-in-law Sybil's favorite sympathizing justifier was "It just *wasn't* meant to be."—because an alternative, more desirable (from our perspective) resolution wasn't in the plan, apparently.

It seems that we find comfort and succor in accepting the mishap, upheaval or loss by calling on our belief that whatever the nature of the occurrence, it wasn't without a plausible reason. Interestingly, like in those alludes to an afterlife—rarely any attempt to explicitly define or elaborate further. More like an implicit acknowledgment that we're all following a script and that we are all on cue.

During those halcyon times when our lives are running smoothly and we're gliding effortlessly through the days—anxiety free—relaxed—secure—completely at peace with the world with no turbulence whatsoever and none in the forecast—the last thing on

## The Direct Connect

our mind is "What's it all about?" Why shouldn't it be, things are just hunky-dory as they are—why risk rocking the boat by questioning it?

Our lives are not always as tranquil and placid as we'd we would prefer them to be however, (this is the land of duality after all), with no effort whatsoever on our part and without any warning we can suddenly find ourselves beset by a string of challenges, setbacks and vexatious problems, even that "biggy"—losing a loved one. That last one can have us despairingly wringing our hands, shaking our fists towards the heavens and screaming hysterically "Why have you done this to us? That beautiful being didn't deserve this. What's the meaning behind it?"

Julian Baggins is the co-founder and Editor-in-Chief of *The Philosophers' Magazine*. In his book *What's it all About; Philosophy and the Meaning of Life*, he writes "For isn't the meaning of life the most profound and elusive mystery of all, unknown to even the greatest of minds? Surely anyone who tells you they have the answer is joking, mad or simply mistaken."

Well, thanks to mediumship, we have the answer. It was gifted to us by none other than our friends in spirit—that most eminently credentialed of all sources. And no, they are not clowning around, nor are they candidates for the funny-farm, and they couldn't possibly be mistaken—they're in spirit for goodness sake, they are *directly connected* to all this wondrous stuff now. They have informed us, via the mediums, that the meaning of life is embodied in what they refer to as our *soul plan*, and for those who have been gifted with the capacity to recognize its scholarship, the meaning of life is no longer "the most profound and elusive mystery of them all." (And here am I thinking that title belonged to how a Pez dispenser works.)

## Our Soul Plan

It is not an overstatement to suggest that studying the principles of our soul plan and reflecting on how our life and current circumstances relate to it and, importantly, together with learning about the reasons behind our loss, could very well turn out to be that key element that liberates us from the vice-grip of grief, and assists us greatly in our struggle to get our life back on track. Equating our soul plan to an explanation of 'the meaning of life" is entirely appropriate, but from the bereaved persons' point of view, it would be just as fitting and equally as helpful to also refer to it as "the meaning of *death*"—the meaning behind their loss that they've yearned for.

The following are two examples of how the mediums have typically come by this profoundly enlightening information over the years, directly from spirit—that truly unimpeachable source.

The world renowned Scottish medium Gordon Smith shares with us the input *he's* received from spirit throughout his career. In his highly informative book *Spirit Messenger* he writes "Having witnessed people's emotional hurt as much as I have, I often put the question of human suffering to the spirit world. The answer is almost the same time and again: 'It is through your suffering that you grow.'" In much the same vein, George Anderson relates what the spirits have said on this subject in his best-selling book *Walking in the Garden of Souls*. They told him that "not only is it incumbent on us to accept there was a good reason for all the suffering we and they endured, but experiencing the difficult times and living on here provides the greatest lesson of our lifetime—to rebuild hope after it has been shattered." As amazing as that may appear to be, we know it to be true because it came straight from the horse's mouth, so to speak

The spirits clearly place a lot of importance on sharing this knowledge of our soul plan with us and go to great lengths to deliver their message. They're also obviously aware that we seek readings with mediums hoping to receive confirmation that they are now free of pain and suffering and that they still love us, because these are invariably the issues they make sure to address early on. They also know about the intense pain we've been in over their passing, and they eagerly share what they've learned regarding our soul plan because they know that it will go a long way in eventually assuaging *our* pain, *our* suffering and free us from any feelings of guilt we may be harboring. They want us to know that there actually is a valid reason behind all aspects of our circumstances and that *everything* we are experiencing is all strictly in accordance with our soul plan—a plan that we co-wrote and signed off on before we came here.

I'd like to share with you two examples ( the mediums' books are replete with them), of how the spirits avail us of this magical phenomenon in readings with the mediums. They don't as a rule make a singular issue of it, rather, we're more likely to learn about it during their explanations regarding the circumstances surrounding their passing.

In her book *Everything Happens for a Reason*, the renowned medium Suzane Northrop tells us about a lady named Marjorie who came for a reading. She was eager to make contact with her deceased sister because she'd been so wracked with guilt about what she considered to be the part she'd played in her sister's tragic death.

Despite the fact that her sister's occupation required her to make frequent business trips to Europe, she'd always suffered from a dreadful fear of flying. In a conversation with Marjorie shortly before

## It's Much More Than Just "A Reading"

an upcoming plane trip to Paris, she confided to her that for some reason she was especially fearful of this one. Marjorie suggested to her that she fly with *Swissair* on the grounds that they had never had a single fatality in its entire history, that way she was bound to be safe.

That was how her sister had come to be on board Swissair Flight 800 when it crashed into the Atlantic Ocean off the coast of Long Island, killing everyone on board. Hence Marjorie's terrible feelings of guilt, convinced that she'd been responsible for her dear sister's death.

When she came through in the reading, her sister quickly assured Marjorie that she had nothing at all to feel guilty about. Since she'd crossed over she'd learned that her lifelong fear of flying had stemmed from the fact that her soul had known all along that it was her fate to die in a plane crash—it was part of her program and had nothing at all to do with Marjorie's advice.

Apparently, by explaining the details of her own program, the sister in spirit provided Marjorie with information that allowed her to become aware of the original choice *she* had made to come into this world as the sister of this particular person.

In his book *Reaching to Heaven*, James Van Praagh also writes about one of his readings in which the spirit who came through made reference to the workings of soul plan. This example speaks in particular to those with "special needs" and those who are incapacitated by disease, but also their families, those devoted intrepid souls who have been fated to serve as their care-givers.

Five members of a close and loving family had come to James for a reading hoping to make contact with their deceased father. One of the family members was a young man of twenty or so who was confined to a wheelchair, having been stricken with muscular dystrophy and was barely able to speak. The reading proceeded in typical Van Praagh fashion—very successfully, with wonderful validation from the father in spirit.

Towards the end of the session, the father speaking to his wheelchair-bound son, told him "You were put on this earth with a debilitating disease in order to teach people around you about unconditional love." This close family were apparently getting good grades on their tests, because upon hearing this the whole family joyously declared "Alleluia."

If any members of that exceptional family, under the weight of their ongoing arduous burden, had ever asked the question "Why?" They had just been lovingly gifted with the meaning behind their situation—straight from the horse's mouth—as a result the weight of the load they're *all* carrying has been substantially lightened.

As these examples demonstrate, we all, each and every one of us, incarnate into this physical plane for the express purpose of soul growth—our own certainly, but not necessarily exclusively so. These two instances serve to demonstrate how the spirits have made reference to the fact that the soul plan, the blueprint we draw up, can frequently be integral to the soul plans of fellow soul-group members—a sharing—a joint venture—car-pooling if you like.

## Duality

A famous philosopher (my high school woodwork teacher), after reminding us about the price of lumber, used to impress upon us that it's quite okay for us to make mistakes. That in order to learn how to do something, it helps if we do it wrong. The only thing we learn from doing something right is that we already know how to do it—it's from our *mistakes* that we learn.

## It's Much More Than Just "A Reading"

Experiencing a lifetime on earth, the physical plane, is sometimes the only way our soul can grow in the specific areas prescribed, because the lessons we need are only available in a system of duality. In the non-physical realm on the other side of the veil, duality doesn't exist—there are no such things as mistakes—right versus wrong—honesty versus deceit—harmony versus—acrimony. Unlike this physical plane, where life for the majority of us is rarely *anything but* duality. We all have those days when we spend all our time swimming against the current, when *nothing* seems to go right the entire day—but on reflection at the end of the day we have to admit that we're actually wiser, if only a little, than we were when our day started. Similarly, we may at some time have had a co-worker or a boss who seemed dedicated to making our life a misery, but in retrospect later, even years later, we've had to grudgingly admit that they'd been the best teachers we could have wished for and we wouldn't change the experience for anything.

Life here on earth can, for the most part, be summarized by the concept of the Yin and Yang of Chinese philosophy—the "interconnection of opposing forces." There is no day without night—no positives without negatives, and so on. It's only in our "hands-on" management of these conflicting forces—duality, that we can experience what we need to learn in order for our soul to grow in that particular area and bring it into compliance with our soul plan. The principles embodied in such philosophies are at the core of most religions and cultures throughout our world. Devotees of Buddhism for instance actually welcome life's challenges and view them as opportunities to grow spiritually.

This physical plane, earth, being a veritable wellspring of all things negative qualifies it as the ideal classroom, equipped as it is with the most superior teaching-aids available for our needs. We can't, for instance, *really* appreciate the importance of honesty without having been the victim of *dis*honesty, and by the same token, neither can we expect to really comprehend the value of loyalty until we know what it's like to be hurt by the betrayal of someone we've trusted or, conversely, if *we ourselves* have been guilty of hurting someone by being dishonest or have betrayed someone's trust. We cannot fully appreciate the desired positive aspects of anything at all if we've never had any experience of its negatives at some juncture in our life. In the super-perfect non-physical realm, any lessons that call for us experiencing any type of negativity are simply out of the question because it just does not exist in any form.

Our enrollment in this course we've elected to take has not been entered into lightly, the syllabus is very specific—it's our soul plan. It's a *blueprint* we designed that maps out, in exceedingly fine detail, the various lessons we're required to learn for the furtherance of our spirituality. We compiled our soul plan before we incarnated with the aid of an advisory board, so to speak, consisting of our spirit guides, all experts in their respective fields. Input was also contributed by members of our "soul group," some of whom, as we saw earlier, have been known to volunteer to incarnate along with us in order to participate in our plan at specific predetermined junctures of our life—even to the extent of playing an adversarial role (that mean misery making character who we all know and love and whom we spoke of earlier).

Nothing is left to chance apparently, hence the expression "there are no accidents." We've taken on a heavy load—a "tough row to hoe" as they say, and life seems only too aware of why we came here because as soon as we arrive here, as we don't need to be reminded, the lessons and tests never seem to stop presenting themselves throughout our lifetime. Some can often be artfully disguised and difficult to recognize then there are others that sneakily ambush us when we least expect them. Fortunately for us there's usually that ubiquitous wise soul around to remind us that "if they were too easy—they wouldn't be called tests."

Robert Schwartz has written an outstandingly informative book on the subject titled *Your Soul's Plan.* Working with four gifted mediums and channels, Schwartz conducted psychic sessions with ten subjects in which they discussed the details of the pre-birth plans they'd made before they incarnated. After learning about the explanations and reasons behind their choices they were now able to understand, for the first time, the significance of matters like the loss of a loved one, severe accidents and various physical disabilities and addictions, and how they had played out when they had subsequently manifested in their lives—events that they'd found to be deeply troubling at the time and about which they'd been puzzled for years.

The result is an assemblage of thought-provoking case studies that contain many aspects which, when we relate them to our own current circumstances, go a long way in helping us with our own recuperative yearnings. This newly acquired knowledge of a soul plan, confirming as it does that there are meanings and purposes surrounding the loss of our loved one, can prove to be just what we need to help us in accepting and coming to terms with our loss. Grief though is an extraordinarily brutalizing experience to say the least, so it may be unrealistic to expect complete recovery to magically come about overnight (pixie-dust is the stuff of fantasy), but a modest investment in time taken to quietly reflect and contemplate on our soul plan and its various implications can soon have us "sitting up and taking nourishment," as the expression goes. In this case—much needed soul nourishment.

The compelling confirmation that there are definitely valid reasons and meanings behind the loss of our loved one can be the progenitor of a realization that what we've been convinced was a monumentally insurmountable task, now seems much less daunting. For the first time we may become aware of a gentle wave of exquisite alleviation coursing through us—and after the steely iciness we've been in the grip of for so long, it feels like a soft warm shower on the inside. It's early days yet, but even the hint of a thawing is enough to have us daring to speculate on the possibility of it being a sign that we're finally actually *turning the corner*.

## Helping it to Sink In

Some years ago, a talented drama coach taught me a trick to help us get our head around complex concepts, which this notion of soul plan assuredly is, and see them in a form we can identify with. It calls for us to reflect on the path our life has taken up to this point and observe it from the perspective of an objective spectator viewing a movie drama, complete with a cast of characters. We mentioned earlier that, like most people at one time or another, we too in the past have alluded to the course of our lives following some kind of preordained plan. All we are doing now, now that our allusions have been substantiated, is assembling the salient points of our life so that they flesh out a storyline, some form of narrative that assists us in making some plausible sense out of it all. Out of what had been a jumbled mélange will emerge a comprehensible picture that will hopefully provide us with the reasons and meanings behind what has befallen us. It is at this point that we'll come to reach an

## It's Much More Than Just "A Reading"

understanding of how our soul plan has been (and still is), playing out, and by extension—that everything that is happening to anyone at any time, is happening because it should—and even at the time it should.

As the executive producer of our saga, we can track the course of events during our life with our loved one. One way of kick-starting and fueling our imagination to help us achieve this is to pore through our family photo albums. This will help us in recalling events in our life, some of which, while not having been considered to be of much significance before, could now surprisingly, in the light of what has happened, be of great value when they're linked with other occasions. Remembrances prompted by this walk down memory lane can help us more easily identify the significance behind the circuitous route our life-path has taken over the years. Light can be thrown on the possible reasons for all those twists and turns, the ups and downs, the inexplicable zigs and zags, the course adjustments, the forks in the road and all the other intersections that called for us to make decisions—there was meaning behind every single one.

Then there were all those "character-building" challenges, those curve balls that were hurled at us from all directions. What was *their* purpose in the scheme of things? Did the outcomes lead to anything beneficial to anyone? If so, whom, us or "them"? We can reflect on the reasons behind various cast members making their entrances into our life and the circumstances surrounding the timing of their exits. Did they have a significant impact on our life and was it negative or positive? And, importantly, did we enrich *their* life in any appreciable way? Of importance because although we refer to it as *our* soul plan, it is not necessarily all about *us*. There are times when *we're* the teacher and other times when *they* are. And sometimes our teacher can be the

## The Direct Connect

last person we would have expected. That co-worker, boss, or in-law, with the annoying knack of "pushing our buttons," may be our dreaded antagonist here in this *physical* realm, but it's possible that in the *non-physical* realm from whence we came, they were our dearest friend or "soul-group member" who had not only participated in the formulation of our soul plan but had actually nobly volunteered to incarnate along with us in order to play the part of the teacher who helps us learn qualities like tolerance, humility and forgiveness etc., Our loyal friend's part in *our* plan though doesn't preclude him whiling away his time working on *his* soul growth too. There's an old Buddhist proverb that seems apropos here, it says "When the pupil is ready—the teacher will appear." A reference, it would seem, to a teacher with predetermined knowledge of the pupil's upcoming needs, hovering in the wings waiting for his cue.

Our assimilation of this incredible knowledge allows us from now on to better deal with those most difficult of all life-challenges—our relationships with others. From now on, having availed ourselves of the principles of soul plan, and now equipped with the knowledge that everyone's actions are also in accordance to *their* soul plan, our blood pressure will no longer shoot through the roof when we're in the presence of those people whom we may have formerly been convinced had been "sent to drive us nuts." We realize now they could very well be a good friend and ally playing the role of "teacher-for-a-day." In any event whomever it is, we've learned, that like us—everyone else too is also here to learn. As this sinks in, we're likely to become pleasingly aware of becoming much less judgmental of others' traits and foibles than we'd previously been because we now understand that when someone disappoints us, it's due to the fact that their soul plan is scheduled differently to ours and, as C. S. Lewis would have put it, "one of us is further along than the other."

We are now equipped with a yardstick by which our spiritual growth can be measured and contentious situations assessed. It enables us to intuitively screen behavior patterns of both ourselves and those of others, such as petty jealousies, "put-downs" and our tendencies to rush-to-judgment. Boorishness of any kind, previously found to be disconcertingly rankling, now, viewed in the light of "the plan," elicits from us a measure of forbearance we hadn't known we had in us. The expression "We signed up for this," will become our "under-the-breath" mantra, our reflexive rallying-cry whenever challenging and vexatious situations land on our doorstep. Our life, as a consequence, becomes progressively more tranquil and far less stressful. We actually like ourselves more now, in short—we feel more spiritually adult.

It has been made clear to us that no occurrence is ever random, accidental or devoid of meaning—ever. The significance of this to us, right now, in terms of our personal ongoing odyssey of recovery, is that all these pieces of evidence that our lives are operating in accordance with an exquisitely crafted pre-planned blueprint, which a panel of soul family members and spirit guides helped us draft, have now crystalized into an unwavering abiding faith that *there actually IS a perfectly plausible and sanctified reason behind both our loved one's early transition to the angelic realm AND our being left here to soldier on alone.* That's a transformational moment.

We recall those months spent shambling around, dazed, confused and hopelessly lost in the pea-soup fogginess of our grief, until that day when we serendipitously happened upon this controversial thing called mediumship. In six-sensory parlance, we now beam our heartfelt gratitude to our team for having the foresight to write and insert this "serendipity" into our plan. And we also thank the spirit guides responsible for orchestrating the process whereby we were able to muster the courage and resolve required of us to stay true to our convictions, ignore the skepticism of well-meaning friends and stick to the path that has led us out of the befuddling murkiness of our grief to this level of enlightenment. Knowledge, so beautiful in its simplicity, that has imbued us with an understanding of such clarity that we're now able to see that *it really couldn't be any other way.*

Yes, there is more to mediumship than just readings—*much more.*

## Ways In Which Spirit Supports Us

I wouldn't want to leave anyone with the impression that the validations we receive from our loved ones during the course of a thirty minute reading, in any way represent the full measure of connectivity between us. There is inarguably a great deal of incredible knowledge to be derived from mediumship, but as wonderful as a reading might be, because of time constraints, there's only so much information the spirits can pass along to us.

There is a reason why readings are of such a short duration, and it's technical in nature. In the reading process, the connection between the medium in this physical dimension and the spirits in their *non-*physical realm calls for the expenditure of a considerable amount of energy by both parties. Apparently there is a huge difference between their respective levels of vibrational frequencies and for communication to take place these levels have to be perfectly aligned.

In order to achieve this, those on the other side of the veil are required to *lower* their vibration while the mediums simultaneously *raise* theirs. Because of the effort this demands of both sides, the connection can only be sustained for a limited time before their connection weakens and fades away altogether. The exercise is taxing for everyone involved.

This does not mean that we're being short-changed however—on the contrary, the spirits are fully aware of their limited "air-time" and pace themselves accordingly. A few days before my reading with George Anderson for instance, his long-time assistant Andrew Barone told me that it wouldn't be necessary for me to make a list of issues I wanted the spirits to address because they'll know exactly what they are. And amazingly, true to his word, that's precisely what transpired. (Between you and me, I have an idea him and George had maybe done this kind of thing before. You think?). So, along with a few personal references regarding current events in our life about which no one else has any knowledge, in order to validate to our satisfaction that they are indeed around us, that's really what constitutes a typical reading—just a sampler really, but hopefully enough to convince us and make a believer of us. As William James said all those years ago—"…..it is enough if you prove that *one* crow is white."

In order for us to benefit fully from the validation we've received of our loved one's presence in our life, it's important that we remain mindful of the fact that the bond between us is not contingent on our consulting with a medium on a regular basis. And there's certainly no reason we should ever suspect, as some people do, that when the reading is over our loved one's go back to what they were doing before we interrupted them, until the next reading. That is definitely not how it is at all—the fact is, and they remind us of this over and over again in readings, *"We will always be with you—come what may"*

For some sitters, the wonderfully validating pieces of evidence they received from one or two readings adequately met their expectations. The solace they acquired from learning of their loved one's

## The Direct Connect

continued presence, albeit just in the non-physical, was "the light at the end of their tunnel of agonizing grief" for which they'd been yearning. For others though, with their appetite whetted, they now hunger for more, there's a certain correctness that appeals—they sense there's more to this and it's just waiting to be discovered—for them the reading was just a primer and they want to pursue it further. The feeling, rather than fading with time, only grows more intense. They even start telling people around them that "Somebody's trying to tell me something."

The mediums would agree with this wholeheartedly, but they don't just *think* someone is trying to tell them something—they *know* they are, and not only that but *who* they are.

Mediums like Patrick Mathews know. In his book *Forever With You* he writes "Have you ever wondered where that good idea came from that you had or why you had a voice inside your head telling you to do something or not do something? This is actually a loved one in spirit communicating with you telepathically."

Like most mediums, the acclaimed Allison DuBois is a storehouse of information on the subject—these are a few pieces she shares with us in her wonderful books: In *Secrets of the Monarch* she writes "We can't even begin to imagine how often and in how many different ways those we love touch us daily." Then these, from *Don't Kiss Them Goodbye*—"They are all around us and continue to share moments with us all." Then "Allow your loved ones to be a part of you and provide inspiration in your life." And then this little "cockles-of-your-heart" warmer—"Our loved ones who cross over still go through life with us. They act as added energy when we need it."

Ms. DuBois and the rest of the mediums aren't sitting around making up this stuff—they're merely passing along to us what the

## It's Much More Than Just "A Reading"

spirits, in their untiring and loving efforts to reach out, particularly to those of us in our grief, have told them—time and time and time again.

Many mediums are quick to remind us that mediumship isn't about "fortune-telling," like some people expect it to be. There are some spirits however that don't seem to have got the memo. I think it's only logical for us to assume that the spirits have at least *some* idea of our future—how could they not, when they have access to the details of our soul plan? Mediumship may not be "about" fortune telling per se, and perhaps we shouldn't enter into a reading with that being our main expectation, but it's been my experience that some aspects of readings can unquestionably be of a predictive nature, this was certainly the case when a reading I was receiving unexpectedly took a turn in that direction.

The reading was with the late Reverend Eloise Page, considered to be the matriarch of the Cassadaga Spiritualist Community in Florida, where she practiced mediumship for over fifty years. The reading had been replete with accurate validating messages from my wife when Eloise, her eyes closed in concentration and after a long pause, said "This lady who is with us here is telling me she has something of significance to confirm with you. She's telling me that you will be flying soon to a large northern city that begins with the letter "M," and that you will be visiting a friend who's name also begins with the letter "M." And she is saying now that you will be traveling across water—not overseas mind, but she's showing me a body of water like a lake. Eloise explained, "I'm just telling you what she's telling me—I don't know if this means anything to you,"

When she opened her eyes and saw me sitting with mouth agape, she smiled and said "I guess it does Reggie—huh?" Giggling and shaking my head in disbelief, I said "Wow Reverend—you're hitting them out of the park today."

After the connection faded and the reading had come to its end, I explained to her that at that moment, on my office desk, was an airline ticket. In three weeks it would have me winging my way to spend two weeks with a dear friend of over forty years. And to get to his place would entail me *traveling across water* because—here it comes—my friend—*Michel* lives on his private little island, *in the middle of a lake* in Canada, north of—*Montreal*. Nothing predictive of anything I didn't already know, but a genuine validation from my wife nonetheless that she's not just in my life, but in it to an extraordinary degree. For instance, Michel hadn't even given any thought to relocating to an island during my wife's lifetime. That had come up a couple of years after the tragic passing of his beautiful wife Florence.

For me—a mind-blowing red-letter day—one for the books. For the Reverend—just another day at the office. An intriguing connection to this story came about in a reading I had with the well known medium Joanne Gerber about eighteen months later. About halfway into the reading, Joanne mentioned that there was another female with my wife who she proceeded to describe. Her description of both their builds, their hair coloring, styles etc.,was so detailed that I felt sure she was describing Florence. When Joanne went on to say "For some reason, this lady is showing me a lap-top computer and laughing." my suspicions were confirmed. You see, while chatting on the phone with Michel just two days earlier, he'd announced a huge development in his life—Michel had finally been dragged kicking and screaming into the twenty first century—a client had presented him with his first ever computer—a lap-top.

## Reading Between the Lines

I can't recall a reading with a medium, either over the phone or in person, where the medium hasn't said at some point, in one way or another, "Your wife is saying that as close as you two were, you're even closer now." or "She wants you to know she's fine and that you're not to worry," and "She loves you and she'll be waiting for you when it's your time."

Whatever one prefers to call it – conjecture – extrapolation or just plain reading between the lines, to me, when the spirits make a point of gifting us with assurances like these, and the readings are loaded with them, it clearly alludes to an affirmation—a mission statement, if you will.

I see it as their way of confirming that we are soulmates, and as such we will remain forever inextricably intertwined at the soul level. They've already revealed how they now enjoy access to our soul plan—a blueprint, the creation of which they played a key role, and they are indicating to us that they are now in a position to assist us in carrying on with our life in accordance with it in ways that would have been totally out of the question previously.

Their validations that come through in the readings are their way of showing us, from their unique vantage point, that they know everything about where we've *been*—and by the same token, knowledge of where we are *going*—and furthermore—*why*.

Again, I can't help remembering what C. S. Lewis told his friend grieving over the loss of his wife, "....she can help you more where she now is than she could on earth."

In all probability we're still going to find ourselves assailed from time to time by (to quote another quite well known writer) "The slings and arrows of outrageous fortune," or find ourselves "on the horns of a dilemma," (gee, this suddenly took a gory turn). But the difference is, we're now familiar with the rules of engagement governing these inevitable challenges. We know them to be officially sanctioned and we feel thoroughly secure in the knowing that we have the support of our personal supremely skilled entourage of adoring guides watching our back.

In our grieving condition, this realization that we are not alone in our struggle to accept our loss and rebuild our life, can be just the restorative tonic we need right now—the challenge facing us is no longer seen as the insurmountable obstacle we've been perceiving it to be. We've already borne witness to our guides' efforts on our behalf by the ways in which they orchestrated this wondrous enlightenment into our life, at the precise moment in time when they knew we would be accepting of it. This can go a long way in convincing us that we've taken a huge step in the right direction—and that things can only get better from here on. How could they not with this kind of spiritual sustenance behind us?

## Another Myth Debunked

We could say that most of our book so far, has been, as a side issue, about myth debunking. For instance, all those testimonies to the continuance of our love for each other after our loved ones have crossed over, reveal that phrase from the marriage vows *"Till death do us part,"* to be a complete myth. We've clearly seen that death *does not* part us. Having summarily dispatched that one, let's take a look at another myth connected with the change we call death.

Whenever we want to acknowledge something as being an undeniable truth—a universally recognized absolute, we say that "It's chiseled in granite," or "Carved in stone." There's at least one thing though that, for centuries, has been arbitrarily chiseled into slabs of granite, marble and stone but that we now know to be based on a fallacious premise.

I'm referring to the letters R.I.P.—the acronym for Rest In Peace, the solemn sentiment featured on millions of headstones. As consoling and well-meaning as those three little words have historically been, for the spirits, they're a source of amusement. In the light of what they've told us through the mediums—the expression is nothing more than an old wives' tale.

Peace, our loved ones in spirit are quick to tell us, they have—in abundance apparently. But they assure us that the *last* thing they're doing is *resting* in it.

In his must-read book *Walking in the Garden of Souls*, George Anderson assures us this is so when he tells us to "Forget what you might have read or hear about the "dead"—they are not resting, you will never be bothering them by thinking of them constantly, and asking for their help whenever you need it will *not* keep them from moving on the hereafter."

## Angels and Spirit Guides

The one source of Divine assistance that seems to be universally accepted is angels. People love them, angel symbols are everywhere—in the form of figurines—framed posters—key chains—bumper stickers—dashboard bobble-heads—tattoos—you name it. There are stores devoted solely to angel paraphernalia. Stories abound of blonde haired guardian angels swooping in to scoop someone out of harm's way—the stuff of miracles. It's even one of the few things that traverse those most sacrosanct lines of demarcation, religious boundaries.

## The Direct Connect

I regard any kind of belief in the availability of Divine assistance to be a wonderfully healthful and affirming resource. So I find it puzzling that most ardent believers in angels are so proudly parochial. The mere mention of spirit guides in the context of Divine assistance or any reference to our loved ones in spirit helping us, can elicit a blank glassy-eyed stare and a quick change of subject—we just lost another one. To people like this, we've just divulged our country of origin—Woo-Woo-Land.

Dr. Doreen Virtue is a metaphysician and clairvoyant, a go-to authority on all things angelic, and has authored several fascinating books on the subject of angels. In *Angels 101* she writes "Speaking as a lifelong clairvoyant, I've never seen anyone without at least two guardian angels stationed by their side."

As I've yet to come across any reference to spirit guides' activities clashing in any way with people's ideas of what angels are all about, it seems to me to be a question of semantics and that the terms are entirely transposable. I sense some hair-splitting is going on here, and that there's ample room for both. I know the mediums to allow room for both, two medium friends of mine have shelves overflowing with beautiful angel figurines. I have a beauty that takes up residence on my mantel over the Christmas season next to my wife's photograph.

The world renowned psychic intuitive Sonia Choquette has written a very comprehensive book on the subject of spirit guides entitled *Ask Your Guides*. In it she describes in detail the specific functions of not only the various levels of angels but also the entire family of spirit guides—joy guides—healer guides—teacher guides etc.

In another of her always enlightening books, *Your Heart's Desire* she tells us that her own spiritual teachers and mentors revealed to her that we all have a set of spiritual guardians whose sole function is to guide us to our dreams. Furthermore, amazingly, we each have an entire spiritual support team of thirty three guides working with us in specific areas of support at any given time (no outsourcing here apparently).

The specifics of the various guides' functions adds up to a prodigious body of data. If we should find it too overwhelming to remain mindful of it all however, I don't feel that Sonia is implying that a successful connection with them is contingent on us carrying around every detail of each guide's area of expertise in our heads. And from what Sonia says, in contacting them, we shouldn't be fearful of stepping on their divine toes. For instance, no one is going to have their noses put out of joint if we direct a request for assistance to our joy guides when the issue concerned comes under the bailiwick of our teacher guides. That's an "ego thing," and egos, as we've learned, simply do not exist in the angelic realm (remember dualism?)—our "call" will just be gladly and understandingly re-routed.

A personal maxim I try to live by is "keep it simple." So in an attempt to stay in compliance with this, I prefer to think of the process of contacting my guides in terms of my wife acting as my gatekeeper. It's in this capacity that I then picture her—routing my requests to the appropriate departments and coordinating their team efforts on projects when needed. It works like a charm. I haven't experienced a "dropped call" yet and I remain in awe of the countless times I've sensed them extricating me from tight corners I've found myself in.

Our loved ones in spirit are now endowed with the ability to influence and orchestrate our life circumstances in extraordinary ways. Unfortunately, their actions are often so subtle and devoid of fanfare that, in our earthbound five-sensory mode of thought, we

*The Direct Connect*

don't even notice. Not staying attuned and remaining mindful of their efforts on our behalf, is to deny ourselves the pleasures of not only experiencing their feats of totally inexplicable magic but also the undying love with which they're proffered.

The many books available by and about the mediums and psychics are a rich and bounteous source of inspirational first hand accounts of the many and varied ways our loved ones continue to be actively involved in our lives. The following are just a few examples—typical of hundreds—taken from actual readings.

The well known medium Jeffrey Wands, in his fine book *Another Door Opens* writes that the enlightening perception he's taken from all the readings he's conducted is that "the world of spirit is a beehive of activity," and that "Their growth and ours remain intertwined because helping us down here is part of their growth up there."

The internationally renowned medium John Edward also makes reference to this fascinating two-way interaction in his book *After Life*. He writes "With the support they send us, we can carry on in directions they may not have been able to. So in a sense, we continue to take their dreams forward, as well as our own."

Esther and Jerry Hicks co-authored a compelling book entitled *Ask And It Is Given*. The entire book was channeled through Esther by a group of spirit entities, a collective consciousness, a panel so to speak, who called themselves Abraham. Through Esther they asked "Do you understand how much orchestration of circumstances and events on your behalf is available to you? Do you understand how adored you are?

The renowned medium Suzane Northrop, in her book *Everything Happens for a Reason*, treats us to an account of a reading she conducted that demonstrates a typical instance of this dynamic at work. The sitter was a recently widowed lady who'd come to Suzane with the hope of hearing from her husband. He did come through and immediately affirmed his continuing love for her and then went on to attest to the fact that it was he who'd been responsible for sending her a "support team"—a multitude of friends and various people to help her cope with her grieving task. His awe-struck wife confirmed that yes—this had indeed been the case. I've even come across readings where the person in spirit has confirmed that it was they who'd been responsible for bringing their surviving spouse and his or her new partner together.

The spirits tell us over and over in the readings that we should never hesitate to ask for their help—that no problem is too small to warrant their attention and it's never too much trouble or inconvenient. On the contrary, as Jeffrey Wands says, helping us also helps them in their spiritual growth. Amazingly, but true—even though we're separated physically, we continue to be the "Terrific Twosome," the "Dynamic Duo" we always were.

Resting? No such word in their vocabulary. Those chiselers just hadn't been fact-checking.

## Invoking Spirit Collaboration

Many, many reading have shown that spirit help is by no means limited to those who typically come through in readings—the sitters' family and close friends. There are also others who willingly make themselves available to assist us with tasks of a creative or specialist nature. There are many instances on record of artists—writers—musical composers—stage actors—scientists—orators etc., who have been humble enough to attribute their creation or performance to sources outside of themselves. Unidentified Divine helpers of some kind that they're convinced must have been responsible because the quality of a certain piece or performance surpassed what they considered themselves capable of.

I think you'll agree that it takes a special kind of person to go public with an admission of this kind. Dr David R. Hawkins addresses this aspect in his intriguing book *Power Vs. Force*. He writes "It's the vanity of the ego that claim thoughts as "mine." Genius, on the other hand, commonly attributes the source of creative leaps of awareness to that basis of all consciousness—which has traditionally been called divinity." I first read this passage during my pre-dawn reading session then coincidentally, while scanning through another book later, while having a lunchtime sandwich in the office kitchen, I read in a book titled *Incognito* by neuroscientist David Eagleman that the German novelist "Johann Wolfgang Von Goethe claimed to have written his novella *The Sorrows of Young Werther* with practically no conscious input, as though he were holding a pen that moved on its own."

A *Discovery Magazine* article in September 2011 entitled *Secret Life of the Mind* cited the case of a death-bed confession made by the prominent Scottish mathematical physicist James Clerk Maxwell in November 1827. He was famous for his development of a set of equations unifying electricity and magnetism, an achievement hailed as the "second great unification in physics"—second only to the one realized by the illustrious Isaac Newton. Maxwell's confession consisted of him admitting to "not actually having any idea how he'd achieved his great insights" and that "something within him" had made the discoveries. I'm reminded of what Carl Yung is quoted as saying that's apropos here "In each of us there is another man whom we do not know."

## It's Much More Than Just "A Reading"

The talented medium Patrick Mathews bears witness to this in his book *Never Say Goodbye*. He writes "Spirits who had a certain profession or expertise, such as a doctor, teacher, artist or singer, just to name a few, will help those who have the same talent or ability here."

Psychic intuitive Sonia Choquette writes at length about invoking spirit assistance. In her book *Ask Your Guides*, she tells us that we all can actually invoke spirits to help us in our endeavors—when we are painting—writing poetry—sculpting, in fact anything at all in which we utilize the talents of any acknowledged master whose now in spirit. She admits to often calling on the spirit of the legendary medium Edgar Cayce in her work as a psychic, especially on issues of health and past lives—Cayce's specialties when he was alive. She explains "These souls took their talents to a masterful level and are more than willing to share what they've learned from the Other Side."

She goes on to suggest that we embark on the invoking process by obtaining a picture of the person or even simply write down their name. Then, while meditating on their spirit, request that they come forward to help, keeping our request plain and simple and being as specific as we can.

James Van Praagh also refers to the invoking process in his book *Talking To Heaven*. He writes that "Particular guides are drawn to us or will come if we ask for their assistance," and goes on to say that "All work, especially that of the great masters, is inspired by the spirit world."

The artist Henriette Wyeth Hurd, sister of the illustrious Andrew Wyeth knows about spirit assistance. She recounted an experience she had with spirit guidance in a Smithsonian Institution film shown on PBS Television entitled *The Wyeths; A Father and his Family*. The father being the great illustrator and art teacher N. C. Wyeth.

# The Direct Connect

She spoke about the day after her father's tragic death in an auto accident. She told how she was in a friend's garden surrounded by masses of blooming chrysanthemums and became inspired to paint a picture of them because she felt her father would want her to. Speaking emotionally she went on: "I found I was painting better than I knew how. I thought this can't be true. I kept hearing him—'Do it this way—remember about that' and so on. I could have sworn he was talking to me over my shoulder. This painting was the best I've ever done."

As an illustrator myself, I've been invoking the help of my heroes in spirit since I first learned of the process some years ago. Naturally it's difficult to determine whether or not spirit *is actually* responding to our requests—it's not as if they're able to sign their work after all, I just trusted that they were and continued submitting my request, then thanking them—just in case. All I knew was that my work never stopped improving and I was blessed with a steady flow of commissions from all over the world.

So it was that when I eventually found myself heavily invested in a project in a different field entirely, I saw no reason why I shouldn't continue with more of the same.

Well, the response this time was, to say the least, nothing short of breathtakingly dramatic. Seriously—I've had "one-click" orders placed with Amazon that took longer to be confirmed. This was definitely not just a mere "feeling" this time—this went way beyond that. This evidence couldn't have been more compelling if Andrew Wyeth's signature had materialized on one of my paintings. Furthermore, confirmation came in a form that the mediums love—validation from a non-local third party who could not possibly have had prior knowledge of any aspects of the situation whatsoever. I'll be sharing

*It's Much More Than Just "A Reading"*

the details of this little saga with you later—when I acknowledge the many people who are helping and supporting me.

Mediumship is a subject that, unfortunately, hasn't historically received "very good press," and the degrading ways in which it's been depicted by the entertainment industry over the years haven't exactly helped either. So I hope the foregoing compilation of reality checks has served to allay any lingering misconceptions of what mediumship is all about. Let's finally put that caricature of a turban bedecked buffoon with a strange accent and crystal ball to rest (in peace).

CHAPTER 5
# THE JOY OF READINGS—
# IT'S MUTUAL

Ken Akehurst was an English medium. He became quite famous because of a modest but fascinating book titled *Everyone's Guide to the Hereafter*, published in 1985, shortly after he'd written it. The most fascinating feature of this event though is the fact that he'd passed to the Higher Life in July 1978—well *before* the book had been written.

You see, the entire book was dictated to and 'channeled' through a writer by the name of G. M. Roberts using the 'automatic writing' process.

The book abounds with intriguing insights as viewed from his vantage point on the other side of the veil but of course from the unique perspective of a medium. I thought these wonderfully affirming observations to be particularly pertinent to our discussion here:

Akehurst wrote: 'We love to contact our loved ones and friends on the Earth Plane to give them messages of hope and good cheer....."

"...the more contact that we can make the happier we are. So never be afraid to go to a medium, you are doing us both a power of good."

"It is the most wonderful thing for us to know that we can keep in touch with our friends and loved ones once we have passed over. The knowledge that we can still be of help when so many think we have gone for good, gives us a wonderful feeling of still belonging. And this keeps the link between us strong. So instead of letting the dead sleep, as some quaint saying goes, you should make every effort to keep in touch. Do not think of them as being dead but on the end of a telephone."

Regardless of how resolutely we stand by our convictions, it's still always gratifying I feel, to have them authoritatively validated like this—the 'official seal of approval' as it were. It's this very sense of mutuality that it's good to remain mindful of as we prepare ourselves to be in a good and positive frame of mind with which to go into a reading—whether it's the first or twenty-first time.

Just as the quality of the connection between the two principal participants is dependent on their vibrational alignment, the vibrations *we*, in our relatively minor role, put out are an important component also. In this regard, it can be a contributing factor to the success of a reading if we try to position ourselves in the best place we can be, emotionally.

Even after we've made the decision to seek out a medium and made the appointment, many of us can still feel some trepidation for any number of reasons. We may be harboring lingering doubts brought on by the disapproving attitudes of well-meaning friends

## The Joy of Readings—It's Mutual

or the skepticism of family members with lurking suspicions that we're "losing it." Pressures such as these, coming as they do on top of years of societal conditioning, ignorance-based old wives' tales, for instance, can build up to such an accumulation of disapproving negatives that's difficult to ignore. A very special effort on our part is called for if we're to free ourselves of this residue of negative influences. If we should find ourselves beleaguered by this stuff, we have to find a way of brushing it off if at all possible because we need to go into a reading intending it to be a positive, affirming experience and be acceptive of nothing less. It can also help if we stay mindful and trustful of the fact that all messages received from our loved ones emanate from a vibration of pure love—love of the highest order.

Patrick Mathews is one of the many mediums who have learned from spirit through thousands of readings over the years, the reasons why our emotional demeanor is important for the success of our reading. In his book *Never Say Goodbye* he writes:

- Grief is a heavy emotion, one that brings energy to a very low position. It places a block around a survivor that makes it very hard for loved ones on the other side to penetrate.
- For a spirit to be able to communicate with others, those people need to be at a higher level, which can be achieved with happiness or being positive.

There's also another satisfying aspect of this mutuality with which we can fortify ourselves for our reading. It's the knowledge that our loved ones, in all probability, have been responsible for conceiving and orchestrating the entire series of events that have led us to this particular medium at this particular time. As incredible as this may seem, the spirits have often confirmed to the mediums that this is indeed the case.

In her book *Through the Eyes of Spirit* Jenny Crawford writes: "The spirit world always knows prior to your visit that you are coming. In fact, more often than not, they may prompt you to pick up the telephone and make the appointment."

Jenny also tells us in *The Spirit of Love* that "Prior to a client visiting a medium, those in the spirit world have often orchestrated the meeting by visiting clients in their sleep state and implanting the idea to seek out a medium."

There are also any number of instances cited by the mediums regarding spirit contact before their scheduled public demonstrations. Spirits have been known to show up the evening before or even minutes prior to them going on stage for an open demonstration where subjects are approached, ostensibly, strictly at random. (Or are they? Not necessarily—apparently).

So, our loved ones clearly have a keen and vested interest in the success of our reading and their ardent desire for us to "get it right" is indicative, I feel, of their sureness of knowing about the power that the benefits of their messages afford us. They know that their words, sent as they are with such genuine love, have the potential to transport us from what we've perceived to be a bleak, desolate and totally joyless future to a new and glorious life—a life full of possibilities.

## Preparing For Our Reading

It's generally acknowledged by the mediumship community that as much as we'd like to, it's not advisable to consult with a medium too soon after our loved one's transition to spirit. They advise us to wait until "Some perspective has returned and our physical loss is not such an open wound," is how George Anderson puts it. The time this takes

## The Joy of Readings—It's Mutual

of course, varies between individuals and their situations. But there is also another consideration, and again, one that the mediums are in a position to know something about—so it behooves us to take heed.

It revolves around the fact that the spirits arrive on the other side with their souls in varying states of debilitation—especially true in cases where physical death came after a prolonged period of illness at the hands of a ravaging disease. The emasculated condition in which such souls arrive are often such that an extended period of convalescence is required.

The mediums have, over the years, received ample and reassuring evidence to the fact that state-of-the-art clinical facilities exist over there, for the express purpose of providing the best loving care and nurturing we could possibly imagine. In the most beautiful and tranquil of environments, our loved ones are nursed ever-so-gently back to perfect health, with tender loving care administered in massive doses by skilled, devoted and highly empathic Spirit Helpers.

Learning about this process a few years ago turned out to be the missing piece in my own perplexing puzzle. It served to explain the vexatious experience that defined my first reading after my wife's passing.

A male and female figures had immediately come through and the female had stepped forward and told the medium her first name together with the name of the town in England where she came from—unmistakably my wife's parents. But no wife—and not even one word about her. Naturally, I was crushed, to say the least, and remained so for several weeks. It was only after reading about this convalescent period that I was able to snap out of it and gather up the courage to book another reading. My wife, you see, had succumbed

## The Direct Connect

after a valiant three-year battle with breast cancer that had metastasized to the bones, so the convalescence explanation made sense to me. The lingering shadow of that "no-show" disappointment however served to double-the-pleasure of the thrill I experienced when my wife came through the instant the medium finished her opening prayer. Just something to bear in mind when apprehensively embarking on that first venture into the wonderful world of mediumship.

When we've decided that we're in a comfortable frame of mind and ready to jump in, we may want to know how to go about locating a good dependable medium. It's not exactly the same as looking for a plumber after all or even a lawyer—I've yet to see a giant medium's face grinning at me from the back of the bus I'm driving behind. And those directories aren't very helpful—no matter what color their pages are.

And also, despite the fact that we may feel perfectly ready for a reading, we may not yet feel ready to "go public" with it. So that shuts us off from one avenue to which we're accustomed to turning—the personal recommendations of family and friends. We're just not ready for more scoffing and mocking from that quarter thank you.

Fortunately there is one dependable source which I can personally recommend.

The "go-to" specialist for this is Bob Olson. He operates several excellent websites that are dedicated to all matters regarding the afterlife, with lots of links to many other sources of interest. One of his sites, *BestPsychicMediums.com* carries listings and descriptions of established qualified mediums, and importantly, each one has been tested several times by Bob himself. (His credentials as a tester incidentally are excellent—the best kind—he's a former skeptic you see).

## The Joy of Readings—It's Mutual

Over the past ten years I've availed myself of the services of several of his listings and have never been disappointed—with several being simply outstanding.

Also, as we've seen, it's quite okay for us to invoke the assistance of our loved ones in our selection process. And as Jenny Crawford has told us—it's quite possible that the spirits have already made the selection for us and have been patiently waiting for us to align ourselves with their vibration by tuning in to and trusting our intuitive hunches.

## The Reading

I personally regard it as essential to have an audio recording of our reading because no matter how adept we may consider ourselves to be at note-taking, we are just not going to catch every single nuance. I've also learned from experience that our perceptive faculties aren't above playing mischievous little tricks on us.

I know this to have been the case with a reading I had early on with one of our "top-flight" mediums. I was so disappointed with the reading initially that I couldn't bring myself to listen to the tape for a month or more. When I finally got sick of moping about it and braced myself to listen to it, I was stunned. There was hardly any resemblance between what I was hearing this time around and how I'd interpreted what I'd "heard" at the time—colored (or *mis*-colored) by my own false presumptions.

Just a few days after my enlightening experience, I was re-visiting George Anderson's book *Walking in the Garden of Souls* and came across his account of an incident that almost parallels it. A recent sitter had written him a scathing, ranting diatribe of a letter about her reading with him—the lady was not a happy camper. A few days later however, he received another letter from the same lady, this missive written *after* she'd listened to the tape. Apparently George wasn't "a liar for whom there was a special place in hell," after all, and no longer did she "wish she'd never heard of him." To the contrary, she was now apologizing profusely for taking her anger out on him. Anger that apparently had stemmed from the fact that what George had reported her daughter as having said, had actually been all too true.

It's the practice of some mediums to provide their sitters with an audiotape of their reading. Others however prefer not to get involved in this and leave it to us. For our telephone readings there are simple devices available at electronic stores that plug into the line between the phone outlet and our tape recorder. (I realize that by the time we go to press, someone will have by now invented several upgraded generations of hi-tech wireless devices that will be way more sophisticated than my "buggy-whip" stuff).

Reputable mediums all agree that there is one cardinal rule we should stay mindful of during our reading—we should *never volunteer information of any kind.* The one exception is our first name, which mediums, as a rule, ask of us because our spoken vibration is believed to help those on the other side to draw in closer to us. Other than that, the only time we ever need to speak is with a simple "yes," "no" or "maybe" when we're responding to the medium asking us if the information they've imparted to us means anything to us, or if it makes sense. They'll usually ask us something like "Do you take this?" for instance, or "Does this register?" This is in order to forestall any suspicions of "leading the witness," as it were, or charges of eliciting tid-bits of information they can ingenuously use.

It's quite natural for us to go into a reading with preconceived ideas of what we would ideally like to hear from our loved ones. It

## The Joy of Readings—It's Mutual

would be a mistake though to, in our eagerness, try to interrupt the medium with questions. Much better that we remain patient and keep any questions we may have till after the reading, because it's really amazingly uncanny how often the very questions we have on our mind are answered anyway in one way or another. To pre-empt them is to deny ourselves the infinitely more gratifying experience of hearing the validation we've been so eagerly awaiting—unprompted by us.

It's also quite natural to go into a reading with certain expectations, but we risk setting ourselves up for a devastating let-down if those expectations are unrealistically high. It's important to stay mindful of the fact that no medium is absolutely perfect, regardless of whether they have their own television series or have written a dozen best selling books. To expect any medium to interpret communications from spirit with a hundred percent accuracy would be akin to expecting a major league batsman to hit a home run every time at the plate (The great Babe Ruth's career batting average was .342).

By the same token though, there's such a thing as having our expectations too low, lowering our vibration in the way the mediums warn us to beware of. An example of this would be not to have expectations of a relative coming through because they died thirty years ago and believing that's far too long for them to come through. John Holland, in his book *Born Knowing* writes of a sitter who had expressed this fear regarding her father. "But he's still dead, right?" John asked her. Then gently explained to her "If he's over there and wants to come to you, then it doesn't matter how long ago he passed."

The mediums suggest that we avoid going into a reading with compellingly fixed ideas of what to expect, but to relax and put ourselves trustfully in their hands and those of our loved ones in spirit. We are in *their* domain now—and this is their wheelhouse after all. We should also bear in mind though that although mediums possess these extraordinary abilities, they are still basically only human. And like us, they too can be prone to having the occasional "off-day" when, for some unfathomable reason, we just don't feel on top of our game.

## Messaging—Spirit Style

To the uninitiated, it must seem the height of incredulity that mediums have this ability to "talk to dead people," as they like to put it. And moreover, that they actually attract followers. In their view, that *really* calls for an unrealistically inordinate amount of faith and trust—or, in their view, even madness.

So I couldn't help recalling that back in 1602 Shakespeare, in *Hamlet*, had Polonius say; "Though this be madness yet there is method in it." So it struck me that breaking down the "mechanics" of the reading process into its component parts would bring about some clarity for non-believers, threshold-believers or any fence-sitters who may be watching.

There are six main methods of communication by which those in spirit communicate with us through the mediums. The first five are quite easy for us to relate to because they pretty much align with the five senses we already instinctively use every second in this dimension, they are:

*Clairvoyance*—A French word meaning clear-sightedness. This method entails the medium actually "seeing" images in their minds-eye in sufficient detail for them to identify what spirit is conveying. For example, the spirits will hold up items and objects, sometimes with a literal meaning, but at other times items in the form of universally recognized symbols. Take roses for instance, red ones are

## The Joy of Readings—It's Mutual

the obvious logical expression of love. But white roses, in spirit lingo, symbolize celebration or congratulations. In my reading with George Anderson he told me that my wife was showing him red roses for me, but then also showed him white roses for our daughter, signifying her congratulations on her recent job promotion—indicated by an image of a flight of stairs. (I hadn't told him I had a daughter by the way).

The promotion was news to me, but on calling our daughter Bev, following the reading, she confirmed that she had been promoted—earlier that very day. I chalked that up as a "hit."

*Clairaudience*—Hearing. The spirits often actually speak audibly to the mediums and use expressions that they know will unmistakably establish their identity to the sitter—unique words or catchphrases usually known only to them.

Spirits have also shown an ability to conjure up sounds that relate to an event of some significance that will serve to convey their day-to-day presence in our lives. During one of my readings with Carole Lynne she said she was hearing the distinct sound of a bird chirping and asked me if we'd had a pet bird. When I told her we hadn't, she went on to say "Your wife is being very insistent about this. She keeps telling me to ask you about the bird. Has a bird flown close to you recently in an unusual way?" It then dawned on me that this had been the case. After the reading, I explained to Carole that the morning before, I'd returned from my beach walk and discovered a sizeable blackbird in my house, chirping his head off. And then, after I'd opened all the windows and taken my shower, was still there, on a window sill, and showing no intentions whatsoever of leaving.

*Clairsentience*—Clear-feeling. Mediums have told us that it seems important to the spirits to confirm in detail the circumstances surrounding their passing. They seem to have a knowing that this will clearly verify who they are by the way they reference aspects of their illness that only we could have knowledge of. Out of all the readings I've had over the past ten years, there have only been one or two where the medium hasn't asked me something like "Did your wife pass with breast cancer? Because I'm aware of a dull pain around that area on the left side." Always, correctly, the left side, never once the right. In their books, the mediums frequently refer to examples of this, covering a range of traumas from head to toe. It's a wonder they don't limp home battered and bruised and it's quite understandable why they can only handle a limited number of calls in a day.

*Clairalience*—Smell. I've often read and heard it said that the power of smell is the most underestimated evocative trigger to memories of past events and locations. Most of us have experienced a time when, out of the blue, just one whiff of a fragrance has immediately whisked us back to a place we haven't given a thought to in years. Oliver Wendell Holmes, talking about this power of our sense of smell said: "Memories, imagination, old sentiments and associations are more readily reached through the sense of smell than through any other channel."

The mediums have attested to this many times. In an excellent reading I sat for with Carole Lynne, she asked me "Are you by any chance baking cookies right now?" When I answered that I wasn't, she said "Well, that's interesting because I'm getting a definite wonderful fragrance of cookies baking and I know it's not coming from this end because I don't have any cookies in my house at all." Then, following a short pause, she said "This female figure here is quite adamant about this, she's telling me you've been *talking* about cookies with someone recently."

## The Joy of Readings—It's Mutual

I could hardly wait to tell her after the reading, that less than an hour before our reading, one of my sisters in England, Mo, had called me, and yes—we'd been talking about cookies of all things. A particular English brand known for over a hundred years for its distinctive fragrance.

*Clairgustance*—Taste. This method that spirits sometimes use to verify their identity, entails borrowing the medium's taste buds. They have been known for instance, to take the unique flavor of a sitter's favorite pudding his wife used to prepare for him, or the distinctive taste of a mother's favorite recipe for carrot cake, and transplant it temporarily into the medium. A friend of mine, in a reading he sat for following the death of his father, was able to identify that the spirit coming through was undoubtedly his dear old dad. The reading had only been in progress for a few minutes when the medium suddenly began smacking her lips and remarked that ever since this, as yet unidentified, male figure had stepped forward, she'd been getting the unmistakable taste of beer. For my friend Tom, that was a clincher—he'd been born and raised in a country pub his mother and father owned.

*Telepathy*—The transference of thoughts by extrasensory means. Mediums tell me that unlike the other five methods, telepathy defies explanation, at least in terms that we "five-sensory" beings can really relate to very well (hence the expression "sixth-sense" I suppose). Understanding it calls for an advanced level of enlightenment that not many can genuinely aspire to. For us to fully understand the process by which messages are communicated by just thoughts alone would require us to be endowed with the same multi-sensory abilities as the mediums themselves.(We all *are*, to a degree, but more on that later). The mediums' unique abilities however, allow them to automatically and instinctively align their vibrational frequency with that of spirit in a way that precludes any possibility of them having emanated from any other source. We, on the other hand, also have thoughts pop into our heads—they never stop—we just have no idea where they come from.

I think you'll agree that this is quite an extensive array of tools the spirits have at their disposal. When we consider the fact that conveying their thoughts and messages to the medium can entail drawing on any or all of them, almost simultaneously at times, and further, that spirits are said to communicate at a pretty speedy pace (as if they're trying to ensure optimal use of their "calling minutes," I'm told), we begin to get some idea of how easy it must be for the medium to miss or miss-hear an item from time to time.

No one has yet been able to definitively explain how any of these methods of spirit communication work—what the nature of the forces at work here, is. The mediums however, from their vantage point, have formed their ideas on the matter, intuitively educed from the pointers they've received from those occupying that most unique of vantage points—our spirit friends on the other side. The following are a few gleanings from our reliable source.

## Electricity—the 'Light' in Enlightenment

> Is it a fact – or have I dreamt it – that, by means of electricity, the world of matter has become a great nerve, vibrating thousands of miles in a breathless point of time? —*Nathaniel Hawthorne,—From The House of the Seven Gables. – 1851*

George Anderson says "We can assume what we think it is, or how it's working, but the other side has said that it works off electricity."

Then, later: "There's obviously some sort of electrical energy working here, and I don't think we've even tapped into it yet."

These quotes are from the book *We Don't Die*, one of several remarkable best-selling works co-authored by Joel Martin and Patricia Romanowski. Based on years of research, two of them, *We Don't Die* and *We Are Not Forgotten*, are predominantly centered around George Anderson and his extensive experiences as one of the world's leading mediums.

George has been known over the years for enthusiastically making himself available for all manner of testing and investigative procedures—including the breakthrough scientific research conducted by Gary E. Schwartz, Ph.D. and his team at the University of Arizona and documented so thoroughly in his widely acclaimed book *The Afterlife Experiments*. Again, in *We Don't Die*, Anderson says "I'm skeptical, I'm cynical about it. I want constant reassurance that this is for real and it's really happening."

Electricity, in some form or another, figures quite frequently in Anderson's accounts of his readings. He refers for instance, to interruptions in spirit communication during readings caused by thunderstorms. He cites one case where he was unable to receive any communication from spirit at all for some time while an electrical storm was passing through the area. This seems to be quite plausible to me because I've read of how the electrical forces associated with geomagnetic storms play havoc with radio and radar signals and also disrupt navigational systems—including those of racing pigeons apparently. I grew up among many pigeon racing enthusiasts in the English Midlands, and I recall the disappointment of these "pigeon fanciers," as they were called, when only a small percentage of their valiant little aviators made it back to their loft—their comrades having had their homing instinct mechanisms scrambled by such storms. Victims have been known to show up weeks later in lofts on this side of the Atlantic.

There are other evidential factors that give credence to the notion of electrical energies being an integral element of spirit communication, in ways that clearly demonstrate their ability to keep abreast of our technological advances. Consider for instance, the multitude of ways by which they're known to gift us with signs of their presence by mischievously manipulating those electronic devices that play such a large part in everyone's daily life these days. Radios—clocks—CD players—television receivers—answering machines etc. There have even been numerous incidents reported of messages being left on cell phones along with the call-back number of the deceased. And of course the one at which they seem to be particularly adept—causing light bulbs to flicker. They can drive anyone pleasingly nuts with this one—it hardly ever stops around my house. In fact my desk lamp here has been at it ever since I started writing this section. Hi darling.

So, it would appear there's a general consensus that it's likely electrical energies that are behind what is at work here. Is it too much to hope that learning this will serve to satisfy the skeptics and convince them and the fence-sitters to come in out of the cold and join the party—so that they can confidently go about availing themselves of the awesome benefits that mediumship offers? They really have nothing to lose, to the contrary—the rewards that the simple act of swallowing their pride can bestow are bounteous beyond belief.

## The Games Those Dead People Play

Acquainting ourselves with the reading process, in effect, living vicariously through the mediums' accounts of them in their books,

## The Joy of Readings—It's Mutual

is an excellent way of preparing ourselves for our own foray into the field.

We learn for instance that the sprits can be quite mischievous at times in the way they dole out snippets of information in what amounts to their version of charades. It's as if they're playing games with the medium, because there are times when the medium is so earnestly intent on doing his job, he has no idea what's going on. But to be fair—in our own intenseness, neither do we, until he looks up and asks "Your wife had an impish sense of humor didn't she?" And then we realize "Yes, that's my gal." The mediums tell us that our loved ones retain their personality to a large extent when they cross over, and whenever this becomes apparent it provides them with a key that helps them to cohesively assemble the often disparate array of tid-bits coming through.

Allison DuBois confirms this in her book In *Secrets of the Monarch*. She writes "Our personality traits are not gone once our body is no longer a part of us. Our humor, sarcasm, or whatever we are inside is attached to our soul."

Sir Arthur Conan Doyle, discussing the ways in which spirit communicates with us, in his book *The New Revelation*, published in 1918, asks us to imagine some wise angel on the other side saying "Now don't make it easy for these people. Make them use their brains a little." Almost a hundred years later—they're still up to their tricks. We can only assume it's a required course they take in an effort to get us to lighten up.

As we've seen, messages from spirit are by no means limited to any one method, so when they're used adjunctively, the phrasing of messages can easily become a multi-faceted affair—which can make them quite complex at times, but always impressive.

## The Direct Connect

To assist in familiarizing ourselves with this unique communication style (Texting or Tweeting it's not), here are a few examples I'd like to share, taken from the books by various mediums and readings I've had myself.

In her book *Spirit of Love*, Jenny Crawford tells of the puzzling way by which a sitter's recently deceased husband was able to identify himself. He'd spent some considerable time pointing persistently at Jenny's neck, which didn't register with Jenny at all. It was only when he started also repeating the word "Neck" that she finally realized he was trying to tell her his name—Nick.

The spirits are also adept at conveying their identity by their manner of speech—tonal inflections—the habitual turns of phrase they'd used and their reflexive body language and gestures they'd lapsed into while saying them. It's like the familiar expression "It wasn't what he said as much as the way he said it." Doris Stokes, in her book *Voices in my Ear* writes of how she'd once successfully identified a family matriarch in spirit with an impression of how she was sitting up straight with her arms folded tightly and bristling because she was very cross. Leaving the assembled family with no doubts whatsoever that this was indeed their mother (We can only imagine the number of times they'd all been subjected to "That look" over the years).

In another of her books, *Innocent Voices in my Ear*, Doris cites an example of how effective a single three-letter word can be. During one of her visits to the United States, she was reading in the home of a family who were hoping to connect with their son who had died of cancer. After explaining that the husband had made it clear that he—"Didn't hold with any of this nonsense, he'd only agreed to it to please his wife." Doris tells us that his, "Waves of disbelief and doubt were streaming from him, making it difficult to concentrate."

## The Joy of Readings—It's Mutual

Her "Gotcha" moment eventually came though when she relayed to them that their son was talking about a vacation. "We went to New Zealand," the son said, "We had a marvelous time didn't we pal?"

On hearing this, his father broke down. Apparently they had *always* called each other "Pal." Just that one little word was all it took to cut through all his skepticism about "this nonsense."

Medium Jeffrey Wands, in his book *Another Door Opens* recounts a similar incident, this one involving three little words. A man in spirit had come to him in a dream the night before a scheduled reading with the man's widow. In the dream, he'd told Jeffrey that his wife had been debating whether to have some work done on their home and had said "It's a go." When Jeffrey repeated this to the man's wife the following day, the very surprised lady explained that "It's a go" had been one of her husband's favorite expressions.

Whenever I come across instances like these—and there are many—where definite identification of a loved one in spirit could easily have hinged on just a single simple piece of evidence, I'm reminded of that succinct observation made by Dr. William James way back in 1885, *"If you wish to upset the law that all crows are black, it is enough that you prove that one crow is white.* (If only more "people of science" would be as succinct). Dr. James' wise words are surely something for us to stay mindful of when going into our reading, for this reason.

If it was possible for the mediums to be able to confidently guarantee the accuracy of every piece of evidence they present us with, it would indeed be "perfect world." But we've seen how complex and confusing communicating with spirit can often be, so it can be comforting to know that a low percentage of hits, even *just one* hit could, following Dr James' dictum—actually constitute a successful reading. So in this context, if the "It's a go" catchphrase had turned out be the only hit the widow had received, it would still have been, in effect, her white crow.

In several readings I've had, the medium has, after acknowledging a female figure's presence, demonstrated or described the same hand gesture that, to me, unquestionably identified her as being my wife, usually before she's even said a word. In life, to emphasize her disapproval or rejection of something said or done, she would raise a forearm with palm facing outward and wave from side to side—"like a windshield wiper," is how medium Patrick Mathews described it in a reading he was giving me. "Was your wife a schoolteacher?" he then asked, (She was), "because while she's doing this she's telling me firmly to slow down and listen."

Another excellent medium by the name of Harry Byard, also picked up on this just two weeks later. When he came to me in a message service, he simulated the same gesture while saying "Your wife is saying you're taking too much on, you're pushing yourself too hard—slow down." (Like I"d never heard that before). I chalked up both instances as definite "Hits."

I realize that all of these examples represent the type of instances that the skeptics scoff at as falling way short of being proof of an afterlife, and of course they're right—but to the sitters, at the time—they represent all the proof *they* need—they are to them, at that moment—priceless.

I don't think any kind of evidence offered by spirit has greater impact on the sitter than when the medium correctly identifies the spirit coming through by name, and from the creative ways in which the spirits often go about this, suggests they too are fully aware of its significance to us.

## The Joy of Readings—It's Mutual

George Anderson successfully discerned my wife's first *and* middle names when he read for me. When I asked how he'd done that, he explained that she'd used the same trick that spirits use on him all the time. Apparently, they're in habit of using his mind like a filing cabinet and delve into it seemingly knowing where to retrieve pieces of relevant information that will help clue him in to what they wish to convey to the sitter.

In this case, my wife, after telling him her first name consisted of five letters beginning with 'D', then slipped into the game-playing mode with which he's become all too familiar. The clue she gave him was "Your mother's sister," How that lead him to Doris was remembering that his aunt had always been known to the family as Aunt Dar—short for Doris.

Examples of the ways spirits use George's "filing cabinet mind" are sprinkled liberally throughout his books. They clearly know for instance, that one of George's passions is classic movies (of which he has an encyclopedic range of knowledge), because this particular file folder is the object of their retrieval hunts time and time again.

Dr. Gary Schwartz in his book *The Afterlife Experiments*, cites an example. In a reading conducted by George as part of Dr. Schwartz's research, spirit showed him images from the Tennessee Williams classic *The Glass Menagerie*, in regard to spirit who'd come forward. What George surmised from this (correctly) was that the character in question had been "A little on the domineering side." Clearly, a reference to the play's domineering character Amanda Wingfield.

It seems that my wife also once familiarized herself with the contents of a medium's "mental filing cabinet." Because mid-way through my sitting with Joanne Gerber, after a minute or so of indistinct whispers aside, she asked me straight out of the blue, "Is your wife's name Doris?" When I—astounded, affirmed that it was, she told me that there had been a famous English medium named Doris Stokes and that my wife must have known Joanne knew of her too because she'd showed her a poster of Doris Stokes with her name boldly displayed.

One must admit that this is truly a wondrous phenomenon that's constantly playing-out here. An assemblage of gifted and caring souls, working creatively in sublime cooperation, to bring about a healing and disburdening comfort, not just for the loved ones left behind on this side of the veil, but as we've seen, also for those who have made their transition to the other side.

To not avail ourselves of the mediums' accounts of it at work, in their books, is to deprive ourselves of an extraordinary enlightening treat for our hearts and souls.

## Separating the Wheat from the Chaff

Although I admit to being an unabashed fan of mediumship, not for a minute would I imply that all mediums are simon-pure. The field of mediumship unfortunately, in common with most fields that involve the exchange of services for money, has it's share of opportunistic bad apples. These can range from those whose level of expertise is questionable, but masquerading as legitimate and accredited anyway, to those who are genuinely officially accredited—but ethically challenged. There are also those who are colloquially, and disdainfully, known as "storefront-psychics" which are usually taken to comprise those who set up their tent at the Fall Fair and Funnel Cake Festival or on the pier at the seaside. But don't be fooled, there are some impressive readings on record from mediums in this category—my wife had a stunner one time.

## The Joy of Readings—It's Mutual

I know—it can get a little confusing, this is the reason I'm pleased I was able to recommend Bob Olson's website. Whichever approach we take, when we have made our decision and settled on a medium, there are a few considerations I'd like to suggest regarding the reading process.

First of all, as we discussed earlier, it's important not to enter into a reading with our expectations too high. Our reading, in all likelihood, will not be one hundred percent—I think it's safe to say that this has never happened. It's not a case of us being knowingly short-changed, it's just that there are simply too many variables inherent both in the spirits' ability to convey information and the ability of the mediums to accurately interpret what they receive—as we've seen earlier, it's anything *but* a regular translation process.

It's true that the medium's function in a reading is that of a "conduit", a tube through which the messages from spirit pass, hence the expression the mediums use to describe it "I'm just the messenger." But it still stands that the success of the reading is contingent not only on the abilities of both parties, but also any unanticipated anomalies that can occur, over which the mediums have no control.

So, all things considered, the mediums clearly have their work cut out for them in just being "the messenger," and that is all that's expected of them, so in the event they veer away from this path, which they're apt to do at times, they're not acting in the best interests of us or the spirits. It's all about the facts—be square with us. No editing—no filtering—no suppositions—no personal embellishments—just the straight dope.

Many mediums offer spiritual counseling as an ancillary arm of their business, and I've known them reflexively drift into this area and start playing psychologist. They should make the effort to keep the two activities separate (unless of course our loved one *was* a psychologist) otherwise, not only are they wasting the spirits' time, it's not what we're paying them for. I can't honestly say I've ever known how to best handle this and any other frailties, other than mark them down in my mental debit column as a future reference for when I'm asked if I can recommend a medium. I will however, always try to "cut them some slack" if their reading has passed muster in other regards (Remember that "one white crow').

There are several other "giveaway" signs that reflect on a medium's level of competence and professionalism. Notably the irrelevant nuggets of cautionary advice they sometimes can't seem to resist doling out. For the most part, these are nothing more than fillers—designed to mask the fact that they don't have anything from spirit due to the poor quality of their vibrational alignment. But presenting them as if they're messages from spirit? Well, to say the least, that's just downright disingenuous. For instance, they'll say things like:

"You need to have your tires checked."

"There's a light switch in your bathroom you should have checked out."

"Check the locks on your doors."

These are just three of several such items about which I've received dire warnings—of course on "good authority," over the years (Has anyone ever gone broke selling fearfulness?). Anyway, it's an old trick from the early days—the kind of seedy hucksterism that could get you run-out-of-town-on-a-rail in the day.

I once accompanied a friend to a message service conducted by an accredited medium—a Reverend no less. When he delivered the customary mini-reading to each member of the congregation, one of

## The Joy of Readings—It's Mutual

the supposed "messages from spirit" he passed on to about 80 percent of those gathered involved them relocating either to another town or even another state. After he'd advised my super-fit friend to move to Utah for health reasons, she turned and quipped to me "Remind me to call my broker tomorrow. I think this guy owns stock in Ace Van Lines."

Is it any wonder that we have trouble getting our message across and convincing people to take us seriously, when we have jokers like this around still playing silly games? Come on guys, cut it out—your clients, in the main, are aggrieved, vulnerable and often fragile souls—they deserve better—they've been through enough for heaven's sake.

No doubt these less than stellar performers do, on occasion, get lucky (even broken clocks are precisely correct twice a day, after all). Or maybe they're on a learning curve and could conceivably become proficient and no longer feel the need to resort to these cheesy tricks.

In the meantime though, every case of this pseudo-mediumship stuff is not doing anyone any favors, and is reflecting negatively on what is otherwise a potentially noble and sacred calling—an unerringly positive force for the universal good.

There are enough skeptics and debunkers lurking out there, looking for the slightest hint of phoniness, fraudulence and breaches of integrity to pounce on—we don't need to provide them with more ammunition.

## Spirited Counteractivity

One of the most frequent charges leveled at mediumship by its many debunkers ever since its inception, has been that the mediums' validations are merely based on knowledge they've obtained about their clients prior to the reading. The theories they've floated

## The Direct Connect

regarding how they go about this, have run the gamut from the patently absurd to the truly bizarre.

In the last few decades, many of their theories have of course featured computer technology (seeing as how there's apparently nothing this much revered idol can't do, wink, wink). Like, for instance, the guy I met who just *knows* that mediums are linked to a vast central database and are able to access all the information they need on anyone who shows up on their doorstep. Seriously?

I was discussing mediums with another dyed-in-the-wool skeptic recently, and he too had it all worked out—I could tell he'd put a lot of thought into it—he was a nice enough chap, but according to him, "The mediums are well and truly busted. This is how it is you see," he explained, "the mediums have a team of cohorts equipped with scanning devices, and when people attending their public demonstrations have parked their cars, they go around scanning their license plates." He went on to proudly assert that "From the data this gives them access to, with a couple of passwords, they can obtain all manner of stuff about those gullible fools."

Take down your shingles you shameful charlatans—the party's over. He assured me he was deadly serious. I told him I was one of those fools and he had the IQ of an after-dinner mint.

But, let's face it, we can't deny or ignore the phenomenally aggressive growth of this information gathering technology with its mind boggling undreamt of potential. I don't see how anyone can say with any certainty that the field of mediumship can remain immune to these kinds of charges. As this age of microchip technology has been consistently demonstrating to us, things may not be as kookily far-fetched as they appear to us right now, in just a few short weeks. It seems at times that literally *anything* is possible.

## The Joy of Readings—It's Mutual

I sense though, that there are reasons to believe that no one is more aware of our vulnerability than those in the spirit realm. And I think it's more than likely that "the cavalry have already been dispatched," as it were, and even as we speak, "They're heading them off at the pass." We only have to consider the ways in which they have, for some time now, been making references to contemporary technological devices to know that they make a point of keeping abreast of earthly affairs and adapting to changes.

I also have a notion that for some time now, we've been in the throes of a very intriguing evolvement that's taking place in the world of mediumship, and it is, what else, spirit driven. One cannot help noticing for instance, that many of their validating pieces of evidence they've been giving us in the course of our readings, have had a definite currentness to them. This has manifested in the ways they've referenced significant events that, amazingly, occurred as recently as a mere few minutes before—as if they're saying to the skeptics "Okay—Google that!"

The books are replete with such instances these days, and again, not necessarily of major import (as we've seen, the most meaningful to the sitter often aren't), but undeniable evidence of a loved one's presence nevertheless. So, for the sitter—pure 24-carat gold.

The renowned Scottish medium Gordon Smith had an experience that serves as a perfect example of what we're talking about, he writes about it in his book *Spirit Messenger*.

It occurred as a client, who was hoping Gordon would be able to connect with her son in spirit, arrived for her reading. At the very moment she was entering his home, Gordon heard her son calling out to him "Ask Mum about Macbeth." So straight off he said to her "What about Macbeth?"

A very surprised and momentarily taken aback client, with widened eyes replied "I've only just bought a copy of the book on my way here this morning."

And no, Mister Skeptic, she wasn't holding the book in her hand. But, fortunately for Gordon, she had failed to notice that guy in the bushes—scanning her license plate.

So obviously, those wonderful spirit friends of ours have our backs. They're wise to the games those wily debunkers play, and in order to stay ahead of them they're diligently manning the ramparts 24/7 while updating and refining their messaging techniques to counter them.

In the following chapter, dealing with my own readings (or messaging sessions, as I prefer to call them), I'll be discussing several of the "current event" validations I've received.

CHAPTER 6

# MY READINGS

I've discussed earlier how it was that my involvement with mediumship grew out of a need for relief from and healing of the grief I was experiencing over losing my wife (ten years ago at the time of writing). My immutable belief in the legitimacy of psychic reading though had been sparked originally by the first six words uttered by the medium conducting my very first reading—over thirty years before that.

Interestingly, but to anyone familiar with the quirkiness of this phenomenon for very long, not all that surprising—there's a synchronous link between those six words spoken over forty years ago and the book you're now holding.

For the genesis of this connection and its relevance to us now, we have to go back to the early seventies. That was when a publishing company approached me with a request to write a "how-to" book on architectural rendering—the field in which I'd been heavily involved for several years. I was flattered and definitely interested.

When it came to putting my signature on the contract they later sent me though, I became beset with doubts as to whether it was in my best interests to commit to what I knew would be an arduous task. For one thing, I was fortunate in being constantly hard-pressed to keep up with the demands for my services as it was. Would I be taking too much on? I didn't want the added time constraints to jeopardize the quality of either my illustrations or a book.

I spent two indecisive months incessantly haggling back and forth with myself, which was uncharacteristic of me—I usually had pretty good instincts about what was best for me. On the one hand I felt that maintaining my level of illustration production while at the same time producing a book would be far too burdensome. On the other hand, the architectural profession *had* been inordinately good to me and the opportunity to give something back, by passing on what I'd learned to young people coming along, was something that appealed to me greatly.

I continued though to agonizingly go back and forth on the matter, until I received a call from the publishers that brought things to a head—I must, as they put it—"fish-or-cut-bait."

Over, appropriately, a seafood dinner later that evening, quite out of the blue, my wife suggested that I consult with a psychic medium. "Where on earth did that come from?" I asked, surprised and somewhat bemused. It turned out that back in England years before—two weeks before we'd first met—she'd received an unbelievably accurate reading from a medium.

And so it was that the next morning found me driving slowly around Cassadaga Spiritualist village—without an appointment—peering out

*My Readings*

at a succession of mediums' signs in the gardens of their cottages. As I rounded a bend a lady hanging out washing came into view. As she turned, cheerfully waving to me, the sign on the picket fence identified the smiling lady as "Donna Chan—Medium." After I'd parked my car and got out I quipped that I thought her sign should be amended to read *"Happy* Medium" seeing as how it was such a beautiful drying-day.

In just a matter of minutes we were sitting across from each other in her study. After lighting three candles, she sat—head bowed—eyes closed in concentration, with her hands in her lap, while all the time passing a strand of beads to and fro between her fingers.

After three or four minutes she slowly raised her head—opened her eyes, and looking intently directly into mine, said softly, but very matter-of-factly: "I see you writing a book."

I was just stunned in disbelief. Had she really said that?

A mere five minutes ago we'd been complete strangers and the only words I'd said to her besides my lame happy medium crack had been "Would you by any chance be available for a reading?" My introduction to the world of mediumship had been just six words that, right off the bat, had *explicitly* addressed the very issue I'd been struggling with for over two months.

The session continued with several more impressive validations, one in particular that I'll be telling you about later, after which, with Donna waving me good-bye, I drove away—in a haze of serene giddiness. I was basking in the glow of a sure and certain knowing that I had just been gifted with nothing less than Divine guidance.

I called my relieved wife immediately on returning to my office then put in a call to the publisher (*My* publisher from now on), to tell him the signed contract was in the mail.

I'd been right about the upcoming extra burden—three years would pass before I'd see my house and family in the daylight again.

## Thirty Years On

It would take the ravaging effects of grief over my wife's passing, thirty years later, for me to feel the need of a medium's talents again. Unfortunately I learned that Donna Chan, my first choice obviously, was no longer in practice as a medium, but a synchronous string of events led me to Vicki Monroe and I made an appointment for a telephone reading with her.

Naturally, as with my first reading thirty years before, I had definite ideas about what messages I would like to receive, and I was not disappointed in that regard. The very last thing I'd been expecting however was a reprise of that first reading. But amazingly, here was Vicki Monroe, a scant few minutes into her reading, asking me: "Who's the writer? Are you a writer? Because the lady I have here wants me to tell you that you must write a book about your experiences, because it will help a lot of people."

Definitely did not see that coming. That, or anything remotely resembling it, was not on my list. And I admit to initially discounting it out of hand—Vicki must have misinterpreted a communication. Writing another book—that's the very last thing on my agenda.

It was only when it became an unmistakable recurring theme in subsequent readings that I began to get that feeling that had been a feature at significant junctures in my life in the past—that had prompted me to conclude that *someone was trying to tell me something.*

A case in point was a reading I had around this time with Mary Rose Gray at Cassadaga. The very first words Mary Rose said to me were those that I was no longer surprised by, that I'd almost come to expect even, "Are you writing a book?"

At that time I couldn't honestly say that I was. What I did have, since I'd heard this so often by now, were a lot of scribbled notes I'd jotted down on half a dozen pads scattered at strategic points around the house, even in my car. When I explained this to her, she leaned forward with a hand on my knee and said very matter-of-factly: "Trust me—you're writing a book."

Expanding on this, she then went on to say "I'm being shown a traffic-light, it's turning green, that's telling you that right now is the time to go forward. I'm being shown a glass wall, there's a door opening—again I'm hearing 'Right now is the time.' I'm being told it's a book of an advisory nature—guidance—helping people. I'm seeing an arm extended—pointing, signifying 'Go for it.' Everything is illuminated by a green light."

Reflecting on Mary Rose's reading over the ensuing days, I figured that that "someone" who'd been trying to tell me something, must by now, be wondering what on earth it was going to take to get this boy off his duff. We were both about to find out.

## The Clincher

What it would take came in the form of another reading I had a few months later, with no less an authority than the world renowned psychic intuitive Sonia Choquette.

The first half of the reading consisted of a series of impressively spot-on validations that spoke to the significance of and the reasons for the various twists and turns of my life path—all the way from previous lifetimes through to the present time.

Then, as if the foregoing had been thoughtfully and craftily designed to establish the credibility of the spirit guides sourcing the information that was to come (which they had certainly succeeded in doing), she went on to say "Your guides are clearly—*clearly* suggesting that your next assignment is to write another book," and even proceeded to furnish me with its title.(Incidentally, I hadn't divulged that there *had* been a previous book). She then went on to tell me "Your guides, led by your wife, are going to download and download and download to you, information to get this on paper in the most beautiful and glorious way."

It would seem that those indefatigable spirit guides, working in conjunction with Sonia this time, had at last succeeded in finding what it would take to get this boy off his duff.

A major shift had just occurred. The notion of a book in order to "spread the word" was no longer an option—a possibility on which to ponder. I had, without a doubt been definitively served with my marching orders—I'd better put my paint brushes away and write a book.

Within the hour, I was on my way to the office supply store where I stocked up for the upcoming big haul with two dozen legal pads and a couple of boxes of ball-point pens. The boy can take a hint—eventually. By the way, fair warning—if you're looking for "writing in the most beautiful and glorious way," I suggest you read any of Sonia Choqette's books.

## More Readings—From the Highlights Reel

It goes without saying that to receive a positive "hit" in a reading is always a thrill. But the validations I get the biggest kick out of are those that have an up-to-the-minute nature about them—a

## My Readings

currentness, like those I wrote of in the last chapter. For instance my wife's reference, in my reading with Carole Lynne, to a bird, the day after I'd had a wild one in the house. And in the same reading, my wife prompting Carole to bring up cookies, fifteen minutes after I'd been talking about cookies on the phone with my sister.

Validations of this type, I think, indicate an awareness on the part of the spirits that regardless of what validations they gift us with, they're going to be subjected to the scrutiny of those ubiquitous naysayers who are going to trot out their usual stock imputations that what the mediums tell us are either generalities that could apply to anyone or, if that doesn't fit, then they're using information that they'd acquired beforehand.

To me, validations that have a definite currentness about them are the spirits' way of pulling the rug from under the scoffers and making an end-run around their nonsense. The following reading was a classic example of spirit confirming a current event.

Medium Joanne Gerber enjoys, deservedly so, a national reputation. I discovered her on Bob Olson's website BestPsychicMediums.com. My telephone reading with Joanne was scheduled for twelve noon. Normally, before a reading, I make a point of avoiding any activities that call for creative thinking and try to quiet my mind by doing mindless chores—rainy-afternoon stuff. To this end, I've made a habit of keeping a few such projects around the studio and I chose one that I thought would be ideal. It was a shoebox into which, for over four years, I'd been tossing photos of my illustrations—over 400 of them—waiting till I could find the time to crop and sort them into a dozen or so categories ready for pasting into various albums. It was a relaxing and pleasant activity that my wife had been glad to help me with many times. It kept me suitably occupied and hassle-free from 8.30 am until just before noon when Joanne's call came in.

We were only ten minutes or so into the reading when Joanne told me that my wife, whose name she'd already given me, was saying that she had been watching me *sort through photos!*

Wow! Big fist-pump!

These kinds of up-to-the-minute validations of our loved one's presence have an electrifying now-ness to them. They're not in the form of a vague reference to an event in the dim and distant past, possibly clouded by time, distance and a selective memory, this is in meaningfully sharp focus—up-close-and-personal.

Validations of this currentness not only attest to the presence of our loved one, in our living room—*right here and now,* they also gift us with the realization that their presence in our lives is not solely contingent on a medium being present—they are with us whenever *they* want to be, or whenever *we* want them to be.

As the great Doris Stokes reminded us—over and over—"They are a mere whisper away."

Please allow me to share a few more brief highlights with you.

## My White Crows

*Donna Chan:* Returning to the lady we first met earlier in this chapter and with whom I'd had my very first reading. I'm afraid the message Donna delivered following the one about writing a book didn't register with me at all—not one single word of it.

She referred to a male figure standing behind me with one arm placed protectively on my shoulder. "He's smartly dressed in a grey business suit and wearing a tie," she said, "and he's of East Indian descent—very westernized and cultured. He's a religious leader and came to this country as a member of a missionary outreach. He's now expressing his gratitude to you for what you did and wants you to know he's watching over you."

When I told Donna that none of this meant anything to me, she said "That's okay, just put to one side for now. This gentleman was communicating very strongly and concisely though, so it will probably make perfect sense in due course." I had to take her at her word. To not do so would have refuted the veracity of her previous validation—I had no interest in doing that.

Well, "Due course" turned out to be just a few days later at the local supermarket, where I met Helen, a neighbor of ours. She said she was glad she'd bumped into me because she had a question for me. Her question took me, to say the least, completely by surprise. To explain why, I have to go back in time a few weeks.

Helen was aware that a mutual neighbor, Pearl Wilson, a dear widow friend and occasional baby-sitter of ours, had recently passed away after being hospitalized with a severe heart attack.

We'd known she had two sons but we'd never met them, as they both lived in other states, so it would be a few days before they would be able to come and be with her. In the meantime, my wife and I would sit with her in the ICU, holding her hand and generally doing whatever we could for her. One of the things in this regard involved the pride and joy of her well-tended garden, her Camellia Trees. They happened to be in glorious full bloom at the time, so we took selected blooms for her and the nurses placed them in dishes on her bedside table and around the room. Sadly, the day after her sons arrived, Pearl passed peacefully away. I was honored to be a pallbearer at her funeral.

Remember, all this had taken place weeks before my reading with Donna had even been thought of, so what I was about to learn from Helen completely floored me.

Her question was "You were at Pearl's funeral, tell me, are her sons like their father?"

"Mr. Wilson had died some years before we moved here so I have no idea." I answered.

"Well what I mean is were they—you know—were they black?"

"I had no idea Mr. Wilson was black."

"Oh yes." she said, *"He was from India you see. He'd been a missionary and was head of a mission in Jacksonville.* That was how he and Pearl had met."

The mediums love these types of validations. They belie the belittling accusation that the skeptics like to use—namely their claim that one way the mediums get information is by reading the sitters' minds. And let's face it, when people have witnessed the extraordinary performances of mentalists like The Amazing Kreskin, it's quite understandable that they could wonder about the possibility of mediums having this kind of ability too.

But thankfully, instances like the one I've just described completely rule out that possibility. Donna couldn't have possibly read my mind, for the simple reason I had no knowledge whatsoever about Mr. Wilson's background.

*Lauren Thibadeau:* No type of message thrills a sitter or a medium more than getting a spirit's correct name, nothing seems to more effectively verify the genuineness of a reading.

What occurred in this otherwise good reading illustrates how easy it can be for a medium to miss or misinterpret what could be a significant message. After the reading Lauren said she could kick herself for missing what, in hindsight, had been an obvious clue. Her concise description of a male figure who had stepped forward had unmistakably identified him as my father-in-law. She then asked me "Was he a hunter?" When I said he wasn't she said "I ask that because he's showing me a hunting jacket. Well, make a mental note of it, it might come to you later."

My wife's father was definitely not a hunter—but his name *was* Harold *Hunt*.

In the same session, Lauren told me she saw parrots as being a symbol I should look out for. It could be in the form of a parrot painted on the side of a van on the highway or a poster–a figurine or even a real parrot. Such a sighting would be the world reflecting my wife's presence, "I'm seeing an Amazon Grey." she added.

Just two mornings later, as I was crossing the boardwalk on my way to my beach walk, my attention was drawn to a lady sitting at a table in the picnic area—feeding a parrot. Perched on top of his cage in the morning sun, he was a dazzling sight to behold.

Now I'm not in the habit of approaching strange ladies on the beach, but my curiosity got the better of me. I went over and said "Good morning ma'am—that's a beautiful bird you have. If you don't mind me asking—what kind is it?" She replied, in a very English voice, "Oh, my William is an Amazon Grey aren't you baby?" William was busy dissecting a grape.

I never did get to the beach that morning, we spent most of it in conversation. I learned she'd been born and raised in Bristol, the same English town as my mother-in-law. She had tickets for a psychic Message Service at a Spiritualist Church for the following evening, to which she invited me to join her. And she, William and I became good friends for over three years when she had to go back north.

## The Direct Connect

*George Anderson:* My reading with 'The Great One' was, surprise-surprise, replete with authentic validations. There was one sequence though that was notable for it's uniqueness.

Midway into the reading he said "Oh, your wife just brought my attention to my cat who's walked into the room, ( I heard his meows), she pointed to him and said 'Oh what a lovely cat.'"

Now I realize this has no significance at all to anyone else, but as lifelong cat lovers, if I've heard my wife say those exact same words—and in the exact same way George said them—once, I've heard them a thousand times. But there was more cat stuff to come.

"And this is interesting," he went on to say, "I have a figurine here in my living room and your wife is pointing at it and telling me 'Tell my husband about that—tell my husband about that.' She's being very insistent about this. What it is, is a figurine of the Egyptian Cat Goddess Bastet. It's solid bronze, about ten inches high and stands on a mahogany base. Now I'm just passing along what she's saying—I have no idea if this means anything to you."

If he could have seen me at that moment, he would have seen that it clearly did.

Throughout the session, you see, I'd been strolling, phone in hand, around *my* living room, and at the very time he was describing *his* Bastet figurine—I was standing no more than two feet away from *our* exact same Bastet figurine.

Allowedly, nothing of major significance here at all—to anyone else that is. To the recipient though—priceless stuff. Chalk up yet another white crow sighting.

*Mary Rose Gray:* The reading with Mary Rose I described earlier was the first time I'd ever met her, but it wasn't the first time I'd been the recipient of her remarkable abilities. The first occasion

*My Readings*

had been in the form of a mini-reading at a Message Service a few weeks prior.

Message Services in the Spiritualist Church are separate from the reading demonstrations that are a traditional element of the regular Worship Service. For a modest donation, those attending receive five to ten minutes of messages from the medium presiding. This was only the second such service I'd ever attended.

When my turn came around and Mary Rose approached me, she immediately embarked on a description of a gentleman who had come forward. She described the man in such detail that any competent artist present would have had no trouble depicting him. I already had—on my mind-screen, and the resulting likeness was undoubtedly a portrait of my father-in-law.

She then described him as standing at a table on which were spread several large thick ledgers with three pencils placed neatly alongside.

That evidence completely confirmed my expectation. As County Administrator for the village of Leintwardine and surrounding rural areas of Herefordshire, England, ledgers were a major part of Harold Hunt's life. All transactions concerning County Public Services—tax collection, licenses, permits, water treatment, besides serving as quasi-ombudsman for local farmers were all required to be recorded—in *large thick ledgers!*

On three evenings every week, at the 17$^{th}$ century Hunt residence—after supper had been cleared away, out would come those ledgers, and he and my future wife, still at Grammar School at that time, would sit at that table and work on the ledgers.

Fast-forward fifty odd years, and here he is Harold, on a Sunday afternoon in Florida, showing all this to a lady in order to identify him as the sender of a message he wanted Mary Rose to deliver to me. She reported "He wants me to tell you that he couldn't have wished for a better husband for his daughter—and that you are a great, great man."

Phew! Serious case of 'lump-in-the-throat', goose bumps and the welling of tears at this juncture. Because my mind went back ten years to the time when my wife had phoned me at the office to tell me of her father's passing. My final words of our ensuing mournful and sorrowful conversation had been "Darling—your father was *a great, great man!*" As Mary Rose said those same words, an image of Harold's characteristic puckish, mischievous smile flashed onto my mind-screen.

On my drive home, I couldn't help wondering why it was that Mr. Hunt had chosen to come through so strongly today. He hadn't after all, come through with anything like this level of clarity before. Then it dawned on me—today was Father's Day.

Such is the beauty and wonderment psychic readings can gift us with.

My euphoric idolatry notwithstanding, to their credit, the mediums have always been forthright in assuring us that we don't really need them in order to establish communication with our loved ones in spirit.

In the following chapter we'll be discussing some of the ways that the souls, speaking through the mediums, have told us we can facilitate this unique connectivity with them.

CHAPTER 7
# FACILITATING CONNECTION

We'd just completed the fourth psychic reading I'd received over the four years since my wife's passing and, as affirming as the previous three had been, this one had been even more so—with several quality "hits"—about as good as one could wish for, I remember thinking.

I told the medium this in expressing my gratitude to her, and was a little taken aback by her response. It wasn't her "Oh. I'm just the messenger,"—I'd gotten used to this admirably humble and self-effacing line by now—it was what she followed that with.

"You know," she said, "most everyone has psychic abilities to some degree, you don't always need a medium, you can learn how to connect with spirit yourself."

Parroting a line from a television commercial running at the time, I quipped "Are you crazy? Are you totally lacking in business acumen?"

We both laughed and I then went on to say "I rather think you're being overly modest—I haven't been gifted with anything like your abilities."

She then went on to further explain "I suspect you're already familiar with meditation right?. Well, by meditating daily you could possibly, in time, connect directly with those in the angelic realm. A genuine daily commitment will itself be enough to draw them closer and encourage them to lower their vibration in order for it to align with yours when meditating regularly eventually succeeds in raising it.

And so it was that I embarked on my quest to learn as much as I could about something that held such an enthralling promise.

My illustration and design commissions were now beginning to flow in again, and my ability to handle them was also showing tentative signs of a possible return to some kind of normalcy. I had a strong intuitive sense that meditation could be the augmenter that could clinch it.

I just had to find a way of fitting a daily meditation regimen into my schedule.

## Meditation—It's as Old as the Ills

The mere word "meditation," to the uninitiated, conjures up images of shaven-headed mystics sitting in the lotus position while chanting mantras—you know, *"new-agey."*

But in fact, meditation is far from being a new idea. Its benefits as a healing modality have been recognized for over 5000 years. Various meditation techniques were mentioned in Hindu Tantras—scriptures rooted in the Hindu and Buddhist philosophies. There is evidence too that the ancient Greeks and Romans also knew of its healing abilities.

More current and closer to home, it has been estimated that currently at least 50 million Americans practice meditation.

The numerous healthful benefits derived from regular daily sessions of meditation are generally attributed to the quieting of the mind that it calls for. Our mind (and the rest of our biological system) as a consequence, is gifted with a welcome break from the unrelenting pressures of struggling to hold its own against the intrusions of such elements as the incessant mind-chatter and the myriad thoughts that vie for our attention and threaten to derail the infinitely more desirable trains of thought we'd prefer to have our minds occupied by.

The mind/body conditions for which meditation is being prescribed, comprise a range so broad and extensive that any attempt to discuss them here would not only fall outside the purview of this book and would hardly be pertinent to the book's intent, which is to help us in our recovery from grief. That being said however, I don't think it would be amiss to make note of a few of the therapeutic benefits of meditation I've come across that attest to its powers:

- In the burgeoning field of health in the workplace, management consultants are regularly turning to meditation as a viable stress-management tool. Oprah Winfrey told *The Huffington Post* recently that, based on her personal experiences with meditation, every member of her staff now incorporate meditation into their daily schedule.
- A study showed that the areas of the brain associated with the prefrontal cortex and the anterior right insula (I'm sure we're all familiar with those) were thicker in people who meditate regularly.
- Dr. Rick Hanson, a San Rafael neuropsychologist and author of *Buddha's Brain* says, "It's like exercise for the brain—making it stronger."

- Dr. Herbert Benson is a well known cardiologist. He founded The Mind/Body Medical Institute in Boston and authored the book *The Relaxation Response.* He conducted a study that compared the genes of people who never meditated with those who did. It showed that the meditators' genes were, in Dr. Benson's words, "Essentially telling the body to stress less and age more slowly."
- In his enlightening and informative book *Meditation as Medication,* Dr. Dharma Singh Khalsa tells us that during meditation our metabolism is in an even deeper state of relaxation than when we are sleeping. And writes that "Long-term meditators experience 80 percent less heart disease and 50 percent lass cancer than non-meditators."
- Studies have shown that the calming effect of meditation actually lowers blood pressure and strengthens our immune system.
- Then this one—one that we're not likely to see any mention of in any ads for prescription pain relievers. 34 percent of people with chronic pain significantly reduce medication when they begin meditating.

To this authoritative list I'd like to contribute a few of my own persuasive features. Collectively, they deprive us of any lame excuses we may have planned on using for *not* meditating. Because, unlike most other activities we get goaded into, with meditation there's no special equipment required—no special clothing to buy—no membership dues—no personal trainer involved—it doesn't cost a cent—we can opt to stay in our favorite armchair—(for which the only competition comes from our cat)—and finally—drum-roll—it doesn't involve sweat!

## Facilitating Connection

But the premier benefit for our purposes here, that transcends all others, is the knowledge that a regimen of meditation is universally regarded by the mediumship community to be one of the most powerful means by which we'll ultimately become multi-sensory beings. It's in this state of inner calmness, peace and quietude that we will become no longer fettered by the lower and denser vibration of the physical five senses. It is at this higher vibrational multi-sensory level that we will become accessible to the magic of spirit-connectivity and guidance.

I think it would be a bit of a stretch to think that this aspect has been on the list of meditation's benefits down through the ages. I think the realization of it being a facilitator to spirit connection is most likely the outcome of the development of mediumship and information subsequently garnered from the spirits by the mediums. There's a phenomenon that social scientists have grappled with for ages—it's known as "The law of unintended consequences." It's the term used when an effective use for a product, for which it wasn't intended, is discovered, often serendipitously. This would surely appear to be the case here.

Orchestrated all along by spirit perhaps? There's a consensus that supports that likelihood.

Medium Jenny Crawford tells us in her book *Spirit of Love*. "I have found meditation to be the key to a positive pathway of love and guidance from the higher realms." It has also often been said that "Prayer is *talking* to God, but meditation is *listening* to God."

The 13th century German philosopher and theologian Meister Eckhart seems to have presaged this aspect when he said "Nothing in all creation is so like God than stillness."

The great medium Doris Stokes said that the spirits told her, over and over, that our loved ones in spirit are "just a whisper away." It's up to us to create the level of quietness and stillness that allows us to hear those whispers and thereby facilitate the direct connection.

## Meditation—Simple but not Necessarily Easy

Anyone who's ever had what had promised to be a productive and rewarding weekend, utterly ruined by trying to assemble something like a Room-Divider Kit that came in a carton with the slogan "Very Simple—Very Easy" emblazoned across it, has learned that the words *simple* and *easy* don't necessarily equate.

With meditation, yes—the process is simple—so simple it can be adequately described with one simple word—relax. What it takes to become an accomplished meditator however, can also be summed up with one word—*practice*. And *easy*, for most of us, is hardly the first word that springs to mind when we hear that word (one can hear the groans). But practice is what it takes to become proficient at anything, so once we've accepted this—yes, simple *will* equate with easy.

The bounteous rewards alone that meditation promises should be all the motivation we need but we're fortunate to also have a formidable built-in incentive going for us, and that is—our earnest desire to recover from our grief. This is what our loved ones in spirit also want for us, so it will help us stay enormously inspired if we remain mindful of the fact that they have a vested interest in our success. And to this end, they will be with us in all our endeavors every step of the way—our personal cheering section, so to speak.

Teachers of meditation often help to allay any apprehensions we have and bring some perspective to the situation, by noting that we've probably all been in what is virtually a state of meditation many times through our lifetime and not even been aware of it.

## Facilitating Connection

For example, during those times when we've been absorbed in an activity to the exclusion of everything around us, to the extent that those around us referred to us as "being off in her own little world." Such times can be when we're completely engrossed in a hobby like our stamp collection—or 'around the house" stuff such as baking a batch of cookies—waxing the family sedan—ironing—planting out the annuals, etc. Literally anything to which we give our rapt but relaxed attention, and that doesn't require a great investment of serious brain power.

On completion of such spells, we're very often aware of a heightened sense of gratification, together with a self-satisfying warm glow of well-being that stays with us for some considerable time. This is all due to the fact that for this period of time we have actually been in a deeply relaxed state of mind, and that is essentially what meditation is all about—an altered state. Unfortunately, that term spooks many people out—they connote it with "loss of control." This is just not the case at all—we're simply totally immersed in planting our petunias and loving it.

What *has* happened, is that our normally over-worked, hyperactive mind has experienced the rare luxury of a condition that doesn't come its way very often—a state of tranquility. For a blissful period of time, it received permission to kick back and enjoy some well deserved down- time—free from fretfulness and anxieties about the past and the future. In short, we have been "in the moment"- "in the now." A much-desired place of peace and groundedness, but in the clamorous world in which we've chosen to live—seldom achieved.

Is it any wonder that our friends in spirit have been reluctant to venture into this madhouse we know as our mind? I'm reminded of Yogi Berra's famous remark "Nobody goes there anymore—it's too crowded."

Meditating is our crowd dispersion stratagem. Masking, quelling or eliminating the incessant "don't-matter-mind-chatter," as a friend of mine calls it, is tantamount to clearing our work area of the annoying hindrance of unwanted useless clutter and creating space in which something more spiritually substantive can form and flourish.

Meditation transforms what we'd previously known only as a place of discord, certainly a rowdy house that spirit wouldn't have been interested in patronizing, into a place of such serene quietude that spirit is only too happy to access and connect with us.

The souls have told us repeatedly through the mediums, that it's here, at this exalted vibrational level, that we will be effectively gifted with the ability to reach beyond our five physical senses. A level at which a dialogue between spirit and our higher-self—our soul, will form and ultimately flourish.

As a consequence—sheer magic will ensue.

Such are the benefits of our investment in this unique therapeutic activity called meditation.

## Choices Aplenty

The number of methods of meditating isn't exactly a bewildering amount, but like in everything else calling for a decision, we tend to get anxious as to whether we're choosing the right one for us. What I've said before about making choices bears repeating here. I firmly believe that it pays to stay mindful of the probability that the spirits are ahead of us and are already gifting us with their guidance on the matter. Like we also said before, they have a vested interest in establishing a connection with us, so it follows that whichever method we choose to go with is going to be the right match for us. If it doesn't seem to work out that way—well, there was a reason for that too—and it more than likely involved a lesson of some kind.

Personally, I don't feel anyone could do better than defer to the mediums' books—most of them give us a detailed guide to the method favored by them, and that they have successfully taught in their workshops for years. Some even provide us with a transcribed version that we can tape for ourselves. (This puts it in the category of a "Guided Meditation," which we'll go into later). There's no rush, we can take all the time we need to check out as many methods as it takes to determine which one *feels* correct—which one *"calls out"* to us.

The bottom line is—there really is no right or wrong way to meditate. It comes down to whichever method we feel works for us, is the correct way—for us.

## Manner of Procedure—Taking Our Meds

I'm a longtime devotee of all things simple, so meditation's simplicity is a feature I've always found highly pleasing. There are those though who favor complexity—they eschew plain and simple and won't have it at any price. And price is often at the root of their fondness for the bells and whistles and frills because they're in the business of selling such accoutrements, and meditation hasn't escaped their attention. I get their glossy catalogues in the mail—pages of "must have" meditation paraphernalia comprising meditation cushions—meditation kneeling pads—meditation silk robes etc. All richly embroidered, and all—surprise-surprise—richly priced.

For me, this kind of mind-set runs counter to what meditation is all about, but should anyone feel that any of these items will help them to relax and go within, then by all means go for it, I wish only the best for you. I question whether spirit will be impressed though

*The Direct Connect*

(What was it someone once said about a camel passing through the eye of a needle?).

Regarding *where* we meditate, it's nice if we can have a designated area to spread out in, a spare guest room for instance would be ideal, but failing that, it doesn't call for anything more elaborate than a corner in any area of our home. Any place really, as long as we can be out of mainstream traffic and be assured of twenty minutes of uninterrupted peace and quiet.

Some meditators like to personalize their area with meaningful items such as photographs, figurines and small objects with a loved-one connection. Burning candles or incense is also popular—literally anything that, for us, gives off a positive and peaceful vibration. We are, in effect, creating our "personal altar" here, an aspect that should be impressed on those around us.

Since I learned from mediums about the negative role electricity can play in the quality of spirit connection, I've made a point of turning off all devices in my den when I meditate, items such as the computer—photocopier—printer—etc. Who knows what electrical interference they put out—why chance it? (These things have always held a grudge against me anyway).

Regardless of which method we've decided on, we'll probably find ourselves adopting a set of procedures that we soon get into the habit of following—rituals if you will. This is consistent with the rituals of one kind or another that have historically been integral to ceremonies across all religions down through the ages. They're a component of some significance, in that they bring an ordered coherence to the proceedings and serve to deferentially reinforce our faith in and fidelity to our beliefs. I think it's fair to say that our "daily devotions" fall within the same purview.

## Facilitating Connection

Our first procedure could be to put ourselves in the desired positive mind-set before we even enter our meditation space. We need to shake ourselves free from whatever else is going on in our life at this time—convince ourselves that our world is not about to fall apart because we're depriving it of our hand-wringing attention for fifteen minutes. Carrying any of those ubiquitous five-sensory lower vibrations into our meditation area could easily nullify the higher positive ones which we wish to attract

Another preparatory ritualistic step we could initiate could be to recite a short prayer of protection or the Lords Prayer, our favorite verse from a Psalm or, of course, their equivalents from any other religion.

The spirits have told us that connecting with us is as equally rewarding for them as it is for us, so they're eager to assist the connection in any way they can. The ritualizing of our procedures, even the time we enter our meditation space each day, helps to establish an identifiable pattern that signals to those on the other side that we're making ourselves accessible—putting out the welcome mat, so to speak.

Speaking of the time of day, Eastern religions have and interesting custom. The Hindu and Sikhism religions for instance, regard the most desirable and effective time of day to meditate to be between the hours of three a.m. and six a.m. They call this period "the ambrosia hours."

My dictionary defines ambrosia as: "Worthy of the Gods—heavenly—Divine—ethereal—glorious—celestial—of the immortals." I think that's all pretty apropos. It's also believed to be the time of day when the world is at its clearest, quietest and most fluid, making it the ideal time for prayer, yoga, meditation and the cleansing of our subconscious.

*The Direct Connect*

I once saw it referred to somewhere as "The time when lucidity and clarity seems to be in the very air—ready and waiting for us to tap into." (Sounds something like Wi-Fi). I know there to be something special about the pre-dawn hours in regard to creativity, I've worked with many writers, artists, designers and producers through the years who've attested to the hours around daybreak as being the most conducive to their creativity, so it could be worth considering. In any event, the importance of following the "same time each day" regimen is also an aspect that's invariably emphasized by experienced meditators.

Let's now discuss the widely acknowledged ways by which seasoned exponents recommend we meditate. Beginning with the stage that forms the basic foundation of whichever method we choose to go with.

## Our Watchword is......Relax

So we're now safely ensconced in the cloistered retreat we've created—ready to go and as we prepare to take up position, ideally, wearing loose clothing, because we need to be as comfortable as possible in every way. Speaking of which—it was a comfort to learn that the iconic symbol of a figure in the lotus position is not, thankfully, an indication of how we're required to sit. That choice is ours, lotus away if you prefer, but we can lie, sit or recline—it comes down to whatever feels right to us.

The quieting and calming of mind that we seek is only attainable if the rest of our body is also in a deeply relaxed state. A way of embarking on this stage that I was taught some years ago, involves systematically tensing then relaxing each of our various muscle groups. Starting with our toes, followed by our feet—ankles—calves etc., and then working our way up through each area in turn—torso—chest—shoulders—upper and lower arms—hands—fingers and then on all the way up to our face and scalp. We were told that this process, which should only take us two or three minutes (it's not gym class), acts as a "wake-up call" to areas that we don't normally focus on to any great extent, but are about to get our attention now, for a short time at least.

Another highly effective way of achieving the desired level of relaxation is through something we've been doing every second from the minute we came into the world and never had to think about—popularly referred to as breathing.

It's been said that the simple act of putting our attention exclusively on our breathing connects our conscious mind to our subconscious. So it is, that by closing our eyes and taking rhythmic deeper-than-usual, gentle measured breaths, we almost immediately experience a pleasing calmness coursing through us.

(This is a quality, by the way, that we can turn to whenever we feel the need to engage our personal pressure-relief valve. When we're stuck in a stop-and-go traffic jam for instance, or when standing exasperatingly in line at the Post Office or when we're trapped in one of those mainly pointless staff meetings that's dragged on ad nauseam and we're about to pop our cork).

Accompanying our breathing by silently repeating a simple mantra such as "I am at ease" or "I am relaxing," can also help the process along. Also helpful is if, with each breath, we imagine relaxation entering us as we inhale gently but deeply through our nose, followed by *feeling* all stress, tension and heaviness leaving us when we exhale through the mouth. When we can add to this assemblage, thoughts and feelings of weightlessness—"floating feather-like on a cloud," was one teacher's favorite phrase, our journey to our inner world will be well under way.

*The Direct Connect*

This stage has probably only taken as long as it took to read about it, but it forms the underpinning upon which all other methods are built—including both of the following.

## Meditation—The Guided Type

Not to disparage the more traditional approaches at all, but there are many seasoned meditators who think there's a lot to be said for *guided* meditations, and they cite a range of reasons for them being their method of choice. The most frequently heard rationale is, again, that unremitting mind-chatter. Try as they might, they've found it to be totally untamable, and the desired state of silence called for, to be frustratingly unattainable. I applaud them for their perseverance in discovering CD's, they're a perfectly viable alternative.

It's unfortunate that some people can't stay the conventional course and end up walking away from meditation altogether, when there's such a perfectly good alternative option available. That's okay, I know of a store that specializes in the sale of used tennis racquets and golf clubs—and interestingly, most of them in "almost new" condition. Hopefully the hapless previous owners are having better luck with something else—like meditation.

There are a number of other reasons why some people are unable to achieve the desired level of peace and quiet. A condition known as Tinnitus is one of them, sufferers of this are subjected constantly to an annoying noise in their ears, in the form of a buzzing, ringing or a shrill high-pitched whistling, and affects over 50 million people in the United States. This doesn't entirely preclude our ability to meditate, but we do need a little help—"a spoonful of sugar to help the meds go down," to paraphrase the Sherman Brothers in Disney's *Mary Poppins*.

## Facilitating Connection

Devotees of the guided types of meditation have told me they like the ways by which the word images created by the narrators' invariably soothing and well-modulated voice, produce a perfect point of focus to zone in on which helps them ignore those intrusive noises. So, for many of us, the guided type is the meditation of choice, and there are lots to choose from—they cater to all tastes. Naturally, again, it all comes down to what we feel comfortable with.

A guided meditation typically takes the form of a narrator walking us through a thoroughly delightful landscape, an "otherworldly" place of beauteous enchantment. Wonderful word-pictures of idyllic locations—flowers and trees in full bloom in unbelievably glorious vibrant hues, and all bathed in a wondrous soft-focus golden-white light. The narrations are invariably accompanied by a suitably subdued layer of music with an appropriate ethereal quality. For me, the style of music aspect has sometimes been the deciding factor, "new agey" drums and gongs are just not my cup of tea. But as I said—there's something for every taste.

I've tried many CD's over the years and have settled on a few that I switch between every few weeks. My favorite for some years has been a two-track CD by the well-known medium John Holland titled *Healing Relaxation and Opening Your Psychic Awareness*. He makes use of the brilliant Divine white light that has become a universally acknowledged salient feature of meditation methods, but he artfully, and successfully I think, couples this with colors of the chakra system as an augmentative healing modality. I reach for this CD often, but always whenever I'm feeling out-of-sorts, under-the-weather or just in need of a spiritual pick-me-up.

We begin to get the idea that a certain CD is right for us, when we become aware of its ability to magically transport us to a place of such peaceful allurement that we begin to eagerly anticipate our escape to our sanctuary for twenty minutes every day.

An outcome entirely concordant with our requirements—I'd say.

## The Silent Type

My reason for saying earlier that we can't do better than turn to the mediums' books for guidance on meditating, is because, for me, the commonality between their prescribed methods gives them all credence we need. I've found that when there's little or no commonality between tutorials on the same subject, it's usually an indication that egos and/or personal agendas are in play—the desire to be different for different's sake.

It's encouraging to know that there's no such disingenuousness among the mediums, they're of one voice—all in accord. No inferences that their way is the only way and is superior to everyone else's—none of that here—we're in good hands.

The mediums are generally quite honest and open up front regarding the business of ignoring the incessant mind-chatter to be *the* big bugaboo we face. They're under no illusions—they fully understand the reasons why it's never easy to get the mind/body to do anything for which it doesn't have a natural proclivity.

The 19th century English novelist Charlotte Bronte made reference to this. Though not referring to meditation per se of course, she wrote that "It is vain to say human beings ought to be satisfied with tranquility: they must have action: and they will make it if they cannot find it."

So we need to understand from the get-go that it's quite natural and there's no need to get unduly impatient with ourselves if we feel we're not progressing at the rate we feel we should. Cut ourselves some slack—it's a process—if we stick with it, our success is assured.

Dr. Dharma Singh Khalsa has studied extensively under the master gurus. Writing about the intrusive thoughts and mind-chatter in his book *Meditation as Medicine*, he says "The thoughts represent a release of energy from the subconscious mind, to the conscious mind. Each time it happens, accept it. I've been meditating for twenty five years, and this happens every day."

This, in his characteristically self-effacing manner, is a *master* speaking. So you see, no one is claiming meditation is easy, it's just that like anything that's worthwhile and that holds the promise of such bounteous rewards, *it does take practice*. And practice, it's been said, is just another word for repetition, and repetition is at the core of all learning. If we're not very competent at something, it's probably due to us not having done much of it, if, on the other hand, we're good at something—it's because we've done a lot of it. It's really that simple.

Anyway, we are now ready to start doing it, meditating by what has become accepted as the universally favored method. It's quite straightforward, unpretentious and free of unessential frills. There is one feature that most teachers whole-heartedly endorse and recommend that we acknowledge and establish at the outset of our relaxing stage. It calls for us to inhale a brilliant golden-white light of spiritual protection, and to visualize its radiance coursing lovingly and sequentially through every nerve, cell and fiber of our being and filling every space.

Writing about this white light in her book *We are their Heaven*, The nationally renowned medium Allison DuBois says "I let in this white light because it reminds me of the spectacular white background that surrounds our loved ones when they appear from the other side."

This single act of focusing our attention on this all-embracing loving presence should itself serve to put the constant mind-yammering garbage on notice that it's no longer welcome.

## Taking Out the Garbage

Although it's our aim is to eliminate unwanted intrusive noises and thoughts, we can't eradicate them completely. That would create a vacuum, and as we learned back in elementary school, nature abhors a vacuum—empty spaces are against the laws of physics. So, it's not a case of reducing the undesired intruders to nothingness as much as it is *replacing* them with something else—something more amenable, innocuous and preferably simple. Not anything our sneaky, scheming mind can pick up on and make an issue of.

And so it is, that a general consensus has emerged that an effective and simple way of achieving this is to simply concentrate solely on the soft sounds of our breathing while at the same time, silently counting the sequential pattern of its ins and outs (Its very rare that we have cause to regret giving a respectful nod to Occam's razor—simplicity, you've gotta love it).

We start then with the few minutes of tensing, relaxing and breathing our way to the weightlessness we discussed earlier while remaining cocooned in our bubble of golden-white light. But we now start to help our mind replace the ever-present threat of outside distractions by following a regular pattern of silently counting 1-2-3-4 as we breathe in and out. We breathe in for a count of four, then hold our breath for a count of four, followed by breathing out for a count

## Facilitating Connection

of four then complete the cycle by again holding what's left of our breath to a count of four.

When we've repeated this pattern for fifteen minutes, voila—we've meditated.

It's the simplest of procedures yet quite flexible should we feel the need to modify it. For instance, if we find the repetitious aspect becomes so automatic that the counting continues of its own volition, creating an opening for outside thoughts to sneak in and take over, we can thwart them by slightly changing the *way* we count. A friend of mine alternates periods of regular counting with stretches of counting backwards. Another person recently told me that for her, switching from numbers to the letters a-b-c-d, forwards and backwards does the trick. Anything that helps us stay focused on nothing of real consequence, that keeps those yammerings at bay and conveniently overlays our pattern of gentle deep breathing is permissible.

## Whoa—Not so Fast

Having harped on about ignoring those outside thoughts that drift in, it needs to be pointed out that when we've attained a respectable level of proficiency, which we surely will, we'll need to stay mindful of our motive for learning how to meditate in the first place—to ultimately be able, through our higher self, to connect with the realm of spirit. At some point, through our new-found intuitive abilities, we may start to sense a subtle but discernibly curious way certain thoughts strike us—almost call out to us.

If we become aware of a pattern emerging here, it may indicate the first glimmerings of a a connection—even the whispers from spirit we've been seeking. The British comedy actor Russell Brand is a long-time devotee of meditation and he spoke of such an instance during a television interview. In discussing the benefits of his twice-daily meditation regimen, he divulged how during one session, he'd received an idea for a movie which he'd subsequently sold.

So as we get more experienced, we will eventually evolve to a point where we can trust in our intuitive abilities to tell us when it's no longer a good to dismiss those stray thoughts out of hand, without first giving them at least a cursory once-over—we never know.

## Are We There Yet?

It's quite natural for us to wonder how we're progressing—how we're doing, We implore ourselves "I've been doing this every day for six months now—is it working?." This may be a legitimate concern, but a discipline like meditation, unlike most other fields of endeavor, doesn't lend itself to our rate of advancement or level of proficiency being quantified. We don't have the benefit of things such as hi-tech monitoring devices strapped to various parts of our person or progress reports—grade point averages—credits—hours of coursework etc.

We can only "keep soldiering on," as they say, and just *trust* that it *is* working, together with an eventual sure knowing that, in due course, we'll receive affirmation that it is—but only when spirit decides that we're ready (or if *they* are, for that matter).

This mundane preoccupation with "progress reports" is all five-sensory stuff, which we no longer have much use for anyway. We're in the process of evolving into multi-sensory beings now—our regular meditation practice has taken us "within." Resulting in us being pretty immune to those lower vibrational influences and more attuned instead to our "inner voice."

This inner voice is our "higher self," and it's through its higher vibration that alignment with the corresponding vibration of those

## *Facilitating Connection*

on the other side of the veil is able to take place. A direct connection has been established and our life from here on will take on a very special, uniquely enthralling quality.

This will result in the emergence of an unmistakable sense of our loved one's presence, manifested in the form of signs of various kinds and also synchronous events that occur with some frequency. Phenomena that we'll be discussing in the following chapter.

All facilitated by the simple act of meditating.

CHAPTER 8

# SIGNS—LOVE MADE MANIFEST

We've seen how receiving evidence of our loved one's continued existence, obtained through either a psychic reading of our own, or vicariously through the readings shared by the mediums in their books is, inarguably, a truly wondrous gift.

This knowledge alone can be an effective restorative on our path back to wholeness. However, as empowering as it may be to receive this through a medium via books or readings—confirmation of their continued existence through actual signs is equivalent to a "free upgrade." Without the need for an intermediary, signs are delivered directly to us—at any time—to any place we happen to be—and no matter what we happen to be doing. Signs, in essence, affirm that our loved ones are not only still with us, but will be walking lovingly in lockstep with us every step of the way on the remainder of *our own* journey when we'll be reunited.

The resultant sense of connectivity with our loved ones in spirit that the ongoing receipt of signs affords us, raises us to a level that is surely concordant with the observation that George Anderson relays to us from spirit, when he tells us that having our loved ones back with us would obviously be the best thing, but with that not being possible, proof of their continued presence is a good *second best*.

As we begin to recognize signs, we begin to appreciate more the fact that, in a sense, our loved one, never *really* left us after all. And furthermore, they're now omnipresent and consequently able to be on the other side of the veil while simultaneously being with us—they have told us this. Could we possibly wish for a more ameliorative gift?

It goes without saying that the love bond between two people is a potent force—an energy, and as the physicists tell us, energy doesn't die—it transforms. So it assuredly follows that the vibrations inherent to a love bond are not about to be phased by something as mundane as one of us relocating back to that plane because it happens to operate at a different vibrational frequency.

Back when we were both on that plane, prior to us incarnating to this one, we co-authored and signed off on a soul plan—it was, in effect, a sacred Divine compact between two inextricably intertwined souls. Because that soul plan didn't die either, don't we remain bound by its original articles of agreement? And if that's so, surely it's safe to assume that when our loved ones make their transition back to that plane, they adapt to their new vibration and learn how to lower its frequency to meet up with ours in order stay in compliance with our joint plan.

The alignment of our vibrations though, is contingent on us raising *our* vibration to meet theirs. But spirit has informed us that the heavy and dense vibration of our grieving condition is

## Signs—Love Made Manifest

not conducive to our mutual alignment, so, before they're able to communicate with us using signs, *they* need to receive a sign from *us*. And the sign they hope to receive is one that clearly indicates that we are making the effort it requires to free ourselves from the grip of grief. Apparently, they understand our suffering, but it really does pain them to witness it, especially knowing as they do now, that it's all so unnecessary—hence their desire to connect with us.

There are medium's readings on record in which the spirits tell us that, in common with other aspects of their new life, skills such as creating signs for us and communicating with mediums, have to be learned and even then the execution of them calls for considerable effort on their part.

Doris Stokes, for example, cited such an instance. In her book *Innocent Voices in my Ear,* she tells of the time when she was the houseguest of a Connecticut family who had lost their teenage daughter in a tragic accident.

When their daughter came through to Doris, she brought her attention to a wooden chopping board located on a kitchen counter and spoke of how she planned to knock on it one day to let her mother know of her presence, "They're teaching me how to do it," she said. A few days later, the family were gathered in the kitchen when they were suddenly startled by a loud rapping noise. A hollow insistent knocking sound that soon had everyone looking for its source. Sure enough, they finally tracked it down to the chopping board—as the daughter was excitedly confirming into Doris's ear, "It's me."

There may be times in the early days when we can't be sure whether an incident had been an actual sign or not, it may seem to have been too indefinite or lacking the clarity we feel a genuine sign would have. So it's worth bearing in mind that its vague nature could have been due to the fact that it was an early tentative attempt by our loved one—operating with a learner's permit. Whoever it was that coined the phrase "We never stop learning," couldn't have had any idea how literal the word *never* was.

It shouldn't come as a surprise that the very notion of this kind of relationship with our loved one in spirit will have its naysayers. I came across a reference to the naysayer species in general in a magazine recently. The author wrote "Any promising invention will have its naysayers, and the bigger the promises, the bigger the nays." This being the case, we'd be well advised to equip ourselves with a really good pair of ear-plugs—thicken our skins and brace ourselves. Because the promises of what signs from a loved one in spirit can do for the bereaved are huge.

The well-meaning expressions of disapproval we can expect to be subjected to, by those in whom we confide our beliefs, will undoubtedly, just as they did when we went public with our belief in an afterlife, center around how our convictions stack up against what they "know" constitutes "acceptably normal behavior." So once again we're going to be admonished with statements like "You've got to move on," and "You have to let go." (Evidently ersatz experts are one thing that's rarely in short supply).

However, we have *genuine* experts like Linda M. Cherek. She is a well known Bereavement Therapist and a President-Elect of the National Catholic Ministry to the Bereaved. I love what she wrote for AmericanCatholic.org regarding us asking our loved ones in spirit for assistance. Ms. Cherek writes "If we pray to saints with a big "S" – such as St. Therese of Lisieux – to help us with life's problems, why not our deceased loved ones? They're saints with a small "s."

## Signs—Love Made Manifest

What is probably the most prevalent source of anguish that can haunt the bereaved are those unresolved issues that sometimes exist at the time of a loved one's passing. Often quite silly piffling differences at the time, but that now, in our grief-addled state of mind, can easily get blown up out of proportion and consume us with survivor's remorse and self- recrimination.

The realization however, that signs from our loved one are actually confirming expressions of their unconditional and (literally) undying love, can magically deliver us from this toxic torment and restore us to a centered place of peace that's infinitely more favorably disposed to the acceptance and healing that we know we should be working toward, and that our loved one too also fervently wants for us.

This doesn't mean we won't still have a rough patch to deal with periodically—a wave of deep heavy sorrow that can swell up out of nowhere when we least expect it, and that still has the power to knock us off balance for a while and induce a tear or two. But the spirits have told us that the signs they gift us with are analogous to loving hugs, a reassurance that, if we stay mindful of it, will serve as a great source of comfort and support on our road back, and will always be there to help us weather the inevitable challenges of life along the way. Signs are proof that not only are we are never alone—we're still the dynamic-duo we always were.

## Sign Types

The types of signs that recipients have reported over the years, and the multitude of forms they take, cover such a vast and varied range by now that any attempt to classify or categorize them would be futile.

Literally anything goes—it's open season on the entire gamut of life experiences. The ways in which they've been known to manifest

## The Direct Connect

range from barely perceptible to in-your-face, from the softest of whispers to the loudest of yells—and everything in between. And the skill levels of creativity and innovativeness the spirits are capable of is just staggering at times.

Did I mention that when we've developed an awareness of them and become adept at perceiving and detecting them, it's very possible our lives could get to be "quite interesting" from then on and, more importantly—decidedly less disconsolate as a result?

As an "old hand" by now, I've often been surprised by how restrictively unimaginative many people can be regarding what constitutes a sign from spirit. For instance, I've often heard descriptions along the lines of "I was standing at the kitchen sink, when I felt a chilly draft on my arm," and another trite type frequently heard, "When I entered the living room, I couldn't help noticing her picture over the mantel was hanging a bit squiffy." Really? I'm hoping our discussion here can succeed in broadening our horizons on the subject a little, because to go around with such a limited range of expectancy is to deny ourselves access to a wondrous world of possibilities.

If anyone *does* happen to derive comfort from such examples, then that's totally fine and dandy—I'm genuinely happy for them, after all a sign, no matter how trivial, is still a sign, and qualifies as a bona fide miracle as much as any other. That said however, I do like to verify whenever can. So in such cases, rather than delude myself they're authentic signs, I would first check out the proximity of both locations in relation to such things as open windows and air conditioning vents. If only because I wouldn't want our loved ones to get the impression that we consider lame instances like these as exemplifying what they're capable of—as we'll see, their creativity and skill levels can run pretty high—much higher than mere "squiffy."

If we get into the habit of practicing the raising of our awareness as we go about our day, we will soon become more well versed at recognizing our loved one's individual style, and distinguishing, say, whether a situation is an actual sign in the form of an answer to a request we've put out there, or a case of our loved one just dropping by to say "Hi."

Although, as we've said, the seemingly limitless range and variety of sign types precludes us categorizing all of them, we can at least discuss some of the most frequently reported types—examples from the highlight reel that merit the title "classics."

## Spirit Assistance

The spirits have told us many times that, as part of their own continuing spiritual evolvement on the other side of the veil, they're assigned certain tasks. Apparently, one of their missions calls for them to assist us in our recovery from grief and our return to wholeness, while also assisting us in *our* spiritual evolvement, but only in ways that are congruent to both our joint soul plan and our personal soul plan. Regarding the latter, those trials and tribulations that challenge us from time to time are often tests that we're required to pass for purposes of our soul growth, so these they cannot help us with, other than being there for us to help us get back on our feet if we should trip and fall. Helping us with a test would be akin to a parent doing a child's homework for them—the only thing anyone learns, is that daddy got an "F"—for parenting.

There will inevitably be times when our mindfulness of this process lapses and we get dejected because we feel our prayers and requests haven't been answered. But we've been assured by spirit that *they have* been answered and *always are*—just not necessarily in the ways we'd expected or hoped. It is always about lessons and our soul growth, and it's quite possible we could receive signs that have been designed specifically to acknowledge this.

It could become apparent to us at some juncture, that signs don't always manifest in a form that's detectable with our physical senses—such as squiffy picture frames. There could be times for instance, when we're beset by a challenge that proves to be a source of considerable anxiety for a while, but then becomes magically resolved in an unconventional and unexpected way that leaves us pleasantly perplexed. Knowing what we know now however, we're also left with a sure and certain knowing that we had very little to do with the outcome—but have a very good idea who did, so we humbly offer up a prayer of profound gratitude.

## Electric Signs

As we noted in chapter five, probably the most frequently reported method by which spirit gifts us with signs of their presence in our lives, is through various kinds of electrical devices, they seem to have a natural propensity for manipulating electrical forces to suit their needs.

There have been hundreds of documented reports of telephone calls from deceased relatives, phone numbers belonging to deceased people appearing on caller ID screens, messages left on answering machines etc. It's going to be interesting to see how spirit adapts to the ever continuing proliferation of smart phone technology, not to mention devices yet to be conceived.

Their standout preference though, if the number of times it's been cited is any indication, is without question, the flickering light bulbs. Maybe because more opportunities present themselves due to

## Signs—Love Made Manifest

the light bulb's ubiquitous presence in our lives, or maybe it's because of their proven effectiveness. Who knows?

The single instance of a bulb flickering can itself be a sign of course, especially when it's a new bulb and we know it's firmly screwed into its socket. But it's when the flickering uncannily coincides with something else that's perfectly germane to the narrative, that it becomes uniquely noteworthy—as in the following example—typical of hundreds reported over the years.

A fellow plane passenger once kindly related to me how a flickering light bulb incident he'd experienced, a few months after his wife's passing, had turned out to be highly meaningful.

Being both voracious readers, he and his wife had customarily spent most of their evenings together in their library/den. And having found, since her death, that whenever he was in this room he felt far less anguished, and more at peace, than anywhere else in the house, this was where he had slipped into the habit of gravitating to at every opportunity.

So on this particular evening, he was leafing through a newly arrived magazine when he came across an article featuring a resort where he and his wife had spent a long weekend in celebration of their silver wedding anniversary. One of the most treasured memories of what had been a wonderful weekend, and which they'd often reminisced about since, had been the elegant and enchanting historic 19$^{th}$ century mansion they'd stayed at. Naturally he was soon engrossed in the article, but then, at the very moment he started turning the page to continue, the lamp he was reading by suddenly began flickering on and off like crazy.

And lo and behold there on the next page, as if on cue, was a beautiful pen and ink drawing of that very mansion—a framed print of which just happened to be hanging on the wall—no more than two feet away from where he was sitting.

He said the experience had served to confirm what he'd always sensed whenever he'd been in that room—that his wife was indeed right there with him.

He went on to explain that during the two weeks prior to this happening, he'd been going through a particularly grievous time over his wife's passing, and had been praying his heart out for a sign of some kind. So having his prayers responded to in this way had proved to be of inestimable value in helping him attain a reasonable level of acceptance of his wife's passing.

## The Signs of Music

If signs involving electricity are the most frequently reported, signs using music must be a close second. I think it's very interesting how the two fortuitously come together through the ways in which they're able to use radios and recordings etc.

Music, in its myriad forms, has always been recognized across all cultures as a powerful communicant. At the individual level, most every love-bonded couple I would guess, has, as one of their mutual gestures of affection, a meaningful song or tune that they've adopted as a symbol of their feelings for each other. "They're playing our tune," they'll say.

So it's hardly surprising that the spirits have included music in their repertoire of sign types. And with music these days being conveniently transmitted via radio and television receivers, satellite radio piped ubiquitously into restaurants and elevators etc., the spirits don't appear to have any trouble at all not only devising ways of manipulating them to create easily identifiable, customized signs, but delivering them using a whole range of situations and locations.

Renowned medium Patrick Mathews tells of a classic example of this in his book *Never Say Goodbye*. During a reading he was conducting for a man who had lost his wife, she asked him, through Patrick, if he'd noticed the music sign she'd sent him.

When the man drew a blank on this, she asked Patrick to tell her husband that it had been she who'd persuaded him to get gas. Patrick was somewhat nonplused by what the connection could possibly be, but that was soon revealed when the husband recalled that on his way to the reading, the notion had come to him to stop and get gas. As he was standing at the pump, he'd heard a radio somewhere playing the song *Don't Worry, Be Happy*. Although it had struck a chord with him at the time, because he'd always hated that song, and his wife had often teased him with it, the fact that it was a direct sign from his wife just hadn't occurred to him.

The spirits have told us that on those occasions when a special meaningful song or tune comes into our head, seemingly out of nowhere, it's very often been induced by our loved one using their unique vibrational skills—in amazingly creative ways at times.

Other frequently reported classic examples involve what, until we learn differently, are commonly regarded as coincidences. For instance, "our song" coming over the car radio at the very instant we turn it on after we've been wondering if there was a chance we would hear it. Or we're dining in a restaurant with a friend or relative and at the very moment they mention our loved one, the piped-in background music starts playing "our tune."

Accounts of similar instances, many of them truly amazing, abound to such a remarkable extent that they just couldn't *all* have come about as a result of random coincidences.

## Old Habits—They Really do Die Hard

The mediums have been told by the spirits that although they've changed in certain respects since they made their transition, most of the changes were mainly for purposes of their spiritual growth. Other than that they still retain much of their individualism—their core personalities and traits, particularly the more endearing qualities by which they'd been defined.

So it follows that they won't hesitate to incorporate any of their foibles and traits into their signs if they feel it will help us to positively identify them as the source.

A frequently reported example of this involve aromas. The spirits have the ability to re-create the fragrance of a favorite perfume or after-shave lotion for instance, which they know for sure we'll recognize. A medium once told me about an example of this that he'd experienced. A gentleman came through during a reading he was conducting, and the moment he appeared, the room became permeated with a smell that everyone immediately recognized and at which his assembled family howled with laughter, as one of them explained "That's Daddy alright, we nicknamed him Benny." It turned out their father had suffered with rheumatism for many years and their house had constantly smelled of Bengay.

If our loved one had been known for a marked sense of humor, there's a good chance his, or her, trademark style will be evident in the signs they gift us with. In the quirky off-beat way they're delivered for instance, and customized according to where we are at the time, who we're with or what we're doing—their signature type of humorous comment or wisecrack that those situations would have evoked when they were alive will come forth in some way. Through *our* mind, by us thinking about them, or by "borrowing" the mind and voice of someone present.

If our loved one had a predilection for playful pranks, some of the signs we receive may be consistent with *this* aspect of their personality. They could play out, as many many people have reported, in the form of radios and televisions coming on by themselves with no one anywhere near them, or even finding them turned on in a room that we haven't been in for a while. Then there are those times when an item that we need—eyeglasses, car-keys, cell phone for instance aren't where we remember leaving them, and when we locate them somewhere else, we put it down to our memory playing tricks on us. Well, certainly tricks are being played, but not necessarily by our memory—sometimes it's our prankster spirit friend up to his old tricks and actually moving things around when we're not looking.

I know something of these sign types—I've experienced both of these last two examples, and others similar to them, several times—and they can certainly make life pretty interesting, but bless their hearts—it's just their endearing way of saying "Hi," so by all means—be my guest and feel free to prank away anytime.

## Signs of Synchronicity

I read about a man in England a few years ago who'd been trying on and off for several years to locate his daughter who, as an infant, his ex-wife had been awarded custody of when they'd divorced.

Then one day, out of the blue, a relative called to tell him that he'd heard that she was now living in a city quite some distance away.

## The Direct Connect

So, despite not knowing her new last name and never having ever visited that city, he decided to follow up on this lead and try his luck.

Through a serendipitous series of twists and turns, a young reporter on the local newspaper learned of his quest and arranged to photograph him standing in a public square in the city center to help him get his story out.

When the photo appeared in the next edition of the newspaper it caught the eye of a young lady reader, mainly because she recognized it as being taken in the square where she'd walked the previous afternoon and was curious about what could possibly have happened there to merit it making the front page.

So she looked more closely at the photograph, and to her amazement she recognized herself in it. There she was, walking along the sidewalk not more than three feet away from the photograph's main subject—a man who the accompanying caption identified as—you guessed it—the father she hadn't seen since she was a toddler. Altogether now....." That's amazing!"

It's known as synchronicity. And it occurs so often that most everyone has a synchronicity story of their own that they'll gladly share at the drop of a hat. Making them an infallible conversation starter at any gathering, and guaranteed to garner a "That's amazing!" response.

I well remember a Dick Cavett show some years ago in which the universality of synchronicity was attested to. His distinguished panel that evening consisted of five leading novelists and playwrights and Mr. Cavett, in his trade mark "devil's advocate" role, asked them how they respond to the charge often leveled towards writers that their use of coincidences as convenient plot devices make their stories too implausible and not true-to-life.

To that, one of the panel, with the rest of the guests smiling and nodding in agreement, explained that in the thousands of interviews he'd conducted in the course of his research over the years, he'd never encountered one person who hadn't had a fascinating synchronicity story to tell. So with extraordinary coincidences being so commonplace in everyones' lives, *not* to include them would render stories involving people *not* true-to-life.

The term synchronicity was first coined by the Swedish psychiatrist Carl Jung in the 1920's to describe what he'd been referring to as "meaningful coincidences that are not related to any causal events." Jung's fascination in the subject had come about as a result of the many puzzling stories of coincidences his patients had shared with him, and he couldn't bring himself to believe they'd just been random events. He wrote "What I found were 'coincidences' which were connected so meaningfully that their 'chance' concurrence would represent a degree of improbability that would have to be expressed by an astronomical figure."

He came to realize that synchronicity explains certain forces in the universe, and what we regard as coincidences are actually signs that we can utilize to help guide us on our life path.

Jung always credited the development of his concept to a series of encounters he'd had with no less a personage than Albert Einstein—who himself once said "Coincidence is God's way of remaining anonymous."

With a divine connection being clearly implied by two such illustriously distinguished figures, and from what we've come to know about the spirits' abilities to create and deliver signs, surely it's quite plausible that they're involved in the orchestration of synchronistic events. As we'll see later, there are many who would concur.

## *The Direct Connect*

The salient feature common to all synchronistic events is undoubtedly the exquisite timing on which they invariably hinge. Most times, a deviation of a mere second or two in either direction and there just wouldn't be an event of any kind worth mentioning.

When we re-visit our father and daughter story and "reverse engineer" it, so to speak, we'll see that it's a classic example of this. The one element crucial to the story of course, is the girl being in the photograph, or in other words—within the frame when the camera shutter was pressed. A difference of just a few seconds, the time it's taken to read this paragraph, and there would have been no daughter in the picture and as a consequence—no reunion and no story.

So, let's consider just a few of the many things she could have done, or not done, during her walk that could have either delayed or advanced her by a few seconds leading up to those pivotal moments in time when she was fortuitously walking those twenty or thirty feet of sidewalk. She could, for instance, have been held up at a pedestrian crossing—or stopped to chat with a friend she'd bumped into—she could have casually sauntered along for a while window gazing—stopped to pick up a magazine at a newsstand—or stood in line for some time for a coffee. When we factor in the thousand and one "could-haves" at all the junctures she'd been required to negotiate since she awoke that morning, not to mention those of the other people involved in this scenario, we begin to really appreciate what Jung said: "their 'chance' concurrence would represent a degree of improbability that would have to be expressed by an astronomical figure."

This reunion of father and daughter was massively meaningful to both of them, and would forever remain so. It's a fact that similar extraordinary events occur every day, to hundreds of people worldwide and they do not just come about, as some would have us believe, as a result of random happenstance. They are undoubtedly spirit orchestrated and the result of the kind of exquisitely crafted time-management that only spirit could be capable of.

## Attestations

Although synchronistic events come in all shapes and sizes and in varying degrees of complexity, from the simple to the convoluted, each one is a miracle. Many people have kindly shared their synchronicity stories with me, and they all alluded, in one way or another, to a feeling at the time that there was a connection to the Divine at play here.

Recipients of synchronistic happenings and even witnesses of them, invariably attest to the very pleasant comforting feeling they'd been aware of at the time, and that had lingered for several days afterwards. Some people described it as being so pronounced that they'd been convinced it could only have been the work of a higher power "deigning," as one recently widowed lady put it, "to reach out to assure her that all is well."

Another lady told me that she'd always regarded her many experiences with synchronicity as "A validation from on high, designed to let her know that not only was she exactly where she was meant to be on her life-path, but at the exact time she was supposed to be there." She added that she took this as "An assurance that everything is in Divine order—and everything is cool."

An elderly gentleman acquaintance said he and his wife had actually first met as a result of a series of incredible synchronistic happenings, and had been intrigued by the many they'd experienced over the ensuing years. He added that he'd never known them to be anything but spiritually uplifting and always having a decidedly positive and encouraging aspect to them—with several of them being so predictive in nature they just had to have been signs from above. His wife added that every experience had left them with a sense that someone was assuring them that they were protected by a caring and loving higher intelligence.

These spiritual explanations offered by recipients are entirely concordant with what the spirits have also told us is the motivation behind the signs they gift us with. So I can't help but feel it's highly probable that, at the very least, our loved ones in spirit play some kind of active role in orchestrating these synchronistic scenarios on our behalf.

As one would expect, the mediums have knowledge of this Divine alliance. John Holland for instance, in an online article he wrote for *Hay House*, tells us that "Synchronicities are clear signs that the Divine source is knocking at your door." I love what he calls them—"Divine nudges."

## Oracle Cards

I have to admit to originally being rather ambivalent about even bringing up this sign type, due mainly to the way in which oracle cards are sometimes categorized in reference books. They're commonly listed under "Tools of Divination," which they usually define as "crystal ball gazing, reading tea-leaves and other occult and supernatural means of foretelling the future," and rarely fail to also mention (just to spook us out even more), the reading of animal entrails—yikes.

You see what I mean? We already have images of wizards, witches and ducking stools scrolling our mind-screens.

## Signs—Love Made Manifest

However, knowing that there are many adherents (me being one of them), who have proven to their satisfaction that oracle cards are a perfectly legitimate and highly effective method of facilitating spirit communication, I concluded that they're far too valuable a resource to ignore and decided to make an end-run around that other stuff. We can all relax though—I locked the ducking stool in the barn—then threw away the barn.

Divination, in its multitude of forms, has been practiced in all civilizations and cultures from ancient times and continues up to the present and the use of oracle cards as a divination tool has been traced back at least to the 14$^{th}$ century—in Italy, with the creation of tarot cards.

When we use oracle cards we are, in effect, providing our spirit guides with a system they can access in order to communicate their messages of guidance and even acknowledgments of things currently going on our life.

Tarot of course is still going strong, in many versions, but they do tend to be rather too complicated for some people to interpret. So much so, that many people prefer to consult with a professional practitioner. Instructional books abound, but I know that *my* personal guides just giggled at *my* prospects of understanding them, so they led me to oracle cards instead.

Oracle cards have evolved out of tarot and there are now a wide range of decks to choose from. Most of them have been created by well known established psychic mediums and psychic intuitives, working with the assistance and at the urging of their own personal guides with whom they work closely on a regular basis. All decks come with a comprehensive guide book detailing how to creatively use them in order to achieve the desired level of

## The Direct Connect

vibrational alignment with our guides, enabling them to more easily communicate with us.

Typically, the illustrations on each card are expressly designed to symbolize a whole range of universally acknowledged situations that provide spirit with a compatible vocabulary that enables them to cogently communicate their guidance, insight and any affirmations they know will address our needs. We can communicate these needs to them either verbally or by mentally focusing on them while we're thoroughly shuffling the deck prior to drawing the cards.

I've been using two decks every day for the past four or five years, and I've been gifted many times with remarkably perceptive counsel regarding irksome issues I was facing at the time. There have even been occasions when I've drawn three cards that actually combined to form a narrative, a storyline, that was uncannily germane to the issue at hand. I've often described my card experiences to friends as being tantamount to having my own personal medium-in-residence. I'll be sharing some of the highlights with you in the following chapter.

In a conversation with Sonia Choquette some time ago, I mentioned how her cards had been helping me handle various business matters. Issues that my wife had always handled so expertly, but which, since her passing, had had me utterly bamboozled—until that is, I began consulting with my medium-in-residence—Sonia's *Ask Your Guides* deck.

When I explained that "It's as if she's there in the room with me." The world renowned psychic intuitive responded "Reggie—she *is*—that's what the cards are all about."

As we become better acquainted with the ways by which spirit is able to ingeniously communicate with us through oracle cards, we'll come to appreciate that they are clearly, a unique formidable force for the good. A Divine vibrational energy that we can have working on our behalf at any time, and it's right at our very fingertips—quite literally.

For an authoritative and comprehensive description of both tarot and the other, more contemporary, oracle cards, I don't think anyone could do better than refer to Sonia Choquette's books *Ask Your Guides* and *The Psychic Pathway*.

Confirm that the bulb in your reading lamp is firmly seated in its socket, then shuffle away and prepare to be enlightened—and hooked.

## Animal Signs

We've seen how creative the spirits can be in utilizing various types of mediators to deliver messages of guidance and support for those they've left behind. In this sign type, the intermediaries we'll be discussing are our friends from the animal kingdom.

The belief that animals, through both their presence and through images, have the innate ability to connect us with a stream of knowledge not of our limited and strictly physical plane, has been deeply ingrained in the lore of societies and cultures going back to ancient mythologies, mysticism and shamanism.

Variously referred to as "animal symbology" or "totemism," it is known to have been a key element of many ancient cultures, including the lost civilization Sanxingdui in Sichuam Province, China more than 5000 years ago.

The images of the many species of birds and animals featured worldwide down through the ages, on items such as coats-of-arms and flags are all symbols of what that particular animal has universally come to represent in people's minds.

## The Direct Connect

In ancient Rome, there existed a level of appointed officials known as "augurs"—Julius Caesar was an augur at one time. They were responsible for interpreting animal and bird omens to assist them in the foretelling of future events in order to determine public affairs—hence the term still used today, "It doesn't augur well."

Native American lore, being so intimately aligned with all aspects of nature, is particularly rich in animal symbology. One of their beliefs for instance, is that we're all guided through life by nine different animals at various times. In their ritualistic dances, they connect symbolically to the realm of spirit by imitating animals.

One group of people who've traditionally had a thorough understanding of animal symbology, out of a pragmatic need are those who live and work close to the soil. They are the inheritors of a voluminous body of insightful observations passed down through the generations regarding the messages and omens behind the behavior of various birds, animals and even insects. Many of them have their roots in agrarian societies, and are naturally centered around possible future weather conditions, both short and long-term—the progenitors of the present-day TV Weathercasters you might say.

My wife was born and raised in a small village in a region of family owned farms in the English county of Herefordshire, and she and her sister Sybil could have compiled a sizable Farmer's Almanac of such pearls of wisdom, many of which are still heard to this day.

For instance, did you know that whenever a rooster crows while he's perched on a gate, it's bound to rain the following day?

But cows lying down in a field is a sure sign of good weather to come.

## Signs—Love Made Manifest

Make the most of it though because that other expert harbinger, the spider, might spin his web high off the ground. In which case—rain is surely imminent.

And those dark brown furry caterpillars we see in late summer—if they're more furry than usual, we'd better get more firewood chopped because it's going to be a hard winter. A nugget of wisdom that also applies to the relative bushiness of squirrels and foxes tails.

Actually, it's quite amazing how often and how accurate many of these sayings proved to be. If you're ever fortunate enough to be sitting in an English village pub enjoying a pint of ale, you'll often hear them trotted out by the locals—they swear by them to this day.

There are thousands of instances on record of animals being the bearers of specific personal signs and later confirmed by spirit in readings. And although having a bird or animal coming into our purview could legitimately be interpreted as spirit just saying "Hi," we must credit the spirits with having more creative ability than something so commonplace would require.

A bona fide sign delivered by an animal will, in all likelihood, reflect the influence of spirit in a way that's sure to get our attention. They'll often achieve this by inducing the animal to act out of character in our presence—performing in ways that are clearly incongruent to what we know its normal behavior to be. For example, when a wild or semi-domesticated creature that's known for its timidity and reticence whenever humans come within a hundred yards, comes surprisingly close to us—maybe even brushing against us. We know this not to be normal and we're nonplussed by it initially, but when a pleasant feeling of peace and calmness courses through us, we can't help but recognize it as being of spirit origin.

There *are* times however when there's no call for them to behave in an overtly theatrical way because their species-type is enough to achieve the point they want to make. Because their appearance has been designed to coincide with us mentioning them in connection to our loved one—that key element of *timing* again.

A lady once told me of an experience she'd once had that illustrates this. A few months after she'd lost her husband, a friend had kindly offered to accompany her to a State Park, just to get her out of the house for a while. During a stop at a scenic overlook on the trolley tour, she was telling her friend how terribly remorseful she'd been feeling lately regarding a dispute she'd had with her husband a few weeks before his passing. He'd been angry with her for spending what he regarded as more than they could afford on a fine-art reproduction of a painting of her favorite bird—a Snowy Owl. After his passing she'd been profoundly regretful that she'd been denied the chance to admit she'd been at fault and to apologize.

At this point, her friend, smiling, took hold of her hand and gestured towards what the rest of the group were already watching. Silently soaring majestically past them, not more than forty feet away, was a gorgeous Snowy Owl. The Park Ranger in attendance told them later that it was the first one he'd ever seen in his twelve years on the job.

No out-of-character behavior needed here, all he had to do was what Snowy Owls do anyway—soar majestically. The role he played in delivering a sign from spirit though, did call for perfect timing on his part. For it to succeed, he had to be precisely where he should be, at the precise moment he had to be there. He'd succeeded apparently, because the lady told me that the moment she'd realized it was a sign from her husband, she'd immediately felt the heavy burden of guilt being lifted off her heart leaving her with no doubt in her mind whatsoever that she'd just received her husband's love and forgiveness—the very things she'd been fervently praying for.

Due no doubt to their unique power of flight, birds have historically been held in extra high regard by the many cultures who believe all animals to be mystically attuned to the spirit realm. Andrea Wansbury is a chartered physiotherapist in South Africa and an expert on animal symbology. She has been successfully incorporating her vast knowledge of it, particularly as it pertains to birds, in her healing practice for many years. She writes about the reasons for this lofty status accorded to birds in her wonderfully informative book *Birds: Divine Messengers*;

"…..ancient cultures believed birds were the link between heaven and earth—they could fly to the heavens where the gods resided, taking human prayers with them, and then fly back with the divine answers and other messages."

Earlier, in chapter five, I mentioned my own encounter with a wild bird, when I returned home from my daily walk and was greeted by one flying around my living room, an incident that my wife referred to the following day in a reading with Carole Lynn, I've also had other, more substantive, "close encounters of the bird kind" (ouch). The first two of which were connected, and together served to play a recuperative role of some significance, not only concerning my own recovery but also that of a friend. I'll be sharing them with you in the following chapter in which I'll be discussing some of the signs I've been gifted with.

It's not surprising that there are people who, ordinarily, have trouble accepting the notion that animals can act as message carriers from the world of spirit. But there's one occasion that rarely fails

## The Direct Connect

to induce the doubters to hedge their bets, so to speak—and that's a funeral.

Stories abound about various kinds of animals showing up at funerals and memorial services and "performing" in ways that attract the attention of everyone gathered—who then, quite happily and unhesitatingly, link it to the proceedings at hand. A tacit inference, it would seem, to the incident being some kind of sign, with the animals involved symbolizing a welcoming committee of protective guardian angels for the deceased perhaps—explanations such as this do appear to be implied, but are rarely, if ever, expressed.

Some of the accounts I've come across, in conversations and in my reading, over the past few years have been quite amazing. A few examples: a sizable group of butterflies circled the casket at various junctures of the funeral service—a pair of swallows flanked the hearse and flew at window height for several miles—a bird-type (there are many bird examples) associated with the deceased, perched on an overhanging tree branch at the burial site and sang his heart out for the duration of the proceedings—at a service for a known cat-lover, an unidentified cat walked purposefully down the center aisle of the chapel and sat in front of the casket throughout the entire service—a bird actually flew into a church at the start of a funeral service, alighted on the edge of the lectern as the preacher took up his position at it, and stayed until the very end.

There are many excellent books on the fascinating subject of animal totems and their meanings. But I'm not suggesting that animal totemism be used in lieu of what we've come to accept as spirit communication with us. It just seems to me that a unique congenial overlapping of two disciplines is at play here (with totemism in an adjunctive role) that we shouldn't ignore.

## Signs—Love Made Manifest

A few final words on receiving signs: We have the spirits on record as saying that it really disappoints them when the signs upon which they've expended so much effort in orchestrating, seemingly go unnoticed.

So we should try to remain mindful that every sign we receive—from the faintest feeling of their presence—to those that are palpably manifest, are all wondrous gifts. Each one nothing less than a miracle that merits appreciation. It's a matter of common courtesy therefore, to always express our heartfelt gratitude to them. A gesture that they've often indicated to the mediums, they find greatly gratifying, and encourages them to continue gifting us.

CHAPTER 9

# THESE ARE A FEW OF MY FAVORITE SIGNS

In common with most everyone who's ever had a loved one taken from them, after my wife's passing, I too yearned for a sign of some kind that would serve to confirm her continued existence. In consequence, I found myself constantly scrutinizing pretty much everything that occurred anywhere around me hoping to detect anything that could be construed as a sign.

In hindsight though—also in common with many people, I had the mistaken mind-set and expectation of signs from spirit being in tangible form—corporeal—the "squiffy-picture-frame" type of cliché way in which signs from spirit are typically depicted in movies etc. 'How else could spirit possibly get our attention?' was my five-sensory rationale at the time—I would soon become better enlightened about the many creative ways they can and do.

## The Direct Connect

I hope that sharing some of the more notable signs my wife has gifted me with since she made her transition, will help mitigate some of the misconceptions most of us can have about the nature of signs, because they can cause us to overlook them and deprive us of their magic. This first example illustrates how my own enlightenment on the subject came about.

I'd spent more than eighteen months 'barking up the wrong tree' after my wife's passing before I finally became clued in to how ingenious our loved ones in spirit can be. And, as is often the case, it was right under my nose—quite literally—on my dinner plate to be precise. My wife you see, had been a Home Economics teacher, and naturally the kitchen had always been *her* domain and a place in which I'd only been allowed at dish-drying-duty time. (These days, it seems as if I'm rarely out of there).

Throughout the horrifying illness she so bravely fought, her chief concern had centered around how I was going to take care of myself when she was no longer there to do it. I must admit to being more than a little terrified at the prospect myself—but I tried my best not to show it. So it was with some considerable trepidation that, after a few months, I'd turned my back on the cans of soup and jars of peanut butter and embarked on my mission to take care of myself, hopefully in a way my wife would have approved.

To my amazement, right from the get-go my meals weren't bad at all. But while I became progressively even more pleased with my efforts I had to admit to being quite puzzled, because I'd honestly never felt that I knew what I was doing—hardly had a clue really.

After a while, I got into the habit of treating myself to a special meal on week-ends. And one Saturday evening, following a particularly satisfying dinner—my most ambitious culinary effort yet,

## These Are a Few of My Favorite Signs

I reflected on a strange feeling I'd been aware of throughout its preparation. It had been in regard to the ways in which the correct combination of ingredients, their measures, even their cooking times, consistently just popped into my head, out of the blue and right on cue—with little or no conscious prethought on my part.

It had been markedly similar to the eerie sensations I remembered experiencing when the quality of my painting was flowing flatteringly much higher than the level of mental effort I was contributing at that time should have reflected—as if, I'd concluded, I was receiving spiritual guidance. It was when I realized that it had been that same palpably comforting glow and the accompanying feeling of well-being I'd felt coursing through me this evening, that it finally clicked. There *had* been considerably more to it than key ingredients mysteriously "popping into my head," in the kitchen, and prior to that, at the food store. That would imply random coincidences—an inordinate number of them—this went way beyond that.

After ruminating for some time on the various elements involved, it seemed to me that there could only be one explanation—not only was the kitchen still my wife's domain—she'd been my cooking mentor me all along. I could have kicked myself for not having been more aware of what must have been a constant stream of signs that had gone unrecognized, and in my apology to her I promised that from now on I would set my sights higher and stop examining things for their squiffiness—that can get pretty insulting I would think.

I continued my ruminations on the series of events for a while, and would soon be glad I did, because I was about to be gifted with an unexpected outcome that gave soul-gladdening substance to the entire episode.

I'd recently re-embarked on a regular meditation regimen and carried this subject with me into my meditation space early one morning. As I was coming up out of what had been an especially deep session of relaxation, I recalled, with striking clarity, an exchange between my wife and I a few days before her passing. She'd expressed her deep concern regarding my ability to take care of myself after she'd gone.

I'd thought of that moment countless times since, but try as I might, I had never been able to figure out where the words came from—but what came out of my mouth was: *"You're not to worry about that darling—you'll still be able to take care of me—just like you always have."*

It goes without saying that to have my unwitting predictive assertion confirmed in this way was not only a meaningfully restorative step in itself, but it turned out to also be the precursor to many more—and they continue to this day.

I feel the foregoing chain of events serves to show why we should try to stay mindful that those faint and indeterminate signs that may appear at first, to be nothing more than mere whispers-of-a-thought—tricks of our imagination—and not worthy of our attention, can sometimes blossom and burgeon into messages of great importance. It's almost as though they're by way of being exploratory "feelers" put out by spirit, to ascertain whether or not we're amenable before they invest more time and effort in us. If this is indeed the case, then it surely behooves us to give our consideration to anything that can be construed as a sign—it's such a modest investment for something of such potentially inestimable benefit to our recovery.

Please allow me to share a few more signs that I've been gifted with.

*These Are a Few of My Favorite Signs*

## Our Friend Flicker

That cliche of signs, the flickering light bulb, has often been a comforting companion around me. Of course, lights flicker for other reasons too so I try to limit my acknowledgment of them to when they coincide with situations that are undeniably germane to my wife in some way.

For instance, while visiting her village in England with my daughter Bev a few years after her mother's passing, we found a delightful book about the village's history in the little village shop. It was a few weeks however before I had a chance to really look through it—after I'd turned in one night. The moment I began flipping through the pages of articles and photographs of people and places with whom my wife had been so familiar, my bedside light began flickering like crazy and didn't stop until I closed it and called it a night thirty minutes later.

Many other occasions come tumbling forth where my wife took advantage of available lighting to confirm both her presence and acknowledgment of what I was currently engaged in—here are just a few of them—typical of many:

While I was reading a beautiful touching letter from her sister Sybil—addressing Christmas cards using her lists—while I was working on a portrait of her that I'd come across half-finished in the studio cupboard, and again two weeks later, when Medium Vicki Monroe referred specifically to the portrait in a reading I had with her.

A "highlight-reel" example that was uniquely meaningful happened just recently. It's become a custom for me on wedding anniversaries and birthdays, to celebrate in a way we always had—by dining at one of our favorite special restaurants. At the one I'd recently deemed special enough for our latest anniversary, I was glad to find the low-level of the general lighting was tastefully supplemented by a low hanging pendant light over each table, as I'd brought along a book to read.

From the moment the maître d' seated me, the light over my table began flickering and continued spasmodically throughout the meal. None of the other lights were doing this, and later, looking back from the lobby—the one over my table was no longer flickering either.

## My Musical Signs

With my wife being a trained pianist and our daughter Bev a successful electronic music producer, recording artist and composer with an international reputation, music has always filled our home. So, if I had to name one message delivery system my wife would have a preference for, it would be through music. And, true-to-form, seldom a day passes that I'm not gifted with some form of music sign—the two following instances merit a mention here.

A favorite piece of ours had been Tchaikovsky's *Romeo and Juliet Fantasy Overture*, and we had several CD's of it, one of which we kept in the car—I was about to be blessed with a reason to be thankful that we had.

Soon after I'd started taking on work again, an assignment came in that I had mixed feelings about accepting because not only would it entail an eight hundred mile round trip, but I would be staying for three days at the same Gulf Coast marina resort where my wife and I had spent many wonderful vacations over the years—our second home really. I wasn't looking forward to that one little bit—too many memories right now—I wasn't sure I could handle that *and* be as creative as I needed to be. By the time the day came around, I'd sunk

## These Are a Few of My Favorite Signs

into quite a depressed and melancholic state—hardly conducive to the whimsical creativity my client was expecting of me.

I'd always liked and respected this client a lot, he was a good man—we'd worked on many exciting projects together. After working off of these thoughts for a while I decided I owed it to him to use the driving time to work on myself and fight my way out of this sorry mess.

Since my wife's transition, the Tchaikovsky album had been a virtual fixture in the car's CD player because it never failed to take the edge off my grief and lift my spirits. But unfortunately, also on this CD was his *Symphony No. 6,* two movements of which, I'd never cared much for, so whenever they came up I'd reach for the "skip" button and bypass them. Annoyingly interruptive perhaps, but the soaring melodic grandeur of *Romeo and Juliet* was well worth it.

I gradually became aware of the music starting to work its magic on me, so well apparently that it took an hour or so for me to realize that I hadn't once had to hit the skip button—it was skipping the two offending tracks automatically. Amazingly, it remained in that mode throughout the trip, and for several months after, even though everyone I asked told me it was impossible.

The upshot was that by the time I reached my destination, the despondency had not only completely dissipated but had been replaced by a level of ebullience that I hadn't experienced in a long time—an aspect that was clearly reflected in the resultant quality of the work produced. My pleasurable sojourn couldn't have been more successful—and all due, I'm convinced, to my wife's expert disc-jockeying.

A CD and CD player also played a leading role in the delivery of this sign I received—along with a supporting cast of synchronicities.

## The Direct Connect

I just cannot work at the board without music—just as long as it agreeably echoes the mood of the subject I'm painting, which, as I'm painting for the light and frothy end of the entertainment spectrum, means lilting, sprightly, uplifting—you know—light-hearted stuff.

One of the pieces that fits this profile and that I've come to love for another reason too, is an orchestral suite that I'd originally recorded on tape years ago from a college radio station in a town where we'd lived at the time. After I'd lost my wife it doubled as a very effective mood-lifter whenever I found myself beset by those inevitable despicably disconsolate spells—so consequently it got a lot of "air-play" on those days—so much so that it soon began letting me know that it badly needed replacing.

Unfortunately, I'd never known the title of it. I had an idea it was French but the student announcer's mangled pronunciation rendered it unintelligible. I tried writing it down phonetically but the music store staff weren't able to figure it out either. My in-house guru-of-all-things-musical however—my daughter Bev, succeeded in tracking it down and had it sent to me.

What it said in the accompanying liner notes could very well have been a gift in itself. I learned for instance that the French composer Maurice Ravel had written the orchestral suite *Le Tombeau de Couperin* as a memorial to friends who had been killed during the First World War. And when he was criticized for treating such a somber topic with such light-heartedness, Ravel replied "The dead are sad enough, in their eternal silence" That certainly aligned with how it had always resonated with me so effectively whenever I'd called on it for spiritual upliftment.

Eager to hear it in High Definition Stereo after years of only hearing it on my beat up mono tape cartridge, I put it on the player

## These Are a Few of My Favorite Signs

and hit the play button. Then sat back bathing in what was, for me, the previously unheard splendor of this exhilarating piece that so evocatively conjures up sound images of the blissful existence that those in the afterlife are now leading. "Sadness begone," is the reassuring message that spirit seems to be conveying to us—through Ravel.

As the layers of melodic trills were tapering away however, I was jolted out of my sweet soporific state by an announcer telling me I'd just been listening to *The Ulster Orchestra*. 'What?' I thought, reaching for the CD case, 'This says *London Symphony Orchestra*—and hey, wait a minute—what's an announcer doing on a recording—what's going on here?'

What was 'going on' it turned out, was that I'd been gifted with a synchronistic sign. What I'd been listening to, hadn't been my CD at all, it had come through my digital radio receiver which was tuned to a radio station and connected to my CD player's "auxiliary port." In my excitement, I'd forgotten to flick the switch back to the CD player.

For this to come about, at the exact moment when I pressed the play button to hear a recording of such special significance to me, a radio station a thousand miles away had to begin playing a recording of the exact same piece. Again—what were the odds?

The "Le Tombeau" still continues its ongoing connection. For instance it was my wife's birthday two weeks ago, a day on which our thoughtful daughter never fails to call me. As I picked up the phone, the classical music station was playing, so I reached for the remote to mute it. As I was about to do so, Bev asked "Is that Le Tombeau I hear playing?" I'd failed to notice, but sure enough—it was, and sure enough her reaction was "Wow, what are the odds?"

One of the cards in Sonia Choquette's *The Answer is Simple* deck of oracle cards is titled *Listen to the Music*. I draw it quite often, as I had that morning, and almost every time I do, I can almost bank on "Le Tombeau" coming on the radio at some point during the day.

## Synchronistic Signs

I've been gifted with so many signs that have revolved around a chain of meaningful coincidences that they warrant a category of their own.

In this example, about two years after my wife's passing I woke up one morning and knew immediately that I was in for a bad day—those who have been bereaved know the symptoms only too well. There are times when the wave of grief wells up out of nowhere for no apparent reason, at other times we know exactly what sparked it off—that was the case here.

In a book I'd been reading the previous evening, a so-called "grief expert" had been chastising those bereaved people who hang on to thoughts of their loved ones for an inordinate amount of time after they have passed. "It's an act of self-indulgence," he authoritatively stated, "And it's only holding them back." (Yikes, that "gotta let them go" mantra again).

Well, I'd allowed those words to get to me, and now here I was with a full day of errands scheduled and no stomach at all for any of them. Try as I might, nothing from my extensive list of affirming mood elevators worked, and I felt myself getting increasingly fearful of sliding back down into that dark dank pit of despair where I'd already spent too much time. What if this idiotically pompous man of letters knew what he was talking about after all?

## These Are a Few of My Favorite Signs

In between obsessing on this, it didn't help that the universe was obviously conspiring against anything going right for me today—it was one wild frustrating goose chase after another all morning. Being informed by the bookstore customer service (?) lady that the book I'd ordered hadn't come in, despite them having called me to say it had, was the last straw. As the exit doors were sliding open for me, the thought struck me (actually my inner voice, I would learn in due time) to check the "New Age" section for any new books on mediumship, so I turned to head in that direction. I hesitated for a moment and considered changing my mind because I hadn't found this store to be very strong in that department in the past, and I'd had my fill of fiascos for one day. But that little voice insisted that I look anyway—there's always a chance I could come by something that will help me deal with this "Gotta let her go" thing I was still grappling with.

Ten minutes later I was standing in the check-out line with a book that was new to me and who's title had piqued my interest—*Never Say Goodbye* by a medium named Patrick Mathews. It was the only positive thing that had happened to me all day—the silver lining perhaps? It gave me hope that there could more good stuff in the offing. As I was leaving the store, on a car parked directly in front of the door was a tag plate that read "AAA—Access An Angel." 'I feel I just did', I remember thinking.

I had a strong sense of there being a good reason this book had come into my purview in the uncommonly arduous way it had. Eager to find out—I hurried to a nearby restaurant—after not having eaten a thing all day, I'd suddenly found an appetite.

At the first chance I got, after the preliminaries of being seated and placing my order, I was finally able to open the book at the introduction page.

The very first words of the introduction were:

*"Your husband, Fred, is saying that he wants to clear up something that you've read."*

*"He is telling me you were reading a book that stated that by you continuing to talk with him, you are keeping him with you, and not allowing him to move on."*

This was by way of a preamble to a detailed account later in the book, of a reading Patrick had conducted for a lady who had lost her husband. The excerpt went on to explain how the grieving widow had tearfully confirmed that she had in fact been upset by what she'd read about our loved ones in spirit only staying around for a short time before they move on. Her husband though, firmly assured her through Patrick that he wasn't going anywhere and doesn't care what those books are telling her.

BAM! Right off the bat—it couldn't have been more pertinent to my situation.

A chain of synchronistic events had culminated in me being magically gifted with the precise words I needed to read in order to help me combat a devastating piece of misinformation.

## Synchronicity at Work

I suppose it's only to be expected that with me spending so much time on the job over the years, that so many of my own synchronistic experiences have revolved around various aspects of my work. The fact is, they were so habitually present that I came to regard them as being almost akin to having the services of an assistant—such was the extent of their helpfulness, and rarely anything but positive and perfectly appropriate to the situation at hand. Synchronicity occurred with such frequency that I became

## These Are a Few of My Favorite Signs

borderline arrogant about it and found myself able to remain surprisingly cool, confident that the elusive critically important photograph would show up.

Most of my working years were way before internet search engines were even imagined, so the tracking down of information in the form of specific images, often of unusual and obscure subject matter, involved ferreting through mountains of books and my own extensive files of photographs, slides and magazine clippings—it can be a very interesting and enjoyable activity actually. *Except* when the illustrations have to be completed to a deadline of like—the day before yesterday—which was the case, more often than not. So, if there was one area of the process where assistance was welcome, this was surely it—and this was where, time and again, at the proverbial eleventh hour, synchronicity saved my bacon.

I'd always suspected that some kind of Divine source was behind such events, I had no authoritative word on this at that time—it was strictly just a "feeling" I had that they couldn't possibly be random coincidences The feeling I have about them these days, is that my wife is also involved in the orchestration of them now. As I say, it's just a feeling, but to me her touch is discernably all over them, particularly in these two examples that happened quite recently.

I'd been assigned to create several illustrations of a proposed attraction involving the famous *Purple People Bridge* that spans the Ohio River in Cincinnati, but I'd hit a snag. I'd been furnished with several color photographs of the bridge, but purple is a notoriously tricky color to replicate photographically and sure enough, the prints showed the color ranging from light brown to a medium grey. The artwork was going to be photographically enlarged to twenty feet wide and pitched to a downtown ballroom audience—with most of them, if not all, being thoroughly familiar with the bridge, it was imperative that I get this right.

After a weekend of agonizing over this predicament, I was still distracted by it early on Monday morning as I drove to my dentists office for a routine cleaning—an appointment I was now wishing I'd cancelled and instead used the time to work on my purple problem.

As the hygienist was entering the room, a co-worker called out to her "Hi Julie, did you enjoy your weekend in The Nati?"

'Oh, sweet Jesus,' I thought to myself—'If I heard what I think I heard, I have a few questions for Julie.' So I asked her "Julie, when you were in Cincinnati, you didn't happen to see the Purple People Bridge did you?."

"See it? Are you kidding me—my boyfriend's apartment is about a hundred yards from it—we must have walked over it a dozen times. I sat on the balcony yesterday afternoon just looking at it. Why do you ask?"

I explained my dilemma to her, and with wide eyed amazement she smiled and said "I know *exactly* what shade of purple it's painted—you're wearing it—that bib is a perfect match."

I left the office later carrying, courtesy of an astonishing piece of synchronicity, my "manna from heaven"—a bag of color swatches in the form of a bib, a napkin and a plastic cup. I had the idea someone had a liking for the color lavender—my wife's favorite color too, incidentally.

The following example wound up being a family affair. A well-known illusionist/magician and long standing client had handed me the pleasurable task of designing a theater for him. One evening while I was sketching some ideas to submit to him, he called me during the intermission of his performance with an idea *he'd* had. We'd considered various exotic motifs during an earlier conversation

## These Are a Few of My Favorite Signs

and he'd come across a photograph of a piece of architecture that appealed to him. It was of the Royal Pavilion in the English seaside town of Brighton, and he wondered about us "borrowing" some of its striking Indian architectural elements.

I had a vague idea of the building he was talking about but I certainly wasn't familiar enough with it to be able to start manipulating its elements in an articulate way. So the following morning I embarked on a search for images. Unfortunately, those I located on the internet—surprisingly, were either too small, too blurry or poorly exposed—for my purposes. My picture books yielded three photos that were so-so, but they too had issues—I had the feeling, from what I remembered about the building, that I could do much better. So I did what the mediums have told us to do—I put my request "out there" and went about my business.

This was what I was still pursuing later in the day, when my daughter Bev called—from England—I had no idea she and a friend had "gone tripping" across "the pond." I told her what a coincidence that was because at that very moment I was surrounded by stacks of picture books of England. When she asked what I was working on and I mentioned Brighton, it was her turn to say "Wow, that's a coincidence," before going on to explain "We were there just yesterday—do you need any photos—I took lots of the Royal Pavilion."

Less than an hour later, I was holding a dozen or so great photographs she'd emailed to me, showing all the elements I needed and from the various angles I needed them.

Coincidences? I've long since stopped believing in them. For me, this was just another day at my one-man office. One-man—but not alone, apparently.

## The Direct Connect

This next example of synchronicity at work involved a show that was billed as an "action drama," an appellation, it turned out, that was equally applicable to the creation of my illustration for it—it turned out to be a truly nail-biting "eleventh hour" rescue mission that redefined the term "nick of time." And for a while, had me fearing that my Grandma's habitual admonition "Pride cometh before a fall," was about to becometh manifest.

I'd been hired by a sea-life theme park to illustrate all the scenes of an action packed lagoon stunt show, all compiled into one picture in the style of many movie posters. The principal sponsor of the show, was the manufacturer of the latest model of jet skis featured, a major financial commitment. So understandably, it was essential that the machine be accurately and prominently featured and showcased in the best possible light.

There had been a teeny-weeny snag however, apparently, those responsible for providing the illustrator with the necessary informational visuals either hadn't "gotten the memo," or were convinced he possessed clairvoyant abilities. In any event, he'd been left swinging in the wind without any images of the said jet ski.

Mister "expect-a-miracle" however refused to be fazed by this potential catastrophe. I'd simply spend the week painting all those water-skiers, speedboats and explosions and anything else that wasn't a jet ski, leaving all of two days to locate jet ski magazines with all the pictures I needed (Remember, this was BG—before google), and finish painting the piece in time for the client to pick up early Tuesday morning. Piece of cake—this *is* Florida after all—jet skis are everywhere. My Saturday search however, from early morning till nine at night, yielded absolutely nothing—zero—zilch. It was obviously time for another prayerful plea to my friends.

# These Are a Few of My Favorite Signs

As we were leaving church on Sunday morning, my wife suggested we walk over to my office as she'd like to see the rendering on which I'd spent so much time all week. It was a lovely morning for a walk along our quaint, and today, unusually vehicle-free main street.

The entrance door to the second story offices over the stores was about thirty yards along a narrow bricked street that ran off the main thoroughfare, and as we were turning the corner the sight that greeted us brought us both to an abrupt halt.

Parked right in front of the office door and directly under my studio window, was a Jeep, the only vehicle in sight, and hitched to it was a trailer, and perched on it—gleaming dazzlingly in the early morning sunshine, was a resplendent yellow and lavender colored jet ski.

We looked at each other, eyes and mouths agog, as my wife exclaimed "Oh my God—it couldn't be—could it?" A quick scurry down the narrow sidewalk confirmed—by its name emblazoned along its side—that indeed it was.

I raced upstairs for my camera while my wife kept watch on our precious quarry lest the owner returned and drove off with it. Another day at the office—another dollar and another prayer answered—through synchronicity.

Before the advent of internet search engines, I'd often spend many hours foraging for vitally important photographic images in used bookstores and thrift shops. Over the years I'd found them to be veritable gold mines, not only of the images I'd been looking for, but also the fascinating synchronistic events that had to occur in order for our paths to cross.

A few months ago for instance, I found precisely what I'd looked all over for in a thrift shop even before the door had closed behind

## The Direct Connect

me. It was the top volume on a stack of books sitting on the counter situated right at the door—the very first thing to meet my eye. I later discovered, as I was paying for it, that the stack had been donated by a lady not more than five minutes before.

The circumstances that justify this outcome as being synchronistic had actually played out the previous day. That was when I'd driven to this same shop, way out on the outskirts of town, but I'd been delayed by a business meeting that had dragged on interminably, and by the time I got there it had closed for the day.

The book turned out to be a rich mother lode of pertinent imagery that contributed greatly to a series of illustrations that helped sell what later became a highly successful award-winning show. Although I'd been more than a little miffed by that long-winded gentleman at the meeting who'd waffled on and on for so long—I admit to beaming him my heartfelt gratitude. Without his unwitting synchronistic contribution, that book and I would have never met up—and the show, conceivably, might never have happened.

This following example didn't involve the kind of convoluted chain of events and cast of players that characterize most synchronistic occurrences, if it *did* contain any kind of message, it completely escapes me. But I try to stay mindful that, as is the case with regular signs from spirit, there are times when a synchronistic event is nothing more than just their way of saying "Hi, I'm here—everything is okay." One thing that *did* grab my attention though was its immediacy—the relevant connection was almost instantaneous.

I received a telephone call one morning from the Assistant City Manager of a neighboring city, inquiring of my availability to paint an illustration showing how the city's famous historic pier will look after its renovation back to its original 1920's splendor, after having

### These Are a Few of My Favorite Signs

sustained considerable hurricane damage. When I'd assured her I'd consider it a privilege to work on it, she gave me instructions on the correct wording to use when filing the required Vendor's Application form on the city's website.

At the time she'd called, I'd been in the process of downloading a blank "Cryptic Crossword," (one of my favorite jogging-for-the-brain exercises), from the internet, so I decided to continue printing that first.

As the columns of crossword clues were forming on the monitor, I was actually holding, and glancing fleetingly at, the notes I'd taken down for filling in the bureaucratic inquisition. First on the list was "Name of Project:"—*Pier Renovation,* I'd been told to write.

When I looked back at the monitor to check whether it was okay yet to hit the print button, one of the clues just about jumped off the screen at me. I sat staring at it—mouth agape, for two or three minutes, completely mystified, and wondering if I was "seeing things."

Clue No.12 across, you see, was: *"Seaside feature ripe for renovation.(4)*

And the answer, in the "cryptic crossword" style, is an anagram of "ripe." Which is "pier."

For this to have happened by chance, as Dr. Jung famously said, "...would represent a degree of improbability that would have to be expressed by an astronomical figure."

With "random chance" being ruled out, it surely follows that this was a spirit communication of some kind. Reflecting now however, on what the message here may have been, I can only assume that it was by way of an acknowledgment by spirit to having had a hand in steering a nice, project my way. The rendering after all was certainly a

## The Direct Connect

delight to work on and was well received—an oversize photographic enlargement of it now graces the august lobby of City Hall.

But it doesn't end there, another intriguing synchronistic aspect of this project, for me at least, was that while working on it and visiting that particular stretch of beach, distant memories surfaced of the times I'd attempted to depict it in paintings when, as a child in England, I'd often painted pictures of Sir Malcolm Campbell's *Bluebird* car. The car in which, in 1931, he broke the world land speed record on this very same beach.

In yet another layer of "coincidence," when a visitors attraction at Daytona International Speedway was being designed, I was commissioned to create several interior views of it. Directly in the foreground of the one showing the main gallery I had to paint that same *Bluebird* car. Finally, after sixty years, I'd sold one of my paintings of it.

I'd like to share two more instances, where similar synchronistic links took many years to eventually play out.

## Synchronistically Forward to the Past

Carl Jung defined synchronicity as "A psychically conditioned relativity of time and space," and also described synchronicity as being "...an acausal connecting principle. Since it goes beyond causation, it goes beyond time and space, and is not limited by such relations."

And Einstein apparently, didn't even *believe* in time, at least not in the way most of us have been conditioned to regarding it. To him, referencing any situation in terms of past, present and future was "Newtonian thinking." For instance, following the death of his lifelong friend Michele Besso, in a letter of condolence to Besso's family, he wrote to the effect that "Michele's death means nothing because us physicists know that the distinction between past, present and future is nothing but a persistent illusion." Devotees of parapsychology have long believed that those in the non-physical realm—those in spirit—exist outside the constraints of what we know as the space-time continuum. The spirits have often made reference to this in readings with mediums when they tell us that "Fifty years in your physical earth-time, is but a "blink-of-an-eye" in our non-physical time."

It seems to me, that viewed in this context, it's quite possible for synchronistic occurrences to be entirely "open-ended" and not circumscribed by an arbitrary limited time-span in the way we've traditionally thought of them. As we've seen, according to the universally venerated Professor Einstein "Time is of no consequence." He's also reported as holding the jocular view that "The only reason for time is so that everything doesn't happen at once."

It surely helps then, I think, to stay mindful of this when we examine a current event that we "sense" is somehow linked to a situation of significance in our past, the reason for which has always eluded us. We may discover for instance, if we are able to mentally eliminate the intervening years (that stuff of no consequence) as if only hours or days separated them, that a puzzling occurrence years ago was in fact prophetic in nature and has been patiently hovering around in the wings awaiting the current event to be placed in our path in order for a coherent narrative to finally emerge. It may be a wonderful Divine message of guidance or just a nurturing assurance that we are at the right place on our soul path and fulfilling our life purpose.

The following two examples exemplify this "straddling of the years" scenario. Both instances are coincidentally linked and in both cases those "inconsequential elements" consisted of thirty years in time and 4,200 miles in distance. And again, they're both work related.

## The Direct Connect

The first segment of this saga took place during my high school years, a few years after the end of World War II. At that time most consumable goods were still under the wartime imposed rationing, including, to the chagrin of us kids—candy.

A lot of good old-fashioned bartering went on during those days, at every level, and the young yours truly saw an opportunity to exploit my emerging artistic abilities. One thing I'd acquired an adeptness for was drawing the Walt Disney characters—especially Mickey Mouse, I could literally draw that cute rodent with my eyes closed. When I discovered that classmates were willing to part with a valuable rationed toffee or stick of licorice in exchange for a portrait of Mickey, I unwittingly became a "start-up" black marketeer—a punishable offence at that time. Business was pretty brisk, and I was destined to become the pimpliest kid in class.

Business must have been slow one day however, because I spent a good part of the lesson stupidly doodling Mickey Mouse in the margins of a school text book. Some straight-laced dutiful fink in the class following ours came across the doodles, turned me in to the teacher and I wound up being summarily dispatched to the headmaster's study. The second tier of punishment was then duly administered in the form of the dreaded "six-of-the-best"—six hefty wacks across the backside with a hefty bamboo cane.

Fast-forwarding at this juncture, through thirty of Einstein's "illusory years," brings us up to the 1980's and 4,200 miles away in Central Florida.

Thanks to a series of career lucky breaks, I'd become a moderately successful illustrator by now, and I was about to embark on my initial foray into the specialized field of theme park conceptual art (a field in which I had no previous experience whatsoever), with an assignment

## These Are a Few of My Favorite Signs

for none other than The Walt Disney Company—the parents of my old friend Mickey Mouse.

They were in the process of preparing to announce their plans to build the Euro Disney theme park with a suitably lavish open-air VIP presentation on the site on the outskirts of Paris, and they wanted me to paint a large birds-eye view detailing the proceedings. One particularly important element of this, prominently displayed "up front and center," in my picture, would be their newly acquired, ten story high, hot air balloon which, in the trademark Disney style of wordplay is named *Ear-Force one*. It's a very impressive sight with its shape taking the form, as it does of a gigantic Mickey Mouse head.

When I was asked by one of the producer's if I'd ever had occasion to depict Mickey, I couldn't resist telling them about my short-lived candy racketeering days. Later, as the meeting was winding down and I was gathering my notes together, his assistant, who'd booked me in earlier, entered the conference room carrying the huge candy-jar from her desk and said "This is for you, we thought you'd like to be paid up-front this time."

Oh, and that text book in which I'd doodled Mickey Mouse thirty years prior? It was titled—*French for Beginners*!

The spirits with a propensity for this brand of time-delayed synchronicity gifted me again three years later. This too was connected to an event in England, thirty years before.

I came home from the office on a Friday evening with a dozen illustrations I'd just completed, and placed them on the easel in the den where my wife liked to look at them. This set represented a blisteringly intense month of twelve hour days and I was eagerly looking forward to a relaxing weekend around the pool with my family.

# The Direct Connect

A short time later I was cooling off in the pool, paddling lazily around in the floating lounger, when my wife joined me bringing with her a tall cool drink. As she was handing it to me she said "Darling, those renderings are fantastic—so colorful and lively, they're gonna be pleased with them—and talk about coincidence."

When I asked her what she meant, she said "You remember—that story you told me once about a Mr. James." It took awhile "for the penny to drop," as we English say, but when it did I almost choked on my drink and roared with laughter so hard I almost tipped the lounger over.

The story she'd referred to was about my first day of a twelve month art school course I'd enrolled in, when I was in my mid teens. I'd missed the first six weeks of classes due to an injury I'd sustained in a soccer game, as soon as I was allowed to sit up though, I had them send me a list of subjects for me to illustrate. One of the six items was "Tropical Fish," a subject I was attracted to but for which the only access to reference sources I had were my memories of a few tropical fish in an aquarium my dad had once built. I remembered them as being brightly colored so that was how I'd depicted them—the brighter the better, was my thinking. When I'd finished them all, I looked forward to submitting them to my teacher, I was so pleased with my unsupervised efforts—particularly the tropical fish.

Mr. James however, wasn't at all pleased—not one bit. To the extent that he had me out in front of the entire class while he proceeded to berate me up one side and down the other. With his critiques getting progressively harsher, with the rest of the students enjoying this no end, and with me feeling a foot tall, he went through them one after the other, until he finally got to

## These Are a Few of My Favorite Signs

the pick-of-the-bunch—my tropical fish masterpiece. And oh my word, that triggered such a tizzy—I thought he was about to have a seizure. "What on earth do you call this?" he bellowed, "It's like a bloody rainbow exploded." Before ending with "Don't you dare show me stuff like this again—and in future, leave gaudy garish fish to that Walt Disney chap in America."

Our derisive outburst and subsequent toast to Johnny James now, thirty years on, was due to the fact that the client who'd commissioned the illustrations I'd just completed was none other than that "Walt Disney chap's" company.

They were scenes you see, of a proposed lavish extravaganza—a stage version of the mega-hit Disney classic movie *The Little Mermaid*. And of course—*gloriously gaudy and garish fish were everywhere!* Later on, I also worked on a *Finding Nemo* show—talk about gaudy fish.

I'm happy to say that by the end of the school year, Mr. John James and I had become firm and mutually respectful friends. We often hear expressions like "If only he could have been alive to see this." One of the countless wonderful things that knowledge of the afterlife avails us, is the assurance that they *are* seeing this—we don't just believe it anymore—we know it. Interestingly, in a reading with Joanne Gerber two years ago she recognized my teacher Mr. James's presence by name—I pictured him, smiling proudly and approvingly—thoroughly enjoying the irony.

The synchronistic aspect of both of these next examples also involved signs—street signs.

I'd been asked to paint an architectural rendering of a multi-story medical facility that was of extreme importance to the community it was designed to serve. Also of extreme importance, to local preservationist and environmental groups, was a certain tree—a magnificent

# The Direct Connect

specimen that the community had held sacrosanct for generations. They needed affirmation that their treasured tree would be protected. No matter from which angle we showed the building, the tree would be prominently featured, so naturally, accurate depiction of it was key to the presentation.

Unfortunately, not for the first time, the people in other states on whom I was reliant for information, were apparently under the impression that illustrators possess clairvoyant abilities, and hadn't furnished me with a photograph of the said tree like they'd promised to do, and time, as usual, was something we were rapidly running out of.

Fortunately however I had a wife with an incredible memory. When I was telling her about my latest "predicament du jour" over dinner one evening, she recalled that we'd driven through that very town a few years before and I'd taken slides of various tree-types in the event I got work from the architects I'd called on in that area.

Thanks to the cool slide retrieval system we'd devised, we were able to locate that cluster of slides and on the edge of one of them I noticed a street sign at an intersection. Under a magnifier, I was able to read the names of the main highway and the cross street, and amazingly they tallied with the site plan. I was holding a slide, taken four years before, of the exact tree I was required to, in essence, paint a "portrait" of. It was certainly highly distinctive in character, I couldn't possibly have faked it.

The synchronistic street sign that "saved my bacon" in this next example was closer to home—a mere two blocks from my house.

I'd painted an illustration of how an iconic Civic Auditorium would look after a proposed major refurbishment. All the city officials and everyone connected with the project were pleased with the painting, it

## These Are a Few of My Favorite Signs

seemed the only person who *wasn't* was one of the architects involved.

When he brought the original to my office, he complained that he'd never seen a sky like that, it didn't look natural and he wanted me to re-paint it.

I've always considered the skies to be one of the most important components of a rendering and accordingly, as always, I'd done my homework on this. My wife and I had attended many evening symphony concerts at this venue, and that was how I'd elected to paint it—smart fashionably dressed audience members arriving for an evening performance, under the pale delicate rosy hues of a placid Florida evening sky, softly streaked with silky golden wisps of Cirrus, as one looks north—magical stuff.

When I suggested to him that not ever having seen such a sky, might be due to the fact that he hadn't done as much looking as I had, he responded that his living room faces north, and he'd spent many hours sitting there looking at the evening sky and he'd never seen one like this.

I hated to do this to the man in front of his wife, I really did, but he'd tried my patience just a tad too much, besides, there were so many elements painted on top of this delicately rendered sky, that painting it over would have taken a couple of days. It only took a minute to flip through the binder where I stored my sky slides to retrieve the one on which I'd based the sky in question. I showed him what I'd written on the slide mount:- 'August 27$^{th}$—7pm—Looking north'. I then put it in the viewer and passed it to him, with the suggestion that he read the street sign.

The street names on the sign clearly proved that when I'd shot the slide, three years before, I'd been standing on his front lawn—not forty feet from his living room window! Magical stuff.

## Oracle Cards—Our Personal Medium-in-Residence

Having consulted with oracle cards for several years now, I can attest to them being a singularly effective way of providing our loved ones in the angelic realm with the means to communicate with us—especially, I've found, when used in conjunction with a regular meditation regimen.

Back in chapter one, we mentioned how losing our partner was described by author Madeleine L'Engle as being akin to losing a limb. Then later on we discussed the difficulties of coping with life's daily challenges single-handedly, with job-sharing no longer an option.

Since I've been consulting with the cards, I've found the messages of encouragement and moral support we receive through them, to be of tremendous help in both nullifying these added burdens and alleviating those disheartening feelings of aloneness the bereaved endure.

Mediums and psychics tell us that when the spirits attempt to convey a message to us using a sign, and it fails to resonate with us, they will "raise their voice" so to speak, by repeating it. If that doesn't work, and they repeat it a third time, they are in effect, yelling their heads off. And so it is with the way in which they manipulate the cards, I soon found.

For instance, drawing the same card on consecutive days means that we've replaced the card in the deck after the first time, then on the following day, after thoroughly shuffling the deck we've drawn the same card again. That is quite interesting enough, but *then*, when the same thing happens a *third* day—well, it should be patently obvious that someone has something important to tell us—and like the mediums tell us, they're yelling their heads off. It was this aspect, that sold me on oracle cards, and it's far from being limited to three. The streak of consecutive times that the same card is drawn can continue for several days—when that happens we just *have* to know that it's not a random coincidence—there *is* someone on the other end of the line. And they have a message that it would be to our benefit to listen to.

How about the same card 76 times in 78 days? That was the rate at which a certain card showed up for me—now that, by any measure, is simply astounding. Especially when, over the 269 days prior to that, it had only shown up 21 times. That was a whole lot of yelling—and yet again, Carl Jung's "astronomical figure" quote come to mind.

Naturally, I can't speak for anyone else or even for any of the other card decks available, but these are the two decks that I strongly felt I was "led to." I've believed, since being gifted with so many successful readings, that we *are* led by our guides to various life-activities and experiences for specific reasons and although it might be difficult for us to comprehend at the time, we just have to trust implicitly that this is the case and that it will all make perfect sense in due course.

I'd like to share with you then, some of my experiences with the two sets that I felt I'd been led to. They are Sonia Choquette's *Ask Your Guides* deck and her *The Answer is Simple* deck. I'm hoping these accounts help explain why oracle cards, in their varied forms, are still going strong after hundreds of years, and also explain why I told Sonia that "It's like my wife is in the room with me." To which she answered "Reggie—she *is*."

I should clarify that the quotes referred to in my accounts are only brief pertinent excerpts taken from the respective guide book entries—the actual guide book descriptions are far more extensive.

*"Celebrate You"*

I've found that the message a chosen card imparts can, despite initially appearing to be obscure and ill-defined, turn out to be predictive in nature when we discover later that it held the key to aid us in resolving a vexatious situation. This was the case in the two following examples.

For three or four days, I'd been quagmired in one of those "deep blue funks" we bereaved can become all too familiar with. On two consecutive days of this spell though, I'd drawn the card titled *Celebrate You* from *The Answer is Simple* deck. It counselled the recipient to "Acknowledge your efforts and feel great about what you've accomplished......" My unspoken response to that, in my depressed state, had been "Phooey—I've never accomplished a thing."

Later that morning I received a call from an art dealer who'd acquired an original illustration I'd done some years before. He'd learned that it was one of six I'd painted of an attractive Gulf Beach Resort and wanted to know if I'd kept any copies of the others to help him in tracking them down. I was finding it aggravatingly impossible to be creative right now and the idea of getting away from the board for a while appealed to me.

So, for the first time in ages, I found myself ploughing through half a dozen photo albums of my work over a three years period. I'm almost embarrassed to admit it, but after a while I gradually began to realize that I was becoming genuinely impressed, not only by the number of paintings I'd churned out, but the quality of them—it was blooming good stuff.

After two hours I'd located the prints the gentleman wanted, and looking over them while savoring a freshly brewed pot of English

## These Are a Few of My Favorite Signs

comfort (Earl Grey Tea), I became aware that the ugly black cloud of despair had not only more or less dissipated but was palpably being replaced by a pleasurable feeling of satisfaction with the world.

It dawned on me that, just as the card had counseled—I'd unwittingly acknowledged my efforts and was feeling great about what I'd accomplished—thanks to the fortuitous timely prompting of a stranger asking for my help.

This next example turned out to be another case of the cards prophetically providing a welcome spirit-lifting piece of advice. Joani, a friend of mine, came by the house one afternoon with a birthday gift for me. While I was making cups of tea for us, she came into the kitchen holding up one of my oracle cards, and asked "Is there any special reason behind this being propped up in your writing space?"

*'Just Laugh"*

It was a card I'd drawn from the *The Answer is Simple* deck that morning. It's titled simply *Just Laugh*, and shows a laughing child happily popping open a Jack-in-the-box toy. The opening sentence of its guide-book description reads "It's time to brighten your mood." The advice couldn't have been more timely, because having felt down in the dumps for a day or two, it served to remind me that that was exactly what I needed to do, and that was the reason I'd decided to keep it in front of me all day.

When I explained this to her, she smiled, and without taking her eyes off me, reached into the gift-bag she'd been holding, while saying "That's a cute picture, but I think the real thing will work much better," as she handed me a resplendent colorfully decorated classic Jack-in-the-box—uncannily similar to the one depicted on the card. She explained that she'd sensed I was feeling down when we'd met a few days before, and thought of me later when she'd come across it in a store. I chalked-up another "hit" for the cards.

I wouldn't want to give the impression though that predictive messages conveyed by the cards are all sweetness and light, and confined only to the "perfect world" expressions we *want* to hear. There *can* be a "real world" aspect to them—foreboding and ominous at times perhaps, but never lacking in love and always with affirmative assurances of a successful outcome. As the following example illustrates, they're really nothing more than an informed "heads-up" that a challenge of some kind may be in the offing, that we may want to prepare ourselves for. I think this "real world" aspect gives a healthy credence to the oracle card process—we wouldn't want to think of them as being the result of a Pollyanna and Mary Poppins collaboration after all.

*"Suffering/Divine Teachers"*

I have to admit to wishing they had been though on the morning I drew the card titled *Suffering/Divine Teachers* from the *Ask Your Guides Deck*. "Sickness may be at hand…" and "…your physical body may be challenged and pain may follow," were just two of the daunting phrases that jumped off the page of it's guide book page—Yikes. I suppose I could have spent the rest of the day in the house, cocooned in a cozy corner, but I had some shrub-trimming to do.

The following day, an area on my arm appeared slightly inflamed, swollen and itchy but that was only to be expected after pruning back the notoriously thorny bougainvillea.

Well, I can't say I wasn't warned. Forty eight hours later I was in a hospital room with tubes attached to me, I was receiving intravenous injections of several antibiotics—my arm having blown up to twice it's size due, I was told, to a severe infection—from a scratch or insect bite.

## These Are a Few of My Favorite Signs

The upshot of this episode was, my firm conviction in the cards being a vehicle by which communications from spirit are conveyed to us remained justifiably intact.

*"Family/Holy Spirit"*

I've found the most highly valued cards I've drawn have been those that carry a comforting message of assurance during times of stress and anxiety, particularly when they arrive at the very moment we need them most, as they most always do. As was the case in the following instance.

I suspect it's a universal truth that we parents never stop being concerned over our children's safety and welfare—it's what we do and continue to do long after they've "left the nest." So I was no exception to the rule when the region where my Bahamian-born, Florida-raised daughter Bev lives, was being subjected to one of the worst winter snowstorms in living memory. Power outages were widespread, a driving ban, together with an official state of emergency were in effect. This was serious stuff—naturally, father was somewhat anxious.

At the height of this, after my evening meditation, I drew my customary single card from the *Ask your Guides* deck. It was the card titled *Family/Holy Spirit*. The operative phrase that leapt off its guide book page said: "There's no need to fret over your children's safety. All is well." Is it any wonder I often refer to my card drawing sessions as "My goose bump break"?

There have been many other occasions when that same assuring phrase on this card has obligingly lowered my anxiety level. For instance, Bev makes business trips by plane from time to time, and of course I get apprehensive whenever I hear reports of chaotic airport

*The Direct Connect*

situations and flight delays due to adverse weather conditions. But I don't think there's ever been a time when I've failed to draw the *Family* card during such times—there have even been occasions when I've drawn it when I had no way of knowing that she was even traveling.

*Purpose/Master Teacher*

Messages of assurance and caring are delivered to me on a regular basis in a variety of ways, and always pertinent to what's going on my life at that moment. One card in particular has long been a recurrent theme at weekends—Friday evenings and Saturdays. The sender is obviously familiar with my bordering-on-workaholic tendencies (I wonder who *that* could be).

The card is from the *Ask Your Guides Deck* and titled *Purpose/Master Teacher*. It assures me that throwing my heart and soul into my efforts "will pay off in the long run." But then goes on to advise me to not "overlook the importance of taking a day of rest at least once a week." Interestingly, it's final admonition "Pace yourself," has also been delivered to me in two readings with mediums over the past three years, after confirming that it was my wife coming through.

*Give Yourself the Best*

Since my wife made her transition, it's become the "family" tradition for my daughter and I to spend every Christmas week together. Our itinerary for the two days before "the day" usually follows the same pleasurable pattern of self-indulgent activities. Typically, dining well at our favorite restaurants—shopping—an evening at the theater—maybe a theme park etc.

*The Answer Is Simple* deck contains a card which is a veritable salute to self-indulgence titled *Give Yourself the Best*. It advises us to ignore our ego when it suggests we're not worthy of the best, and

## These Are a Few of My Favorite Signs

give it to ourselves. Then offers a litany of suggestions—the best and most nutritious food—the best clothes—the best of entertainment and so on and so on.

The fact that I, unbelievably, drew that card on the evening before our scheduled spree and again the following morning, would suggest that "someone" wished to acknowledge that she was thoroughly familiar with our annual tradition and wanted us to know that not only did she approve, but that she would be there enjoying it all along with us.

*Thank God*

This final example of oracle card magic illustrates how a message can sometimes be embodied in the artwork that embellishes the cards and be just as psychically significant as any written description of it.

Thanksgiving Day is inarguably a wonderful holiday—a joyous family celebration. But with it's emphasis on family get-togethers, it's a notorious bugaboo day for the bereaved—with their families having been rended asunder. The mere prospect of it can have we "aloners" wishing we could fast-forward through it. Accordingly, a few years ago, determined to avoid the disasters of previous years, I decided I'd spend the day at a relatively little known stretch of beach about sixty miles along the coast.

So, equipped with a cooler chest, carrying an "almost' traditional Thanksgiving feast, plus a great book, great music and a comfortable lounger chair, I spent a splendid day on a quintessential tropical palm-fringed beach. With perfect weather—calm ocean—a sailboat just offshore and surprisingly, a dozen or so fellow "aloners." All resulting in what was by far the best Thanksgiving I'd experienced since my wife's passing.

After arriving home that evening, I drew my usual single card from *The Answer Is Simple* deck, and I thought it's title—*Thank God* was singularly apt for the day—the accompanying text too was germane to Thanksgiving. However, it was the *illustration* on the card that *really* caught my attention, it showed a lone Robinson Crusoe type of character, on a tropical palm-fringed beach, fronting a calm ocean with a sailing ship off shore and the about-to-be-rescued Crusoe on his knees offering a prayerful thanks to God.

There couldn't have been a more literal pictorial rendition of my day—minus my picnic hamper of course, and I took it as a definite message acknowledging that I'd actually attended a Thanksgiving Day family get-together after all.

So those are just a few of my experiences with oracle cards. Back in the first chapter, we discussed how burdensome it often is for the bereaved to have been dispossessed of the benefits of job-sharing—that aspect of our aloneness is a cruelly constant reminder of our loved one's absence that can greatly encumber our recovery. I hope I've been able to demonstrate how being gifted each day with such compelling evidence of our loved one's presence in our daily life, through the cards, can negate this hindrance to our progress and help in substantially lightening our load on our journey back to wholeness.

In this next sign segment, I'll share a few examples of signs I've received that show that carrier pigeons aren't the only members of the animal kingdom who deliver messages.

## Animal Signs

I had no way of knowing it at the time, but the following incident was my initiation into the field of animal totemism that we discussed briefly in the previous chapter. Having lived for a number of years

## These Are a Few of My Favorite Signs

adjacent to a small lake that attracts numerous species of shore birds, waders, pelicans, ducks etc., it's possible I'd already been the unwitting recipient of animal signs—but in my ignorance hadn't recognized them as such.

About eighteen months after my wife's passing, I returned home one lunchtime from a business meeting and pulled onto the drive. After gathering together an assortment of sketches and documents from the passenger seat, I turned and started to open the door to get out but abruptly slammed it shut again.

The reason being, from out of nowhere, seemingly, but now standing just inches away from me, was a Great Blue Heron—his huge head level with mine, with a long pointed bill and a large eye staring piercingly at me. This was much too "up-close-and-personal" for my comfort—I had no intention of leaving the safety of my car with him around, I'd often seen how they can strike with lightning speed to snare their supper—that bill could put your eye out for goodness sake.

After about twenty minutes of trying to induce him to leave by banging on the window and honking the horn, all to no avail. I finally decided to end this "Mexican standoff" and scooted over to the passenger side door and hightailed it out of there to the relative safety of my front porch—hoping I wouldn't see him again.

Returning from my morning walk two days later, I noticed that several shrubs at the side of the house needed trimming back and fetched the hedge shears from the garage to deal with them. I'd been leaning over and clipping away for about ten minutes when I became aware of an eerie feeling of being watched. As I was gingerly straightening up I was half expecting it would be a neighbor, but as I started turning to look round I almost jumped out my skin.

## The Direct Connect

Standing not more than a foot and a half away was a Great Blue Heron—the same one I presumed. Whether it was from a flustered nervousness or what, I have no idea, but I found myself mindlessly saying "Hello mate—you again?" followed by me inexplicably blathering on about something or other as if I was channeling Doctor Doolittle.

After ten minutes of my best stuff—either out of sheer boredom with my material, or he had more important things to do—he turned and walked dignifiedly away (I get that a lot).

At that time remember, I had no knowledge of totemism whatsoever, or that when animals behave outside of what we know to be their character, it's often because they are the bearers of messages from the spirit realm. My enlightenment on the subject though was in the offing.

When I told my friend Simon about the heron incidents over lunch the following day, it turned out that he had some knowledge of totemism. Apparently he'd been gifted with a book on the subject the previous Christmas, but hadn't had time to do more than casually leaf through it. I received it in the mail a few days later, as promised.

It was Andrea Wansbury's *Birds: Divine Messengers*. Attached to the cover was a note from Simon that read: "Re our conversation of the other day—it seems that heron had a message for both of us Reg—see page 115."

The listing he'd referenced dealt specifically with herons and what it means when they come into close proximity to us. The sentence he'd highlighted said "...you have isolated yourself from others, and now is the time to re-establish friendships or to pursue a social life."

The uncanny relevance of this observation wasn't lost on either of us. You see, having both lost our wives a few weeks apart, we'd been getting together now and then for lunch—a "birds-of-a-feather" kind of link, and would inevitably wind up comparing notes on how we were coping without our wives. It's almost as if someone had been eavesdropping on our most recent conversation that took place ten days before my first encounter of the bird kind, because it had mainly centered around a situation we were both grappling with—the lamentable isolation of widowhood. The result of, as we noted earlier in the book, the social "invisibility" and "stiff-arming" to which the bereaved are often subjected. And to which, thanks to our heron friend, were both now receiving a timely "psychic nudge" to make an effort to do something about.

There have been numerous other times since, when I've had occasion to consult with *Birds: Divine Messengers* following instances of "birds behaving oddly"—with ducks often being the message bearers. Ms. Wansbury tells us that the unusual behavior or closeness of a duck can be a sign that we "...are being reminded that there is always Divine spiritual support." and also that "...your angels and spirit guides are always there guiding and protecting you," ( Mickey and Minnie were so relieved to learn that).

There have been many occasions when I've had good cause to be mindful of these comforting assurances when ducks acting out-of-character around me has coincided with spells of low-spiritedness. For instance, when three ducks took up residence for nine days under a shrub just three feet from my front door. Then there were two occasions, on the same day, when a duck came flying directly at me at head height, for some distance before veering off sharply in a flurry of feathers—that certainly got my attention. Maybe that's how they got the name "duck."

The message this next bird gifted me with was as 'on-point' as any I've ever received.

I'd had an idea for a series of whimsical illustrations and had pitched it to a client who had responded to them favorably enough as to encourage me to develop a set of sketches at a higher level. Whenever work didn't call for the studio facilities, I liked to work outdoors on the screened-in deck overlooking the lake, so that had been where I'd been engrossed, hunched over my sketch-pads for most of the morning. After about three hours, I received a phone call from a neighbor who asked me if I was aware that I'd had an audience for at least the past hour, and suggested I turn round. Sure enough, there was my audience—two large Wood Storks. Standing motionless, up-close to the screen and studying me intently from about six feet away—looking for all the world like a pair of art connoisseurs one might see at the Louvre.

I could hardly wait to see what Andrea Wansbury had to say about my "groupies"—I wasn't disappointed. She says: "The stork may be telling you that you have a talent in the creative arts and now is the time to start using your abilities. If you have good ideas in your mind, now is the time to give birth to them and bring them into physical reality."

I can't imagine that anyone could read about this fascinating subject and ever look at any kind of animal in the same way again—it really is astonishing.

This final example also happens to involve a bird, but not the feathered variety this time. I was not involved in this at all, but the lady who was, Marilee is a friend of mine and it's such a classic that she's kindly agreed to let me share it.

Marilee had been deeply anguished, naturally, by the passing of her beloved mother Mary Ann, with whom she had always been extremely close. One day, with her thoughts dwelling on how much she missed her mother, she recalled having read and heard accounts about bereaved people asking their departed loved ones for a physical sign of some kind—a butterfly for instance, and actually having their requests and prayers answered. So with nothing to lose, she decided to give it a try. After giving it considerable thought, she settled on a sign that she thought would be kind of out of the ordinary, not too commonplace—a ladybird. And moreover, that it would be delivered within the next three days ( She has some nerve, that Marilee).

Consequently, whenever she was outdoors (which she made sure was often) over the following two days she scanned every surface in sight—hardly a shrub, leaf, or twig escaped her scrutiny—as she tried to "intend" a ladybird into existence. On deadline day, when she drove into the parking lot across the street from her office, she purposely parked in the furthermost space, then sauntered slowly around the landscaped perimeter taking everything in. But again— not a thing. "I suppose it just wasn't meant to be," she thought to herself as she dejectedly made her way to the crosswalk leading to the office where she'd be penned up for the rest of the day, well away from anywhere a ladybird was ever likely to be seen.

She actually welcomed having to wait for the pedestrian light to change—she could use the time to work on clearing the fog of utter despondence that overwhelmed her right now.

She was abruptly shaken out of this meditative state however, by the roar of a bus that suddenly came barreling around the bend in her direction. As she quickly stepped back from the curb, shocked and glaring at the perpetrator, she could hardly believe her eyes—printed along its side was the most resplendently beautiful ladybird she'd ever seen.

## The Direct Connect

Marilee continues to be gifted with signs from her mom, but apparently, having got her attention so dramatically, she no longer sees the need for such flamboyancy. Opting instead for something more low-key—in the form of a three digit number. It shows up in her life with amazing frequency, and in an astonishing array of ways, for instance even in the hospital where her grandchild came into the world. When her excited brand-new-papa son called to break the news, he told her that at some point during the proceedings the digital wall-clock in the delivery room had stopped—but it wasn't showing the customary 12:00 flashing on and off, instead, it was displaying their familiar three digit number, with its "Hi, I'm here" message from formerly mom, and now—great-grandmother.

A set of specific numbers of significance were also the way through which Michel, my dear and valued friend of forty years or more, received a sign, from his beloved wife in spirit, Florence, a few years ago. For several years since her passing, by way of paying homage to her, Michel had been using a password that consisted of the numbers that made up her birth date, something no one else had any knowledge of, of course. When Michel decided to relocate to a different area some years after he'd lost Florence, his youngest son agreed to be at the new home when the telephone company came out to connect him up. When the engineer had completed the hook-up Sebastian called his father to give him his new number, which a stunned Michel took down with understandable disbelief—they were the same birth date numbers.

"This just in," as the newscasters say. While I was writing actually this passage I received a "Hi" message. One of my reference sources for correct grammar usage is an excellent website called *Word Hippo*. Just two minutes ago I referred to its "Words in a sentence" section to check on the word "homage"—should it be "homage *to*" or "homage *for*?" It responded with seven examples, the second of which said *"And we're content to think that we're paying homage to the good people of Florence."*

What where the odds of that being the result of a random coincidence? As Jung said: "an astronomical figure." And it wasn't as if this was an isolated connection, Michel has been gifted with many visitations from Florence over the years, experiences of such intensity that they leave him with a highly detailed and pleasurable impression that lasts for weeks afterwards. Another connection occurred after a telephone conversation we had several years ago, in which he'd excitedly told me that he'd just acquired his first laptop computer. During a reading filled with accurate factual references the following day, with medium Joanne Gerber, she told me that my wife had come through with another lady who had shoulder-length wavy blonde hair and who was saying something about a laptop, and smiling while holding one up to show her.

## My Golden Crown Affair

I regard the following incident to be the most notable of any sign I've yet been gifted with. If there was one sign that I could credit with making a true believer out of me—this was surely it—my golden crown of signs. The brief sequence of events occurred just short of two years after my wife's passing.

I'd finally succeeded in getting more or less back up to speed with my illustration work, my energy level and motivation were coming back and nice assignments were flowing in a steady stream once more. Unfortunately, my productivity was being frustratingly hindered by an allergic rash on what I call "my money-digits,"—the thumb, index

## The Direct Connect

and middle fingers with which we grip brushes and pens etc. All area dermatologists I'd called were booked solid for weeks ahead, and the ointments I'd tried had hardly helped at all. My fingers had become so sore and tender by now it was seriously affecting my ability to achieve the finely detailed brushwork this particular multi-billion dollar theme park project demanded. Furthermore, the pieces I was working on were crucial to the presentation in Tokyo in ten days time and I was falling behind schedule.

This was the predicament I was meditating on one morning as I was robotically going through my morning chores preparing for my day at the office. I was finishing up, when out of the blue I recalled something a medium friend had once told me. He said he'd learned from the spirits that they are available at any time with guidance to help us with life's challenges at any time—providing it's consistent with our soul path and our soul growth. And all that's required of us is to explain specifically what our needs are, then simply leave the matter with them, put it out of our mind if we can, and then go about our day.

So that's what I did. Talking to my wife's portrait over the mantel, I explained my situation (as if she didn't already know), and asked her that if she knew of any other ointments around the house to please lead me to them, then I headed for the studio—via the kitchen.

By way of the kitchen, because that's where I keep the visor I have to wear to shield my eyes from the glare of the lights I work by and that are positioned just inches away. I can't work on these kinds of paintings without it so I've made it a habit to leave it on the corner of the kitchen island nearest to the studio, so that I always know where to find it.

When I reached for it this time though, it wasn't there—even though I *knew* it had been there earlier. There are only ever two other items on that countertop once the meal preparation paraphernalia has been put away—a bowl of fruit and the current book I'm reading, on which I place the visor. In the event I *had* misplaced it, it would be the first and only time.

A forty minute search of all the places it could conceivably be yielded nothing except more frustration. But I did get a sudden flash of an idea that there may possibly be another visor somewhere, one that had belonged to my wife. It was a long shot because by then I'd donated my wife's clothes to a couple of local church thrift stores—but I vaguely recalled a visor she'd only worn two or three times, and incredibly I could now picture it and its location in my mind.

I opened a drawer in the dressing room vanity somewhat gingerly, I was still vulnerable to those dreaded waves of mournfulness when I came across any of her things. But I needn't have worried, amazingly, there was only one thing in there—a visor—a pretty thing, decorated with rainbow colored dolphins.

As if that wasn't amazing enough however, something infinitely more so was awaiting me when I picked it up. Lying underneath it was a white tube, and on it, in bold red letters were the words *LOTIL CREAM—For Skin Rashes*. To say I was nonplussed as I donned my new visor and walked back through the kitchen would be greatly understating my response. Even that was about to pale however in comparison to the sight that greeted me when, as I was passing, I reflexively glanced at the countertop—because *there*, where it hadn't been three minutes before—*was my original visor!*

This extraordinary turn of events was, for me, irrefutable proof of my wife's presence. And all aspects of it had been so wholly consistent with her nurturing nature and caring personality.

Those were qualities of hers I was naturally thoroughly familiar with. But conjuring tricks? Well, honestly—you think you know somebody.

No matter what form signs take—and whether we rate them as being of huge significance or just barely so, each and everyone is a full-blown miraculous gift. A divine, exquisitely crafted expression of deep abiding love that our loved ones have worked diligently to deliver to us. They can undoubtedly play an incalculable remedial role in the healing they desperately desire for us.

In the next chapter we'll discuss various other recuperative measures we can adopt to also assist us on our path back to wholeness.

CHAPTER 10
# DIY RECUPERATIVE MEASURES

Having devoted a large portion of the book so far to what I regard as by far the most compelling restorative of all to our recovery—knowledge of the afterlife and the ongoing role our loved ones in spirit play in our lives, in this chapter I'd like to discuss a few augmentative steps that we can also adopt to assist us on our road back to wholeness.

These measures that I'm putting forward are in no way intended to replace, conflict with or in any way challenge the universally acknowledged immutable stages of grief that the bereaved are required to go through. Grief experts and counselors are in accord that grieving in a way that's correct for us, is itself a task so formidable that it warrants us giving it the first order of priority over everything else—graduating from this level is a must if we're to progress further.

## *The Direct Connect*

There are many excellent books on the subject of healing grief, and they're written by experts who are inordinately better qualified than I to offer advice on coping with this most formidable of tasks, the critical grief-stricken period when we're so severely debilitated. So it's with respect and reverence, plus a modicum of shameless cowardice, that I'll skirt the "intensive care" stages and leave you in their hands. I'll skip to sharing the measures I *do* feel qualified to discuss, the steps I found to be effective in helping *me* through the ensuing period of recovery that we're also required to navigate on our road to accepting our loss, our return to wholeness and the meaningful life our loved ones in spirit fervently desire for us.

The books written by the eminently qualified grief experts, teach us how to best deal with the various early stages of grief that have become the universally accepted "five stages of grief." These were first introduced by Elisabeth Kubler-Ross in her seminal book *On Death and Dying,* published in 1969, and comprise stages of denial—anger—bargaining—depression and acceptance (not necessarily always in that order), and they remain the "gold standard" to this day.

Earlier, in the Introduction, I described the chain of synchronistic circumstances that led me to James Van Praagh's book—*Healing Grief,* which proved to be the gateway to the support and encouragement *I'd* been seeking. That experience, together with what I've learned since from the mediums, prompts me to suggest that when we're confronted by the dizzying array of books available on the subject, we relax and stay mindful of the distinct probability that our loved ones, responding to our needs, will lovingly create and orchestrate ways of guiding us to *the* book, or books, they know to be the most suitable for us at this time.

## DIY Recuperative Measures

I believe that studying the experts' books before embarking on any measures like those we'll be discussing could very well be some of the most crucially important reading we've ever done, so with that in mind we should ensure we get the best return on our investment of book study time—a few thoughts about which I'd like to share.

"Hitting the books" may be something we haven't been involved in for a while, so an adjustment of our reading techniques and habits may be called for. Many of us for instance, conditioned by the daily deluge of emails and text messages, have gotten into the habit of treating any form of the printed word to little more than a begrudging cursory glance at best—as if we're fearful that letting any content of substance sink in would lead to complications we don't need.

Absorbing and inwardly digesting what we read calls for us to focus on, and give due consideration to what we're reading, it helps if we mark relevant passages using a system, like "XXXX's" in the margins, or using various highlight colors or underlining, to denote their comparative degrees of significance. This makes it much easier to review later, which we'd be well advised to get into the habit of doing—again and again—in order for the information to embed itself in our subconscious and allow us to derive lasting benefits from our reading. Repetition, repetition, repetition *does* work—just ask anyone in the advertising industry.

Back now to our proposed measures. The debilitative effects of our grieving condition can physically and emotionally benumb us to such an extent that it will be a while before we feel motivated enough to even *think* about getting involved in any recuperative activities. This connotes action and an expenditure of energy, at a time when, in our thoroughly depressed and lethargic state, and with our emotional

*The Direct Connect*

and physical resources already stretched to their limits, it's all we can do to get through our day.

When we *do* feel motivated to do something, it's important to do so at a pace *we're* comfortable with, be patient for instance and ignore outside pressures such as other peoples' naive preconceived notions on how long our recovery should take and their insensitive exhortations to "get over it." It's also perfectly okay to take things easy and not feel guilty about resting when we feel exhausted—be self-nurturing, you know—be our own best friend.

In his novel *The Silver Chair*, C. S. Lewis makes this observation about the transitional stage that we face when we've put the worst behind us. He wrote: "Crying is all right in its way while it lasts. But you have to stop sooner or later, and then you still have to decide what to do."

Although we'll find that the crying doesn't just conveniently stop on command, like he seems to be simplistically implying, there does come a time when, allowing for some overlapping, we have to at least start giving some thought to what our options are and give some thought to what we want to do.

In the course of time, our faculties and our survival instincts will be restored, and our vibrational energy raised. As a consequence we're now more likely to be bolstered by our spirit guides and helpers, who will help us prevail over this unnatural condition. In response to the telepathic urging and support of our ever-present cheering-section in spirit, we'll muster the required resolve to shake off the fragility that's frustratingly impeded us and supplant it with a desire and commitment to do whatever it takes. With our new-found mental clarity though, we'll also sense that realistically, no one—no one outside of ourselves anyway, can do this for us. We've arrived at the

## DIY Recuperative Measures

moment of decision stage to which Mr Lewis referred when he said "we have to decide what to do."

What I'll be sharing with you is a compilation of the things *I* eventually started doing when I'd, more or less, stopped crying—they were garnered from all manner of sources over a year or so. They include one or two that I rejected after a reasonable period of "road-testing," but I included them anyway because various friends felt that they helped *them*. I'm not suggesting for a minute that these are the *only* ways to go, they just happen to be what I'd strongly felt I'd been "led to," and I'm certainly not suggesting they're better than the measures or paths to recovery that anyone is already following and has a preference for. With all of us being so different to each other, and with our individual grieving situations consisting of such a multiplicity of factors, there plainly is no "one size fits all" here and certainly no "magic pill."

While I was mulling over this aspect when I was planning this chapter, it occurred to me that there's a marked similarity here between this approach and the healing modality that's currently gaining in popularity known as holistic healing—holistic clinics are springing up all over.

In contrast to conventional western mainstream medicine, which has traditionally tended to focus on treating just the *symptoms* of a condition, holistic medicine, in an effort to get down to the *root cause* of the ailment, takes the *whole person* into consideration. Factors such as physical, emotional, spirituality, life-style, to name just a few, are taken into account. Resulting in the prescribing of a broad array of alternative and integrative healing disciplines, and includes such things as nutrition and diet, physiotherapy, acupuncture, homeopathy, reflexology, aromatherapy and even our friend meditation, to name just a few. Pretty much whatever is deemed to be required to effect a more permanent healing.

So, I suppose this is our introductory course to "Holistic Grief Healing 101."

With the exception of the first two, the measures are not in any order of importance, and I'd be very surprised if they all appealed to everyone—we all have different needs—but I'm confident a majority of them will. They're all intended to be flexible, allowing us to be creative and cobble them together into what amounts to our own customized curriculum. A personalized graduate program we're free to carry out at our own pace and not beholden to considerations such as "semester credit hours" and "grade point average tables." Just a self-monitoring of how we *feel*, and no one is more qualified to be the arbiter of that than we ourselves.

Of all the pieces of advice I received from well-meaning friends during those crushingly agonizing months after my wife made her transition, the one that proved to be the most helpful was the simple suggestion to "stay busy." Apparently, the literary icon Mark Twain found this to be a remedial aid for *his* grief after his treasured daughter Susy died of meningitis at the age of 24 in the summer of 1896. For the rest of his life, he referred to it as the most devastating loss of his life. In the following January, in a letter to his close friend the Rev. Joseph Twitchell, he wrote: "I am working, but it is for the sake of the work—the 'surcease of sorrow' that is found there. I work all the days, and trouble vanishes away when I use that magic...."

Most of the measures I'll be discussing are, as an added bonus, wholly consistent with Mr. Twain's explanation of how focusing our attention on projects and tasks can magically distance us from the grievous thoughts that unrelentingly beleaguer us.

In our grievously depleted state we can easily convince ourselves that the colorless and totally joyless grind in which we've become enmeshed, defines how our life is destined to be like from now on. So it's possible that the mere thought of taking part in an activity of any kind can be daunting. When that's the case, one proven way of surmounting this hurdle is to work at *faking* enthusiasm—"fake it 'til you make it." the slogan goes, it's a confidence building and positive reinforcement therapy technique that's been borne out in many studies.

Mark Twain also had a suggestion on the subject for us, he said: "The secret of getting started is breaking your complex overwhelming tasks into small manageable tasks, and then starting on the first one." Even that man-of-few-words President "Silent Cal" Coolidge splurged on a few words on the subject when he said: "We cannot do *everything* at once, but we can do *something* at once." (Multi-tasking had yet to insinuate itself apparently).

Once we *are* able to get rolling, it's imperative that we adopt and maintain an attitude of single-mindedness. We'll no doubt encounter set-backs—periodic bad days are inevitable—but when we experience them we have to summon up the resolve to "soldier on." As the illustrious great man Sir Winston Churchill told us, in his trade-mark forthright manner: "If you're going through hell, keep going."

A determined stick-to-itiveness is required of us, and I well remember a remarkable young lady who had a unique take on that. She was a guest some years ago on *The Tonight Show Starring Johnny Carson* following her feat of becoming the first woman to climb the formidable sheer granite face of El Capitan in The Yosemite National Park—an amazing accomplishment, and a gruelingly lengthy one.

## The Direct Connect

Johnny asked her what kind of thoughts were going through her head during all those long, lonely arduous hours, and her response has stayed with me ever since. She told him that what had kept her going more than anything else was repeating over and over something her father had once told her: "You eat an elephant one spoonful at a time." I've had occasion to call on those words many times over the years, they've served me well whenever I've been faced by *my* "El Capitans"—insanely unrealistic deadlines in which to produce an equally insane amount of work. Which of course I always succeeded in doing—one brushstroke at a time.

Regarding the genesis of the measures I'll be discussing, it was when the heavy cloying pea-soup fogginess of grief began to intermittently dissipate and the crying began tapering off that I started to notice blocks of media coverage dealing with a wide range of health and fitness matters crossing my path in curiously synchronistic ways. Enlightening television segments, articles in reception area magazines, product brochures in my mail, casual conversations with strangers, snatches of conversations overheard, website links emailed by friends with whom I hadn't been in contact for ages.

It's difficult to explain, but there was a certain commonality about the way they resonated with me, the meaningful way they all pertained to my personal situation and the coincidental ways I'd come across them. Then one evening, following my meditation, the notion came to me to compile a list of them. And again, that sense of something special in the air—despite the fact that these incidents had spread over a year or more, remembrance of them came flooding in at such a rapid pace that I had trouble keeping up. There simply had to be some kind of Divine involvement here because this hard-drive between my ears has become quite clogged with information by now and my powers of retrieval no longer respond with the greased lightning promptness they once did—this clearly transcended what has frustratingly become my norm.

By the time I'd completed the list of health and fitness exercises, there was no doubt in my mind that I'd been the beneficiary of spirit guidance because this was nothing less than a list of recuperative measures that were uniquely applicable to my situation. I was left with a strong sense that I'd been given my marching orders and I'd be well advised to follow through on them. Sure enough, when I subsequently began putting them into practice, it wasn't long before their remedial benefits became apparent and I made them my daily regimen.

The experience, for me, has served to underscore the value of staying mindful of what those in the spirit realm have told us repeatedly in readings—that we are never alone and they will always be there for us whenever we need them. An assertion that itself, when we stay mindful of it, is immeasurably comforting and spiritually sustaining.

We've also seen in the preceding chapters how the spirits have this extraordinary ability to orchestrate the most convoluted and exquisitely timed synchronistic connections between people, objects, and locations in order to bring forth a seemingly boundless array of magical outcomes. So it surely behooves us to stay alert to the possibility that anyone, or any thing, that comes into our orbit is potentially delivering a message from them designed to guide us to specific measures we can take that they know will assist us greatly in our recovery.

I met a lady named Nora at a Spiritualist Church event a couple of years ago who told me how glad she was that *she'd* been alert to this process when she'd been in deep mourning over her mother's passing.

## The Direct Connect

She remains convinced that her mother had been responsible for the synchronistic way by which she was guided to an activity that she'd previously regarded as nothing more than yet another passing fad, but that surprisingly turned out to be the thing she credits most for helping her eventually cope and come to terms with her loss.

It all stemmed from one of the ways in which she'd memorialized her mother. For years, her mom's pride and joy had been the beautiful display of African violets she kept on the sill of the deep bay window off the kitchen dining nook. After her passing Nora had learned about caring for violets and had lovingly maintained them ever since, the protective cover on the sill though badly needed replacing and she'd been unable to locate a suitable material.

On the recommendation of a friend her search took her one day to a department store in the next town, a store she'd never visited before. She'd barely got through the doors on entering when her eyes were drawn to a display of colorful panels of some kind. When she went over to take a closer look, she discovered that they were made of a rubberized material—not only ideal for her needs, but one of them in her mother's favorite dusky pink color.

It wasn't until a lady behind her in the check-out line said "Oh, I see you're into yoga too," that she learned she was about to become the owner of a yoga mat of all things. The lady's ensuing testimony to the many wonderful benefits of yoga, resulted in Nora's conversion, the purchase of another mat and her enrollment the following day in a yoga course.

She's been delighted with the healing powers of her regular yoga class and, having no doubts at all that she has her mom to thank for orchestrating it, sends a prayer of gratitude to her every day. The following measures are the ones I know *I* was similarly guided to.

## Suggested Measures: Our Health Matters

We saw in chapter 1 how the stress stemming from our bereavement can severely compromise our immune system, leaving us vulnerable to a whole range of physical disorders. So it follows that the level of our general health, being of paramount importance, should be the first thing we address regardless of what other steps or measures we feel guided to.

Consulting with a doctor would be beneficial of course, but particularly one who is qualified to advise us on the curative benefits of vitamins, supplements and an optimum diet regimen. Most doctors of osteopathy (DO's) are ideal in this regard because although they are equally as qualified as MD's, they also practice a holistic approach to healing and regard the body as an integrated whole. I'm fortunate to have been blessed for many years with a brilliant DO doctor.

Good health food stores normally carry a line of unique and effective natural medicinals called *Bach Flower Essences* several of which can help we bereaved in coping with and overcome our emotional pain. They are the result of years of extensive research and testing carried out in Oxfordshire, England in the 1930's by Dr. E. Bach, formerly a distinguished Harley Street consultant for over 20 years. They work by gently correcting those emotional and psychological imbalances that can adversely affect our physical health and impede our recovery from illness. They are entirely safe, benign and completely compatible with other medicines and are used worldwide with great success by medical practitioners and the general public alike.

Consisting of 38 homeopathically prepared essences derived from the flowers of wild plants, trees and shrubs, each one is specifically designed to restore balance to emotional discords including those the bereaved are only too familiar with—the ones resulting from the traumatic psychological stress we've been subjected to. Brochures are available where the essences are sold that comprehensively describe the various symptoms each of the essences is specifically designed to alleviate, allowing us to accurately identify the ones appropriate to our needs.

For instance, the description for the essence named after the flower *Star of Bethlehem*, reads:

- Have you suffered a shock in your life such as an accident, loss of a loved one, terrible news, illness?
- Are you numbed or withdrawn as a result of recent traumatic events in your life?
- Have you suffered a loss or grief that you have never recovered from?

A perfect match for us—wouldn't you say? There are several others that also pertain to our situation, and they can be conveniently combined with each other.

Regarding the level of our general health, experts on nutrition exhort us to follow, as best we can, a sensible balanced and healthy diet—preferably free from processed foods, i.e. junk foods and factory made stuff. Fresh fruits and vegetables are what they customarily recommend—and despite what some of us would like to think—ketchup on our French fries do not constitute the "two vegetables" guideline often suggested by nutritionists.

In the event we find the discipline this calls for difficult to maintain, it helps enormously to stay mindful of the fact that our return to good health is what our loved ones in spirit fervently want for us—that alone could be all the incentive we need to stick with it.

## Our Soul Plan

We talked about our soul plan earlier in chapter 4 and I've given it prominence in this compilation of suggested steps we can take because, for me, becoming enlightened about this extraordinary process, first via the mediums then by Robert Schwartz's excellent book *Your Soul Plan,* was *the* defining experience in *my* journey back. To over endorse it would be impossible.

Most grief experts and counselors are in agreement that acceptance of our loss is absolutely crucial to our recovery. That being the case, finding a reason or the meaning behind what has befallen us is precursory, it seems, to achieving that goal. Learning about our soul plan helps us do just that because it provides us with the explanation to which Dr. Viktor Frankl was referring when he said: "If there is meaning in life at all, then there must be meaning in suffering."

Dr. Frankl had reached this conclusion when his studies revealed that his fellow Nazi concentration camp survivors all had the ability to find meaning in their suffering. It follows then that acquiring knowledge of the soul plan we ourselves formulated before we incarnated, can provide us with the meaning behind both *our* suffering and that of our loved one, and can greatly assist us in *our* survival and recovery too.

It teaches us, for instance, the reasons why learning in one form or another is embodied in *all* our life experiences. Every challenge, every hardship and every obstacle we're called on to surmount is a potential opportunity to grow and spiritually evolve. As Elisabeth Kubler-Ross told us: "…everything in this life has a purpose, there are no mistakes, no coincidences, all events are blessings given to us to learn from." In other words—as difficult as it is to accept sometimes, everything that is happening, is happening because it should.

*The Direct Connect*

The 19th century English novelist George Eliot said: "Deep unspeakable suffering may well be called a baptism, a regeneration, the initiation into a new state." An observation echoed in the frequently heard aphorism: "Every ending is a beginning."

As we absorb the intriguing insights that knowledge of our soul plan affords us, and then extrapolate from them in the context of our own current circumstance, we could become aware of a narrative emerging that reveals the meaning behind it. Maybe even an explanation, for instance, of the reasons why our loved one—this wonderful being who was our whole life, was so cruelly snatched from us. Remember, this is *our* plan—it was of *our* making—*we* co-authored it and signed off on it, as amazing as it may seem, in essence we elected to experience every aspect of what has happened. It's hardly likely then that we would we have gone to all that trouble if there was a chance the outcome would be anything other than positive, righteous, virtuous and beneficial for everyone involved. So clearly, it's now incumbent on us to search for what that could be—when we find it, we will have been gifted with *the meaning*.

Again I'm reminded of C. S. Lewis's words of condolence in a letter to his recently widowed friend, in which he wrote: "She was further along than you, and she can help you more where she now is than she could have done on earth." Surely a reference to the meaning behind both his friend's sufferance and that of his wife.

Making ourselves receptive to the mind-bending possibilities, while also taking into account the fact that our loved one too has now been apprised of his or her role in all of this, can bring about a warm feeling of inner peace coursing through us, suffusing us with a sense of finally being freed and revitalized. Our new level of comprehension can not only throw light on the previously puzzling why's and wherefore's of situations gone before, but it can also enable us to better discern our life's purpose, our very reason for being even. In fact, in the course of time, we'll likely come to view many life situations and relationships in a different light from now on.

I well remember some years ago, bristling and being quite angered by a medium's suggestion that there would eventually come a time when I would view my wife's passing as a gift. "A gift? Are you out of your mind?" was my perplexed reaction at the time. I must admit now however, from the perspective of having since acquired some knowledge of what soul plan is all about, to having a much clearer understanding of what he meant. In fact I've become so acceptive of it that I'm convinced it simply couldn't have been any other way.

Evidential instances of this dynamic are scattered throughout the mediums' books, there are many examples of spirits attesting during readings that they're now assisting and guiding their surviving loved ones with their careers, business matters, relationships etc., in order for them to fulfill their life-purpose in ways that weren't possible when they were in their restrictive physical form. In short—we continue to be the team—the awesome twosome, we always were. Surely, this alone is enough to arouse within us all the impetus we need to do our utmost from now on to ensure that we don't squander the unique opportunity their sacrifice has gifted us with. With our commitment to do so, we're also honoring and gifting our loved one in return, bestowing meaning and purpose to *their* life too in the process—a satisfactory completion of the circle.

This highly illuminating revelation about our joint soul plan, providing us as it surely does, with the meaning behind what has occurred, can prove to be a gigantic therapeutic step on our road back to wholeness. By any measure—that's powerful stuff.

## Hitting the Books

For me, books are sacrosanct, because it's not an exaggeration to say that between their covers there is often magic to be found—pure, life-changing magic, and that's a commodity we have an urgent use for right now. Book study may be a pursuit some of us haven't felt a need to involve ourselves in for a while, but we could certainly use some wizardry now, so with many excellent books available we might want to consider pressing some of them into service.

I've had six careers over the years and was fortunate to be pretty successful in all of them, but it was books that equipped me with the required wherewithal, so I have a few thoughts and ideas on the subject I'd like to share. Most of them are fundamental in nature but I feel they're considerations it pays to be heedful of if we're to benefit from our investment in reading time.

During several years as a college lecturer for instance, I found there were invariably some who came to my classes with the idea that it's enough to more or less scan their way through a book as if it was a chore that they were in a hurry to rid themselves of. So I had to instill in them early that deriving optimum benefit from our books calls for us to read *into* and *through* each word, phrase and sentence by focusing and pondering on the information the writer is diligently trying to impart to us. Full assimilation can then be achieved by further reflection on the content, *after* we've given it sufficient time to percolate down and sink into our subconscious. What I then found of course, was that our capacity to absorb information varies between individuals, some of us can only handle small chunks at a time for instance, while others are able to take in practically an entire book. So in a class setting, maintaining some sort of balance in an attempt

## DIY Recuperative Measures

to be fair to everyone is an ongoing challenge and inevitably there are those on both sides of the fulcrum who get short-changed. But in our case here we're not disadvantaged in that way, it's all about just *us* now, this is *our* curriculum, *we* created it—for *us*. We're not hampered by having to follow a pace set by others and the only rules we have to be in compliance with are those we set for ourselves, so we have the luxury to move along at the tempo we're most comfortable with.

There are people who are gifted with the enviable ability to read something once and they've "got it," my twice valedictorian daughter Bev is one of them, but I, in common with others I've known, usually have to revisit a book—often. Which is fine by me because I can't get enough of this stuff anyway, so I've got into the habit of rotating my reading list of favorites. And an aspect of this process I find fascinating is the way a certain sentence or paragraph that I've read several times over the past two years or so, but that I'd never really got my head around to my satisfaction, can unexpectedly jump off the page with a clarity that I hadn't been aware of before and what had formerly been murky at best, magically becomes crystal clear. Several friends have acknowledged having experienced this and they too find it encouraging because it indicates a measure of growth and evolvement has taken place, triggered by knowledge acquired from the other books in the period between readings of the current one—a progress report if you will, confirming that we're moving in the right direction.

"Never judge a book by its cover," wrote George Eliot in her novel *The Mill on the Floss*. It's possible that truer words were never written—or more quoted, but it seems that many book marketers these days assume that we *are* influenced by a book's cover. Why else would they, in order to appeal to that "raven gene" that many of us have—our attraction to shiny objects, embellish their book covers with flashy neon-like colors and eye-catching glittery metallic embossing to the extent that they visually yell at us from across the bookstore.

What I'm suggesting, is that while there are times when books marketed in this way *can* undoubtedly live up to such hype, it does make them "low-hanging fruit" and we shouldn't overlook a related and frequently heard maxim: "looks can be deceiving," because the fact is, between the tattered covers of an old used book we can often find, among its yellowed dog-eared pages, nuggets of pure gold. I can't recall one instance when I've been *totally* disappointed in a book that has a few miles on its clock—to the contrary, I've invariably been able to find a few morsels of wisdom that have made the book well worth the measly dime or two it cost me.

A case in point is a copy I have of Sir Arthur Conan Doyle's book *The New Revelation,* originally published in 1918, that I came across it at our local library's annual book sale some years ago. It has seen much better days—for instance it was missing its back cover when I found it and what was left of its front cover was literally hanging by a thread. But I had it fixed and have since made a point of revisiting it from time to time and more often than not I come across some tidbit, some insight, that uncannily resonates with me in a way it hadn't previously.

There is one thing about books "of a certain age" that may take some getting used to at first however, and it's an aspect of older books that several people whom I've met admit to having had a problem getting past, and the reason they sometimes give for being dismissive of them. What I'm referring to is the inherent outmoded, even archaic, style of writing that distinguishes books from bygone eras.

But I always encourage people to stick with it and try to convince them that they're bound to find the rewards for their perseverance well worth the insignificant amount of effort it takes to not be put off by Conan Doyle's "...from we know not whence," for instance, or his occasional "verily."

## Fear, Begone

The impediments to our recovery are quite numerous, but the one we bereaved often find most troubling is the fearfulness that has dogged us since our loved one left us—there doesn't seem to be any aspect of our life that isn't negatively affected by it. The lack of self-confidence this induces is a new and unnerving experience for us and naturally soon becomes a constant source of puzzlement and frustration. We attribute it to our fragile and depleted state that, so our reading about grief informs us, heightens our vulnerability to a host of sub-par health issues—fear being one of them presumably.

Mulling over our plight only serves to reawaken our awareness to the specialness—the quality of what we had, all features of which were representative of our security and orderliness, in the form of just our loved one's physical presence for instance, our togetherness, our mutual supportiveness, the intrinsic wordless communication we'd enjoyed since the moment we met, and the just always being there for each other.

All of them of a uniquely special quality and all of them unceremoniously snatched from us, taking with it our self-confidence along with the feelings we'd had of being in control. We had formerly not only taken ordinary everyday tasks and challenges in our stride but had actually derived pleasure and satisfaction, inspiration even, from their ordinariness. But even these inexplicably completely overwhelm us now—causing us to be even more fearful and sickeningly daunted. The thought that, deprived of the moral support of our life partner, we may now forever lack the inner resources and the fortitude needed to cope, simply terrifies us. It was at this juncture that I came to realize that I'd somehow become ensnared in this constant state of fear and if I was ever going to be able to extricate myself from it I needed to learn something about the nature of fear. I'd like to share some of what I learned.

It's universally acknowledged that *some* degree of fear is a *good* thing and a necessary, even healthy, component of the human condition. Fear of failure for instance is often cited as being the motivating factor behind our ambitions and the pursuit of our goals. Fear also automatically mobilizes us to react appropriately to danger—the classic "flight-fright-or-fight" response we're all by now familiar with.

But, as we've seen, in what appears to be either a quirky ambiguity of nature, or a subtle deficiency in our language, under certain circumstances fear can turn against us and get quite belligerent (sounds like an uncle I once had). We bereaved became only too familiar with this other face of fear when we lost our loved one, because by any measure, this was for us—a traumatic event, and traumatic events bring on abnormal emotions such as distress, helplessness and *fear*. The great Dr. Martin Luther King had this to say on the subject:

> *"Normal fear protects us; abnormal fear paralyzes us. Normal fear motivates us to improve our individual and collective welfare; abnormal fear constantly poisons and distorts our inner lives."*

Most of us are aware of the condition known as "post-traumatic stress disorder" (PTSD), through accounts in the news media of its

## DIY Recuperative Measures

devastating effects on our combat veterans afflicted by it. Not to disparage or diminish in the slightest, the sufferance endured by our courageous warriors, but research has shown that PTSD isn't confined to only those who have done tours of duty in foreign war zones. The fact is, anyone who has gone through a traumatic experience can become severely distressed—mentally, physically and emotionally.

Literature on the subject lists the types of events that qualify as traumatically stressful, they include natural disasters such as forest fires, earthquakes, floods, tornados etc., plus man-made disasters like those involving airliners, trains, highway accidents and criminal acts such as domestic violence. Then there are traumatic events of a more personal nature, for example, job-loss, divorce and the one we're the victims of—*bereavement.*

Fear brought on by our traumatic event, can change us in ways that may not be readily apparent. It can, for instance over time, weaken us to the extent that we create all manner of false and scary scenarios in our mind. Dreads that can become irrationally amplified by the sight of disturbing images, accounts with an unnecessarily exaggerated negative slant that we read or overhear, can ricochet endlessly around in our mind—making the often heard expression "grip of fear" quite appropriate. In this state we can also become more susceptible to the negative vibrations emitted by people we come into contact with, exacerbating our fearfulness and weakening us even further in the process.

None of these influences are exactly conducive to our recovery and the return to some degree of normalcy we desire of course, but there *are* measures we can take, adjustments we can make to assist us in resisting the insidious impact of these "crazy-makers." I'd like to share with you a few steps that I was led to take.

*The Direct Connect*

The 19th century American essayist, philosopher and leader of the Transcendentalist movement Ralph Waldo Emerson said this about fear: "Fear defeats more people than any other one thing in the world." One can only speculate on what the Sage of Concord—if he were alive today, would have to say about what must be *the* most powerful inciter of fear and that "defeats more people than any other one thing in the world," these days.

## Television: Commercials

The inciter I'm referring to comes to us via an appliance that I doubt Mr. Emerson ever even envisioned, but that almost everyone now owns—and often have one in every room of their home (yes, even *that* room), and yes, it's the television receiver, or *"deceiver,"* as a cynical but pragmatic friend aptly calls it. It's not the television per se that offends however, that can be quite an attractive piece of furniture, what defeats people are the emotionally charged messages and images that it emits when we turn it on. Mainly, but not exclusively, in the form of commercials that are expressly designed to sell us stuff, and preferably lots of it, regardless of whether or not we have a need for any of it in the first place.

To that end, advertisers play heavily on our emotions of course and always have. It's likely been the marketing tool of choice since cave dwellers wanted to persuade someone to take stuff off their hands in exchange for a clam or two. In more recent times the emotion they've trained their sights on, and honed in on more intensely than any other, is our fear. Our fear that, as the messages invariably insinuate, something catastrophic will befall us and those we love if we *don't* buy what these hucksters are pitching—and behold it works, and works very well indeed, and furthermore, when it's

## DIY Recuperative Measures

employed along with that other odious sales practice of repetition upon repetition, it's even *more* successful. Also, human nature being what it is, advertisers have bought into the notion that if something is worth doing it must be worth *over*doing, consequently, the fear factor in advertising has been "notched up" incrementally to an astonishing degree in recent times. I read recently of a study that estimated that anxiety disorders affect almost 40 million adults in the U.S. It may be that there's no connection, but one can't help wondering.

Several years ago, an advertising executive with an agency I'd done business with for some years treated me to lunch to tell me that he would be resigning from his position soon. In explaining his reasons for this surprising career shift, he confided something that stuck with me and that I often recall when commercials come on while I'm watching television. He said "Never forget that whenever someone has something they want to sell you these days, whether it's pharmaceutical drugs, retirement advice, burglar alarms, insurance, pet food or even politicians selling themselves—they will tell you absolutely *anything*—and the scarier the better. They've discovered that nothing induces us to part with our money more readily than scaring the bejeebers out of us." He explained that he'd resigned because the agency had just taken on several accounts that would take them down that path, and he wanted no part of it.

It turns out that this stance was mainly due to his sister having lost her husband two years before and then subsequently witnessing how the resultant fearfulness she'd suffered from since had not only triggered a host of health issues but had wreaked havoc on every aspect of her life including her relationship with her children.

Emotionally stable, well grounded people may well be inured to the round-the-clock blitz of scare tactics, but for those of us already weakened by our fears it can only be further detrimental to our emotional health. It's obvious we'd be better off without this low energy in our life and thankfully we have the solution right there at our fingertips—in the form of our TV remote.

The fact that the unprincipled perpetrators seem to take a Machiavellian delight in having this hypnotic power over us, while all the while making loads of money from it, should surely make it easier for us, and also be pleasurably satisfying, to figuratively "pull the plug" on them and "unfriend" them by hitting the "off" button on our remote or switch channels and seek the sanctuary of commercial-free programing. Taking either of these actions though would, as the saying goes, be "cutting off our nose to spite our face," because we'd then be depriving ourselves of the source we rely on for our information—the news programmes. So it's a trade-off issue. At least news programmes are less ubiquitous than commercials in that they don't rudely interrupt what we're viewing every ten minutes, but they *are* proven fearmongers too—so taking a closer look at them may help us understand how we might better protect ourselves.

## Television: Newscasts

The innate desire that most of us have to keep up on current affairs—aka staying informed, has historically been acknowledged as a commendable trait—good citizenship. Unfortunately the lines of demarcation between objective reporting and plain old fearmongering have always been a little blurry. And there's also that thing known as editorial bias, where important pertinent points on issues can wind up being skewed so that the information we receive doesn't necessarily square with the facts—formerly call lying. We can find this

## DIY Recuperative Measures

unsettling, and it can leave us feeling scarily insecure and wondering 'what *can* we believe?' and 'where *do* we go to get the truth.

It's a fact that newscasts, like other programmes, are ratings driven, so there are times when we can't help cynically suspecting that a story we're watching that strikes us as not being very informative, hadn't been considered newsworthy at all until someone had seized on some aspect of the story and taken liberties with the truth in order to enhance and sensationalize it in gratuitously violent and/or scary ways. I've been told that, as a ratings booster—this rarely fails. If this is so, those in the news business must really be "over the moon" about globalization.

In recent years most every aspect of everyone's lives have been impacted to some degree by the ever burgeoning phenomenon of globalization that's been taking place since the mid 1980's, and television news is no exception. Mind-bending technical advancements have taken place in the ways news is gathered and disseminated these days—resulting in a world that is now considerably smaller than it once was. For instance, all of us are now figuratively as close to people and events on the other side of the world as our forefathers were to people in the next valley. In some respects even closer, because high-definition images of a wide range of events taking place in the farthest and remotest areas of the world are now, amazingly, being beamed directly into our homes—*as they are actually happening.*

Certainly on the face of it, a wonderful thing to behold—which it would undoubtedly be if it wasn't for the fact that not everything that is happening around the world is exactly what we could call positive, uplifting and suitable family viewing. To the contrary, widespread famine, social upheaval and appalling atrocities are what is often happening and what someone decides constitutes suitable viewing. But "suitable" is hardly the word *I'd* use, for imagery that can be so devastating to our western sensibilities that some of us can easily become debilitated by the fears it can instill in us.

We've never been naive enough to delude ourselves that we live in "perfect world" of course—we haven't been living in a vacuum after all, so naturally we *had* heard of such things. It's just that when we witness this stuff night after night, in the sanctity of our own home, and *in real time* no less, and then re-runs of it ad nauseam, the accumulative effect of these negative vibrations can bring it all so compellingly "up-close-and-personal," that we feel far less separated from it—far less detached than when we'd only learned about such events after the fact.

We certainly don't have a need for anything so abhorrent in our lives, and mentally ingesting a steady diet of this kind of fare isn't exactly conducive to our recovery, so we might consider cutting back, or even, again, pulling the plug on it altogether. It's getting increasingly difficult to avoid these disseminators of fear though—they seem to be everywhere—if they were carriers of any other kind of transmittable health threat, quarantine precautions would likely be in effect.

One of the odious ways they reach out to us now is through those TV monitors in public waiting areas, where we're a captive audience. Where I live they're invariably tuned to a 24 hour "Police Blotter" news channel that reports on every nefarious act that's been committed in every precinct throughout the tri-county area. In recent weeks I've been subjected to monitors churning out this stuff in my car dealership customer lounge, all three waiting areas at a medical clinic, two banks, my post office and even above a shoe-shine man's station in a hotel lobby.

## Other Media Fearmongerers

When I was growing up in the English industrial Midlands, it was quite common to see people walking along the street eating their fish and chips in the time honored way—straight out of a newspaper. Even back then a credibility gap must have existed between the news print media and their readers because a sardonic expression frequently heard was "Never believe what you see in a newspaper laddie, except fish and chips." It's counsel that still holds up.

In an otherwise fast moving world there remain some things that don't change very much. A few years ago, tired of and exasperated by, the kind of TV news fearmongering we've been discussing, I imposed a personal embargo on TV newscasts and for a month or so relied instead on newspapers and weekly news magazines for my news. Having spent several years on the editorial departments of a national magazine and a major newspaper, I've long held journalists in high regard and I found much of their coverage to be professional. But I still have notes I took of some of the more dopey items that someone other than the news department thought belonged under the heading *News You Can Use*. The following examples are just a few of many:

- — A daily Doomsday Countdown on the latest expert-deciphered date on the fabled Mayan Calendar predicting the end of civilization—again. A prophecy that would have more credibility if they'd predicted the collapse of their own civilization.

- — An article in the English newspaper *Daily Mail*, under a headline quoting the head of Amsterdam's health service as saying "Sugar is the most dangerous drug of our time and should come with smoking-style health warnings.

## The Direct Connect

— A dire warning in the *Home and Leisure* newspaper section regarding the real possibility of the "Dreaded Lurgy" lurking in our kitchen sponges—the likely progenitor of a pandemic.

— A magazine article by a scientist, complete with computer generated images, showing how the sun will swell enormously. Causing the earth temperature to rise by a 1,000 degrees, incinerating all life in the process (including, presumably, that thing living in our sponges). I could have gone all day without knowing that—the scientist who came up with that must be a joy to be around don't you think?

Stories like these, and others like them, would have had me taking to my bed, if it hadn't been for another article detailing the activities of pesky dust mites and bed-bugs—as they chomp down on us throughout the night.

Such Stygian portents are, it seems to me, wholly in line with the old aphorism that tells us "There is nothing new under the sun." Consider this pearl of pessimism from an essay by Thomas Malthus, an English economist in which he posited that because the earth's population was growing at a faster rate than the food supply, war, disease, and famine were necessary in order to prevent overpopulation. Sound familiar? Something heard on the news or read about recently perhaps? Hardly, Mr Malthus wrote this in 1798.

Over the years, great minds have attested to the destructive power of fear time and again, and it's clear that the blame for its perpetual presence in our daily lives lies squarely at the feet of the news media, it's very seldom we receive our information about current global events from anywhere else after all. No one's implying there's intentional malevolence involved however, because it's obviously the logical outcome of the "over-the-top" sensationalism in which they've chosen to indulge—in their relentless battle for the biggest market share of viewers and readers, regardless of how it impacts on us. There *are* ways we can shield ourselves from their scaremongering and stay composed though, for instance, just recognizing this dynamic at work and seeing it for the silly sham it is, allows us to summarily dismiss the shrill "the sky is falling" tone of news items like the proverbial "water off a duck's back." This makes it easier for us to keep it in perspective and focus on the features we consider more plausible. As someone once said, "We may not be able to change what we see—but we *can* change the way we *look* at it."

## Fear: It's Like WiFi

Fear, like WiFi, is in the air—it's *everywhere,* just hanging there waiting to administer its daily dose of fear into our collective psyche. There's no doubt that this is most often a consequence of the actions of those with a vested interest in exploiting fearfulness to their financial advantage, resulting in a ceaseless barrage of fear laden messages that permeate all aspects of our society.

I can't imagine that there's anyone who has more effectively drawn our attention to how prevalent this insidious activity is than Barry Glassner. He is president of Lewis & Clark College in Portland, Oregon and was formerly Professor of Sociology at the University of Southern California. To date he has authored seven books dealing with contemporary social issues, one of them being *The Culture of Fear.* Published originally in 1999 and revised and updated in 2012, this thoroughly enlightening work was the result of five years of research on the pathology of fear and its negative effects on all levels of society. Citing numerous examples in factual detail, he exposes the organizations that habitually exaggerate and embellish the direness of events and documents the extraordinary ways in which instances of fearmongering, under examination, can often turn out to be based on unfounded myths that then proceed, via the media, to burgeon forth and inflict extended spells of national hand-wringing that can border on mass hysteria.

It's a compellingly enlightening read—and one that ensures us that from now on, if we *do* watch the news we'll be able to do so safe in the knowledge that we need no longer allow ourselves to be fooled by the disingenuous ways in which news is often presented.

'No, the sky is *not* falling dear Chicken Little—it was just a leaf landing on your tail.' We made mention earlier that there's nothing new under the sun, apparently various versions of John Greene Chandler's famous 1840 Chicken Little fable have been traced back 2500 years or more.

## Other People (Don't Get Me Started)

A good friend of mine, a sociology major, once explained to me that it's universally acknowledged that human relationships are notoriously one of life's biggest challenges for the vast majority of us. I had cause to recall our conversation early in my new status of widowhood several years later, while I was driving home following my baptism into the insensitive and oddly inappropriate things people are apt to say when they're in the company of we bereaved. It had occurred at my wife's memorial service no less—just six days after she'd made her transition.

As the service ended and with the chapel seemingly still echoing with the sweet dulcet tones of our treasured friend, the nationally known singer Lisa Moscatiello, mourners were gathering around me and my daughter Bev to kindly offer their expressions of condolence.

## DIY Recuperative Measures

One of my wife's dear friends Lillian, a widow herself, gave me a hug while compassionately assuring me that "It *does* get better after a while Reggie." At which, on overhearing this, a woman whom I knew had lost her husband a year or so earlier, belligerently elbowed her way up to me and emphatically declared "No it doesn't!" 'Ooh, charming' I thought—'am I glad *you* came.'

If I'd harbored any benevolent expectations that this incomprehensible outburst was an isolated case of a seemingly intelligent adult just misspeaking, I was being naively optimistic, because for many months afterwards similar demoralizingly insensitive remarks were voiced by these "grief experts" with such unsettling frequency that they appeared to be the rule rather than the exception. Comparing notes with fellow grieving friends and acquaintances during this time revealed a general consensus that the dismissive attitude of many people towards the bereaved is unfortunately "par-for-the-course," and one of the reasons many of us give for our journey back being so emotionally arduous.

I'd understood of course that life without my wife would obviously never be the same and that the path back to recovery would be an uphill slog, fraught with the challenges of acquiring new skills. What took me aback, probably more than anything else though, was the discovery that the steepest part of my learning curve was going to be—of all things—people.

My sociologist friend suggested that uncomfortable encounters with people that culminate in we bereaved having our feelings trampled on is oftentimes due to the fact that in our emotionally thoroughly debilitated and fragile state, any remarks that are inappropriate or are delivered in anything other than soft, gentle and genuinely commiserative tones can easily be amplified out of all proportion—compounding our misery still further.

He went on to suggest that I should make the effort to resign myself to the fact that this, for the moment at least, is simply the way it is, and will continue to be until I've attained the level of emotional healing that will allow me to more easily differentiate between those that I presently *misperceive* to be hurtful and unwarranted assaults on my sensibilities and those encounters that are unmistakably so. It was then that I decided I was a long way from achieving that level and that for the time being, I'd be better off avoiding situations and people whom I felt could be problematic for me—I didn't need this hurt-upon-hurt. Taking this approach however can entail maintaining a delicate balance, because the last thing we want is to be completely isolated, but on the other hand, being compelled to be constantly on the defensive around people isn't exactly conducive to the tranquil state of mind our convalescence would benefit from either.

Sure enough, as I slowly but surely recuperated towards some degree of normalcy, I eventually found it getting progressively easier to be more magnanimous towards people whose propensity for insensitive remarks would have previously upset me no end. I attributed this to the fortuitous ways in which various indicators had been trickling into my life that collectively led me to the understanding that most of our beliefs and attitudes, in the absence of personal experiences, are largely the result of our individual societal conditioning. So it's reasonable to assume that there are many people whose life experiences just haven't exposed them to the same kind of ravaging emotional toll of losing a loved one that *we* have experienced. Plus, the subject is not only seldom mentioned, it's also consciously avoided—and rarely, if ever, taught to us. I find it ironic that although we often hear the term "people-skills" these

## DIY Recuperative Measures

days (there are college courses on the subject for heaven's sake) there's one subject I have yet to see on any school curriculum, it's "*dead*-people-skills."

So in all fairness, with such a scarcity of learning opportunities on the subject, it's hardly realistic to expect everyone to know how to comport themselves in the approved manner when they find themselves in the presence of the acutely susceptible sensitivities that can define we bereaved. Any more than many of *us* could have honestly claimed to have known—prior to *our* tragedy. The old adage about "walking a mile in someone else's shoes" comes to mind here.

After giving this a lot of thought and discussing it with friends, I eventually concluded that adopting a more tolerant stance, with sincerity, could be mutually beneficial, in that not only would it make for a more peaceful life all around, which is undoubtedly conducive to our healing, but it's also possible that arriving at this point was no accident, that it had in fact actually been part of *our* soul plan to emerge as *their* teachers—at this juncture of *their* soul path. At last, something about this wholly inexplicable and damnably demoralizing situation felt *right*.

I must explain though, that in referring earlier to my own slow but sure recuperation, I was acknowledging that this agreeably satisfying and desirable outcome regarding my more charitable attitude towards other people was not by any means arrived at overnight. The degree of emotional centering and grounding required to help get us through our convalescence *does* take time, but we can achieve our goal sooner and easier if we work on inuring ourselves—thicken our skins, if you will—against those types of people whose inappropriate attitudes and hurtful remarks could distress us in ways that can, accumulatively, impede our progress. No doubt it was these kinds of people who prompted novelist C. S. Lewis to wonder, in *A Grief Observed,* if "the bereaved ought to be isolated in special settlements like lepers."

The examples following are typical of many such encounters that various friends and I have experienced over the past several years.

## People: They Can Say the Darnedest Things

While lunching with a friend a few weeks after my wife's passing, he naturally asked me how I was coping. Feeling that our relationship was such that I could be open and honest, I told him that the past couple of days had been tough going but that I was pretty good again today. I was quite shocked when he responded by finger-waggingly asserting "Listen to me, when you wake up in the morning you have two choices. You can choose either to be happy that day or you can choose to be sad—simple as that!" "Wow," I thought to myself (later, of course, while driving home), "what a concept? Why hadn't *I* thought of that?"

He wasn't to know of course that the "couple of days" I'd referred to had actually been three days of uncontrollable bone-aching sobbing, and I realized there was no conscious intent on his part to inflict hurt, but I thought that with him being a church deacon and counselor, he should have known better, because what he said was tantamount to telling a marathon runner who's fallen and broken their ankle, to just get up and finish the race. Why is it so difficult for people to understand that we bereaved are similarly incapacitated? Choice? That's a luxury we just simply do not have. The exchange however did serve to show me how ignorant many people are about how our debilitated condition can heighten our sensitivity to their careless comments.

## DIY Recuperative Measures

Throughout history, it's been the custom in various countries and cultures for the newly bereaved to symbolize their situation to others in some visible way, wearing black for a certain period of time for instance is considered proper mourning attire in some cultures. When I was growing up in England, it was the custom for family members of the deceased to wear a black armband or a small diamond shaped patch of black material sewn onto their coat sleeve.

Such customs are rarely still upheld here in the western world but I've often thought that with many people needing a little guidance on "death etiquette," it would be a good idea if we bereaved adopted the practice of wearing a button bearing a concise and to-the-point slogan such as *"Keep It Simple"* or *"Less Is More,"* just to remind them of whose company they're in.

"Simple" is always a good thing, that's why many great minds have extolled the virtues of it over the centuries. Leonardo da Vinci for instance referred to simplicity as being "the ultimate sophistication," while Albert Einstein said "Everything should be made as simple as possible, but not simpler." So whenever someone is presented with the opportunity to offer their condolences and express their sympathy to the bereaved, be it at the funeral or when they happen to bump into the them at the mall, "simple" would seem to be the watchword. There's just no good reason to subject both ourselves and the bereaved to discomfort and embarrassment when all that's required are a few simple appropriate words that show someone genuinely cares and shares their sorrow. Simple phrases along the lines of the following are quite sufficient:

*"I'm so very sorry this has happened to you."*
*"Please let me know if there's anything at all I can do for you."*
*"He/she was a beautiful being, and will be greatly missed."*

I find it interesting that while most people will admit to finding it difficult to know what to say to the bereaved, and with brevity being so desirable, there are always those who become tediously verbose, maudlinly philosophical or overly dogmatic in lecturing the bereaved, on not only *how,* but for *how long* they should grieve for example. Anyone having the temerity to force their opinions on the bereaved in this way at this juncture, is hijacking the circumstances and making it about *themselves.* The bereaved is the lead player at this moment in time—*everything* should be about *them*—not us, our involvement in the proceedings is that of a supporting role.

There *are* those who do speak sparingly, but unfortunately when they do it's often in the form of quite thoughtless banal platitudes and clichés such as:

*"It was God's will."*

*"Time heals all hearts."*

*"He/she's at peace now."*

*"It was his/her time."*

*"He had a good innings."* Quite appropriate I suppose—if the deceased had played baseball.

*"Just think of the happy times you had together."* What a cringe-inducer this one is. Seriously? The happy times we once *had,* but will *never* have again? That is *precisely* what the newly bereaved are trying *not* to think about right now. There will undoubtedly come a day when they will find it extremely heartening to do so, and what a magical day that will be, because it will signify healing. But we realize only too well that that's not going to happen anytime soon, and certainly not in the way the thoughtless advice implies—by a mere snapping of the fingers to summon up pixie-dust. Honestly, where do they get this stuff?

## DIY Recuperative Measures

*"Life has to go on you know."* Yikes! Who doesn't get tired of hearing this one? It's a pity there isn't a way it's use could be legally restricted solely to only those who have recently successfully applied the Heimlich Maneuver?

*"I know what you are going through."* Whenever someone says this to a bereaved person (and it's said an awful lot), they clearly do *not* know—not a clue. Because if they *did* truly know what we are going through, they would have some idea of how irritating such a presumptuous statement can be, particularly when it's repeated over and over, like they tend to do.

While I was going over this list with two fellow widowers it occurred to us that all the foregoing statements share the same characteristic—each one, in its own way, is actually a conversation closer. In that none of them either invite or allow room for a rejoinder or encourage any furtherance. "I have said my piece—I have spoken!"—end of conversation.

So any hopes we may have had that we were in the company of an empathic friend with whom we could maybe share a few supportively assuring thoughts, have been unceremoniously dashed—a disappointing outcome that falls short of what our anticipations had been. One can't help but wonder if this is, subconsciously, the rationale behind the form these statements take, after all "closers" do conveniently end their discomforting contact with us. Just wondering.

Whatever their motives, I do feel that it helps if we recognize and admit to ourselves that during those dreadful early days, we ourselves are not exactly the easiest people in the world to be around either. Looking back, I can recall occasions when not only would *I* have not wanted to be in the same room as me—I wouldn't have wanted to be in the *same town*. So in the event our relationship with someone whose friendship we truly value shows signs of becoming strained due to this condition, we would do well to find a way of explaining to them how the emotional and physical battering we bereaved have been subjected to can at times addle our faculties of perception, causing them to turn a little quirky and render us super-sensitive and brittle at times.

In the meantime we'd do well to find ways, early on, of steeling ourselves against such inappropriate and thoughtless remarks because they come with the territory, and until people become better enlightened there'll surely be more to come.

## People: They're Known to Use and Abuse

The numerous fellow grievers with whom I've discussed how vulnerable we are to people taking advantage of us have found it ironic that while many people seem to be unable to sense our heightened sensitivity to things said to us, like we've been discussing, they don't seem to have any trouble at all sensing our *neediness.*

Sir Bernard Williams is widely acknowledged as being the greatest British moral philosopher of his era. There's one of his legendary pearls of wisdom in particular that I've often thought that we bereaved should have printed up on calling cards—it goes:

"We grow a little every time we do not take advantage of somebody's weakness."

Theoretically, handing these out to those who show signs of having opportunistic tendencies could maybe nip them in the bud. What actually happens though of course, is that by the time we learn in what ways these people are capable of taking advantage of our good nature—they not only already are, they're probably well along that road. What these types of people don't seem able to realize is that what they perceive as weak-kneed neediness on our part is nothing

## DIY Recuperative Measures

but the perfectly understandable desire we have to be socially reconnected, and accepted—partly in order to compensate for the hurtful evaporation of those former "fair-weather friends" who elected to distance themselves from us, but another reason we actively seek social connectivity is because we understand that it can play a helpful role on our recuperative road back to wellness.

Unfortunately there are those who completely misinterpret our motives which can then easily render us vulnerable, because it's these types of people who are not above taking advantage of us, *particularly* if we happen to possess special skills or a talent that they can use. If we happen to own our own company, we're probably not going to be inconvenienced in terms of time, we can delegate any anticipated favors to staff for instance. It's when we're self-employed freelancers that time consuming favors inconsiderately expected of us can get to be a real burden.

I well remember a widowed lady named Molly, a member of a grief counseling circle I once attended. She was a retired seamstress, and one evening when this subject came up, she tearfully recounted how, after her husband's passing, her attempts to reach out socially resulted in a constant stream of requests for her sewing skills from these so called friends who acted like they were doing *her* a favor by keeping her busy. She laughingly likened her feelings at the time to those of the gazelles that we see on TV animal programs, who become conscious of their gait because they are being stalked by a lion who's looking around for one that's walking with a limp.

The following account that an acquaintance, Joani, shared with me also illustrates how our perceived neediness can seemingly be sensed by people who then unscrupulously seize on it as an opportunity to take advantage of us.

Joani was a talented interior designer and she and her husband Roger had operated their own successful business together for several years before his tragic passing. She'd stoically managed to keep it running through the dark days of her grief thanks to the help of a loyal and compassionate staff, but when she realized after a few months, that doing so single-handedly, while also raising their young daughter, was going to be far too stressful, she decided she had to sell the business and pursue something less burdensome.

One evening, while sitting quietly contemplating her options, she suddenly recalled how, before Roger made his transition, she'd enjoyed painting the occasional mural for clients of their company and how her work graced the walls of numerous upscale homes around their town. That sparked her remembrance of how Roger, whenever she'd finished one of her murals, would invariably comment that she'd never be without a back-up career, and it occurred to her that reigniting her passion for the murals could not only provide the income she badly needed but would also be an ideal therapeutic aid in helping her with her ongoing struggle of working through her grief.

She spent the next two months or so testing the waters by putting the word out to friends and contacts in the interior design community and had been greatly encouraged by their positive reactions to her presentation. However, when she responded to the requests for her services that started pouring in, she discovered that some people had misconstrued her gesture as nothing more than using what had been a pastime anyway as a way to stay busy and take her mind off things ("you know, like those pitiable grieving people do," as Joani put it later). So, as it had with Molly, it turned out that those with that kind of mindset, seemed convinced that they were actually doing *her* a favor when they handed her a simple task, such as transforming

## DIY Recuperative Measures

their dining room into a veritable Palace of Versailles—with a deadline of an entire week.

For months, in order not to jeopardize valued friendships, she dutifully complied to their demanding and often niminy-piminy requests and, being the consummate professional she is, never once allowed her bruised feelings to prevent her from doing her best work. Fortunately, she was able to overcome her emerging resentment by philosophically rationalizing that at least she was getting valuable experience, and besides, there was always the potential bonus of possibly benefitting from the exposure her work would get by having it surrounding the town's "movers and shakers" who would likely be future dinner guests in the "faux palaces" she'd created.

Thankfully her strategy paid off as she was able, eventually, to diplomatically extricate herself from their clutches and put this sordid phase behind her, leaving her free to enjoy her passion—only on *her* terms this time—being fairly compensated for her skills. Joani confided to me that this turn of events was mainly due to her remembering something her wise father had once told her, "People who make a habit of using people almost always wind up being used themselves, and the irony is—they rarely realize it."

Fortunately for Joani, her experience ended happily, but that's not necessarily always the case. Our weakened condition can make us highly vulnerable to this kind of manipulation and although it's an admirable attribute (some would say "it's incumbent on us") to share our God-given talents and skills—we don't have to allow ourselves to become *anyone's* doormat. And neither would *they*, if their friendship was genuine, *want* us to be demeaned in this way.

Our spirit friends have told us through the mediums that our soul growth is the reason we're all here, and the lessons we need to help us accomplish this are custom designed and presented in the form of challenges we're called on to face and hopefully overcome. As Joani's experience serves to illustrate, when our being taken advantage of can be attributed to our weakened and vulnerable condition, we've actually been gifted with a unique growth opportunity that can not only assist in our recovery but also contribute to our spiritual evolvement. This would certainly appear to be the case here, because the chances of *us* taking advantage of anyone in the future, in the way we were, are now pretty slim—as Sir Bernard Williams said:

*"We grow a little every time we do not take advantage of somebody's weakness."*

Joani's so-called friends were presented with the same opportunity for spiritual growth as she was, but they blew it. It's doubtful if those who habitually take advantage of vulnerable people in this way will *ever* grasp it—as long as life for them is all about acquiring free stuff.

I feel it's also the "soul growth lessons" aspect of these types of challenging experiences that Elisabeth Kubler-Ross must surely have had in mind when she said:

*"The most beautiful people we have known are those who have known defeat, known suffering, known struggle, known loss, and have found their way out of those depths."*

So let's see—as I see it, the upshot of this whole exercise, along with others that we bereaved can expect to encounter on our way out of the dreadful "slough of despond," is that we are "most beautiful people" in the making. Isn't that a wonderful "light-at-the-end-of-the-tunnel" thought from which we can all derive much needed spiritual sustenance?

## People: Spread the Word By All Means—But Carry an Umbrella

The world renowned medium George Anderson refers to our acquiring knowledge of the afterlife as nothing less than "The greatest gift we will ever receive while we remain on earth." When we ourselves have received all the evidence we need to convince us that this is so, whether through undeniably genuine messages from our loved one via a medium or an unequivocally genuine sign denoting their presence, we're hit by the realization of what a powerful restorative this knowledge can be for the bereaved—and accordingly we can hardly wait to share it with everyone. We want to shout it from the rooftops and (in present-day speak) viralize it—tweet it—just get the word out in any way we can. After all, how could anyone *not* be excited to learn that the thing that almost everyone in the world fears, namely—death, not only doesn't exist but never did and never will. Interestingly, there *are* such people, and for reasons known only to them they can be inordinately begrudging of the happiness of anyone who *is* excited by the discovery of something that holds such wondrously meaningful ramifications for all the world.

I suppose it's due to our optimistic expectations (what's *not* to like about it after all?) but we can be really surprised and more than a little puzzled by how openly hostile these people can often be in voicing their condemnation of us. Although they don't seem prepared to inspect the evidence of an afterlife themselves, they will go to great lengths to inform we who have of how stupid, misguided and downright evil we are. It's as though these Grinch's lives are so joyless that they're only happy when they're raining on other people's parades. I was mulling over this very thing a few weeks ago while walking on

## The Direct Connect

the beach to which I'd retreated after I'd been on the receiving end of one of their rants, and I passed a young lady who appeared to know something about this because her tee-shirt was telling the world that "When momma aint happy—ain't nobody happy." I think she'd come to the beach looking for peace and quiet too.

Any hopes we may have had for intelligent discourse with such avowed adversaries can understandably be shattered by this level of antagonism directed at us. It's as though their long-held cherished beliefs, political leanings and their views on social issues have become so narrow and rigid that it's impossible for them to be tolerant of opinions that don't precisely align with theirs, and they become unreasonably enraged as a result. Words like "zealous" and "fanatical" come to our minds at this point, and things can quickly get quite ugly—several friends and I have experienced many such uneasy confrontations and we've concluded we have two options—stand our ground and be totally eviscerated or rapidly retreat to a more peaceful place—like the beach.

In our daily lives we interact with people all the time, co-workers, neighbors, customers, relatives (especially relatives) with whom we don't see eye-to-eye on everything, but thankfully, being adults, when it becomes clear we're not going to change each other's minds on certain issues, we're able to just accept it and respectfully agree to differ—mutually recognized boundaries have been established and peace reigns. But for some inexplicable reason, just the mere utterance of the word "afterlife" in the presence of some people and it's "Katie bar the door," because ain't nobody gonna be happy around here—peace will definitely not reign.

And that's just *mentioning* the subject, any attempts by us to enter into a rational discussion and hopefully enlighten, can give rise to outbursts of mockery, sneering sarcasms, derisively disparaging insults that question both our mental stability, our parentage and that of our ancestors and a whole litany of snide barbs that impugn the integrity and intelligence of anyone who even *thinks* that an afterlife is possible, especially those "phony mediums who claim they can talk to dead people." Here are just a few examples I've had directed at me over the past few years:

"That is totally stupid, when you're dead, you're dead—period!"— "Those psychics are agents of the anti-Christ," is one that I especially remember having screamed in my face the very first time I'd attempted to describe the epiphinous experience I'd been gifted with by a world renowned medium. "Nothing but quacks, the lot of "em. I can see I've got a lot of work to do on you," was my "friend's" parting shot. ( I'd heard that last part some years before—when I was in pre-school). And then there's my favorite gem, "You do-gooder liberals are all alike." That reminds me—this "do-gooder" must remember to ask these people over for dinner sometime—a fabulous evening of fun and fellowship is promised.

It's always possible that contentious confrontations such as these are intended to be growth opportunities—lessons, where at times we're the pupil and at other times the teacher. But when any unbelievers with whom we debate are so steadfastly determined to stick to their convictions that they refuse to even consider *listening* to our reasons for believing in the afterlife, and talking any further would clearly be an exercise in futility and conceding the floor to them would just be inviting them to make us their whipping boy, it might be prudent to settle for peace and cancel classes today. Saying something along the lines of "You know what? You may very well be right—thank you for your words," should be enough to allow us to gracefully make our exit.

We should also never let anyone make us feel that our belief in an afterlife is contingent on their approval. And what anyone thinks of us for adopting this stance is strictly *their* business—and is nothing to do with us. Neither are we obligated to make apologies for who we are, and if this makes us an eccentric in their eyes—so be it.

The renowned philosopher Bertrand Russell had some wise and appropriate words that pertain to this, he said: "Do not fear to be eccentric in opinion, for every opinion now accepted was once eccentric."

In other words—it's not that we're round the bend after all—it's just that we're ahead of the curve. We might also do well to remember the famed advice Polonius gave his son, in Shakespear's *Hamlet,* he said: "This above all: to thine own self be true."

## Acts of Kindness—The Other Best Medicine

It's perfectly normal, maybe even a natural defense mechanism, that throughout the early months of our inconsolable grieving our thoughts have been inordinately directed inwardly—to the exclusion of most everything and everyone else. In a word—it's been all about *us.*

So the suggestion that we make the effort to go out of our way to reach out to others may not be very high on our agenda right now—presuming we have one at all. This type of apathetic response is quite understandable, even allowable, it's a recognized stage of grieving. But stages are defined as "phases of a journey" after all, and with our journey consisting of our eventual healing, remaining in this static state of self-absorption is akin to us taking a seat on a bus that's up on blocks. No matter how long we sit there—we're not going *anywhere,* despite what it says on the destination board.

When we do recognize that we need to become socially active once again, in our benumbed state just thinking about it can be daunting. We're fearful of the expenditure of energy, mental and physical, that it would require, neither of which we've had a surfeit of for a long time. It's at this point that it helps if we recall that thing we were taught at school, that said "with every journey, whether it's just a walk around the block or around the world, one single step is all it takes to launch us on our way." We're also no doubt familiar with what the revered 6th century Chinese philosopher Lao Tzu said: "The journey of a thousand miles begins with one step."

When we feel up to it, our first step could be for us to take a leaf from the book of those in the self-improvement field, who tell us repeatedly that in order for us to love others, we must first learn how to love *ourselves*—be our own best friend, if you will. When we accept this premise and also intuitively feel that this is the path we've been led to, then we will have taken that all-important first step, and "voila,"—we're on our way—piece of cake.

Telling ourselves the most comfortingly consoling things we can possibly imagine our consortium of friends either saying or writing to us, or even things we know our loved one in spirit would say to us, can be a wonderful and spiritually uplifting exercise—a highly satisfying sense of self-worth emerges. In effect we now have our personal cheering section—on call, anytime we need them. We can make it a habit to repeat these inspiring soul nourishing words out loud to ourselves every chance we get, when we're driving alone in the car for example. Also, borrowing from the mantra of those in the advertising field when they want to embed their messages in our minds: "Repetition-repetition-repetition," we could print them up on cards as affirmations and post them in places where they're

## The Direct Connect

sure to catch our eye, on the various mirrors we use around the house for instance and in our work places, especially in areas and on surfaces that come into view immediately on waking. A friend of mine carried a set of his around with him so he could flip through them whenever he found himself waiting in line anywhere.

Once we've succeeded in getting the ball rolling, we could begin to feel its momentum prodding us towards other indicators that affirm that the regular practice of genuine acts of magnanimity make for a highly desirable level of spiritual nourishment for all involved.

The prodding that eventually propelled me in the right direction came from a stream of aphorisms that serendipitously came to my attention over a six or seven week period. For instance, a television public service announcement whose sign-off line said *"Feel good—by doing good,"* was one I remember. Then this sprinkle of "pixie-dust" that caught my eye while doing research for a production I was working on. It was a quote by the Scottish novelist and dramatist James M. Barrie, the creator of Peter Pan, he said: *"Those who bring sunshine into the lives of others, cannot keep it from themselves."* Then I came across this appropriate Chinese proverb on a card at a florists: *"A bit of fragrance clings to the hand that gives the flowers."* In a book I was reading the same day about my compatriot Sir Winston Churchill, I learned that he once said: *"We make a living by what we get. We make a life by what we give."* A maxim that also resonated with me soon after that was featured on a desk calendar I came across, ironically at my bank. It was by no less a personage than His Holiness the Dalai Lama, who'd said: *"If you want others to be happy, practice compassion. If you want to be happy, practice compassion."*

Interestingly, a magazine I'd been reading while waiting to see the bank officer to whom the calender belonged, carried an article by a social psychologist on *The Principle of Reciprocity*, a social construct that as far as I could make out, basically means "giving in order to get." Quite a few notches down the scale from the altruistic acts of giving we're talking about, furthermore it's more aligned, I feel, with the narcissistic "Me Generation," whose pseudo acts of kindness are often disingenuously motivated by such expectations as monetary reward, career advancement or social status upgrades—the kind of conduct that comprised those "friends" who were so sneakily adept at taking advantage of Molly and Joani's good-heartedness.

The type of giving we're discussing here is strictly a "no strings attached" gesture. Any "getting" or reciprocity that may result from our actions, come solely in the form of the mutual soul nourishment that they create and is not contingent on the giver receiving anything at all in return—nothing of a material nature anyway.

This is by no means fanciful wishful thinking, there have been numerous scientific studies that support this phenomenon. Research into the causes of our mood changes for example, has shown conclusively that mood balance is modulated by a chemical that's created by our body and known as serotonin. It's one of six known neurotransmitters and is popularly referred to as "the happy hormone." When there's an increase in the level of it our mood becomes elevated along with it and we feel happier—the higher it rises, the happier we become.

Modern neural imaging techniques have now allowed scientists to study the relationship between the rise in serotonin and the receiving of acts of kindness. On looking further into this they discovered, through brain scans, that there was also the same dramatic rise in the serotonin levels in the brain of the person *responsible* for the kind act—the giver.

Amazingly, they then also discovered that the serotonin levels of someone just *witnessing*, or even *learning* about the magnanimous gesture rose by the same amount as the primary participants. By any measure—an act of kindness is clearly a powerful vibration, so who *wouldn't* want to avail themselves of something that promises a payoff with such uniquely therapeutic benefits, and all for such a modest outlay? Evidently there *are* people who are aware of the benefits of practicing kindness because a poll conducted by *Time Magazine* showed that helping others was cited as a major source of happiness by an impressive 75 percent of American people. And research into volunteerism in England indicated that people who help others not only have lower rates of depression and heart disease but also enjoy better health all round.

It has to be emphasized however that this level of mutualism afforded both givers and receivers, is only possible when it emanates from a source of pure sincerity—a quality that some people seem to have a problem comprehending. Like the Hollywood producer, for instance, who I once heard voicing this self-parodistic axiom: "The key to making it in this town is sincerity, and anybody who can fake that has it made." I realize it was probably spoken half in jest, but it's a cynical view that's often taken literally by opportunistic people. Which is unfortunate because anyone living this way would be denying themselves access to the magical consequences that sincere acts of kindness can bring forth—just as long as they're authentic—simon-pure—and guile-free. That producer? Judging by the check I received, he was obviously living by his own creed because it was the rubber variety—the bank did eventually clear it—after two bounces.

## Kind Acts: More of 'Less is More'

The "Less is more" slogan which we referred to earlier could also apply to acts of kindness. The grand expansive (or expensive) gestures of charitable largesse are fine, in their place of course, but the acts of kindness we're discussing could be defined as being of a broader spectrum and of a scale that would allow them to become habitual, reflexive, and able to be appropriately dispensed at the drop of a hat, to friends, strangers and anyone with whom we come into contact as we go about our day. And, importantly, in casual, humble and unassuming ways—free from showboating of any kind, that would be about *us*, and that is *definitely not* what this is about.

Kind acts cover a wide range of possibilities and the value and significance of them to the recipients, being entirely relative, varies considerably. For instance, something as commonplace as offering to pick up a suit from the dry-cleaners for one person, while appreciated, may not be seen as all that big a deal because they didn't need it for another three days, when they would be passing by there anyway. But, the exact same trip can make us a shining hero in the eyes of a lady who happened to badly need that special dress for a formal function that evening but with their car in the shop, had no way of getting there. For us though—both acts are equally fulfilling.

Compliments too, of course, are always welcomed, and again, sincerity is the word. We probably all know from our own experience how a simple compliment, artlessly expressed at a propitious moment, can give us just the psychological boost we needed at that moment.

There are also times when just a simple "Thank you" is all it takes to make a welcome positive impact on someone's day. William A. Ward, the author of *Fountains of Faith* and one of America's most

## The Direct Connect

quoted inspirational writers, had a few words to say on this—he asks us: "God gave you a gift of 86,400 seconds today. Have you used one to say 'Thank you?'"

I think that's pretty inspiring food for thought, we might wonder who could possibly argue with such insight—well, I came across such a person recently. A gentleman on a TV News(?) show introduced as a "Time Management Consultant," was talking about his list of biggest office 'time wasters'. He said "The one that really drives me up the wall is email replies that just say 'Thank you'." Seriously? A 'Thank you' offends him? Evidently it hadn't occurred to him that besides being a desirable social nicety (what my daughter refers to as 'internet etiquette') that 'Thank you' actually doubles as confirmation of having received the initial message—a receipt, in the event the sending of it is brought into question later, a perfectly sensible business practice, but one that our friend would ban apparently. I hope he's not too disappointed when the deluge of 'Thank You' notes he was expecting from the clients who paid for his expert advice doesn't materialize, due to them being mindful of his advice about that being a big time-waster.

We've touched on how a simple "thank you" can qualify as a kind act, but there can be occasions when a kindness is even simpler than that, in that no words are needed at all. In fact all we have to do is summon up the humility it takes to refrain from stealing the spotlight from others by keeping our mouth shut. For instance, by resisting the urge to top a proud parent's account of their child's solid "A" minus grade by making it known that our own pride and joy just graduated valedictorian. I had the good fortune to witness such a scenario actually play out one Sunday afternoon. The kind and humble part was played by my good friend Tommy, and I've been familiar with this admirable character trait for many years now—he never fails to inspire me, and hopefully, everyone else with whom he comes into contact.

## Kind Acts: Instant Karma

Although we've been viewing acts of kindness strictly from the standpoint of pure and altruistic selflessness with no expectations of receiving anything in return other than the inner glow they leave us with, there are times when, with no effort at all on our part, we receive positive feedback—and we must admit, nonetheless, to finding it gratifyingly affirming.

The following accounts are of two such instances of this speedy delivery system we call "instant karma" that I've experienced.

Two years ago, when my sprinkler man was servicing a couple of heads on my lawn irrigation system, he suggested that I might also consider upgrading the underground connectors on the rest of the heads, and I asked him to go ahead. A few days later the sun had barely cleared the horizon when he arrived on the job. Over the course of the day, as I went about my own work, I'd had occasion to catch glimpses of him hard at work under a blistering Florida sun. So when he handed me his invoice at three thirty, impressed by the hard days work he'd put in and having reason to believe he'd also gone the extra mile, I went to my office and wrote a check for quite a bit more than what he'd billed me.

He thanked me profusely when I handed it to him through his van window and I explained that I'd had a piece of good fortune that week and whenever that happens I like to share it. Then as he was pulling away from the curb and I was about to go back into the house, I noticed my mail carrier's van approaching round the bend and went back to collect the mail she was about to deposit in my mailbox. Two pieces were junk, but I recognized the other as being a check from a client I'd designed a building for. The pleasure one gets from opening that kind of envelope is something I never seem to tire of, but this one doubled my pleasure. The check was attached to a photocopy of my invoice on which my client had written: "Everyone here is so thrilled by the magnificent job you did I rounded off the amount you billed us." You guessed it, the added bonus equaled exactly the one I'd handed over a minutes earlier—classic instant karma.

I've since made a point of relating that account whenever the opportunity presents itself with the hope that it could inspire someone to follow suit and discover the magic for themselves—(it truly is an affirming experience, for everyone involved). In the same way the following chain of events had served to inspire not only me, but, I found out later, the person I was with at the time.

This instance occurred when I was driving a show producer back to his office one afternoon after visiting the workshops to check the progress of some stage sets I'd designed. We were stationary in the left turn lane awaiting the green arrow that would put us on the road back to the expressway when a piteous looking individual approached the passenger window. He was carrying an empty coffee can and a scrawled sign indicating that any money dropped into it would help feed him. I know what you're probably thinking, but one never knows about these things, there are many unfortunate souls out there who are genuinely down on their luck and in need of a helping hand. And anyway, the gentleman sitting next to me, besides treating me to a great lunch at his Yacht Club, was about to pay me, for that day's consultation, the equivalent of what would have been a months salary just a few years before.

So, in an effort to do my bit to balance the world's social inequities, I reached into the little change compartment on the dashboard and handed the coins it held to *my* benefactor for the day and asked him to pass them along to our friend. As I was closing his window after he'd dropped them into the fellow's can, he said:

"Are you nuts, did you know there was all of two-fifty there?"

"So what?" I answered, "That's no big deal, did you notice what your club charged you for that coffee you said was awful at lunch?"

"The point is, you shouldn't encourage those people, you know he's only gonna spend it on booze or weed don't you?"

"No I don't actually, and neither do you."

"But you may as well have thrown that two-fifty down the drain."

"Nah, every cent of that will come back to me before the end of the day."

"Humph. Didn't they make a movie about you once—Pollyanna I think it was called."

Well, the upshot of all this was that less than ten minutes after our philosophical debate, there we were, me wearing a smug smile, and my friend staring at me incredulously and wide eyed while jokingly saying "I don't believe you Stanton—you are something else, you know that. Tell me, what's the color of the sky on that planet you're from?"

You see, just a few minutes after the panhandler incident, we'd wound up in quite a long slow moving line of vehicles at a toll plaza, with my friend going on and on about how this was all my fault because if I hadn't thrown my last change down the drain we'd have been able to use the "Exact Change" lane. All that came to an abrupt halt however when, on finally reaching the toll booth, the toll taker called out to me "The guy ahead of you already paid your toll for you and said to have a nice day."

The toll my good Samaritan had paid for me incidentally, was—as you've probably guessed—two dollars and fifty cents.

Such is the magic of instant karma, and the beauty of random acts of kindness, together with the always present prospect of them inspiring those witnessing them to help spread the word by example, as, I was to discover weeks later, this experience did for my friend.

## Acts of Self-Kindness: Credit Ourselves

Another way we can raise our level of self-liking involves us acknowledging our achievements. (Remember my earlier account of how I credited Sonia Choquette's oracle card titled "Celebrate You" with helping lift me out of a particularly bad patch?) We're most likely not in the habit of giving them much thought, and may not have even regarded them as achievements because they didn't stack up against feats like winning the U.S. Open. Or we may not have gotten that promotion we'd coveted so fervently or been elected class president, but they *are* there and they *were* achievements regardless of how much our ego has tried to convince us otherwise. Personal achievements are relative, they come in all shapes and sizes, they are all significant and we're entitled to be proud of them and by extension—ourselves. Again—*be our own very best friend!* Or, in our modern idiom—our VBFF.

They were, and still are, a form of energy, and as such they've been sitting down there in our subconscious waiting to be called upon and pressed into service, and all it requires to rekindle our remembrance of them is for us to take a reflective stroll down Memory Lane. It's a particularly propitious time to do this, because we're now in a better position to view their significance from a more centered and objective perspective and appreciate them in a more realistic representation than we could before. When we've succeeded in retrieving them and spent time reflecting on them we will have equipped ourselves with an excellent device with which to defend ourselves against those disheartening setbacks, brought on by such things as those haunting flashbacks of our loved one's suffering or those self-esteem-busting waves of self-recrimination that periodically bedevil us and threaten to further impede our progress.

## Act of Self-Kindness: Supersized

We should never doubt for one minute that we wouldn't have been assigned this horrendously demanding challenge if it was suspected that we didn't possess the degree of fortitude and stout-heartedness required to successfully overcome it. Virtues that, by any measure, rank right up there alongside the higher feats of valor—making us, in effect, nothing less than full-blown genuine heroes. Accordingly, we should never, ever, allow anyone to disparage, denigrate, or in any other way undervalue our efforts to heal and rebuild our life.

## A Brief Pertinent Afterword

Over the past three years or so, when I've been affectionately chided by friends for giving my writing priority over their social gatherings, my excuse has been "Books don't write themselves, you know." A piece of synchronicity that occurred just today however would indicate that there are times when, if you're lucky, they practically do.

The sequence of events began yesterday when I emailed an excerpt of what I'd written regarding the benefits we receive from our acts of kindness, to a friend of mine. When we met earlier today, she handed me a newspaper clipping while saying "Look what my horoscope said today—I'd just read it not more than two minutes before opening your email." Her horoscope said *"You'll be amazed at the satisfaction you get from helping others. Join a humanitarian cause and participate in making the world a better place for everyone."* Having often discussed the topic of synchronicity, we naturally both found this very interesting, for my friend, being an experienced humanitarian, it was a case of "preaching to the choir"—for me, the luxury of having a paragraph virtually write itself for a change.

## Affirmations: Emboldening Words to the Wise

It's inevitable that during our recovery we're going to experience a bad day or two, periodically, for some time, and in our weakened state, and with our minds enshrouded in the grief induced haze that can distort our powers of perception, we can easily become despaired when we misinterpret this slippage as being a sure indication that the efforts we're making to heal ourselves are not taking hold, and that we're about to spiral back down into that dark place.

There's a proven approach that we can implement however that helps us in arresting, then warding off, such negative thoughts, allowing us to restore clarity of thought and help get us back on track and move us more quickly along our path to recovery. It's a simple process, in that all it involves is the regular repetition of selected and appropriately emboldening affirmations.

The word affirmation has it's origins in the Latin word *affirmare*, which means "to assert and strengthen." Although the use of affirmations has sometimes been derisively regarded and written off as "touchy-feely" and New Agey—that's just simply not the case at all. The fact is, the use of them has been traced back to ancient cultures world-wide, and in that sense are closely allied with the long established ritual of chanting that's been practiced by many religions for thousands of years. The chanting of Sanskrit Mantras for instance, has long been considered to have the power to elevate us to higher levels of consciousness and help us to achieve our goals. In other cultures, rhythmic and repetitious chanting is viewed as a way to spiritual enlightenment and better health. Making the practice ideally suited for *our* purposes too—wouldn't you say?

As has so often been the case with other ancient metaphysical beliefs, modern day research methods and techniques have now been able to confirm their validity with factual supportive data—and so it is with affirmations too it would seem. Research by neuroscientists has shown that the repetitive chanting of mantras, either by saying them out loud or by just thinking them, amazingly, actually rewires our brains. In effect, restructuring areas of the brain by forming synapses between brain cells, resulting in the strengthening of their function—the more we affirm our thoughts, the more they're reinforced. One can only imagine how those millions of believers have been derisively mocked over the centuries for their steadfast belief in them.

It's not too much of a stretch, I don't think, to compare the benefits of affirmations with the gestures of that best friend we made mention of earlier, in that they're always there with a figurative gentle comforting hand on our shoulder, along with exactly the right words of reassurance and encouragement, and all dispensed at the precise time they're most needed.

As we've all no doubt experienced, our grief, by its very nature, has a despicably nasty habit of allowing any negative thoughts or behavioral patterns to sneakily take up residence in our psyche, causing absolute mayhem and resulting in them becoming stubbornly difficult to even modify—let alone eradicate altogether. Nothing less than a relentless day-to-day commitment to an appropriate curative is called for—a task for which the application of affirmations is singularly qualified. Their curriculum vitae would show that they can effectively give the lie to those hackneyed pieces of conventional wisdom, that for countless years, have assured us that: "A leopard can't change his spots," "A zebra can't change his stripes," and "You can't teach an old dog new tricks," (Now that last one is personal—I'm operating this computer aren't I?)

The appeal of, and the effectiveness of affirmations, for me, lies in the sheer simplicity of them. Which, as we've seen before, makes their acceptance difficult for those who insist on connoting effectiveness with complexity, and simplicity with "Too good to be true." I once heard a noted self-improvement guru contemptuously pooh-pooh them with the admonition: "Forget that corn-ball affirmation nonsense—they don't work—they're a bumper-sticker mentality."

To the contrary sir. Affirmations are actually concisely worded and right-on-point truisms—pithy encouraging rallying cries, if you will, that, when repeated over and over have proven to have the capability of resonating deep within our psyche to such a degree that lives can be magically and permanently changed for the better. With no unpleasant after-taste and with none of those negative side-effects associated with most other mainstream medicinals these days. I feel sorry for those who find affirmations too simplistic to be effective, but the fact is that many of the best things in life *are* simple, and *are,* as the affirming words of the song tell us—*free.*

Due no doubt to their characteristic short and to the point conciseness, affirmations have been likened to slogans. Those often memorable sayings that have been shown by advertisers and politicians alike, to be such a successful means of embedding their messages into our collective psyche to the extent that they frequently become part of our everyday vocabularies, at least until the next batch catch our imagination—or the fast-food merchant makes a menu change.

Some of the recalcitrants among us learn about the power of repetition early on, for me it was when I was in elementary school in Miss Stephenson's music class. Writing "I will not talk back to my teacher again," a thousand times to the sound of my mates outside kicking a soccer ball around ensured that I would never sass a teacher again.

Another example of the way many of us were introduced early on to the concept was through the children's story *The Little Engine That Could,* that has been produced in many versions since it appeared in a Swedish journal in 1906. The simple story centers around the plucky little locomotive who used the motivating phrase "I think I can—I think I can—I think I can" repeatedly to help him in pulling the train up a steep mountain incline. Analogous, it seems to me, to the uphill path confronting we bereaved.

## Affirmations: The Nature of Them

As we've noted before, this production—this show, is *ours* and ours alone. And any affirmations to which we feel guided are not dependent on the opinions or approval of others.

Our adoption of this mind-set frees us to be as creative and innovative as we want to be—literally anything goes, and furthermore, as we're the only ones who really know what's at stake, we own the exclusive rights to be the sole arbiters of what's good for us—what *we* feel will be healing. The answer to the question "will the embedding of the thought behind this phrase into my subconscious assist in my healing?" is the only criteria with which we need concern ourselves. With that established, we're ready to go into production, unfettered.

Our personal affirmations can be comprised of literally any words or phrases that resonate with us, that call out to us or that we, in any way, feel guided to—regardless of their source or whether they're slang terms, regional colloquialisms or even acceptable cusswords. Sources of appropriate eye-catching phrases for instance, can be found on items such as sympathy cards, get-well cards, and those inspirational cards with their emboldening words of encouragement. I have a friend who spent a lot of time searching through sophisticated and erudite pearls of wisdom, only to find that none of them lift her up more than the slogan on a card that her seven year old son gave to her. It depicts an adorable wide-eyed kitten hanging precariously from a tree branch, with the simple caption *"Hang in There."* She told me the reason it speaks to her so effectively is that she can't look at it, without hearing the words being spoken by young Nathan.

One of my own personal favorite types of spirit-lifters are certain songs. It's well known that the pairing of meaningful words with a rhythmic tune can make for a heart-gladdening mood raiser at any time and in any place. There's also something particularly habituating about catchy songs, evidenced by those days we've all experienced when we just can't stop one of them, a commercial jingle for instance, from going round and round endlessly in our head—even spreading contagiously to other people around us at times. Just the other day I got six people singing along while waiting in line at the Post Office.

The lyrics to virtually every song ever written are freely available to download from any number of websites. Another potentially bountiful internet source of morale boosting expressions are the

## DIY Recuperative Measures

numerous websites that carry quotations by prominent notables. Anything we can glean from any source are grist to the mill, and we don't have to feel obligated to copy them verbatim. For purposes of the desired brevity and succinctness, we can rewrite, edit, modify, paraphrase and customize them in any way we see fit, transforming them into quite powerful tools.

Regarding the thoughts and content of our affirmations, they can run the gamut from targeted expressions of a highly personal nature to universally accepted and long-established aphorisms. There is a tendency for us to sometimes regard the latter as "old hat" and dismiss them as clichés and therefore not to be taken too seriously. This is unfortunate because the over-familiarity that's behind this belittling attitude and the very reason they've been quoted so frequently over so many years is because they happen to be very wise and very true—true down through the ages, and just as true now. In being dismissive of them we take the risk of short-changing ourselves for the sake of appearing au courant. Consider, for example, the frequently expressed: "This too shall pass." This always reassuring adage, has been traced all the way back to the medieval writings of Persian poets. So, let's have a little respect for our elders—y'hear?

As you may have suspected by now, I give great credence to the feasibility of us being "led" or "guided." by spirit at any time. This is because I've found that when I've acted in accordance with my intuitive feelings, they have been on point on too many occasions for them to have resulted from chance coincidences. The process is known as "trust your vibes," which, coincidentally, is the title of an excellent book in this fascinating subject by Sonia Choquette.

If, after we've incorporated affirmations in our life for a while, some of them don't appear to have the level of relevancy they once had, or they don't seem to resonate with us to the same degree they once did, it could very well be a positive sign—a barometer reading of our progress and evolvement. It could be due to a slight shift in our perspective brought about by a fresh piece of knowledge coming into our purview. A friend of mine, for instance, because of frequent distressing setbacks, had become particularly fond of an affirmation that he referred to as his number one lifeline, it read: "Trust that everything is in Divine Order." After much reading and reflecting however, on the concept of Soul Plan—the life path he and his late wife had jointly drawn up and signed off on before they incarnated, he felt that something not so abstract and less ethereal would be more appropriate and more to the point. So now, at the first sign that a wave of his grief over his wife's passing may be about to overwhelm him, he meditates on and repeats the more pragmatic "Hey, we signed up for this!" He says it helps him to avert his imminent descent into those despicable depths and keeps his head above water. Apparently it's a phrase he and his fellow recruits had often used to help them survive the rigors of Marine Corps basic training.

Taking stock of the various affirmations *I'd* found most helpful over the past few years, the most powerful and consistently impactful one has been a phrase once voiced by a medium at the end of a reading—she said: "Remember—I will *always* be with you—come what may." I can't tell you the number of times those simple heartening words have served as *my* personal lifeline.

## Affirmations: The Mechanics of Them

Positive affirmations, as we've seen, can be a unique method of expression and for our purposes, a wonderful form of supportive encouragement, but there are certain considerations we need to be

## DIY Recuperative Measures

regardful of. For example, with the chanting of mantras, the affirmative messages are expressed vocally, requiring them to be clearly enunciated, with our affirmations being a *visual* communication, it's *legibility* that's a requisite to communicating their messages distinctly.

Readability of course is paramount in conveying any kinds of messages that we're trying to get across quickly and at a glance. A perfect case in point would be those crucially important road signs that are such a ubiquitous feature of our daily lives, where their unadorned clarity and unambiguous legibility are essential for their effectiveness. Conversely, the word "Stop" scrawled on a piece of cardboard at the side of the road is not going to be anywhere near as effective as the clear and distinct STOP signs that have been adopted worldwide. In terms of our affirmations, although a memo-to-self scrawled on a Post-it note on the refrigerator might be adequate in reminding us to pick up a gallon of milk, I seriously doubt if that technique would work very well in badgering us day after day in the way we want our affirmations to. Accordingly then, we should strive to make our affirmations as legible and as attention-grabbing as possible, in order for them to effectively convey their messages to us. I must explain that my harping on this is simply a measure of the degree of importance I attach to our affirmations—we have a lot riding on them. They're a great and invaluable tool.

With so many of us now having access to the typesetting capabilities that our computers afford us, we're able to create and produce a broad range of printed pieces that have quite a respectable professional appearance. It can be very gratifying to watch our favorite affirmations spring to life as we create ways of increasing their effectiveness by, for instance, emphasizing key words through the judicious use of certain eye-catching fonts, italics and vibrant colors etc., and also taking advantage of the seemingly endless variety of colored and textured papers and card stocks available on which to print them.

When coming up with ideas for eye-catching lettering and color combinations, bear in mind that as we're not going to be marketing them we don't have to be ground-breakingly novel, so we're allowed to "borrow" ideas from anywhere and everywhere. A widowed lady at a workshop I once attended, for instance, when showing us the very impressive collection she'd created, admitted to getting most of her ideas about fonts and color combinations from the various labels on grocery items in her pantry.

After we've finished printing them, we need to decide how to best display them for optimum effect. Ideally of course, they should be near at hand and easily visible to us throughout our day, regardless of where we are or what we happen to be doing, because there are times when it only takes a split second for one of those seeds of negativity to be sown, and once sown, can then germinate and take root in the next second after that. Such a level of access calls for them to not only be eye-catching, but be placed where they don't meld with their surroundings, as familiarity has a tendency to do.

For many of us in grief, our thoughts on first awakening can be particularly emotionally wrenching, with our minds consisting of a disturbing murky hodge-podge of dark depressive directionless thoughts swirling crazily around. Whenever this was the case with me, I found that heading for the affirmations I'd strategically taped to the dressing room mirror helped me nip them in the bud and cut through the desultory dross more effectively than anything else I'd tried.

I have a friend whose worst time was also on first awakening, but the long daily commute to his office required him to get into his car almost straight out of bed. So he attached his affirmations to the dashboard and the sun visor but in addition he also recorded a tape of them that he played back repeatedly throughout his trip. Other creative methods people have shared with me include a lady whose available desk space, due to a company policy, was limited to one frame. But she cannily bought one of those five-sided frames that rotate, which she frequently did during the day. Another widowed lady I met had found it just too upsetting to sit down for a meal at the table she'd shared with her late husband for 36 years. But a novel solution to her dilemma came to her out of the blue one day when she remembered something from her years as a restaurant manager. With the help of her graphic artist daughter they printed up colorful layouts of her favorite affirmations on cards that they then folded into variously shaped tent-cards, similar to those she'd placed on her restaurant tables every morning for years. Obviously in fine spirits now, she said "I'm finally able to relax and enjoy my meals—plus I get both my nutritional and spiritual sustenance, *and* feel my Joey's presence, all at the same time."

Affirmations are clearly an invaluable healing ally, and good legibility along with the right placement can ensure their benefits are fully optimized. There will naturally still be times when we're overcome by feelings of despondency, but thanks to our affirmations we are now equipped with a unique personalized survival kit that we can reach into at any time to give ourselves a "booster shot" as it were, to help us arrest any negative trending and put us back on course.

## Photographs: Utilizing Their Energy

I thought originally that the inclusion of a section about photographs in this list of recuperative measures, would be considered unnecessary—a no-brainer, because I think it's safe to say that we all

## The Direct Connect

have them around us and treasure them for the moral support and the good feelings they never fail to engender in us. However, a few days ago I received an email from an old friend with the cryptic subject line: *"Be sitting when you open these attachments Reg."*

I was subsequently thankful I'd taken Mike's advice, on two counts. One—I probably *would* have keeled over while reading them (as it was, I almost fell out of my chair), and two—the contents of them prompted me to decide that the inclusion of a section dealing with photographs of our loved ones was a must. The attachments you see, consisted of two clippings, one from a magazine article and the other from a book, both written by "experts," and both informing those of us in grief about the folly and the dangers of keeping photographs of our loved one around. (I believe I just heard a concerted: "WHAT?").

One of these dire declarations warned that the common practice of doing things such as kissing our loved one's photo in the morning or in the evening ensures that we bereaved will remain in grief which can result in depression.

The other "expert" on the subject stated that keeping photos of our loved one around keeps us linked to the past and is therefore deleterious to our recovery. To me, when people make statements like this it seems as if they're suggesting that in order to heal, we must expunge all thoughts and remembrances of our loved ones from our life—as if they never existed.

Scary stuff huh? So it was, that I decided that in order to allay any concerns that could arise in the event anyone happens to also come across these kinds of, what I regard as deluded and totally unhelpful opinions, I felt it's incumbent on me to share what *I've* learned about the unique benefits of having photographs of our loved ones around

## DIY Recuperative Measures

us, and the significant role they can play in our healing, along with my sources.

We are fortunate to have access, through intermediaries, to sources whose credentials for communicating the facts regarding the energies inherent in photographs, are unquestioningly impeccable. I'm referring of course to our friends and loved ones in the angelic realm, who, via the mediums have enlightened us on the subject quite comprehensively over the years—and needless to say, what they've told us runs counter to the opinions of those who steadfastly refuse to even acknowledge the fact that mediums are gifted with the ability to communicate with those thoroughly reliable sources who inhabit that special realm on the other side of the veil.

Is it at all conceivable that our loved ones in spirit would knowingly steer us wrong on this, or any other issue for that matter? Would they encourage us, as they have over and over in their readings, to openly display their photographs if it wasn't in the best interests of both us and themselves? Not for a nanosecond could I even imagine that to be the case. The following examples of references to photographs are just a few of many that I've encountered both in the mediums' writings and in my own readings with various mediums.

The illustrious English medium Doris Stokes had tragically lost her only child, her infant son John Michael, when he was just five months old., and in her book *Innocent Voices In My Ear,* she writes about how, every night for the rest of her life, she would say "Goodnight—God bless you," to his photograph on the mantel, and "Good morning my love,"each morning.

Her books, and those of other mediums, are replete with accounts of spirits referring to photographs in readings, in the form of accurate descriptions of their placement for instance, and aspects such as the types of flowers displayed alongside them and on which wall they were hanging, together with descriptions of the frames. In her book *Voices In My Ear* for instance, she tells of how a husband in spirit, after admitting to his widow that he'd been responsible for the noises around the house and also the moving of objects that she'd remarked on, asked Doris to tell his wife to "Get my photo out of the sideboard drawer and put it on top where it belongs." Not, as you'll notice, "put it *in* the drawer," or "*leave* it in the drawer," as those "experts" in their ignorance, believe we should do.

In *Innocent Voices In My Ear*, Doris cites an example that appears to attest to the unique inherent energies or resonance in photographs. When Doris asked the sitter what it was her daughter in spirit was trying to explain in relation to a certain flower, the girl's mother told her about the time she'd moved her daughter's portrait away from a vase that held a flower, and the perfectly healthy flower promptly wilted and drooped over. When she moved it back however a few minutes later, the flower completely recovered—and the entire incident witnessed by her husband sitting alongside her.

In her book *Whispering Voices,* Doris recounts numerous instances when spirits came through during her theater demonstrations and referred to their photographs. In one, a lady in spirit expressed her displeasure that her family had put artificial flowers in the vase they kept by her framed photo, instead of fresh ones—a detail that was substantiated by her relatives present. In another stage appearance, Doris told the parents of a 17 year old son in spirit that he was telling them to change that colored photo you keep of him—he doesn't like it. He says his hair doesn't look right.

The renowned medium Allison DuBois is also a confirmed believer in the positive energies emitted by our loved ones'

## DIY Recuperative Measures

photographs and cites many validations to this in her wonderfully enlightening books. In *Secrets of the Monarch* for instance, she tells us that she's learned from the spirits that our loved ones reminisce along with us as we pore over our memories of them depicted in photos taken during happy times together.

Allison is eminently qualified to advise us on such intimate aspects—she relates to us on these matters—she's been there herself. Accordingly, she speaks so poignantly in her books of how, when her beloved father made his transition, she was "emotionally and physically maimed." It's this degree of personal sensitivity to our situation, I feel, that allows her to appreciate the significance to her readers of amazing facts such as the one she shares with us in her book *We Are Their Heaven,* when she tells us that we actually provide comfort to our loved ones whenever we talk to them while looking at their picture, and that doing so also includes them in our lives. Another fascinating facet of our photographic reminders of our loved ones that Allison has learned about during the many readings she's conducted over the years, is that when we pore over our loved one's photos and one in particular stands out, that's their way of communicating to us what they look like now. This is a classic example of spirit influence in our lives.

I well remember two readings by James Van Praagh on his television program *Beyond* some years ago, when the spirits who came through referred to photographs with details that left no doubts about their authenticity. One validation that took the sitter's breath away and that he verified as being correct, described two photographs as being in the same frame, but rather than hanging on the wall, it was sitting on the floor and leaning against the wall.

In the other, the father of two young sons in spirit was stunned and thrilled when James told him that his boys were telling him about three photos of them he'd attached to the sun-visor in his truck, and that he touches and speaks to them every time he gets behind the wheel.

Could anything possibly make a better case for assigning our loves one's photographs such a comforting and supportive role in our lives?

What I've found particularly significant in recent years about the spirits' acknowledgments of photographs, is the degree of specificity in their descriptions. It seems that it's no longer enough for them to just *mention the presence* of their photographs, they do so now with details that leave us with no doubts at all as to their genuineness—the type of frame, color of the matt, even a small crack in the glass that the sitter herself hadn't even been aware of, and had to go and check. This didn't seem at all to be the case in transcriptions of readings I've read that were conducted years ago, validations from spirit in earlier days tended to be in more general terms.

It's been my feeling that this development hasn't come about serendipitously, but rather that it's due to an increased level of astuteness on the part of those in the spirit realm. It seems to me that a concerted effort on their part has succeeded in closing many of those loopholes that had previously served to provide the skeptics and naysayers with "low hanging fruit." It must have been so easy for them to be dismissive of spirit validations with their routine charges that mediums speak in loose and general terms—accusations that have historically been a stumbling block to the universal acceptance of this potentially powerful resource. As we saw in the readings we referenced, such charges no longer hold up when the photo in question *was* in fact in the drawer specified, and the flowers in the vase *were* actually artificial, and the frame with two photos *was* leaning against the wall—hardly vague, indeterminate and ambiguous generalities.

It's my belief that we can look forward to any future contrived reasons that the skeptics' put forward to explain their disdainful rejection of mediumship will assuredly succeed in prompting a similar kind of response from those in the realm of spirit. As we noted earlier in the book, Shakespeare, in *The Merchant of Venice,* said: "but at the length the truth will out."

## Photographs: My Own Validations by Mediums

I've been fortunate to have received several references to photographs of my wife in readings I've had with mediums since her passing, each one describing in detail features unique to the photo or painting in question.

Patrick Mathews for instance, after referring to a portrait of my wife hanging over the mantle on the far side of the living room area, said "Your wife wants you to know that there's really no need for you to call out to her portrait like you do, because when you're working in the kitchen she's always right at your side helping you." This confirmed what I'd always sensed—that when I'm preparing meals, seeing as how I'm in my cookery teacher wife's wheelhouse, she's helping me. If this *wasn't* the case, I'd have probably accidentally poisoned myself by now. Medium Carole J. Obley also referred to the same mantel while accurately describing the placement of a framed photograph of my wife, she said: "Your wife is bringing my attention to a photograph of her—it's in a polished brass frame, and it's on a decorative white mantel between a vase holding a large peach colored rose and a handsome antique mantel clock."

There's another photograph of my wife that the Reverend Mary Rose Gray talked about in a validation packed reading I once had with her. It's one of my favorite photos because, thanks to a few lighting techniques I'd picked up from professional photographers I'd worked with, together with a fortuitous change in the available light, I had the good fortune to capture an image that has quite a remarkable three-dimensional quality. The reason Mary Rose's reference to it was notable was due to the fact that a week prior to my reading with her, my friends Tommy and Nan had dropped by the house accompanied by Nan's sister Sylvia who was visiting from out of state. While Tommy and I were in the studio going over some illustrations I was creating for his company, Nan gave her sister the obligatory tour. When they joined us later, an elated Sylvia burst out "Reggie, that photo of Doris is amazing—she looks so real and so lifelike I felt she was about to speak to me in that beautiful English accent of hers."

Over the following few days, as I passed that photo when I was walking back and forth between the studio and the office, I would often stop, and mimicking Sylvia, quip, "You look so real, it's like you're about to speak to me." So imagine my reaction when, half way into her reading Mary Rose said "Your wife is telling me about a photo of her that's hanging in a hallway, and she's saying that you stop and look at it. And the reason you do is because it's so real it looks like she's about to say something. She says she likes that you take the time to do that."

Is it any wonder I champion the presence of photographs of our loved ones in our lives?

It occurs to me that I've never met, heard or read of any mediums who've ever been known to say or write anything but positive things about having photographs of our loved ones in spirit around us. With their knowledge of such matters coming from such an impeccably reliable source, namely the thousands of spirits with whom they've communicated in thousands upon thousands of readings—who could possibly be more qualified to advise us on this? Put those photos away and forget them indeed! Honestly, where do they get this stuff?

I'm hoping the foregoing testimonials regarding photographs of our loved ones have served to confirm and legitimize their therapeutic value to us on our road back to wellness—a journey on which we clearly have a traveling companion.

## Loneliness and Aloneness: Not Necessarily the Demons We've Been Led to Believe

One of the aspects of our grievous condition that can be particularly bedeviling is the state of abject aloneness in which we find ourselves when our loved one has made his/her transition, frequently to a degree we've never before experienced, and further amplified by, as we discussed earlier, the evaporation of so-called friends who decided we're no longer suitable "hang-out-with" material. However, those around us who *did* remain loyal naturally, out of their genuine concern for our well-being, are eager to advise us on how to deal with being lonely.

Unfortunately, their well-meaning ideas have often been shaped by years of societal conditioning that has disproportionately stigmatized loneliness in ways that, if over-dwelt on and in our vulnerable condition, can cause some of us to develop a phobia. We can imagine that we're unhealthily at odds with the rest if the world, heightening our sense of isolation even further and have us feeling more alone and abandoned than we've ever felt in our lives. Not exactly the kind of place we like being—and definitely not conducive to our healing. As Mother Teresa once said: "Loneliness and the feeling of being unwanted is the most terrible poverty."

## The Direct Connect

So that's the *downside* of our predicament—fortunately for us, there *is* an *upside,* and it centers around the fact that while it's quite common to mistakenly equate *loneliness* with *aloneness* they're actually, as sociologists will tell us, two distinctly different situations, in that loneliness is regarded as basically a state of mind whereas aloneness is a state of being. Confusing them, as we're often apt to do, can cause us to adopt a totally unwarranted self-critical and dire outlook that we could well do without at anytime, and certainly not now.

It's not that one is bad and the other one good however, there *are* times when they can both be positive and, contrary to what we're often lead to believe, we *do* have a say in the matter. There are many people who actually *choose* and *prefer* to be alone, and find aloneness to be both pleasurable and beneficial—the legendary enigmatic actress Greta Garbo for instance craved solitude so much her plaintive cry "I want to be alone," became a national catchphrase. A sentiment often echoed by creative people of all stripes—writers, music composers and artists etc., whose Divinely ordained callings can only be practiced in an environment of solitude. A situation with which they're completely comfortable, and often work for long periods of time in—totally alone in their own magically blissful world and loving every minute of it.

For many hundreds of generations now, the entire world has been blessed with the legacy these "loners" left us, the copious abundance of masterworks from across the entire spectrum of the arts, and all of such magnificence that it's impossible to imagine a world without their awe-inspiring presence—and each one, for the most part—the outcome of *aloneness*. The 18th century English historian Edward Gibbon and author of the epic *The Rise and Fall of the Roman Empire,* acknowledged this when he said: "I was never less alone than when I was by myself."

## DIY Recuperative Measures

It's aspects like this that makes it all the more difficult to understand how and why it is that aloneness has become almost universally stigmatized as being an undesirable condition. (I can picture the spirits of loners like Rembrandt and Beethoven enjoying a few good old laughs over this—and a self-celebratory glass or three of Schnaps).

And regarding loneliness, who hasn't experienced being in a crowded room, a function perhaps, and despite being surrounded by throngs of perfectly pleasant genial people, plus an open bar, we still felt dejected, utterly lonely, miserable, and all the while thinking 'On the whole, I'd rather be at home with my dogs, my favorite beverage and a Grisham novel'?"

Obviously, I'm not qualified to speak with authority on this complex subject, there are numerous excellent websites though that we can access that *can* enlighten us very well and that I've long been urging my friends to visit. Because our feelings of abject loneliness, especially in those critical early months after our loss, can be a source of considerable distress that, if not addressed level-headedly, can exacerbate our already fragile condition in ways that could be a definite detriment to our healing.

In the meantime, in the event we should feel that our feelings of loneliness make us disconcertingly different and at odds with the rest of the world, I'd like to share with you some fascinating statistics that came to my attention recently. I'm confident that you'll find them to be, as I did, surprisingly encouraging and could go a long way in helping us *un*-stigmatize loneliness and aloneness and help us to more healthily view them in their rightful and proper perspective. A step that I feel could assist us in allaying those totally unwarranted anxieties and eliminate any self-reproachful thoughts we're harboring regarding our isolation making us somehow unhealthily inadequate in any way.

## Loneliness and Aloneness: Join the Club—It Has a Huge Membership

It was reported by CBS News in May 2012 that after several years of tracking the seismic spike in "solo-dwelling," Eric Klinenberg, a Professor of Sociology at New York University, had come up with some incredible numbers. Figures that indicate that one is apparently no longer the loneliest number, because he'd not only found that 32.7 million Americans live alone, but also that roughly four out of ten households are single-person homes. Cities for instance like Seattle (42 percent), San Francisco (39.7 percent), and Denver (40.4 percent). It further turns out that on the urban island of Manhattan, almost HALF of all households are made up of just one person.

These startling statistics surely fly in the face of the reasons commonly given by those who are quick to admonish us for spending too much time alone, seemingly convinced that this is a sure sign we're seriously afflicted and bound to soon become weirdo reclusive oddballs. Those figures though suggest that if we do, we won't be short of company. The segment also went on to describe the experiences of the New York writer Kate Bolick. Ms. Bolick's notion that there was a need for some enlightenment on the subject of aloneness proved to be completely justified, because when her article on the joys of living alone was published in *The Atlantic* magazine it turned out to be one of the most widely-read pieces in the magazine's entire history—a feat that was responsible for landing her a major book deal.

Another American writer, the novelist Thomas Wolfe, also appears to have had a realistic and broader view of loneliness. In his essay *God's Lonely Man*, he wrote: "The whole conviction of my life now rests upon the belief that loneliness, far from being a rare and curious phenomenon, peculiar to myself and to a few other solitary men, is the central and inevitable fact of human existence." I guess then, that our loneliness is really another aspect of life—just one among the multitudinous array of facets of which we all consist. So this is what I've been saying to friends who are in the same boat—"Yes we *are* alone right now, and for the time being that's maybe how we prefer to be, but that does not in any way make us "an oddball" or weird or a dedicated hermit. And yes, I suppose that *does* make us "different" to the norm, but it's nothing more than another transitory condition that we need to go through in order to graduate from." Then I like to remind them of what the writer and philosopher Aldous Huxley told us in his acclaimed book *Brave New World*, he wrote: "If one's different, one's bound to be lonely." Another observation that also puts loneliness into perspective goes: "It is strange to be known so universally and yet to be so lonely." You may have heard of the gentleman responsible for this comment—he went by the name of Albert Einstein. That must surely be the ultimate credence to the old adage "It's lonely at the top."

We must admit then, that for the moment at least, we *are* "different" to the accepted norm, so why does it seem so difficult for others to appreciate the fact that with our healing being paramount, we could regard spending time alone to be a self-nurturingly remedial protocol that, for us, is infinitely more preferable to following the herd and socialize for socializing's sake, when we feel that doing so could be detrimental to our recovery. I imagine that one has to have actually experienced what we're going through to *really* appreciate how sickeningly cringeworthy it can be for the newly widowed ("newly" being a relative term, because it can be months or even years) to spend an evening surrounded by happy couples for instance.

The time will hopefully soon come when we actually *will* look forward to such occasions, but right now we shouldn't feel obligated to attend any functions that could potentially set us back weeks because of how our absence might "look" to someone. On the whole, friends—if they're genuinely true and caring friends, will be nothing but respectfully understanding of the courage it requires of us to remain steadfast to our convictions in the face of pressures to conform to social etiquette, and will accordingly allow us all the time we need to convalesce.

And besides, there's really no need for anyone to be so concerned about us, because after all we've been apprised by our private reliable sources in spirit that "We are *never* alone—*ever!*"

So things like aloneness and loneliness? We can handle *them*—piece of cake.

## Reverence for Life: It's a Two-Way Treat

We made reference earlier in this chapter to the classic *Five Stages of Grief* that were the keystone of Eisabeth Kubler-Ross's pioneering work in the field of grief support, and along with millions of others, I've been an ardent advocate of her wonderfully enlightening writings since I was introduced to them some years ago.

To my knowledge though Ms Kubler-Ross never claimed or implied that her groundbreaking *Five Stages* were an absolute, as some of her critics over the years have been known to suggest. On the contrary, to her credit, she never failed to make ample allowances for the multitudinous differences in the ways grief affects different people. One of the aspects of her five stages model for instance, that I've often heard brought up in debates has centered around how people often have unrealistic ideas regarding the transition between

## DIY Recuperative Measures

the stages—that the ending of one stage should more or less seamlessly segue into the next, seems to be their expectation.

Unfortunately, the process isn't always so cut and dried—in reality there's the ever-present possibility of stages overlapping, as those that we'd thought we'd safely graduated from reoccur for no apparent reason. Resulting in us becoming perplexed and somewhat disappointed to realize that we can't depend on our progress being as conveniently predictable as we'd hoped it would be, leaving us with disconcerting fears that we now have a hodge-podge of new concerns—namely the confusing intermixing of the residues of what we'd thought of as "done-with" previous stages—now returning to periodically plague us yet again while we're grappling with the current stage. Having the scattered remnants and residues of denial, anger, bargaining and depression battle it out in this way while we're struggling to make headway is akin to the barnacles that attach themselves to the hull of a racing skiff—in that our progress is impeded.

What we obviously have a need for, should we find ourselves stymied in this way, is something that will provide us with the means to figuratively mop up these troublesome dregs once and for all, and free us from their destructive negativity. The problem is, that with such a wide array of disparate challenges threatening to thwart our progress, this "magic pill" would itself need to be a broad spectrum type of medicine—preferably time-released.

Fortunately there *is* such an alleviative—it's called *reverence*. And while it's possibly compatible with most of the measures we've already been discussing, it is certainly augmentative to those that make up the rest of this chapter.

Although the word reverence usually connotes a strictly religious association in peoples' minds, it's also secularly applicable to literally

*The Direct Connect*

any*thing* or any*one* for which or for whom we have a deep and abiding respect. A broad spectrum of such reverence emits an energy so compelling that, when expressed, not only infuses everyone in its purview with the purest and most wholesome feelings of well-being, but does so in the purveyor of it too.

Albert Schweitzer was himself a highly revered gentleman. He was a German born philosopher, theologian, humanitarian, a medical missionary in Africa and the 1952 awardee of the Nobel Peace Prize. The fact that he also knew something about the "broad spectrum" quality of reverence is reflected in what he once said on the subject: "Just as white light consists of colored rays, so reverence for life contains all the components of ethics: love, kindness, sympathy, empathy, peacefulness and power to forgive."

A budding sociologist friend of mine is also of the mind that cultivating and fostering a genuine reverence for life using components like those listed by Schweitzer, could be the very tool we need to help us expunge the residues of our horrifying grieving stages that obstinately cling leech-like to our psyche, from where they continue to intermittently interject their influence in ways that inhibit and negate any progress we're making. Detaching ourselves from these impediments can give us the freedom, buoyancy and hope we need to advance along our path to healing. So surely we owe it both ourselves, and those around us, to at least explore with an open mind, along with an open heart, any measures that could possibly help us in achieving this.

A reverence for life is by no means just a cynical gambit—a disingenuous means to an end—a manipulative ploy to win someone's approval for instance. Far from it. Reverence of this quality is nothing less than an unimpeachably genuine emotion of the highest order. When it's expressed along with the customary and appropriate solemnity and awe, it's easy to see why reverence is so often mistakenly regarded as the exclusive province of religion (due also in part no doubt, to clergymen being identified by the title Reverend).

When we begin practicing reverence, we soon become aware of a prepossessing sense of purity, unsmirched by any expectations of materialistic outcomes that years of societal conditioning has led us to expect. The Classical Greek philosopher Plato was obviously aware of this dynamic, because he summed the situation up this way:

"Let parents bequeath to their children not riches, but the spirit of reverence."

## Reverence for Life: It's a Healing Golden White Light

In the condition our grief has put us in, having reverence for anything or anyone is probably not exactly at the top of our agenda right now. Having been mired in abject despondency for every waking minute, the only emotion we're capable of is most likely to be along the lines of unrelenting, self-abasing, maudlin introspection. All quite understandable responses to what has befallen us and all perfectly natural defense-mechanisms that will, also naturally, dissipate with time. However, Mother Nature—Spirit—Infinite Intelligence (call it what you will), sometimes needs a little help, and a little nudge from us to this end, never hurts—*if* we should feel up to it. It's a definite help to always bear in mind that all these proceedings, in all probability, are being orchestrated by those in the realm of Spirit anyway—our cheering section.

Those of us in grief, spend an inordinate amount of time engaged in introspection, which is, by definition, all about inwardness, darkness, hopelessness etc., and although we may not like to think so—unhealthily all about *self*. Reverence for life on the other hand, is about outwardness, light, hopefulness and thoughts about—and this is key—*others*.

Visually speaking, (which, being an artist, I frequently am) viewing life's multitudinous aspects with reverence is akin to seeing everything in the enthrallingly enchanting golden white light of late afternoon sunshine—the ambient light historically favored by artists. Whether they're portraitists, landscape artists, still-life painters, cinematographers—in fact any depicters of scenes comprising visually pitch-perfect beguiling idealistic moods and locales—popularly known as "the money shot," in the business—especially apropos for commercials.

It's no accident that this highly congenial golden white light is emphatically *not* the lighting of choice for scenes that are intended to invoke moods such as despair, despondency, anguish and abandonment, in other words the god-awful wretched emotions that have defined every moment of our existence lately. The often quoted maxim "Sunshine is the best disinfectant," seems to acknowledge this correlation. It is credited to no less a figure than Louis D. Brandeis, a highly esteemed U.S. Supreme Court Justice.

With despair, despondency and inconsolable anguish being just three of the numerous debilitating emotions we've had a bellyful of, we'd do well I think to try to acquire the habit of figuratively shining the golden white light of reverence on everyone and everything in our purview whenever the opportunity arises from now on. Easier said than done? No question—but was there ever a worthwhile endeavor of *any* kind that *wasn't*? Surely the potential of this measure to be such a potent soul-nurturing tonic is all the incentive we need.

## Walking: Literally Steps on Our Road Back to Wellness

The fundamental act of walking has been getting a lot of favorable press in recent years because of what those in the medical field have discovered about its impressive health benefits, and as a consequence people are taking to it in droves—whether they own a dog or not. It's now become common knowledge that exercise triggers our bodies to manufacture and release a range of chemicals such as endorphins, adrenaline, serotonin etc., to the extent that they're now casually referred to in conversation as "the happy hormones." A multitude of studies have shown that these hormones are responsible for collectively promoting within us an elevated level of self-esteem together with a highly desirable feeling of well-being—an emotional high, if you will. With the added advantage of course of all this being achieved quite naturally and therefore totally free of the undesirable side effects and adverse reactions associated with the artificial medications usually prescribed for mood enhancement. And all this without the need for specialized equipment, special skills or athletic abilities, and plus—it's all free.

So surely, providing we are physically up to it of course, fitting a walking session of 20 minutes minimum into our daily return-to-good-health regimen is clearly a most beneficial thing we can do for ourselves. And that's just the straightforward, walk—no frills, and also not contingent on *where* we walk—around the block where we live or work—literally anywhere fills the bill and can be perfectly adequate to our needs "as-is." That said however, there *are* measures we can take to augment the benefits still further. Let's take a look at a few of them.

## Walking: A Reverent Stroll in the Park

In the previous section, we made mention of the regular practice of reverence as being augmentative to the other healing measures we're self-applying. In this regard, walking and practicing reverence are made for each other. If only for the slower pace at which the world conveniently presents itself to us when we're merely walking, compared for example to when we're in a vehicle, where everything flashes by, pretty much unexamined, at "fast-forward "speed—we are, as a result, automatically afforded all the time we need to simply *observe* and *revere* what we don't normally have the time to take in to any appreciable degree.

Personally, I can't think of any acitivity that provides us with a better opportunity to take in and revere what we observe than when we embark on a walk in nature—it's nothing less than "a marriage made in heaven, as the saying goes. For the simple reason, whenever we walk in nature and no matter what the locale, whether it's in the woods, an urban public park, mountain areas or the beach—God's gloriousness surrounds and accompanies us every single step of the way. There simply is no way we could *not* be affected by the awe-inspiring majesty of it all even if we were dumb enough to try. And regardless of the weather conditions, there is so much to be aware of—to be reverent towards, that we can't help but feel "at one" with each living, breathing and vibrating molecule of it all. All in all, we are left pleasingly sated by a warm shower-on-the-inside, glow of reverence—reverence in it's purest form. A soul-nurturing encounter to be sure.

Great minds have been in accord on the magic of nature for at least 2000 years, that was when the Greek philosopher Aristotle said :

## DIY Recuperative Measures

— "There is something of the marvelous in all things of nature."

— John Muir, the Scottish-American naturalist and conservationist and founder of TheSierra Club said, much later: "In every walk with nature one receives more than he seeks."

— The Bengali philosopher Rabindranath Tagore, who was awarded the Nobel Prize in literature in 1913 said: "Trees are the earth's endless effort to speak to the listening heaven."

— The English writer Aldous Huxley, son of the writer Leonard Huxley, said: "My father considered a walk among the mountains as the equivalent of churchgoing."

— More recently, Sir David Attenborough, the celebrated English broadcaster and naturalist who a nation wide study showed to be "The most trustworthy public figure in Britain," said in a television interview that "When you are around nature, you are never ever bored."

All these authoritative attestations, and there are many more, have been corroborated in one way or another in countless scientific studies over the years—having shown repeatedly that just being in natural environments lowers our blood pressure and pulse rate, significantly eases muscular tensions and elevates our mood.

E. O. Wilson, is the American biologist known as "the father of biodiversity." In his 1984 book *Biophilia,* he put forward the hypothesis that suggests that there is actually an instinctive bond between human beings and other living systems. For which he coined the term "Biophilia," which literally means "love of life and living systems." His biophilia theory suggests that humans thrive in nature and actually suffer in its absence.

## Walking: Nothing Like a Stroll Through the "Oxygen Factory"

Studies have indicated that many of the beneficial outcomes of a walking regimen are attributable to the ways in which walking stimulates our hearts to pump more oxygen to our brains. So in this regard, that walk in the park, or any green space where there are leafy trees, is a highly healthfully rewarding trip if only to pick up a supply of the oxygen that trees produce, which they do in impressively prodigious amounts. We've all known since way back in kindergarten that "trees are our friends" because they gift us with valuable life-sustaining oxygen, but never did we imagine the enormity of their daily output—day in and day out. And all with no minimum wage and no benefits—an occasional pruning maybe, but paid vacations? Forget it.

Here are a few tree statistics I came across. A tree's oxygen production varies between species of course and is also dependant on it's age (it always seems to come down to that), but the Arbor Day Foundation tells us that "a mature leafy tree produces as much oxygen in a season as 10 people inhale in an entire year," and incredibly, a single mature tree absorbs 48 pounds of carbon dioxide in a year. And the Northwest Territories Forest Management inform us that a 100 foot tree, 18 inches in diameter at its base, produces an extraordinary 6,000 pounds of oxygen.

With payoffs like these it's no wonder we now appreciatively celebrate our tree friends with official Tree Hugging Days around the country—seems to be the least we can do. It's a feeling that seems to be mutual—a quid pro quo aspect, because there are many practitioners in the burgeoning field of Holistic Healing who now recommend a variety of ways of using the actual hugging of trees as a viable healing modality. Is that cool or what?

More credence is given to this kind of phenomena regarding trees by Angela Wansbury in her book *Birds: Divine Messengers,* where she shares an interesting account of her own experience with our tree friends. Apparently she'd felt for some time that she was sensitive to the energies emitted by pine trees, due to the fact that whenever she was around them she felt somehow "more alive." Her suspicions were confirmed when she made the discovery that the energies inherent in pine trees actually pulsate at a frequency very similar to that of the *human* energy field and merely being in close proximity to them recharges our energies. I think it's a good time to get more "Hug-a-Tree" tee-shirts on the market.

## Walking: More Ions in the Fire—(not a typo)

Yet another scientifically proven health benefit we derive from our walks in nature occurs through the fascinating phenomenon of Negative Ions. These are electrically charged particles created quite naturally when molecules of air break down in the presence of fast moving air and water, the very kind of conditions that happen to characterize those locations to which people, for generations have flocked for their vacations—the seashore resorts for instance and hilly countryside regions. A rudimentary explanation for why we come away from these locales feeling revitalized and energized (hence, no doubt, the term 'recharging my batteries'), is that, in the case of the seashore, the negative ions we breathe in are created by the sea breezes passing over the waves and also the action of the waves crashing onto the shore. In the case of hilly countryside areas, these same negative ions are formed by the actions of winds flowing over the undulating terrain and by waterfalls cascading and plunging into the turbulent basins at their foot.

These principles were discovered by a Swedish chemist Dr. Svante August Arrenius, who was awarded the Nobel prize in Chemistry in 1903. Other benefits we can expect from breathing in and being generally exposed to negative ions for a period of time include:

— An increase of oxygen to the brain, endowing us with a higher level of alertness and an increase in mental energy.
— The stabilizing of brain function results in general feelings of calmness.
— Biochemical responses that increase the levels of serotonin—the mood chemical known to diminish depression and reduce stress.
— An increase in the levels of calcium in our bloodstream which helps purify our blood.

Not at all a bad deal for a therapy that's unlimited, entirely free and where the only thing required of us is to just show up—and breathe.

There is also an extensive range of various types of portable ionizer generating devices now available that allow us to conveniently avail ourselves of all these benefits in every area of our life, throughout our home and workplace—I've even had a small one in my car for several years.

## Walking: To the Beat of the Thymus Thump

This potentially restorative measure that we can adopt to help further enhance the benefits of our walking regimen, involves a body-part that we've likely never had cause to even think about before, let alone locate its whereabouts—it's our thymus gland.

## DIY Recuperative Measures

We know that the function of the thymus is to support our all-important immune system, while also playing a major role in controlling the flow of "life energy"—or "spiritedness"—the meaning of the Greek word thymos. It also has a tendency to be adversely affected by stress, something we grievers can certainly relate to, but studies in the field of behavioral kinesiology have shown that it can be stimulated and revitalized by a simple technique dubbed "The Thymus Thump" (more of a series of firm taps really—but you know these smart-alec wordsmiths).

The thymus gland itself is situated under the upper part of the breastbone just below the hollow of the throat. The Thymus Thump consists of simply tapping this area, quite firmly, with our finger tips. My wife and I were taught this process by a holistic naturopath doctor some years ago, and he recommended that we carry this out in two parts early on in our walk, as we're getting into our stride. All the first part entails is to stimulate the thymus by tapping that area firmly with the ends of our fingers, like we were tapping a tambourine say, in a series of rhythmic 1-2-3 : 1-2-3 : 1-2-3's over 20 seconds or so. The other part calls for us to breathe in deeply to a count of 4 steps, then exhale—again to the count of 4 steps, but in the form of a pronounced, almost throat-clearing, HA! with each of the 4 steps. Repeat this second stage 4 or 5 times and do the sets intermittently every 10 minutes or so throughout the remainder of our walk. We shouldn't have any expectation of our revitalized thymus function being dramatically apparent in any tangible way—we just have to trust that it is. Another component in our remedial mix.

## Walking: To Nature's Musical Accompaniment

Some years ago my editor, handed me the pleasurable assignment of covering a major PGA golf tournament—literally a walk-in-the-park perk, one might say. When we'd agreed that our readers might find it of interest to learn something about the considerable amount of preparation required to bring live events like this into our living room every weekend throughout the summer, I arranged to meet up with the television production crew early the following morning.

While waiting around for them to arrive in their big-as-a-house trucks at daybreak, I used the time to familiarize myself with the beautiful manicured course while all the time being treated to the fresh morning air filled with the wondrous chorus of birds as they greeted the dawn. Little did I know that I was soon to receive a fascinating insight into the important role their kinfolk would be playing in the upcoming production—a part that, it turns out, is tantamount to the all-important background music of pretty much every movie ever made. The only difference being, this particular musical accompaniment was going to be provided by our fine feathered friends.

In due course it was explained to me how an overlay of recorded birdsongs from an extensive library, songs known to be specifically appropriate to that particular region, are carefully superimposed over the real-time ambient sound, in order to enhance the pleasing outdoor experience that characterizes the golf experience. When the audio technician obligingly demonstrated identical footage with and without this melodic augmentation, the difference between them was quite dramatic.

I was to recall that enlightening morning years later when I embarked on my walking regimen at dawn around the lake in my local well-wooded park, and came to really appreciate the significant contribution birds make to what, in effect, is actually a live and quite exhilarating soundtrack to our very own personalized travelogue.

## DIY Recuperative Measures

As I was in the process of assembling material for this subject, an interesting article in *The Wall Street* Journal came to my attention. It dealt with the research being carried out into the calming effect of birdsongs, and described how a dessert town in California had been attempting to deal with the troubling high crime rate along a certain stretch of highway. After consulting with a research firm in England, they installed 70 speakers along the notorious stretch, over which, for 5 hours a day, they broadcast the sounds of birdsongs along with the soft sounds of trickling water. After just 10 months, the police department reported a 15 percent drop in minor crimes and a 6 percent reduction in serious crimes. Experts in this field believe that the soothing effect of birdsongs is due to their ability to reduce cortisol and adrenaline—two of our body's hormones know to respond to stress.

Interestingly, the cheerful sounds of chirping birds are also now being played in several of those notorious stress inducing facilities—namely those seemingly perpetually bustling airport terminals—in an effort to relieve passengers' stress.

## Walking: Doing it Mindfully

So, it seems that in order for us to derive maximum physical and emotional benefits from our walks in nature, we would do well to make the effort to remain mindful of our breathing, particularly the breathing in of those negative ions, while staying consciously reverential towards everything in our purview that we can see, smell, hug and hear—especially our feathered friends who contribute much to the specialness of our experience. Practicing, in a word—*mindfulness*.

The practice of mindfulness is one of the cornerstones of Zen Buddhism—focusing our mind on the present to the exclusion of any thoughts that smack of negative brooding about the past and/or the future—*being in the now* is another way it's often expressed. It goes without saying that walking in natural surroundings provides an excellent opportunity to practice it, if only because, as Sir David Attenborough implied, "there's so much to observe in nature that when we're around it we are never ever bored."

We would be hard pressed indeed to come up with a combination of activity *and* locale that is more ideally suited for our special needs than the simple act of taking a leisurely mindful walk through our favorite neighborhood park. For emotions such as ours—brutalized as they've been by grief—and subjected to prolonged periods of confused, scattered and disordered thoughts regarding both the past and the future, gifting ourselves with the time to take a walk in nature will go a long way to helping us extricate ourselves from this maelstrom and try to focus instead on being *in the now—in the moment*. It can prove to be a highly rewarding investment of our time—and the very mollifying balm we've been longing for to help get us back on the road to the level of peace and acceptance that, for us, will constitute the wellness we seek.

## Music: Nutrition for the Soul

The legendary librettist Oscar Hammerstein II famously told us that "The hills are alive with the sound of 'it'." And according to the Scottish composer Fred Hartley "Life is nothing without 'it'," with which he could have unconsciously been channeling the German philosopher Friedrich Nietzsche who asserted, back in 1889, "Without music life would be a mistake." More recently, the Grammy winning Music Director, composer and record producer Peter Rutenberg, faculty member of the Herb Alpert School of Music at UCLA, described music as being nothing less than "The path to well-being, harmony and peace." The path and destination to which we aspire.

It seems that every time I've ever attended a seminar or studied a book on how to attain and subsequently lead a spiritually fulfilling and emotionally centered life, right up there on the list of suggestions of how we can go about this is through music. And all that's required in order to reap it's magical benefits is for us to make a concerted effort to identify the types of music that "speak" to us—that "move" us (and we all have at least one—it's in our DNA), and carve out spaces for it them in as many areas of our daily life as we can. With the resultant benefits being so undeniably significant to our recovery, and with the entire range of music forms so readily available and convenient to organize and download onto our various devices, there's no excuse for not dosing ourselves up with this type of medicine—it's such a sweet pill to take after all, "a spoonful of sugar" not necessary here Ms Andrews.

Music's desirable influence is so broad and multi-faceted that it's frequently expressed in paranormal terms by the mediums. Psychic Intuitive Sonia Choquette for instance, who's oracle cards we discussed in chapter nine, has a card in her *The Answer is Simple* deck titled *Listen to the Music*. In her accompanying description of it she tells us that "Music will calm your mind so that inner guidance from Spirit can be felt." Then further along she says "Music will calm the moment. As you listen to it, the heavenly forces will work on your behalf to bring about joyful resolution and a peaceful outcome." My guide(s) have selected this card many many times now.

There's ample documented evidence too, that indicates that the illustrious Ludwig Van Beethoven also knew something about the spiritual connectivity aspect of music. Signified by his observation: "Music is the mediator between the spiritual and the sensual life."

Speaking of mediators, the renowned medium Allison DuBois is also in accord with the previous two "greats." She writes in her book, *Secrets of the Monarch*, about how she's learned that listening to our favorite music can connect us to our loved ones in Spirit. She tells us that "Music soothes the soul.....it's a powerful way to reconnect with those you love. The vibration of the music seems to be felt by both the living and those who live again."

## Music: It's Magic Disseminated en Masse

There's a weekly nationally broadcast BBC radio program in England titled *Desert Island Discs*. Amazingly, it has now been on the air continuously for 73 years—since January 1942 to be exact. It strikes me that longevity as phenomenal as this must surely attest to the universality of music's power, if only for the way this program has become so deeply and affectionately embedded in the collective national psyche—and all achieved with the simplest of formats.

Each week, a guest celebrity drawn from all fields of activities, chooses eight of their favorite pieces of music that they would like to have in the hypothetical event they were marooned on a desert island—and discusses the reasons behind their choices. Some fascinating and intriguing revelations regarding the significance of each piece in their hearts and minds invariably ensue as a result. A measure of this national institution's continued popularity in recent years has been the ways in which it has become available for download and streaming via desktop computers and a whole range of mobile devices.

Another BBC radio program that enjoyed a long run, albeit a mere 27 years this time, was called *Music While You Work*. It was

## DIY Recuperative Measures

broadcast twice daily on weekdays and ran from June 1940, at the height of World War II, until September 1967. Consisting of non-stop popular music performed live by the leading bands of the day—a different one each day, the 30 minute program was introduced initially for the purpose of raising the morale of factory workers during the stressfully perilous years of the blitz with the added expectation that productivity would improve as a result. A concept that, judging by its extensive run well into the post-war period of economic recovery, was obviously eminently successful—and more testimony to the impressive positive power of music.

Music as a morale boosting element for Londoners being subjected to the almost constant nightly bombing raids of early World War II, was also at the core of another successful venture. With all gathering places such as theaters, art galleries and museums shut down by the government as a measure to avoid casualties, there was a dearth of entertainment and cultural activities, pursuits that would normally provide much needed respite. But the celebrated classical pianist Myra Hess came up with a wonderfully inspired idea. She volunteered to organize the staging of, and perform in, daily lunchtime classical music concerts in the spacious National Gallery in central London for those who worked in the area. The concerts proceeded to take place from Monday through Friday every day, year round, throughout the war and were phenomenally successful as people in their hundreds of thousands sought the respite from relentless stress they badly needed. Some film clips of these performances have survived, and thanks to the internet we can access them.

Such is the marvelous magic of music. For sure, a potent force for the good and so conveniently accessible to absolutely anyone who cares to avail themselves of it.

## Music: The Other Universal Health Care

During the course of my research for this segment on the health benefits of music, I came across several fascinating articles dealing with the life expectancy of members of the music profession, with particular emphasis on those who work in the classical music field. There's almost a surfeit of statistics regarding their longevity for instance, about which Wikipedia lists 56 musicians who merit the title "centenarian." Other impressive age related factoids include:

— Lorin Maazel was appointed chief conductor of the Munich Philharmonic after he'd turned 80.

— The celebrated pianist Vladimir Horowitz played several gigs in his native Russia when he was 83.

— The legendary conductor Arturo Toscanini finally decided to pack it in—at 87.

— Even though English born Leopold Stokowski had conducted his final concert when he was 90, he couldn't stay away from it, and continued to wave his baton around—his magical wand, while making recordings right up until his death—at 95.

No one's implying that data like this, in any way, constitutes a scientific study, or gives us the go-ahead to go online and click a piano, a podium, and a baton together with a 100 cake candles, into your figurative shopping cart. But nevertheless, an insurance agent friend of mine tells me that figures like these certainly attract the attention of those responsible for compiling life insurance mortality tables.

## Music: "Has Charms to Soothe a Savage Breast"

That the English playwright William Congreve made this much-quoted observation the opening line of his 1697 play *The Mourning*

## DIY Recuperative Measures

*Bride,* would suggest that either he had some knowledge of music's magical healing powers or that he himself had equally finely tuned powers of prophecy. Because over the 300 ensuing years since, countless studies have shown it to be an irrefutable fact that music *does indeed* have a unique ability to heal—and soothe.

Although the results of recent studies are often cited to attest to music's healing powers, it's by no means anywhere near being a modern notion. There's evidence for instance, that shows music therapy was commonly used in India as far back as 5000 years, as an aid in the convalescence of the sick. It's also known that Pythagoras, the Ionic Greek mathematician, believed 2500 years ago that music possesses healing properties—referring in his writings to chants, rhythms and melodies as "musical medicine."

No doubt, from his current Divinely exalted location, he's deriving great satisfaction from the findings of modern day studies that show for instance that our levels of antibodies (those proteins that target invading viruses and harmful bacteria), increase significantly after listening to just 50 minutes of uplifting music. And further—that scientists have found that immune system weakening stress hormones show a marked decrease after being exposed to music. As if these findings aren't impressive enough, consider the fact that, in the case of dopamine—the "happy hormone," it's been discovered that not only does *listening* to music cause a release of it, but the mere *anticipation* of music results in a release of it too. Now that, to me, is truly phenomenal.

Dr. Mitchell Gaynor, Founder and President of New York based Gaynor Integrative Oncology, says that he has seen cancer patients actually go into remission utilizing Sound Therapy. And, amazingly, there have been many reports by medical practitioners in a whole range of fields who have found that when they expose their patients to music, it allows them to *decrease* their dosages of pain medication.

The Sing and Hum website reports Dr Raymond Bahr, Director of the Coronary Care Unit of St. Agnes Hospital, Baltimore as saying that listening to classical music for just 30 minutes produces the same effect as ten milligrams of Valium.

This latter I can attest to personally, because I well remember how thrilling and gratifying it was when, during my reading with medium Carole Lynne, she said to me quite out of the blue: "Your wife is thanking you for the music system you set up in her room, so that she could hear her music round the clock—because without it she wouldn't have been able to make it." Well of course she *hadn't* "made it," but we both knew what she meant. The round-the-clock hospice nurses had remarked to me at the time that my wife hadn't required as much morphine as she had previously and also that she hadn't been crying as much during the night.

## Music: Trailblazing its therapeutic benefits

One person who is undoubtedly delighted by the relatively recent burgeoning of the music therapy field (and we do know by now that despite having made his transition—he *is* watching all this), is a gentleman by the name of Theodore Presser. In 1883 Mr Presser founded the music magazine *Etude*, and at its peak in the early 1920's its circulation was an impressive 250,000 copies per month.

Unfortunately it ceased publication in 1949, but the legacy it left the world was the notion, promulgated repeatedly in articles, that music inherently possesses viable therapeutic benefits—in more than a hundred articles over the years. Writers from a wide

## DIY Recuperative Measures

range of backgrounds, all extolling by examples and case studies the health benefits and virtues of music therapy. Quite amazing when one considers that even in this day and age, holistic approaches to medicine are still regarded as controversial and are constantly struggling to be officially recognized. They *will* succeed though, they're all rapidly gaining ground, and when that day comes we can look back and applaud Mr Presser for dedicating more than 50 years to laying the foundations—note by note.

So I was delighted when I learned earlier today from one of today's "torch carriers," namely the American Music Therapy Assoc., of Silver Spring, Maryland, (who, by the way, have great On-hold music) that there are now over 6500 board certified Music Therapists working in hospitals, pain clinics and hospice settings etc. That is very soul-nurturing stuff don't you think?

Anyone would be hard-pressed I feel, to come up with a healing modality that is as broad based as music therapy is. What other disciplines, for instance, can reach so deeply into our hearts, our minds and our innermost souls even, as music has proved it has the ability to do. That is powerful stuff by any measure.

So powerful and far-reaching that it's no accident that in many impoverished and unstable Third World countries, music and musicians are often the first groups to be singled out to be censored and victimized by various measures—incarcerated even—for merely *listening* to music on their usually illicit radios. And all apparently, because of their leaders' irrational paranoia regarding music's ability to capture the very hearts and minds of their repressed subjects at a level they themselves can't possibly aspire to. Music's influence, it seems, can be a veritable multi level changer for the good—both personally and globally.

## Singing: It's Not Just for the Birds

*"He who sings scares away his woes."*
—Miguel de Cervantes

As we discuss the benefits of singing, we'll still be on the subject of music therapy—it merits special attention however if only for the fact that it differs in one significant respect. This being that instead of us receiving it through intermediary playing devices, *we ourselves* are the device—the source. So our doses of its therapeutic powers are, as it were, undiluted. Besides being more personalized and available anywhere, at any time—in effect, timed-released medicine. The results, accordingly, are quite amazing and backed by authoritative studies.

Studies for instance, have associated singing with lowering blood pressure, decreasing heart rate and effectively reducing the debilitating effects of stress in general. Studies have also revealed that singing actually boosts the immune system and fosters feelings of well-being.

A study carried out at the University of Frankfurt in Germany, showed that active members of choirs had elevated levels of cortisol and immunoglobulin A. Cortisol is the hormone that modulates the negative changes that occur in the body due to stress, while immunoglobulin A is an antibody that plays a critical role in mucosal immunity. Antibodies are proteins manufactured by the immune system to fight off threats by harmful bacteria and viruses.

It was reported in the English *Daily Telegraph* in October 2013 that research into choristers by Dr. Bjorn Vickhoff at the University of Gothenburg, Sweden determined that the process of singing together with others has the effect of inducing a level of calmness that is as beneficial to their health as yoga. Choral singers were also the subject of a joint study in 2008 by Harvard and Yale Universities, their research indicated that choral singing had actually increased the life expectancy of the residents in a Connecticut town.

Shelby Sweeten is an accomplished singer from Minnesota and in January 2012 she auditioned for the hit television show *American Idol*. In interviews conducted at the time, she revealed how singing in preparation for the audition stages of the show had helped her immensely in overcoming her debilitating bipolar condition, a disorder that had been diagnosed after struggling with the depression she'd battled with ever since the fourth grade. She went on to share that whenever she'd been beset with periodic hypo-manic episodes, singing, sometimes along with her mother, had really helped her.

Pioneering music therapy techniques incorporating singing have been credited with playing a major role in the miraculous recovery of U. S. Congresswoman Gabrielle Giffords. She was, you no doubt remember, the victim of an assassination attempt in which six others were killed and 13 wounded, at a public forum in Tucson, Arizona in January 2011. The critical head injuries she sustained were so severe that it was initially believed by doctors that she would spend the rest of her life in a vegetative state.

*The Sunday Telegraph* however, reported just 7 weeks later that through an array of various pioneering therapies, together with what doctors described as "sheer willpower" on her part, she had succeeded in confounding all expectations and was steadily regaining her faculties. Working with musical therapists at TIRR Memorial Hermann Rehabilitation Hospital in Houston, her phenomenal comeback had first involved the singing of classic nursery rhymes and gradually progressed to sing-alongs of jazz and rock classics.

Later, in November 2011, ABC News reported Ms. Giffords' music therapist as explaining that her inability to speak was due to the irreparable damage to the brain's language pathway. The process, known as neuroplasticity, was likened to a freeway detour where the act of singing stimulates the brain's ability to pave a new alternative route around the damaged areas—in effect, turning a one-lane road into a super highway. Awe-inspiringly wonderful stuff—and all facilitated by the simple act of singing.

## Singing: Those Lighter-Than-Air Ditties Can Lift the Heaviest of Hearts

We've seen how the deceptively simple act of singing can literally work miracles. I use the word "simple" guardedly because I realize that in our sometimes lamentably heavy-hearted and melancholic condition, to actually sing out loud could, quite understandably, be the furthest thing from our minds or inclinations right now. "Check with me sometime later—like never." "Me? Sing? Are you out of your mind?" Those are just two of the responses I received when I broached the subject to fellow-grieving friends after reading so much about it.

As we've said before however, but it bears repeating, every journey begins with a single step—whether it's across the kitchen to get the phone or across the continent. So please, we owe it to ourselves, those around us and above all—our physically absent loved ones, to find a way to motivate ourselves and take those first steps. We have nothing to lose but our misery.

Sonia Choquette has long championed the power of singing, both in her workshops around the world and in her written words. In her *The Answer is Simple* oracle card deck she has a card titled *Just Sing*. The accompanying guide book commentary on its meaning assures us that "When you sing, you wake up the angels and escort them

## DIY Recuperative Measures

into your life." Then later: "A singing heart is a happy heart—and a healing one." I've drawn that card many many times now, and invariably when my spirits are a little low.

Several friends of mine who at first had felt reticent about opening up in full voice even, puzzlingly, in the privacy of their own homes, overcame their bashfulness by singing along to recorded songs, and to their astonishment—their ceiling didn't come crashing down. It may seem at times that there's hardly a surfeit of happy uplifting songs around these days, but thanks to the internet we have a rich mother-lode of all genres to choose from.

Even those catchy commercial jingles can be effectively utilized for our purposes. We've all experienced those jingles that become "ear-worms" that we can't get out of our heads—quite silly ditties really, but inveterate spirit lifters nonetheless, and for our purposes—all grist to the mill. Song lyrics are also available on many websites in the event the words are uniquely pertinent to our situation and our relationship with our loved one. Sonia Choquette, in her enlightening book *True Balance,* has a few affirming words of wisdom about lyrics that could be construed as affirmations. She writes: "When you sing an affirmation, you engage the power of the heart chakra as well. When you bring these two energy centers into alignment, you release one of the most powerful forces on earth."

Although there's no denying that the song content can have substantial significance, from what we've learned, the actual singing process is the component that appears to contribute to the physiological benefits we derive. So in that regard, what we sing can take the form of pretty much anything, madrigals, Christmas carols, hymns, nursery rhymes, the national anthem even—anything that we feel exalted by when we belt it out. No one need hear us—it's our home, our domain, we're the ones paying for it. Another option we have, and the favorite of a few of my friends, that affords us the privacy we feel we need in order to feel sufficiently uninhibited, is while we're driving. At least it's safer than texting so let her rip—we'll feel all the better for it.

A few of my friends have those film clips of classic songs bookmarked on their desktops, they like the added layer of uplifting images. Three examples they've cited are:

— *Zip-a-dee-doo-dah*, performed by James Baskett from the 1947 Disney movie *Song of the South*.

— *Singin' in the Rain*, the unforgetable song and dance sequence performedby the great Gene Kelly from the film of the same name—which he also directed.

— *Tomorrow,* the show-stopper from the 1977 Broadway musical *Annie,* unforgettably belted out by Andrea McArdle, the youngest ever Tony Award nominee.

I can't imagine anyone *not* being substantially uplifted by any of these, and thanks to the internet there are hundreds more like them readily available—all of them guaranteed to be good for what ails ya. I like the way the late legendary songstress Ella Fitzgerald put it—she once said: "The only thing better than singing—is more singing."

## Laughter: It Truly is the Best Medicine

The man known as one of the finest British poets, Lord Byron, advised us to: "Always laugh when you can, it is cheap medicine." While another highly venerated poet, Robert Frost, opined: "If we couldn't laugh we would all go insane."

Both these highly revered gentlemen of letters would no doubt be highly gratified by the research that's subsequently been done into laughter—studies that have established and confirmed the physiological process behind what they appeared to have innately sensed regarding the healthful benefits of laughing. Much of it, it turns out, runs parallel to what we discussed earlier regarding the benefits of walking—in that those same endorphins are involved here also.

Science Daily reported in 2008 on a study carried out at Loma Linda University, California by a team led by Dr. Lee Berk. They found that hormones that are known to alleviate depression—endorphins, and the human growth hormone (HGH) which helps our immune system, increased by 27 and 87 percent respectively when volunteers merely *anticipated* watching a humorous video. And amazingly, merely looking forward to having a good old laugh—even days ahead, apparently boosts our immune system significantly, reduces levels of stress hormones while also increasing the levels of chemicals that help relax us.

Laughter then is certainly an expression of an emotion that's highly desirable for anyone in our situation but, like many things in our life these days, it's a case of easy to say—not easy to do. Especially when we've very likely long resigned ourselves to the fact that there would never be a time when we'd have reason, or even the desire, to laugh—ever again. It's crucially important however that we give it our best shot to *try* to be happier and replace pessimism with optimism by *relearning* how to laugh again—because it's what our loved ones want—that alone should surely be incentive enough. And thanks to the mediums, we know this to be the case. The renowned Doris Stokes for instance, writes in her book *Whispering Voices,* that she told her sitters: "We all have to go through a grieving period, but it makes them sad to see us so unhappy." And once reported to a heartbroken widow: "He's happy in his new life but your grief is making him sad."

## The Direct Connect

The way I see it is that our life is, after all, *our* production. *We* are sole producer and director. We alone have the authority to rewrite any scene that we're not happy with. For example, there's a neat ploy that's frequently touted by those in the self-improvement field that goes: "Fake it—till you make it." I know, it's one of those cute sounding clichés. But, as is often the case with clichés, it's become a cliché for one good reason—it actually works. If we can break through our inertia by taking those first baby-steps and start acting out this role we've rewritten—and fake laughter—we can, over time, fool our minds into accepting that it's really so and have it responding accordingly. If truth be known, it never has been comfortable with us dragging it down that forlornly futile path anyway.

There can sometimes be a certain amount of social risk in embarking on this tactic however, due to the fact because there are always going to be those who disapprove of us laughing at all on the grounds that "it's too soon," "sacrilegious"—"irreverent" even. I've heard them all. If this is ever the case consider benignantly ignoring them, after all, whatever people think of us is strictly their business, and consequently has nothing to do with us really.

We're probably all familiar by now with the pioneering exploits of Norman Cousins regarding the curative properties of laughter. Mr Cousins, if you recall, was a journalist and the editor of the literary magazine *Saturday Review*. In 1964 his doctors had assured him that the degenerative inflammation disease he'd been struck down with was incurable. He subsequently succeeded in proving them wrong however and wrote a best selling book, *Anatomy of an Illness,* detailing how he'd achieved it.

He did it by checking into a hotel near the hospital and then proceeded to transform his room into what was basically his personal

## DIY Recuperative Measures

entertainment center, complete with a movie projector and a huge library of comedy movies such as those hilarious romps made by the Marx Brothers. He also vociferously read humorous books by his favorite writers.

He found that laughing so long and so heartily had the desired effect of stimulating his body chemistry to such an extent that after each session he was, for the first time, actually able to enjoy several pain-free hours of sleep. This regimen succeeded eventually in him, amazingly and against all odds, actually laughing himself to a full recovery.

A few years ago, after being inspired by and taking a leaf from Mr. Cousins' book, I began regularly viewing the similarly hilarious film clips that are on the internet these days—there are thousands of them, and all available with a mere click of our mouse.

For all our talk about out-and-out laughter however, I should point out that for purposes of our emotional upliftment it's not absolutely necessary for us go around guffawing inanely or rolling around in fits of uncontrollable laughter *all* the time (that could really annoy the neighbors). There have been studies that have shown conclusively that the just the *act* of smiling is all that's required to bring about a desired change for the better physiologically by triggering an appreciable increase of endorphin levels in our brain. Not to the same extent obviously, but an increase nevertheless and something that we can make a habit of doing pretty much all the time as we go about our day (that can also drive those around us crazy—wondering what we're up to).

Dr. Paul Ekman formerly of the University of California, in his capacity as founder of the Paul Ekman Group, is a pioneer in furthering our understanding of nonverbal behavior encompassing

## The Direct Connect

our facial expressions and gestures. He has shown for instance that the exercise derived by our facial muscles get when we smile produces a calming influence on our nervous system, our heart rate and our respiratory system by releasing those same "happy hormones" which we've been speaking of here.

Then there's Fritz Strack, a professor of Psychology at the University of Wurzburg, Germany. In 1998 he and his research team studied groups of people half of whom held a pencil between their lips, while the half held their pencils between their teeth horizontally from one side to the other—this is a position that automatically uplifts both corners of the mouth in basically the same way as they do when we smile. All participants were then asked to rate several cartoons in terms of their degree of funniness. Those who had been "unknowingly" smiling (due to the pencil between their teeth), rated the cartoons as being much funnier than those who'd only held the pencils by their lips. In other words, the "between the teeth" ruse had effectively fooled the brain into assuming those people had actually been smiling—essentially, the "fake-it-till-you-make-it" ploy in action.

There's a gentleman in India whose extensive research and public demonstrations of the healing benefits of laughter have earned him the nickname "The Guru of Giggling." He is Dr. Madan Kataria, and in 1995 he founded the Laughter Yoga Club. It's a movement that originally got its start when he and a handful of other people with whom he'd previously discussed the benefits of laughter, gathered in a corner of a public park in Mumbai and proceeded to just laugh their heads off. Incredibly, it not only caught on locally but spread so widely that by 1998 more than 10,000 members of laughter clubs from all over India gathered at the Race Course grounds in Mumbai and just laughed and laughed and laughed the afternoon away.

It's since become a movement that continues to infectiously spread globally, with affiliated clubs now in the USA, Europe, Australia, the Middle East, South East Asia, China and Africa.

One of our most highly esteemed Founding Fathers also seems to have known something about the restorative powers of laughter. The ever-wise Benjamin Franklin once said: "Trouble knocked at the door, but, hearing laughter, hurried away."

I also like Sonia Choquette's words on the subject, in her book *The Answer is Simple,* She writes: "Laughter is the voice of Spirit. When you laugh, your Spirit is singing. To do so is to align with Heaven."

## Are We There Yet?

When the one-time Mayor of New York City, Ed Koch, used to call out "How'm I doing?'" to passers by on the street, he was doing what we "bent but not broken" heros find ourselves doing after we've been dutifully carrying out any healing measures, such as those I've been suggesting—looking for any indicators that could tell us whether or not what we're doing is actually working. Monitoring our progress, in other words.

If an article in a health news magazine that came to my attention recently is anything to go by, we're hardly alone in this. According to the piece there's a rapidly burgeoning industry developing around a plethora of high-tech wearable devices designed to monitor our progress as we're actually performing our exercise activities—and apparently no self respecting fitness enthusiast would dare to be seen not sporting at least one of them these days.

At the time of the article, May 2014, it had been estimated that there were upward of 84 million such gizmos on the market, with that number expected to top 120 million by 2019, with a whopping $2.2 billion in revenues.

So who knows, with this kind of technology advancing so rapidly maybe there'll come a time when recovering grievers will also be able to have access to some kind of high-tech techniques that measure our progress and tell us how we're doin'—maybe that 1970's fad, the Mood Ring was on the right track after all.

Not that we need them, I hasten to add, because if there's one thing I've learned from my readings and interviews with mediums over the years it's that what we *do* have available to us, and *always* have had, is a constant stream of Divine expert assistance from our loved ones in spirit. They've been informing us over and over again, through the mediums, how they fervently want us to attain a healthy level of acceptance of what's befallen us with grace, and to this end and from their extraordinarily unique omnipresent vantage point, they will lovingly assist and guide us in doing whatever is required to facilitate our healing, freeing us to get on with the task of living out our lives in accordance with our mutually drawn-up soul plan. Surely then, just our knowing and trusting that this is so, precludes the need for any monitoring devices—making an unquestioning faith and trust in our loved one's involvement in our healing all we need really.

That said however, we must admit it is comforting to actually have evidence of progress, so it's only natural that we're going to be looking for signs that indicate that we are. And when we do, it's most likely going to come down to a barely perceptible emotional response to an incident or a subtle glimmer that strikes us as promisingly different—a flicker of light where before there's been a dark murky nothingness but that now, for the merest instant maybe, detaches us from the sullen pall of sadness that's defined our existence since our

## DIY Recuperative Measures

loss—and we become pleasingly conscious of a certain lightness that has us wondering 'could it possible be? And if it is, what can I do to repeat it so that the chinks of light grow into something I can grab a hold of and get it to stay around longer next time?'

A fellow grieving friend of mine, a boater, called these experiences his "touchstone moments" after those channel markers that boatmen rely on to indicate where they are in pea-soup foggy conditions—quite appropriate to our situation I think.

Although it may *seem* that we haven't made much, if any, headway, rest assured that if we've been following a daily regimen of meditating, along with other measures we've felt guided to, we will most likely have subconsciously acquired certain multi-sensory abilities. For instance intuitive abilities that allow us to better discern and identify those subtle shifts that are indicative of touchstone moments. Of particular importance because each instance we can identify and hold on to can, over time, coalesce and collectively form the critical mass needed to establish that we are indeed on the right path back to wholeness.

## Are We There Yet?: Typical Touchstone Moments

During the few years that I've been working on this book, I've discussed and shared experiences with many heroic recovering grievers. And naturally their breakthrough incidents, have been a memorable aspect of their recovery process people were happy to share, with the hope that they would serve as morale boosters for others in the same situation. It is for that same reason that I'd like to conclude this chapter with a short selection of typical stories.

My friend Eric's breakthrough moment took place, quite out of the blue, one afternoon at a shopping mall to which he'd got into the habit of retreating whenever he was hit by one of his periodic bouts of extreme heavy-heartedness over the loss of his wife Lois, fourteen months earlier. He'd just left his favorite book store and was slipping back into the stream of fellow shoppers, when he caught sight of a familiar figure walking straight towards him, but despite having made definite eye-contact the man quickly looked away and veered away as if something in the nearest store window had caught his attention—unquestionably, to Eric, a cold-shoulder snub because by the time he'd drawn level with him he was hunched over, nose against the glass, as if deeply engrossed in the eye-catching window display.

Although it was the kind of dismissive gesture of avoidance that we grieving souls have come to expect from embarrassed acquaintances, Eric said he was quite relieved by this one. He went on to explain that the gentleman in question was a deacon of the church he attended, and in his capacity of grief counselor he's ministered to Eric briefly. Briefly because he'd stopped attending after the third session because, as he put it: "I just couldn't stand how his constant high-minded, sanctimonious, self-righteous pious attitude made me even more depressed."

But there was Eric, in the mall, the man who'd barely been able to raise a smile for fourteen months, turning the heads of everyone around him as he erupted in a spontaneous outburst of uncontrollable giggling. You see, the window that Mr Goody Two-Shoes had chosen to be so raptly absorbed in happened to belong to none other than *Victoria's Secret*.

A still giggling Eric told me: "God Bless him—he'll never know that I benefitted far more from those few seconds than I would *ever* have done from his counseling."

## DIY Recuperative Measures

Laughter brought on by an irony was also at the heart of a significant turnaround moment for a lady I met named Phyllis. She told me how, after her husband had made his transition, she'd become hooked on the mediums' books and through them had been turned on to the concept of invoking Spirit assistance with any difficulties we're facing. After the ensuing string of successes she'd had in locating all manner of misplaced articles around the house and garden, she couldn't help wondering about what other kinds of issues Spirit might be able to help her with. She didn't have to wonder very long—the answer came to her later that same afternoon, while driving to the food store to do her weekly grocery shopping. This was a chore she'd loathed ever since Alan's passing because one: it was yet another one of those things that never failed to remind her of how much they'd enjoyed doing things together, and two: this store had a habit of constantly shifting stock around and he'd always been so much better than she at finding the items on her list.

The upshot was she spent the next hour muttering the items on her present list to him under her breath, and each time, without fail—she was magically led directly to it. Plus, as an added bonus—several generous "specials." She described the experience as her first "turnaround breakthrough" because, in one fell swoop, she'd gone from habitual tearful plaintive outbursts of "What am going to do without you?" to "Honey—what *would* I do without you?"

I've found it interesting, and frankly delightful that people's accounts of their memorable "breakthrough/touchstone moments" have invariably been delivered in such a gigglesome manner. A level of buoyancy that would seem to be a sure indicator of what a hugely significant event that first sign of release from their feelings of sheer despair and utter hopelessness had been in their life.

## The Direct Connect

This was certainly the case for a bubbly vivacious lady named Abby to whom I was introduced by a mutual friend some time ago. At the time she experienced *her* first touchstone moment, it had been almost eighteen months since she'd lost her dear husband Roland, so it was hardly the first time she'd heard such admonitions as: "You have to let him go, you know." The, by now, wearisome line this time was delivered to her, at a church function no less, by a needlessly loud, expansively outgoing woman acquaintance who'd happened to catch Abby in the act of gently dabbing a slightly irritated eyelid with the corner of a hanky. It was the kind of unthinking remark Abby had just about "had it up to here" with by now, and ironically, the reason behind her initial reluctance to attend this event when a friend had suggested she attend a talk at her church on "Healing Grief," delivered by a noted authority on the subject.

Abby's reflexive reaction to the remark was to take a deep breath and work on mentally quelling the slow burn that these kinds of careless words had never failed to evoke. Her concentration was suddenly broken however by the gentleman seated on the row in front of her, with whom she'd exchanged pleasantries earlier, enough to learn that he too had been recently widowed. He'd turned around now, leaned in closer, then speaking discreetly behind the back of his hand said: "Please don't allow that loud-mouth to get to you—she has some nerve speaking to you like that—she's my sister-in-law and I happen to know that my brother bought her that hideous coat she's wearing way back during the Kennedy administration, but she's so miserly, she can never bring herself to part with anything."

The explosive shriek of laughter that this set off and rang through the sparse early-bird gathering in the Fellowship Hall, was of course quite out of character with the demeanor of the, up until now, woeful

## DIY Recuperative Measures

mourning widow—but she simply couldn't help it, any more than she could help the ensuing uncontrollable fit of the giggles it gave rise to.

Between more giggles now, she told me that, as embarrassing as the incident had been for everyone present, she'd been grateful for the way it served to remind her to be watchful for the string of turnaround moments that ultimately succeeded in releasing her from the grip of grief that had held her captive for eighteen months, and put her squarely on the path to recovery.

Despite a touchstone moment being the breakthrough we've yearned and prayed for, and can potentially, as Abby put it, put us squarely on the path to recovery, we must be mindful that, like any road, it's likely not going to be free of bumps, potholes and even a detour or two along the way. But it *will* be taking us in the right direction where before there had been no direction at all, and our first touchstone moment was a chink of light where previously there had been absolute nothingness. But now that light *has* finally emerged, it's akin to a loving caring hand gently taking hold of ours and leading us through a burgeoning forth of even more light until we're eventually embraced in the warm golden white sunlight that will define our return to wholeness.

CHAPTER 11
# THE CASE FOR MEDIUMSHIP —GOING FORWARD

You will no doubt have noticed by now that throughout the book, whenever I've considered it appropriate, I've put forward the notion that our loved ones in spirit are always there for us—ready and willing to compassionately dispense their magical abilities to help us through our healing process. At this juncture I'd like to make the case for the *continuance* of this extraordinary Divine connection going forward, in a world that's awash right now with the often negative, and always complex, impact of this ever-evolving computer driven technology. The fact is, that in the name of "progress" (a term that, for me, has to be qualified more clearly than it usually is), many of us are being left floundering and confused as long-cherished aspects of our lives, features of our daily lives that represent security and peace of mind are rapidly becoming victims of attrition as they are summarily

## The Direct Connect

elbowed out of the way to make room for, ostensibly more sophisticated and technologically advanced devices and methodologies.

With so many treasured aspects of our lives being jettisoned as a consequence (the "baby out with the bathwater" syndrome), it can understandably occur to us that the same fate could befall

Direct Connect/Stanton 341 the field of mediumship—the bridge to, and our vital point of contact with the other side.

I've always marveled however at the ways the Spirits have constantly honed their skills over the years, particularly in how they present their pieces of evidence in ways that hopefully make them more valid. Which naturally in turn, ensures a wider acceptance by the public while at the same time depriving the skeptics of some of their ammunition.

The style of mental mediumship, as it's practiced today, is obviously a far cry from the physical approaches used during the latter half of the 1800's and the early 1900's. I'm referring to methods like those melodramatic seances around large tables conducted in obligatory dark rooms, and tactics such as table rapping, the alarming levitation of tables, the materializing of trumpets and the trance channeling of identifiable voices via a mysterious viscous gel-like substance known as ectoplasm. Spookily pseudo supernatural goings-on here—which unfortunately left plenty of leeway for the public's suspicions of jiggery- pokery. It's no wonder they had so much trouble being taken seriously. More recently the field was awash with ersatz practitioners such as those invariably turbaned crystal ball gazing fortune tellers, palmists and readers of tea-leaves—an ever-popular fixture at vacation venues like seaside boardwalks.

Admittedly a motley collection for any one of them to seriously lay claim to being a progenitor of what we're now solemnly espousing

## The Case For Mediumship—Going Forward

as a perfectly legitimate and noble cause, but nevertheless they each, in their own way, represented stages of evolvement that it was necessary to negotiate in order for mediumship to eventually attain its current status.

This kind of evolutionary process is really not much different to the ways in which other fields of endeavor have evolved. Consider aviation for example, its pioneers flew by the seat of their pants in primitive canvas and wire contraptions but that evolved over time into our modern day jet airliners that can carry 600 or more passengers. In like manner, we now have mediums who regularly fill auditoriums around the world, plus conducting live compelling "close-up-and-personal" readings on well produced television programs, which together with the proliferation of books by the mediums, have undoubtedly served to herald in an unprecedented level of interest in the proven ongoing connectedness between we in the physical and those entities in the non-physical—on the other side of the veil.

Each of the many stages of development through the years are testimony to the Spirits' ability to adapt and adjust to often capricious societal attitudes, fluctuating trends and the unpredictability of peoples' expectations in general—all factors that even baffle expert prognosticators at times. So it promises to be interesting, going forward to watch how the Spirit realm deals with the seemingly unstoppable profusion of high-tech hand-held devices that are asserting themselves so forcefully on society—not all of them, I venture to add—either desirable, welcome, or even necessarily beneficial to everyone. Will the Spirit world's adeptness allow them to come up with a way of using this formidable force to our advantage in spreading the word—as their record would certainly suggest they can? And if so, what form will it take?

I have a theory I'd like to put forward regarding how this might play out, because I'm convinced that the field of mediumship and the entire amazing dynamic of Spirit connectivity between us is on the threshold of one of the most significant periods of evolvement yet.

## The Case For: A Magical Confluence of Energies?

Not for one second do I think it's a random accident that the relatively recent upsurge of interest in mediumship and spiritualism world-wide just happens to coincide with the ongoing technological advancement in communication devices and systems that have allowed the dissemination and exchange of information to escalate so rapidly. It's my sense that these two dynamics are linked, and furthermore, that this confluence of energies couldn't have come along at a more propitious time, and it promises to be very interesting to watch how this plays out if Spirit, as I suspect, has plans to utilize it for everyone's benefit. The fact that there are now numerous reports on record of messages from loved ones in Spirit materializing on voicemail systems, computer screens and intriguingly, on cell phones whose batteries have long since run down, suggests a certain high-tech savviness and that adaptive measures are already underway.

The wide array of communication devices that have become collectively known as the *social media,* have for some time been demonstrating their remarkable powers in bringing people together in common causes—even to the extent of bringing down governments in politically unstable countries—that's powerful stuff. The ability of these devices to allow us to disseminate information to thousands of targeted people simultaneously worldwide, each of whom can then forward it to thousands of other like minds, is surely a feat totally unprecedented in the history of the world, and it's potential impact on society just boggles the mind.

In the marketing field it's universally acknowledged that there is nothing more powerful in persuading people to purchase *anything* than a simple, good old-fashioned word-of-mouth recommendation. Even the 3 billion dollars a year spent internationally on marketing movies for instance can't possible emulate the influence of something as basic as word-of-mouth rave reviews, any more than can all the advertising slogans and reams of copy used in the 180 billion dollars spent annually, worldwide, on advertising in general.

So what else is this social media phenomenon, other than, in essence, the word-of-mouth spreading of information that people consider to be worthy of sharing? I can't imagine that this aspect has been lost on our friends in the spirit realm if only for the following reason: Receiving confirmation of our loved one's continued existence after their "death," either via a psychic medium or through unmistakable personally meaningful signs, is inarguably an amazing and wondrous thing to behold—as noted earlier, it's what the great medium George Anderson refers to as "The greatest gift anyone could ever receive in an entire lifetime." It's an event of such joyously meaningful implications that we want to share it with everyone we know. An outcome totally out of the question previously but that now, thanks to the miracle of social media, is as commonplace as chatting to someone sitting next to us.

Joyful events are *meant* to be shared don't you think? Practically an unwritten law. And one that we're only too happy to comply with—we can't help ourselves, it's what happy overjoyed people feel compelled to do—and who can argue that the universe is always better for it. I have a sense that this is really what social media is all about, and if

## The Direct Connect

we can ignore it's negatives for a moment—it really is the ultimate in the all-powerful word-of-mouth recommendation. The confluence of these two dynamics in this context then, it seems to me, is nothing less than a match literally made in heaven, and I wouldn't be at all surprised if those on the other side of the veil have been guilefully orchestrating this highly propitious amalgamation all along—it has all the classic hallmarks associated with such phenomena.

Historically, down through the years, the word-of-mouth process has been central to all manner of societal shifts involving as they invariably do, the gradual verbal eroding of deep-seated resistance to changes in the status quo. It's what's required to fuel the steady build-up of converts needed to eventually form the critical mass that radical social restructuring hinges on. Traditionally, changes of such significance rarely if ever unfold as quickly as we would like of course, their actual coming about being, normally, a gradual drawn out process, and realistically the quantum leap forward that we're hoping for may not happen overnight. So the process of establishing, once and for all, the fact that those in the Spirit realm—our guardian angels, Spirit guides and our departed loved ones, continue to be involved in our lives on a daily basis, will probably call for patience on our part. It's my sense though, that the final thrust forward to the desired level of universal acceptance and understanding of an afterlife is already underway. Furthermore, thanks to the astuteness of the Spirits the amazing power of the social media will no doubt be playing a key role in helping us to eventually achieve that goal.

The wheels have been set in motion and for the time being we're just going to have to relax in the peace and knowing that, as in all matters spiritual, *everything—absolutely every thing*—is in Divine order. It just couldn't be any other way.

## The Case For: Spirit's Ability to Adapt

I'm not expecting or asking anyone to blindly accept my word that those in the Spirit realm have the ability to influence and adapt to changing circumstances on our physical plane. There's evidence aplenty to be found throughout the books authored by the better known psychic mediums that they can, and in fact do. The books indicate that there have been numerous occasions over the years when, in order to counteract the hackneyed charges by skeptics of charlatanism, adjustments have been made in the ways validations are presented during readings. For instance, in order to counteract and negate accusations that evidential descriptions were too broad and so general that they could apply to anyone, the Spirits have adapted accordingly so that their validations these days tend to be far more particularized than they once were.

Other charges by skeptics have centered around their claims that certain facts presented by mediums such as relatives names, ages, places of birth, wedding dates etc., could have easily been acquired from sources such as public records—even from the license plates on the cars they drove up in, was one that an ardent skeptic once suggested to me. The advent of the internet and search engines of course only served to exacerbate matters to the extent that the all-knowing and infallible internet was credited with being the source of practically every word the mediums uttered. Regrettably for mediumship, all quite plausible really, what with such a veritable mother lode of information now being so readily at hand—literally, with the so-called smart-phones that seemingly everyone now carries at all times.

However, in readings these days validations of Spirit presence in the sitter's life have been noticably more current in nature, to

## The Direct Connect

the extent that obtaining the same information from even the most sophisticated of computer searches would have been absolutely impossible.

I made mention of two such examples of this in Chapter 6 in my account of the reading I had with Carole Lynne. First, my wife's reference to a bird, when the very day before the reading a wild bird had gotten into our house and proceed to spend an hour flying around the living room and den. This certain "hit" was then followed by Carole telling me the precise subject of a telephone conversation I'd had with my sister in England—*a scant 15 minutes before the reading*—for heaven's sake.

Another example came up in a reading I had with Joanne Gerber when, after unmistakably identifying my friend Michel's wife in Spirit, Florence, went on to describe how she was grinning widely and holding up, of all things, a laptop. If there's any truth at all in what the skeptics say, Joanne must have some pretty sneaky spies out there, because it was only the day before that Michel had told me he'd finally been dragged into the 21st century, by his son buying him his first ever computer—a laptop.

But it's an incident cited by the Scottish medium Gordon Smith in his book *Spirit Messenger* however, that must represent the very ultimate in currentness. As a lady client was actually entering his home one day for her reading, Gordon "heard" her son in Spirit say to him: "Ask mum about Macbeth." He did so immediately, and with her eyes wide open with surprise she explained: "I only just bought a copy of the book on the way here." Scotched again, skeptics.

There's another lame claim skeptics often make in their relentless attempts to invalidate the legitimacy of mediumship. It's that mediums, rather than receiving a certain piece of information from

## The Case For Mediumship—Going Forward

the sitter's loved one in Spirit, are actually telepathically reading the sitter's mind. On the face of it, pretty creative reasoning on the skeptic's part. What effectively scuppers this notion however, is when it's proven later that the sitter couldn't possibly have had any knowledge at all regarding the information, at the time the medium presented it, and only learned about it later from a third party. There have been countless documented examples of such instances—the mediums love them because they always make for such a highly cogent argument for mediumship's genuineness in a way that just can't be refuted. The New Zealand medium Jenny Crawford writes about a classic example of this in her book *Through the Eyes of Spirit*.

Unbeknownst to Jenny at the time, the ensuing chain of events were initiated during the course of a reading she was conducting with a lady when she told the sitter that her father in Spirit had come through and wanted her to know that she was not to worry about her brother because he was here with him and he was helping to take care of him. The sitter was quite bewildered by this message for the simple reason she didn't *have* a brother in Spirit. On returning home however, she was informed by telephone that her brother, together with the hunting party he was a member of, had gone missing in a remote area of rugged bush country. The wide search that was mounted finally located his body a few days later when it was determined that he'd died several days prior. Confirming that he had indeed actually been in Spirit at the time of the his sister's reading with Jenny.

The mediums' books are replete with accounts of readings that could be regarded as being in the same category as this "third party" example, in that they also involve information obtained by mediums from those on the other side, but of which the sitter had no knowledge. But these pertain not as much to people, as they do to *things*—objects about which the sitters couldn't possibly have had any knowledge at the time, but were discovered later precisely where the Spirits had said they were. The items cited cover a wide range. Documents for example, tucked away in places where someone obviously hadn't wanted them to be easily found, and things like wills, old share certificates and life insurance policies—any of which could be vital to a surviving spouse who's experiencing financial stress brought on by his/her loss. Then there have been a variety of other items of value that sitters have been fortuitously guided to, things such as jewelry in sock drawers, semi-valuable artwork hidden in the attic, paper money hidden inside books—and on and on. All with, for purposes of our discussion, one thing in common—how could the mediums have possibly obtained the information of their whereabouts by reading the sitters' minds—when that information had never been there in the first place? Nice try skeptics—but no cigar.

I venture to suggest that the emergence and the trending of this newish kind of mediumship, rather than being the result of random coincidence, is the result of a conscious stratagem on the part of Spirit—with the specific intent to thwart and frustrate the skeptics while at the same time helping to mitigate the negative influences that their misguided notions might have on the efforts of those of us who feel we have a munificent obligation to *spread the light.*

## The Case For: Brand Recognition

Anyone embarking on this task however, soon realizes that we can go on all we want about "The truth will come to light," and "The truth will out," and all that high-minded stuff, but the down-to-earth—real-world fact of the matter is, that in this over-commercialized world in which we live, in order for *anything* to catch on, flourish, be universally accepted and get that much coveted all-important "market-share," it's necessary to have what has become the mantra of the advertising profession—"brand recognition," formerly known by the, apparently now prosaic, term "household name." This brings us into the frequently frenetic high pressure world of attention-grabbing logos, slogans, catchy commercial jingles, cute cartoon characters, product placement in hit movies and complex marketing strategies. None of which, it's safe to say, exactly lend themselves to something as altruistic in nature as communicating with those in the realm of Spirit. *But,* there is one requisite component of brand recognition we intentionally omitted and is probably *the* main ingredient—it's what we know as "celebrity endorsement."

Let's face it, when it comes to persuading the masses of the worthiness of virtually anything in the world and making true believers out of us—nothing succeeds more convincingly than a celebrity endorsement. A conclusion supported by the fact that $50 billion is invested on them globally. I have a sense that it is *the one* factor out of this mix that we can comfortably utilize for purposes of furthering our cause and I see it coming into play in the following way.

As more and more people experience the magic of a successful reading and cannot resist sharing their story with those around them and with anyone else who will listen, mediumship will, over time, naturally become less stigmatized. A state which people who had previously shied away from mediumship will now regard as giving them permission to be acceptive of it. Likewise, I see the many celebrities who I suspect of having experienced successful readings, but have understandably been reluctant to "go public" will now, with damage to their "image" no longer a threat, be more open to sharing their positive experiences in order to benefit the rest of the world. And voila—celebrity endorsements—word-of-mouth recommendations with, hopefully, the desired ripple effect.

There are actually grounds for encouragement here, because there are numerous references on record of celebrities coming through in readings where the sitter was someone they'd known and just wanted to acknowledge, or to whom they wished to express their gratitude.

George Anderson for example, described a surprise guest appearance in his book *Walking in the Garden of Souls*. A lady, identifying herself as "Grace" paid a brief visit with a sitter to thank him for a job well done. The sitter subsequently contacted George to tell him how much this had meant to him personally because the drop-in visitor had been none other than Princess Grace (Kelly) of Monaco. He then went on to explain that he'd written a biography of her life and had always wondered if she'd been happy with the way in which he'd portrayed her.

Another surprise guest appearance was mentioned by Doris Stokes in her book *Innocent Voices in My Ear,* in which she recounts a reading where quite a well known gentleman came through and stayed awhile. After establishing that it really was who an amazed Doris thought it was, by citing facts no one else could have known, a John Lennon (you may of heard of him), proceeded to explain how he could help the sitter with a financial problem. He said he'd learned about it the previous evening during a telephone conversation she'd had with his best friend Elton John—all verified by the sitter who was also in the music business. No big names here.

I well remember another super-star coming through in a reading that the great James Van Praagh was conducting on his television show *Beyond* some years ago. The sitter this time was herself a celebrity—the famous English actress Juliet Mills, daughter of the renowned actor John Mills and sister of the actress Hayley Mills. In the course of his reading James had been painting a typical Van Praagh detailed word picture of Juliet's home and garden and was in the process of similarly accurately describing a wall in her den which was covered with framed family photographs, when a familiar gentleman figure came into the scene. It was the legendary actor Laurence Olivier, a close friend of Juliet's father, and he confirmed his identity by indicating the photos in which he was featured, all corroborated by Juliet, and along with an anecdotal commentary on the circumstances behind each one. Which itself, interestingly, further established his identity—peppered as it was with the salty language he was known for.

The celebrity connection however, isn't confined solely to the times departed ones have come through in readings. There are many allusions and references sprinkled throughout the mediums' books to the times when *the sitters* who came for a reading have been the celebrities—famous movie stars, highly revered public figures—even royalty, from all over the world. It's well documented for instance that Sir Winston Churchill consulted with psychic mediums during World War II, particularly with the famous, and notorious, Helen Duncan. So we know for sure that there are many prominent people who obviously believe in an afterlife, notables who's views, by virtue of their fame and social stature, are held in such high esteem that the news and information gathering members of our Fourth Estate virtually hang on to their every word and duly report them to us—over and over, around the clock. A process that over time automatically exerts a considerable amount of influence on the collective psyche—regarding our feelings, attitudes and opinions on a wide range of issues

*But*, unfortunately for us, the readings these pillars of society have received from the mediums have understandably been conducted in strict confidence. Nevertheless, assuming their experience was positive, all of them are now qualified to be precisely what the field of mediumship, and by extension the world, needs right now—high caliber celebrity endorsees.

It's become my belief that this could very well be the fulcrum point on which the desired universal acceptance of mediumship's ability to communicate with those in Spirit is balanced. And who knows, if truth be told—these potential celebrity endorsees could one day be quite amenable to publically sharing their experiences. And all it could take for that event to magically "break the logjam" as it were, is for just one or two members of that high-profile lionized group to decide for some reason to "go public and let the chips fall where they may" Then watch as their reputations not only come out of it totally unsullied and completely unsmirched, but the esteem in which they're held by their public soars as a result. The soul-swelling sense of gratification this gesture would undoubtedly engender could not only serve as confirmation that it was the right thing to do, but also be indicatory to the rest of us that the Spirit realm possibly had a hand in orchestrating this entry into the field of celebrity endorsements from the get-go.

## The Case For: A Television Programming Genre Upgrade

The place where the majority of us are most likely to be exposed to celebrity endorsements, other than on the billboards we drive past, or those that drive past *us*—y'know, buses, is of course in our homes—via the television sets ubiquitously present in every room

## The Case For Mediumship—Going Forward

these days. Firmly establishing the medium as the most powerful and wide-ranging delivery system of information and entertainment ever conceived. So it follows that television shows on mediumship would surely be a "natural" for furthering our cause and spreading the word. This hasn't escaped the attention of various television network executives in the past of course, but unfortunately, whenever they've ventured into this highly competitive arena (and there have been numerous gallant attempts), they've been singularly unsuccessful in attracting loyal viewers in sufficient numbers to "earn their keep," so to speak.

One reason for this lamentable record, I believe, is the ways in which the various genres of programs have been segmented into groupings. Traditionally, in ways that make for very little flexibility for the inclusion of any program type that doesn't already have a proven record, thereby reducing its chances of being conferred with a budget adequate enough to allow it the time to really establish itself—ill-fated from the start, in other words. Particularly when the subject is something like mediumship, a topic that's unfortunately generally misunderstood anyway and about which many people are already conflicted. For one thing, it's been my experience that those who lack a clear understanding of what a psychic reading is all about, seem to instinctively associate it in their minds with heavy-heartedness rather than what it *really* is—a potentially magical reunion that can be as joyous an event for the sitters as we could possibly imagine. Terms such as "over-the-moon" or "deliriously happy" don't come anywhere near expressing the intensity of the bliss that sitters can experience.

In determining which programming format demonstrations of mediumship best align with, so it's probably easier to eliminate the formats with which it's *not* compatible. So after discounting the obvious ones such as drama series, cop shows, news magazine

## The Direct Connect

productions and political "talking heads" panels etc., the group that mediumship shows seem to always wind up in, is the one that encompasses what's come to be known as game-shows or quiz shows. A format that harks back to those wildly popular quiz and game shows of the 1950's, for instance *The $64,000 Question, What's My Line?* and *I've Got a Secret.*

This popular genre however, has naturally undergone a series of substantial makeovers over the years. For example competing networks, in order to attract more viewers, have adopted a standard entertainment device generally known in the business as "production values." Resulting in slick spectaculars that comprise vividly colored and glittery stage sets together with a dizzying array of laser effects, swirling strobe lights and lots of sheet neon dramatically emerging through an obligatory fog and all to the accompaniment of a gratuitously suspenseful musical score that can be counted on build up to an ear-drum-throbbing, edge-of-your-seat crescendo.

With the entire outrageous extravaganza presided over by a highly personable well-coiffed host, supported by obviously coached hyper-excited participants, who are relentlessly egged on by a frenetic over-the-top audience raucously responding to electronically cued signs. Needless to say—bedlam rules. Such are the nature of the types of production values deemed necessary to assure the success of television shows that fall into this category these days.

Not to be snobbish or hoity-toity about it, but they're hardly a treatment that's appropriate to an event as decorous and sublime as a psychic reading. Typically, that involves a guileless, self-effacing medium earnestly linking up people in grief with their departed loved ones enabling him to forward their life-changing compellingly validating messages of assurance. Each one of which is nothing less

## The Case For Mediumship—Going Forward

than a miracle—a prize infinitely more valuable to the recipients than any game show could possibly aspire to.

I'm reminded of something a gentleman by the name of Newton N. Minow once said. He was chairman of the Federal Communications Commission at the time and in a speech he made in May 1961 he famously referred to American television programming as a "vast wasteland." Sadly, after all these years, in some ways it seems it still is—it's just got to be flashier, noisier and more glittery. I have reason to believe I'm not alone in thinking that it's a pity we've allowed ourselves to become conditioned to these styles of presentations. Yes, they have their place, but surely accommodation could also be made for shows that, while entertaining and equally enthralling in their own way, are more temperate in tone—plus, they enlighten to boot.

It's not as if we're without precedents for this after all. In 1980 for instance, PBS Television launched a phenomenally successful series about space, narrated and co-written by the great Carl Sagan. A man who *Smithsonian Magazine* referred to as "The most famous scientist in America—the face of science itself." and a professor of astronomy at Cornell University. Titled *Cosmos: A Personal Voyage,* the program went on to ultimately reach hundreds of millions of people world-wide—the highest rated show in the history of PBS—a record it held for 10 years.

More recently, in 2014, Fox Broadcasting Company aired a 13 episode "re-boot" of the now late Dr. Sagan's masterpiece, now entitled *Cosmos: A Space-Time Odyssey.* Hosted this time by the renowned astrophysicist and Director of the Hayden Planetarium—the vastly popular and super-amiable Neil deGrasse Tyson. And once again—a tremendous success. There have also been numerous other such successes over the years, admittedly not all of them the runaway smash-hit chartbusters the front office might prefer, but even a steady diet of caviar, truffles and foie gras can get to be deadly boring—or so I've been told.

So, having been shown that it *can* be done, that it *is* possible to create quality programs that both entertain and inform *and* attract respectable numbers of viewers, we can only hope that as more "substance-over-form" precedents continue to be established, those policy-making men and women in grey suits will, at some time, no longer be able to ignore the need for, and the opportunities that will then exist, to develop a program or two about mediumship. And along with the appropriate kinds of stimulative production values, even the same template if that what a successful program dictates, but more temperate in nature, less frenetic. A format that entertains certainly, but also exhilarates, stimulates and positively inspires people world-wide with affirmatively life-changing validations of an afterlife.

Coincidentally, Dr. Carl Sagan once made a statement that's uncannily apropos to our discussion, he said: "Personally I would be delighted if there were a life after death, especially if it permitted me to continue to learn about this world and others, if it gave me a chance to discover how history turns out." I have an idea we may have acquired a celebrity endorsee.

*We* know don't we that Dr. Sagan, having now made his transition, *is* indeed thoroughly delighted (I can picture him now—sporting that engaging trade-mark broad grin of his to confirm it). And who can doubt, that with his remarkable abilities and passion to enlighten, he's now using them to do everything he can to spread the word regarding the afterlife to everyone on this physical plane who has yet to be convinced. After all, he also once said: "Somewhere, something incredible is waiting to be known."

## The Case For: Universal Acceptance By Default

When a situation exists that we find undesirable, the fixing of which could benefit millions of people, some of us feel compelled to do whatever we can to rectify it—out of an altruistic desire to halt the needless emotionally debilitating burden its continuance subjects people to, or perhaps to simply help do our bit to make the world a better place. There are always those however who take a laissez faire attitude and prefer not to do anything at all except hope things will work themselves out—by default.

Of course there's always a chance they'll be right—eventually, after they themselves have "shuffled off this mortal coil," as Shakespeare put it. This has been called a "policy of benign neglect," and has had scholarly support, and the observation made by physicist Max Planck, that we referred to in Chapter 3 bears repeating here. He said "A new scientific truth does not triumph by convincing opponents and making them see the light, but rather because its opponents eventually die, and a new generation grows up that is familiar with it."

The cogency of this astute observation was borne out for me when I came across it quite coincidentally the very same day that a friend had forwarded me some published reports regarding the current status of religion in Britain and the United States. From which I learned that CBS News reported in December 2012 that some 45 million people—one fifth of the U.S. adult population say that they belong to no particular church. The study by The Pew Research Center, a nonpartisan think tank based in Washington D.C., revealed that the number of people who check the "None" box when asked to describe their religious affiliation has more than doubled since 1990. Yet paradoxically, sixty percent of them admit to believing in God or a universal Spirit of some kind. An apparent disenchantment, it would appear, with the status quo and a desire for more attractive options—a re-examination—a break with what they consider to be outmoded traditions and a need to exchange them for something better—a discipline that promises to leave them feeling more comfortably in vibrational alignment with.

In an article relevant to this in July 2015, the *Daily Express* reported that 1,000 churches across Britain were facing closure due to the inability of dwindling congregations to fund costly and lengthy repair projects. A trend substantiated by the Royal Institute of Chartered Surveyors, who identified 500 churches that have been transformed into apartments over five years.

The British *Daily Mail* reported on another study by a team at the University of East Anglia, which showed that only 15 percent of British people attend church at least once a month. And, significantly, a large percentage of whom are elderly people.

So it's small wonder that a Senior Pastor in Dallas, Texas told the Pew researchers "We have to realize that the church is pretty much one generation away from extinction." An astute observation that eerily echoes that of Max Plank, while also corroborating one of his assertions on the subject of change in his field, he said: "Science progresses funeral by funeral."

That's pretty sobering reasoning by the illustrious physicist and, in essence—the attrition process of alleviating the undesirable effects of change at its very ultimate. But I prefer to regard his arbitrary "Expiration Date" as negotiable and less absolute, and that the progressive changes we're seeking can come about incrementally and in doable stages—the sooner the better I think. To that end, I feel that the strategies we've been discussing here could all be instrumental in helping us achieve our goal of universal understanding and acceptance of the afterlife. Then, with them securely in place maybe we too can take a proactive laissez faire stance and take delight in watching as the nature we've helped create takes its course. Surely it's the least we can do for the generations following us—they're already inheriting more undesirable stuff than they deserve to as it is—don't you think?

## The Case For: "Keep Soldiering On"

Those of us who are long since beyond needing proof of the existence of the afterlife, and unquestioningly, to the point of *knowing*, accept that mediums have genuinely been gifted with the ability to communicate with those who have made their transition back to that non-physical plane, do so regardless of mainstream science's unwavering insistence on "scientific proof."

And let's face it, most scientists do, as a rule, know their stuff and wouldn't think of lying to nice people like us. That said however, their fallibility *has* been laid bare from time to time, and that proverbial bird we spoke of earlier in the book who walks, swims and quacks like a duck has been embarrassingly misidentified by scientists more often than they care to admit. This is assuredly another one of those times because the common sense duck aphorism certainly applies to science's unflagging negative position on mediumship. Yet how else could the situation possibly be characterized when literally billions of accurate readings, many of them stunningly precise, have been documented by thousands of mediums over the past 150 years or more—in the United States alone? Not to mention the stunningly impressive series of scientifically conducted experiments carried out over several years by professor Gary E. Schwartz at the University of Arizona and documented in his seminal book *The Afterlife Experiments*. In which he and his team rated the odds of the more detailed spirit validations being so accurate by mere chance as one in a *trillion!*

I hate to rain on the naysaying scientists' parade, but for me, and apparently millions of others too, that bird is, without a shadow of a doubt—a real life fully fledged duck. And I find it quite fitting that we're using the duck analogy in relation to this subject, since the great American psychologist/philosopher Professor William James also coincidentally used a bird analogy in confirming the legitimacy of meduimship way back in 1885, when he coined the famous adage: "If you wish to upset the law that all crows are black, you mustn't seek to show that no crows are; it is enough if you prove one single crow to be white."

Naturally, it takes courage to stand steadfast in our convictions, especially when they conflict with those of scientifically credentialed experts, who for some reason, prefer to resolutely refuse to recognize the truth inherent in such seemingly simplistic explanations, doggedly opting instead for their customary complex quantitative analysis—with the results being expressed in their trade-mark tortuous jargon that's usually quite incomprehensible to most of us.

However, as the saying goes: "The truth will out." Albeit at a slower pace than it would with authoritative scientific blessing, but as we mentioned earlier in regard to future prospects, Carl Sagan once said: "Somewhere, something incredible is waiting to be known." It may also help if we bear in mind the advice Winston Churchill often offered the beleaguered Brits during World War II: "Keep soldiering on." In the meantime we should remain true to ourselves while continuing to spread the word whenever the opportunity presents itself.

## The Case For: Possible Prospects for Scientific Verification

I've spent an inordinate amount of time over the past few months reading about all manner of amazing scientific experiments that have been carried out by the world's top physicists at various research centers worldwide for over a hundred years now, and the jaw-dropping wondrousness findings of many of them has, it seems to me, caused a few chinks of light to appear, leaving me with a sneaking suspicion that there now exists in the scientific community an emerging "silent majority." Consisting of a new generation who tend to be more progressive and consequently more open-minded about notions that formerly would have been dogmatically dismissed out of hand as implausible nonsense. And I have a feeling that among them are some who are cagily hedging their bets, so to speak, regarding several pieces of evidence in their findings that suggests it may possible to prove that there's something to this afterlife thing after all and could also provides clues that could explain the ability of mediums to communicate with those on the other side of the veil. They may be some way yet from being convinced enough to be comfortable in going public on the matter, but at least it's a start—a sign that there are now scientific minds who are less likely to reflexively reject heretical sounding notions than "old school" scientists have customarily been. Their reticence is quite understandable of course when "coming out" too early could easily jeopardize their professional standing among their more conservative peers not to mention those research grants so crucial to their livelihoods.

The field of science we have to thank for these thrilling breakthrough possibilities and their potential to end this stand off once and for all, is known as quantum physics. And the ongoing exciting revolutionary strides being made in this burgeoning field has to be tremendously encouraging when we realize that it wasn't all that long ago when scientists were convinced that if something couldn't be detected under a microscope it didn't exist, and outer space (you know, those vast areas out there between those round rocks), well that was just an empty vacuum of nothingness—nothing to concern ourselves with there.

## The Case For: Quantum Physics

Quantum physics evolved originally during the early 1900's out of a theory propounded by the gentleman we've been quoting—the esteemed German physicist Max Planck, work which culminated in him being awarded the Nobel Prize in Physics in 1918. Subsequent developments and amazing experiments have been, and continue to be, carried out by numerous other distinguished physicists worldwide over the years since.

It's a subject that's by no means easy to grasp, so difficult in fact that even the best scientific minds admit to having trouble understanding its concepts. A fact attested to in the quotes on the subject made by two of the world's leading scientists—themselves Nobel Prize winners.

The Danish physicist Niels Bohr for instance, who was awarded the Nobel Prize in Physics for his foundational contributions to the understanding of quantum physics said: "If anybody says he can think about quantum physics without getting giddy, that only shows he has not understood the first thing about them." The American physicist Richard Feynman, also a Nobel Prize winner, went so far as to proclaim: "I can safely say that nobody understands quantum physics."

## The Case For Mediumship—Going Forward

Even "The Great One" himself, Albert Einstein expressed his misgivings about it early on, even going so far as trying to disprove it and modify it and declaring one of its aspects to be: "Spooky action at a distance."

Should anyone feel daunted by the prospect of attempting to absorb and mentally digest any published explanations of a branch of science that even has Nobel Prize winners in the category baffled, please rest assured that there are numerous books and articles on the internet that do an admirable job of explaining it in layman terms. My own primary source of information has been a wonderfully enlightening classic titled *The Field, The Quest for the Secret Force of the Universe*, thoroughly researched, documented and masterfully crafted by the well known investigative journalist Lynne McTaggart. It would be difficult to imagine a book on a subject of such complexity being written with more clarity or a higher degree of intelligibility.

Quantum physics is basically all about the nature of matter and has been responsible for forcing scientists to re-examine many of their long-held cherished beliefs, to the extent that there are now very few aspects of modern life that haven't been impacted by it to some degree.

Quantum theory has succeeded in radically revolutionized our understanding of the *tiniest* things in our world—those subatomic particles that atoms are made of, a principle that's complemental to Einstein's theory of relativity which deals with the *largest* things in the universe, and which also revolutionized our previous understanding, in this case, of space and time, thereby pleasingly completing the circle as it were. A situation that now constitutes the basis of many aspects of modern physics, resulting in a new generation of scientists who are now motivated to expound theories that effectively kick over the traces of Cartesian and Newtonian dogma and revise it's long-venerated but, at times, misplaced beliefs.

The upshot has been that, the coming about of a universal understanding and acceptance of an afterlife may now be imminent, and we'll have quantum physics to thank for moving us closer to scientifically verifying the notion. And interestingly, its findings have served to support what ancient spiritual masters, sages, mystics, shamans, religious bodies and cultures the world over have maintained in their texts all along—for thousands of years. Namely, that the vibrational energies generated by every gesture, every thought, everything voiced and every event on this planet are inextricably interconnected and reverberate throughout the universe in perpetuity as part of an unimaginably complex field (the much alluded to "Life Force").

The possible ramifications of finally having the ability to tap into such an infinite source of information and reveal the universe's elaborate inner workings about which, until now, we've only been able to speculate, simply boggles the mind. A prospect succinctly summed up by the genius Nikola Tesla—inventor and physicist and a man clearly ahead of his time, who once said: "If you wish to understand the secrets of the universe, think of energy, frequency and vibration."

Even I, with my sadly limited grasp of the subject, can appreciate how this extraordinary range of ground-breaking disclosures is contributing to scientists' growing disaffection with Descartes' rigid insistence on strict statistical analysis and frees them up instead to more creatively interpret and philosophize about the data garnered from their experiments, in ways simply not possible with the requisite conventional methods of quantification. In itself—literally a "quantum leap," one might say.

This is just one of several aspects of quantum physics that, collectively, have led me and my spiritualist friends with whom I've discussed it, to firmly believe that the prospects are now extremely promising that somewhere in this complex mix of extraordinary phenomena lies the information that could lead us directly to the discovery of, what is for us, nothing less than the "Holy Grail." The degree of solid, incontrovertible proof required to once and for all convince mainstream science and those debunking skeptics everywhere of mediumship's genuineness.

## The Case For: My Rationale

My first "eureka moment" regarding the possibility of a direct association between quantum physics and the mystery of how mediumship works occurred while I was reading the fascinating accounts concerning our vibrational energies reverberating and affecting everyone and every thing throughout the universe. It struck me when one of the articles was synchronistically followed by one dealing with the subject of *Contagious Magic*. This is another area of paranormal phenomena that has traditionally been dismissively discounted by mainstream science as being nothing but part myth, part superstition and partly an old wives's tale.

The term applies to a belief whose origins are thought to date back to primitive societies, and has been cited by evolutionary anthropologists as consisting of items belonging to a category of third class religious relics. A typical example of Contagious Magic would be a snippet of cloth that's known to have been taken from the robes or vestments of a revered holy personage. The "magic" aspect is centered around the belief that robes and other items of clothing worn by a person, or a lock of hair or even a footprint in the sand,

## The Direct Connect

are automatically infused with that person's energy that then has a contagious magical effect on everyone who subsequently come into contact with them, regardless of distance and time passed. A process that can also be fulfilled by carrying around just a snippet of material taken from their apparel. In similar vein I suppose, I once attended a rock concert performed before an audience of mostly screaming females where the star performers were lucky to get out of the arena with their clothing intact.

So I couldn't help but equate this phenomenon with the aspect of quantum physics I'd previously been reading about, together with another extraordinary piece of quantum theory I'd come across that is similarly germane to the possibility of it one day providing the proof we're seeking. This facet of quantum physics is known as Bell's Theorem after an experiment conducted by the Irish physicist John S. Bell in 1964 that proved Niels Bohr's theories concerning the instantaneous communication between atoms and their attendant ever-spinning electrons—a process known as quantum entanglement.

His groundbreaking experiment demonstrated that when two atoms are paired with each other they remain connected to such a degree that they continue to communicate with each other in terms of their rotational spin patterns, regardless of the distance between them—whether one is in the next room, a thousand miles apart or even light years away on the other side of the universe—all simultaneously, with *absolute zero time lapse*. Small wonder Albert Einstein referred to it as "spooky action at a distance," presumably, at the time, with one eye on the plank upon which his Theory of Relativity rested—that *nothing* travels faster than the speed of light.

Surely then, the acceptance of a definite correlation between these two phenomena, quantum entanglement and contagious

## The Case For Mediumship—Going Forward

magic, could surely—by extension—serve to give credence to one of the controversial facets of mediumship, known as psychometry. Because, coincidentally, this too is based on the premise that objects such as an article of clothing like a glove, a scarf, a tie or an item of jewelry like a wrist watch or a ring, continue to retain information in its energy field, pertaining to the personality and events experienced by the person who had worn them for any length of time. It's long been accepted by believers in mediumship that mediums and psychics with psychometric abilities can, by merely holding and handling that item, psychically tap into its special energy (which some characterize as being of an electromagnetic nature), and accurately divine any information that continues to be imbued in it long after the owner has made their transition to the other side. It's for this reason that psychic mediums who possess this ability often suggest to sitters that they bring to their session an item worn by the person in spirit with whom they wish to connect, and use the information gleaned as an adjunct to the reading.

It seems to me that it's clearly not beyond the realm of possibility that somewhere in the complex mélange of possibilities and suppositions surrounding quantum entanglement could lie the magic key that unlocks all the data we need to establish proof of the mediums' mechanism of thought energy, and that of Spirit, that allows them to intercommunicate so uniquely.

Bearing in mind all the while of course, what Niels Bohr and Richard Feynman said regarding people who think they understand quantum physics. But in any event, it's apparent that a significant chink of light has emerged—one that could very well be the precursor to the dazzling full-blown floodlight of a long awaited universal enlightenment.

## The Direct Connect

Nikola Tesla was an acclaimed genius. A physicist and, as we'll see, a futurist, who famously invented and developed the first alternating current motor (AC), and AC generation transmission technology that remains the global standard for power transmission to this day. He was also a pioneer in the discovery of radar.

Tesla was clearly not as dismissive of supernatural phenomena or of notions that happen to be outside of mainstream science, as scientists predictably tend to be. Tesla once said:

*"Physics, extends beyond what is scientifically known today. The future will show that what we now call occult or the supernatural is based on a science not yet developed, but whose infant steps are being taken as we speak."*

Let us all hope that those infant steps soon mature into strides.

CHAPTER 12

# NO WONDER IT'S CALLED HEAVEN

John O'Donahue was an Irish author, philosopher and Catholic priest. In his 1997 best-selling book *Anam Cara,* a Celtic term for "Soul friend," he wrote:

"We do not need to grieve for the dead. Why should we grieve for them? They are in a place where there is no more shadow, darkness, loneliness, isolation or pain. They are home."

In the course of their readings with mediums over the years, thousands of our loved ones in spirit have gone to great lengths to convey basically the same message to us and often along with a whole range of other reasons why there's no need for us to overly grieve their transition in the protracted and frequently desperate ways we instinctually do. For instance, the well-known psychic medium Patrick Mathews, in his informative book *Never Say Goodbye,* reports on another perspective of their life in the angelic realm that pleases them. Apparently they've told him that they: "Get the best of both worlds, enjoying life on the other side and continuing to be a part of their family and friends' lives here too."

One way the spirits have tried to comfortingly assure us why it's not really necessary for us to grieve for them in the ways we traditionally have, is by "painting" for us wonderful word pictures that describe their new surroundings. Detailed images they hope will serve to preview for us the sheer splendor of the beauteously Divine Realm where they've taken up residence, while they patiently await that day when it's our time to join them. In doing so they never neglect to explain that no verbal descriptions could possibly do justice to the visually flawless perfection that greets them everywhere they go, whatever the terrain. Vista after vista of indescribable beauty from which emanates an ambience of quietude and tranquility of a quality rarely, if ever, experienced on our earthly plane.

Many spirits have also positively gushed over the *colors* of nature over there—blossoms that profusely adorn trees, shrubs and meadowlands, in palettes of iridescent colors and hues they've never seen before. In addition to this prevailing visual beauty they've also referred to sensing the presence of an energy that seems to emanate from the leaves, petals, grasses, the soil and even rocks—resulting in a blissful all-embracing vibrational harmony with their energy.

The celebrated medium Allison DuBois, in her book *We Are Their Heaven,* writes about a characteristic countryside setting, with children running happily through brilliant emerald grass and men fishing from the same river banks that they had during their boyhood, along with the puppy that had died when they were young. And complete with couples who'd been married for 50 years or more, strolling hand-in-hand looking exactly like they had when they were first wed.

The great medium Doris Stokes often wrote about how the spirits had told her that the other side is just as real to them as this physical plane is to us—it's just in a different dimension. In her book *More Voices In My Ear* she treats us to a detailed description of an experience she once had with the phenomenon known as astral travel. This is based on the notion that during our sleep it's possible for our mind to leave our body and float around in time and space on the astral plane, is how she described it. Her tour consisted of meeting up with her son in spirit John Michael, who had died 36 years before during his infancy, and being escorted by him on an extraordinary tour of the area of Heaven where he and her parents now lived—fascinating stuff.

I remember the highly esteemed evangelist Billy Graham appearing as a guest on Johnny Carson's *Tonight Show* some years ago. In discussing what Heaven is like, he described it as being: "earthly but in another dimension, so there could actually be a railroad running through where Johnny's desk is sitting—with locomotives running through as we sit here talking."

## Welcome to Paradise

When spirits arrive in this other dimension, they usually do so after having experienced any one of a multitudinous array of conditions, ranging from dying peacefully in their sleep to, unfortunately, a prolonged period of suffering characterized by the ravages of a painful disease. While the souls of others have been traumatized by sudden violent endings such as those caused by highway accidents or acts of brutality being inflicted on them.

In these types of cases, the souls, on entering the Angelic Realm require appropriate specialized nursing and a period of convalescence, and for this they are brought to a wonderful healing center where they receive the very finest expert care and attention, lovingly tendered by specially trained guides and angels, along with their loving family members when possible. I must say, I've been extremely impressed and encouraged by the fact that the many detailed descriptions of this process that the Spirits have offered us over the years have shown, in the examples that I've encountered, a remarkable level of consistency, which, for me, itself indicates authenticity on an aspect important to our own peace of mind.

Doris Stokes visited such a facility during her astral tour with her son and describes a building with an extraordinary atmosphere about it, occupied by recently arrived souls in rows of beds that faced seemingly transparent walls that looked out onto a beautiful landscape of gently rolling hills, shady trees and brilliant flowers. She writes: One could feel the healing in the air and it seemed to come not only from within the building, but from outside as well. Healing power seemed to wash in on invisible waves from the idyllic scenery outside." Highly comforting words for we bereaved, don't you think?

There's another highly intriguing phenomenon that takes place and that the spirits are understandably eager to apprize us of. It revolves around the amazing fact that we all, on crossing over, magically revert back to how we looked when we were in our mid-thirties. (Which, incidentally, is the reason I've heard mediums give for recommending that we enjoy the old photographs we have of our loved one, since that's how they look now).

Another highly reassuring detail associated with this amazing reversion process, is that on entering Heaven we return back to perfect health. And that encompasses the miraculous healing of all types of afflictions, disabilities—whether major or minor—congenital or hereditary—or incurred during our lifetime. In short—we now enjoy, maybe for the first time ever, optimal physical emotional and physical health in all its many wondrous aspects.

Once the new arrivals have been deemed to be fully recuperated, rested and restored to perfect health in every way, they're free to then ease gently, at a pace they're most comfortable with, and acclimate themselves into the super blissful lifestyle that heaven's residents enjoy.

They are reportedly assisted through the various stages of this process by appropriately qualified spirit guides and helpers together of course with the assistance of several generations of our adoring relatives, friends and even vibrationally compatible acquaintances we may only have known briefly, but nonetheless—all fellow souls who now comprise our "soul group."

## Rest In Peace—and Other Myths

It's difficult for us to imagine how utterly bewildering it must be to awaken in the other dimension but from all accounts, although our period of initiation may consist of a constant stream of surprises, they are all without exception, decidedly delightful and more pleasing than we could have possibly imagined. We touched on one surprise earlier, the revelation that gives the lie to the universally held notion that Heaven is all about R.I.P.—resting in peace, and that not only is it *not* the watchword we've mistakenly been led to believe it is—it's actually a big myth. Wishful thinking for some I expect—but a complete fable. The *"in peace"* part yes, of course, every single aspect of life in Heaven is about peace. But rest? Rest in the "just lolling around" sense? Hardly.

On the contrary, countless spirits have attested to the fact in readings, that everyone in Heaven is actively engaged in everything *but* resting, and are apparently so busy being productive, most frequently in ways that are contributive to spiritual evolvement—their own and others—that the word "rest" is probably only used by musicians and those who play billiards. On the subject of recreational activities, many spirits have spoken of how they're still able to participate in everything they'd enjoyed doing or wanted to do while on this plane—fishing, golfing, snorkeling, stamp collecting, paragliding, whatever they fancy it would seem.

For the most part, their typical normal daily pursuits involve anything that's devoted to the furtherance of their spiritual growth along with tasks and assignments that address the needs of their loved ones back on this physical plane too. They rejoice in being able to assist their loved ones back here with *their* life's challenges and spiritual growth, especially when it involves helping to keep them on track and staying in compliance with the growth lessons they wrote into their soul-plan and signed off on before they incarnated here. For the most part, their assistance is quite subtle but there are times when this ongoing concern and love for us actually manifests, in a way that gets our attention. For instance those scary and hazardous kinds of situations, the dramatically successful climax of which often evoke expressions such as: "Wow! My guardian angels sure saved my bacon there." An inference that, at some level, we all know about this amazing Divine connection.

We're told that those spirits who were fortunate to have been gifted with celebrity status talents and abilities in the various fields of the arts and sciences during their time on this physical plane, can wind up being just as active after they've crossed over. There are many references to instances of them being assigned mentoring stints, in keeping with their particular specialty, in service to aspirants both over there and on this plane too—we discussed a few examples of this earlier in Chapter 4.

I've long believed this to be the reason we should try to avoid overly flaunting our achievements or being too quick to pat ourselves on the back for a job well done, as we are all understandably prone to do—because the possibility always exists that we may actually have had very little to do with that special touch that raises it to the level of "masterpiece." And that in fact, the credit should really go to our spirit guides who, in all likelihood, "stage-managed" the whole affair from the get-go—in other words: "Get over yourself."

We're all probably familiar with a fitting 12th century expression, it's attributed to Bernard of Chartres and was inscribed on a plaque that my early mentor, Bill Simmonds, kept on his desk, it reads: "If I have seen further, it is by standing on the shoulders of giants."

The beauty of staying mindful of this incredible potential resource during our own creative endeavors, is that once we've opened our minds to this Divine connection—and accepted it with sincere humility and reverence, the spirits we're told, will lovingly respond with more of the same. This process was evidenced by the English medium Ken Akehurst in his book *Everyone's Guide to the Hereafter,* which he channeled after his own transition and in which he wrote: "The next time a piece of advice comes into your mind it could very well be your soul group at work, and that goes for some of the strange things that happen and that turn out to be for your benefit." I'll be discussing one of my own experiences with this wondrous procedure later on in the book.

Another intriguing aspect the spirits have divulged about their life in Heaven, revolves around the fact that amazingly, they're able to create their own reality in accordance with their preferred environment and lifestyle, and from the accounts that I've read, their tastes and preferences seem so relatable to those we have on our physical plane that once they've settled down their transition is not really very different to what moving to another town would be here. In fact their descriptions sometimes read like those brochures for new housing developments.

There are numerous accounts in the books that describe customized cottages with gorgeously landscaped surroundings on the picturesque banks of a placid stream spanned by the obligatory quaint rustic bridge—those popular idealistic scenes painted by the late celebrated artist Thomas Kinkade come to mind. I came across one account of a psychic reading years ago where the spirit who came through proceeded to give the sitter a detailed description of a house he was in the process of building. The word-picture he painted moved the, by now "eyes-agog-jaw-dropped" widow, to confirm with certainty that this was her husband because he'd just described exactly the home they'd always dreamed of building one day.

With such a boundless array of options and possibilities at their disposal now, and with no need for sleep, it's no wonder the word "rest" isn't in the spirits' vocabulary.

## Small Wonder It's Also Known As Paradise

Most of us, I would imagine, can recall times in our life when we were blessed with an experience so magical we were lifted to a level of such bliss and utter contentment that, although relatively fleeting, was so intense that just the remembrance of it years later can bring on a wave of goose bumps, accompanied by a highly pleasurable warm inner glow and a smiling heart. But again, frustratingly—relatively fleeting, as we're inevitably slurped back into the mostly mundane realities of day-to-day life.

The spirits have used these exquisitely ecstatic states as a point of reference in their attempt to describe to us what their Heavenly existence is like. *Plus,* in one case, the jaw-dropping addendum: "Well, that's what life here is like—*every single minute."*

I know—when I first read that, I too gasped—followed by a "WOW!"

This stunning declaration may strike us as being "over-the-top," but it begins to appear quite plausible as details emerge regarding an element of life in Heaven that warrants those frequently heard superlatives such as Paradise—Shangri-La—Utopia—Elysian fields—celestial—nirvana etc. Because it turns out that Heaven's lavish profusion of perfection is by no means limited to just the visual aspects—those idyllic rural settings for instance, that the spirits enthusiastically describe and that we've been discussing. As awe-inspiring as those features undeniably are, Heaven's consummate flawlessness is infinitely more far-reaching, particularly in aspects that are more *sociological* in nature.

It would seem to me that we are able to relate to spirit descriptions of Heaven's visually amazing aspects because they are, in essence, super-enhanced versions of what we're familiar with. However, the divide between the sociological climate in Heaven and ours on this plane is, by all accounts, so enormous that this feature I'm referring to, is impossible for us to relate to. Putting it, I'm guessing, at the very top of their "Sources of Culture-Shock" list that the recently arrived surely can't help mentally compiling during their acclimation process.

Most of these standard features of day-to-day-life in Heaven, as reported by the spirits in readings, can only marginally compare

## The Direct Connect

with anything ever experienced during our relatively brief sojourn on this earth plane. Dreamed of, fantasized about, yes, but rarely, if ever, actually realized—and then only momentarily, making bliss on this scale virtually impossible for we earthlings to even imagine. It's a very fascinating topic to reflect and extrapolate on, and also, an understanding of it can benefit us with a desirable spiritual uplift, making it, hopefully, a worthwhile investment of the time it takes to discuss a few aspects of it.

Firstly, it's been my experience that analyzing and assessing a diverse interactive situation, like the one we have here, is often made simpler by reflecting on what elements the factions we're comparing are *free of,* rather than the multiplicity of stuff they *contain.* So when we apply this to examine the incredibly blissful life in Heaven—the element that jumps out, is the absence of the dualism that defines our life on this plane. It's generally regarded as the essential dynamic—the Yin Yang, that Taoist philosophy believes ensures the necessary equilibrium to life on this plane—the ebbs and flows of life, in familiar western vernacular.

Accordingly, the spirits have described Heaven as being *totally free* of this dualism dynamic and have explained why there's no need for it. From their accounts, apart from a few allowable and quite innocuous human foibles and personality traits which spirits are known to carry over with them as part of their personality, there is a marked absence of anything that smacks of any kind of *negativity* in Heaven. As a result, social relationships, generally regarded as being the source of many of life's biggest challenges on our physical plane (the Yin Yang), are, in Heaven, totally free of destructive and disquieting attitudes like malevolence, petulance, animosity, snobbism, phoniness, acrimony, rancor etc., etc. And no one is *ever* guilty of being boastful, envious, pretentious, quarrelsome, vindictive, hostile, disingenuous and the thousand-and-one other instigators of the friction and discord so ubiquitous in our lives here on this plane.

In a world that's totally free of these kinds of negative attitudes and behaviors, and where the prevailing atmosphere is never anything but one of love, civility and graciousness in their purest forms—and where harsh words are never spoken, no one has reason to ever be the slightest bit apprehensive or suspicious of anyone's motives. Ergo—Ying and Yang begone.

Just imagine—all this, plus free cable, WiFi, limitless cell-phone minutes and unlimited breadsticks. Oh—and cake, lots of cake—Angel Cake, I'm guessing.

This social interaction aspect of life in Heaven, as far reaching as it, by all accounts is, is just one facet of the many that form the whole complex composite. And it boggles the mind to conjecture that presumably, they all function at the same giddy height of perfection.

Small wonder the spirits are invariably eager, in their psychic readings, to assure their loved ones they left behind with words that echo those that John O'Donahue insightfully wrote: "There's no need to grieve for them."

## In the Meantime

The spirits, after sharing with us details about what their life in Heaven is like, have also assured us that in their eternal undying love for us, the main thing they want now, is for us to strive to be fully acceptive of what's befallen us and be as happy and contented as they are. So, regardless of the fact that we miss them terribly, and will continue to do so until the day we're together again, we're surely honor-bound to do our very best to be in compliance with their wishes, while trying to overcome any feelings of guilt that this may naturally tend to engender in us. Hopefully, the recuperative measures we've suggested in this book will prove to be helpful in achieving this.

The one thing that I do feel is of paramount importance for us to stay mindful of as we continue on this solo part of our journey, is our soul path—the joint soul plan that we drew up together with the help of our team of spirit guides, before we incarnated here. Keeping that mentally handy can, whenever we feel the need for a spiritual booster shot, serve to remind us—that *everything is in Divine order*, and that *everything* that is happening is happening because it *should*—because it is in the soul plan we signed off on. An appreciable amount of solace and comfort can also be derived from keeping in mind what the spirits have been telling us throughout the book—that *we are never alone—ever*, and, as they've also taken pains to assure us—we are protected at all times by a veritable host of adoring guardian angels and spirit helpers. All diligently orchestrating and stage-managing our affairs while being there for us with the precise amount of appropriate expert guidance that our problematic circumstances call for.

It can be an extremely beneficial practice to keep these comforting words handy in some form—"memos-to-self" to refer to on the fly, whenever we feel the need for a moral-booster.

# AFTERLIFE AFTERWORD

Despite the fact that a belief in the afterlife, and having faith in the mediums' ability to communicate with those who now reside there, can inarguably bring about the restorative solace that we bereaved desperately seek, there are still those who can't even bring themselves to allow us the benefit of the doubt or be acceptive of the process in any way, often going so far as to scoffingly dismiss such a belief as being on a par with believing in fairies and leprechauns.

The stalemated condition this attitude produces is most unfortunate because it can (as it *has* all these years) discourage many agonizingly pained and emotionally broken souls from availing themselves of its benefits. Obviously, this is a situation that is only likely to be resolved when such intransigent naysayers have been presented with nothing less than the absolutely irrefutable scientific proof they insist on.

All attempts to scientifically prove mediumship's genuineness have however, been frustrated by the fact that, as we discussed earlier, mediumship just happens to be one of those things (there are many others) that are simply not *quantifiable*. So this is the stumbling block that, for now at least, makes it virtually impossible for the phenomenon of mediumship to become the universally accepted absolute that would effectively give the lie to the age old myth that "death is so final."

Nothing could convince me though that the scientific proof we need is destined to elude us for ever. I'd wager that the research leading up to every scientific discovery ever made was, at some time, dogged by the same sense of foreboding, (naysayers being historically ubiquitous). So I'm confident that the missing pieces of the puzzle *do* definitely exist—it's just that it hasn't been their time, or ours, to bring them to light yet—but it's only a matter of time before a scientist with the right amount of stick-to-itiveness, plus a modicum of good luck, stumbles across them.

It's not as if solutions resulting from serendipitous discoveries are unheard of after all—in the annals of amazing scientific breakthroughs there have been many notable cases. For example, in an 1890 interview with *Harper's Magazine*, the legendary inventor Thomas Edison, in discussing his invention of the first incandescent light bulb, revealed that: "Every quarter of the globe was ransacked by my agents, and all sorts of the queerest materials were used, until finally the shred of bamboo now utilized was settled upon."

Fast-forwarding to our present-day amply illuminated world, the spotlight of many scientific investigations world-wide has for many years now, centered around the mind-bending field of quantum physics—the subject I attempted to summarize and make a case for in Chapter 11. It's a truly intriguing area of scientific inquiry that, despite its labeling even by leading scientists, as "a weirdly bizarre set of theories," has nevertheless become universally recognized as being "the most well-tested scientific theories in human history." Thousands of experiments have apparently been conducted over the years, with completely unambiguous findings that incontrovertibly confirm the validity of quantum physics.

I admit to never having had a very good head for science, let alone this rarified branch of it known as quantum theory, but from what I've been able to garner from reading about its brain-numbing functions, I can't help but have a sense that our long on-going quest for the scientific proof we need is similar to Mr. Edison's late 19th century global "treasure hunt," in that we too are looking for a figurative "shred of bamboo." The difference is, searches like this aren't confined to just this globe anymore, because the hunting ground whose 'every corner can be ransacked for the queerest kinds of findings,' to paraphrase Mr. Edison, now consists of nothing less than the entire universe, thanks to the amazing field of quantum physics—an acknowledged bizarre field whose surface, so we've been authoritatively assured, has barely been scratched yet.

The following are a few examples of quantum theory's weird quirkiness I've come across:

— *Quantum experiments have shown that reality is an illusion.*
— *A noted professor of physics proclaims that: "At the quantum level reality does not exist if you're not looking at it."*
— *Subatomic particles behave and react to being observed. Hence—where observation ends and reality begins, is up to each one of us to decide.*
— *Particles can be omnipresent and exist in two places at the same time.*
— *In the weird world of quantum, the past, present and future are happening simultaneously.*

## The Direct Connect

Bizarre stuff to be sure, and it would appear that there's even weirder stuff to come because quantum physicists have also discovered that we are all part of an immense field of energy that consists of all possible realities and actually reacts to what we're both thinking and feeling.

It's these kinds of pronouncements that have led me to posit the notion that the scientific proof that's frustratingly eluded us so far, is secreted away somewhere in the ether—waiting to be bizarrely chanced upon by one of these assorted aspects of the weirdly unorthodox behavior of subatomic energies—that "spooky action at a distance," as Einstein referred to it.

In the event my layman's descriptions give the impression that quantum physics is one of those abstract, airy-fairy, esoterically complex theories with which we often associate fantastical sounding claims, let me assure you that this is emphatically not the case. Evidenced by the fact that quantum physics has actually been at the core of the relatively recent developments of any number of things that have actually become "cannot-live-without" features of everyday life. Items as commonplace as computer chips for instance (what *doesn't* contain them these days? I mean—you can't move for them), then there are lasers (our store check-out bar-code scanners, to mention just one of many applications), and also, intriguingly—LED lights. A development which, with characteristic quantum weirdness, loops us bizarrely back to Edison's fabled invention. Because super-ironically, LED lights, after lo these many years, are currently in the process of rendering Edison's incandescent light bulb obsolete—their manufacture prohibited by government mandated energy conservation legislation.

This is an undreamed-of outcome and one which, for spiritualists, raises the question: "Could it be possible that the great Mr. Edison, from his current exalted vantage point in the Spirit realm, has been an active participant in this amazing development all along?" (After all documentation does exist that attests to his interest in the possibility of communicating with those in the afterlife). And that being so, would this be a literal example of what Einstein called: "Spooky action at a distance?' Just asking.

Speaking of whom—Einstein once said: "God does not play dice." But that somewhat imperious statement was presumably made prior to quantum theory evolving to the levels that have since given rise to the kinds of mind-bending examples cited earlier. Because it so happens that a physicist descendant of Einstein's—the highly renowned Stephen Hawking no less, subsequently countered that statement with: "Not only does God play dice…he sometimes throws them where they can't be seen." A concept that is, coincidentally, perfectly pertinent to the notion that hidden somewhere in the weird "roll-of-the-dice" nature of quantum physics lie the clues that could potentially lead us to the scientific proof we covet. It's become my feeling that the figurative dice *are* out there—just not in a place where they can be seen—*yet*.

Our world has gone through many sociological paradigm shifts during its history, but few of them of greater significance than this could potentially be. I don't think it's an overstatement to say that life in a world where everyone is absolutely, unequivocally *certain* that death—rather than being the *end*—is actually the *beginning*, could conceivably never be the same again—in all the most peaceable and noblest aspects it's possible to imagine.

## A Few Final Words

When the medium from whom I was receiving my fifth reading after losing my darling Doris became the fourth one to open with:

"The female figure who's here is saying you must write a book about your experiences, because it will help many people," I was left with a keen sense that a special kind of direct connection had been established and I'd received my marching orders.

So it's my sincere and fervent wish that the resultant book you're now holding has indeed helped you in forming your own direct connections, that in turn have been, and will continue to be, greatly beneficial to your own healing in all the ways you desire—while always knowing that you are never alone—*ever.*

*Wishing you Love, Light, Peace and Wholeness.*

END

# ACKNOWLEDGMENTS

Bringing this book into being would not have been possible were it not for the generous contributions of numerous fine people. So it's to them that I—and by extension—those who will hopefully derive benefit from the suggestions and information shared, will be forever indebted.

A singular debt of profound gratitude however must be reserved for a very special lady, and in explaining how her participation came about, I'll be fulfilling the promise I made earlier—to share my experience with the type of psychic message from spirit that mediums relish delivering. I'm referring to those instances when a spirit with whom the sitter identifies and acknowledges, imparts specific information that just doesn't register and of which the sitter has no knowledge whatsoever, *but* that is subsequently positively verified by a third party in another location. Often hundreds or even thousands of miles away. Thereby effectively ruling out the possibility that the medium obtained the information by telepathically reading the sitter's mind—an accusation frequently leveled by skeptics to support their claim that mediumship is bogus.

My personal experience of such a reading happened this way: When I'd satisfied myself that, after two years of research, I'd amassed enough material to finally get down to some serious (not *too* serious I hope) writing, I recalled Sonia Choquette's assertion that whenever we're involved in a creative project it's possible for us to invoke the assistance of experts in that field who are now in spirit—former renowned artists, writers, musicians, sculptures, for example. Accordingly, I gave this a lot of thought as I went about my weekend and at the end of my Monday morning meditation I'd decided who to invoke and invite into my designated writing space. I'd been led to England's most widely read novelist Catherine Cookson.

My wife had been a lifelong voracious reader, and must have read every word the brilliant Ms Cookson (now *Dame* Catherine) had ever written and I'd enjoyed a dozen or more myself. Over a hundred of her novels had been published during her career, with several of them adapted into major movies.

So it was, that before I put pen to paper I settled myself into a few minutes of quietude—a mini-meditation during which, I invoked my wife's help but also suggested that she invite Catherine Cookson over for a pot of tea (with the obligatory watercress sandwiches and scones) and then, approach her with a respectful request on my behalf for her expert guidance with our book. With my entreaty submitted, I took a deep breath and plunged into my first day of writing.

At that time, I knew that our daughter Bev, who lives with her two cats 700 miles away in another state, had arranged for a psychic reading later that day with a well known pet psychic, hoping to get to the bottom of behavioral issues brought on by their recent relocation to a new home. Diane Roadcap had read for other cats who'd rescued Bev over the years, with many amazingly accurate validations, so I was excited by the prospect of Bev calling me later to let me know how this latest reading had turned out.

She called around noon to report that although it had been another excellent reading, one message had left her nonplussed. Apparently, after affirming that her mom was present, Diane went on to tell her: "Your mom wants you to know that Catherine and Bill are with her."

Remember, having put my gambit into play just that morning it was totally unbeknownst to Bev, but despite being wildly excited and sorely tempted to jump in here—I didn't say a word. Because it occurred to me that although the mention of a Catherine pointedly registered with me, I didn't think it prudent to get into an elaborate explanation of what was at play here until I'd thought it through. After all, for all I knew there may very well have *been* a Catherine and Bill in her mom's past, the discovery of which would preclude this message being necessarily connected to my invoking of Catherine Cookson's assistance.

Anyway, Bev reiterated that neither of these names had registered with her—and having no knowledge whatsoever of either a Catherine or a Bill in her own purview—inquired if I could think of any relatives or friends with those names either her mom or myself may have had, and plus—apparently linked. I duly promised to do some poking around and call her back later.

The ensuing diligent search involving three address books and several calls to relatives in England came up blank. No Kate or Kathy, no Bill, William or Willy—nothing even close. Which all served to

## The Direct Connect

convince me that Diane's Catherine reference was a classic "hit." But what about Bill—who could that possibly be? Catherine's husband naturally sprang to mind.

The very first of the 6.6 million websites that resulted from my 'Feeling Lucky' search for Catherine Cookson that I clicked on turned out to be a magazine correspondent's interview with Catherine together with her husband.......*Tom!*—Darn it—not what I wanted to see.

However, an intuitive feeling said I should press on, and two paragraphs later—bingo! Catherine and Tom recounted a spooky ghost incident that they'd experienced shortly after moving into the large Victorian house they'd bought. A fascinating story that revolved around the strange behavior one evening of their bull terrier dog, named—wait for it now.......*Bill!*

Bingo again! And as they say: "'Tis nice to have friends in high places."

Over the four years since, not a single person among the many I've asked, including two owners of boarding kennels and a vet, can recall *ever* having heard of a pet dog named Bill,—not one. One smart Alec did say he'd once had an uncle name Bill who was said to be 'a bit of a dog,' but not one actual dog—just not a doggie name I guess. Unless, it would seem, you happen to be a highly successful creative writer.

So it's quite feasible to me, that with Diane being so acutely attuned psychically to our friends in the animal kingdom, it's only natural that she would pick up on the vibrations emanating from Bill—he *is* a bull terrier after all.

This validation was doubtless a classic "hit" on Diane's part, and as far as I'm concerned it was clearly Dame Catherine's way of confirming that she was indeed assenting to my request for her assistance. Hence the reason for her heading my list of people whose contributions in the creation of this book I'm happy to acknowledge with profound gratitude. You could say she's been my "ghost writer" after all.

As you can imagine, I've spent an inordinate amount of time in my "designated writing space" a.k.a. my dining room table, over the past four years and I can honestly say that there's never been a time when I haven't had the intuitive sense—a knowing of "a presence." Whether this has been my wife's vibration or Dame Catherine's or both, I have no way of knowing with certainty of course. But what I *do* know—unquestioningly, is that I haven't been alone in this space, because there have been innumerable times when I've started to search through my mental card index for an appropriate word or phrase—and voila, in a mere second or two the precisely pertinent word or phrase would magically plop into my consciousness. And spookily, often words and terms I know I'd never used before in my entire life, but invariably authenticated by my trusty thesaurus. This continued to occur so regularly and so eerily predictably that after I'd confided this phenomenon to friends they dubbed my dining room "that goose-bump place."

Next in this assembly of fine folk to whom I owe a deep debt of gratitude, has to be a certain special lady. This uniquely multi-talented, two-time valedictorian is someone I've been learning from since she was around six or seven years old—and I proudly admit to still doing so. I'm referring to our musician/composer daughter Beverley Joy, who also happens to be one of the most spiritually advanced and inspiring people it's my privilege to know (believe me, the proverbial acorn fell a long way from the tree here). In her unenviable role as my personal guru of all things computer connected, her expertise graces every single page of this book. Just couldn't have done it without you Bev. Muchas gracias.

My sincere appreciation for their various generous contributions is also extended to the following fine folk:

The pre-eminent Psychic Intuitive Sonia Choquette, for gifting me with the very first words that greet every reader—the title.

The team of Guthrie Gifford and Harold Woodbine. For their collaborative machinations that succeeded in inadvertently kick-starting a series of challenging soul-growth events that eventually synchronistically culminated in a revelation that each energy-draining encumbrance inflicted had actually been in perfect accord with the Soul Plan we'd all signed off on.

Mr Bert Summerfield was a brilliant art teacher—a standout in his field. I will be eternally grateful for his patience and encouragement.

Likewise, illustrator extraordinaire Abe Goldman, for his mentorship. Not just right up to the day of his tragic untimely passing, but—and I have reason for *knowing* this to be the case—from his unique vantage point in the afterlife too.

Love and hugs are due to my Spiritual Header and friend Lorraine Peterson for her periodic ministering of the magically therapeutic Golden/White light that unfailingly re-fuels me.

I am also indebted to those who were kind enough to willingly share their inspiring positive experiences in the interests of helping to "spread the word" in order that others may benefit.

My sincere heartfelt thanks also to the mightily gifted sweet-voiced diva Lisa Moscatiello. I will never forget the ways in which you came through for Doris and my family in such generous helpings. Be assured that your amazing albums get lots of air-time around here.

*Afterlife Afterword*

Talking of music-based gifts—it would be remiss of me to allow a unique musical treasure to go unmentioned. I'm referring to the awe-inspiring video footage, accessible on the internet, of the now universally celebrated Susan Boyle's audition appearance on the television show *Britains Got Talent,* where she performed the song *I Dreamed a Dream* from the hit musical *Les Miserables.* This ultra-extraordinary clip has been a highly supportive source of soul-nurturing inspiration in my life ever since.

Lastly, my profound gratitude to my sisters in England, Rita Cubberley and Mo Langford, for comfortingly being there for their beloved sister-in-law, 4,500 miles away—throughout our hideously wretched time. Then later, for me also—during my subsequent prolonged convalescence and return to what now goes for normalcy.

May each and everyone of you be forever bathed in the Divine golden light of Christ-Love.

# READING SUGGESTIONS

Akehurst, Ken. *Everyone's Guide to the Hereafter.* Essex, United Kingdom: The C. W. Daniel Company Ltd., 1985.

Andrews, Ted. *Animal Speak.* Minnesota: Llewellyn Publications, 1993.

Anderson, George, and Andrew Barone. *Lessons From the Light.* New York: Berkley Books, 1999.

———. *Walking in the Garden of Souls.* New York: Berkley Books, 2002.

———. *Ask George Anderson.* New York: Berkley Books, 2012.

Bonnett, O. T. With Satre, Gregor Alan. *Reincarnation: The View From Eternity.* Arizona: Ozark Mountain Publishing, 2005.

Brown, Robert. *We Are Eternal.* New York: Warner Books, 2003.

Choquette, Sonia. *Soul Lessons and Soul Purpose.* California: Hay House, 2007.

———. *Ask Your Guides.* California: Hay House, 2006.

———. *The Psychic Pathway.* New York: Three Rivers Press, 1995.

Crawford, Jenny. *Spirit of Love*. Minnesota: Llewellyn Publications, 2002.

———. *Through the Eyes of Spirit*. California: Blue Dolphin Publishing, 1996.

Dalzell, George E. *Messages*. Virginia: Hampton Roads Publishing Company, Inc., 2002.

Doyle, Sir Arthur Conan. *The New Revelation,* New York: Square One Classics, 2001.

DuBois, Allison. *Don't Kiss Them Good-bye*. New York: Simon & Schuster, 2004.

———. *We Are Their Heaven*. New York: Simon & Schuster, 2007.

———. *Secrets of the Monarch*. New York: Simon & Schuster, 2008.

Eagleman, David M. *Incognito*. New York: Vintage Books, 2011.

Edward, John., with Natasha Stoynoff. *After Life*. California: Hay House, 2003.

Greer, Dr. Jane. *The Afterlife Connection*. New York: St. Martins's Griffin, 2004.

Hawkins, David R. *Power vs. Force*. California: Hay House, 2002.

Holland, John., with Cindy Pearlman. *Born Knowing*. California: Hay House,

Hopcke, Robert H. *There Are No Accidents*. New York: Riverhead Books, 1997.

Lewis C. S. *A Grief Observed*. San Francisco: HarperCollins, 2001.

Lynne, Carole. *How to Get a Good Reading from a Psychic Medium*. Maine: Weiser Books, 2003.

Martin, Joel, and Patricia Romanowski. *We Don't Die*. New York: Berkley Books, 1989.

———. *We Are Not Forgotten*. New York: Berkley Books, 1992.

———. *Love Beyond Life*. New York: HarperCollins, 1997.

## Reading Suggestions

Mathews, Patrick. *Never Say Goodbye.* Minnesota: Llewellyn Publications, 2003.

———. *Forever With You.* Minnesota: Llewellyn Publications, 2012.

McTaggart, Lynne. *The Field.* New York: HarperCollins, 2008.

Northrop, Suzane. *Everything Happens for a Reason.* California: Jodere Group, Inc., 2002.

———. with Kate McLoughlin. *The Seance.* New York: Dell Publishing, 1995

Obley, Carole J., *I'm Still With You.* United kingdom: O Books, 2008.

Occhino, MaryRose. *Beyond These Four Walls.* New York: Berkley Books, 2004.

———. *Sign of the Dove.* New York: Berkley Books, 2006. Plimmer, Martin., and Brian King. *Beyond Coincidence.* New York: St. Martin's Press, 2006.

Rushnell, Squire. *When God Winks at You.* Tennessee: Nelson Books, 2006.

Sharp, Harold. *Animals in the Spirit World.* Essex, United Kingdom: PN Publishing, 1966.

Smith, Gordon. *Spirit Messenger.* California: Hay House, 2004.

———. *The Unbelievable Truth.* California: Hay House, 2004.

———. *The Amazing Power of Animals.* California: Hay House, 2008.

Schwartz, Gary, with William L. Simon. *The Afterlife Experiments.* New York: Atria Books. 2002.

———. *The Truth About Medium.* Virginia: Hampton Roads Publishing Company, Inc., 2005.

Stokes, Doris, with Linda Dearsley. *Voices In My Ear,* also *More Voices In My Ear.* London,

United Kingdom: Time Warner Books,1998.

Van Praagh, James. *Talking to Heaven.* New York: Signet, 1999.

———. *Reaching to Heaven.* New York: Signet, 2000.

———. *Healing Grief.* New York: New American Library, 2001.

———. *Heaven and Earth.* New York: Simon & Schuster, Inc.,2001.

Walker, Jeanne. *More Alive Than Ever.* Virginia: EPM Publications, Inc., 1995.

Wands, Jeffrey A., *Another Door Opens.* New York: Atria Books, 2007.

Wansbury, Andrea. *Birds: Divine Messengers.* Scotland: Findhorn Press, 2006.

www.ingramcontent.com/pod-product-compliance
Lightning Source LLC
Chambersburg PA
CBHW071644090426
42738CB00009B/1419